THE HAWK AND THE DOVE

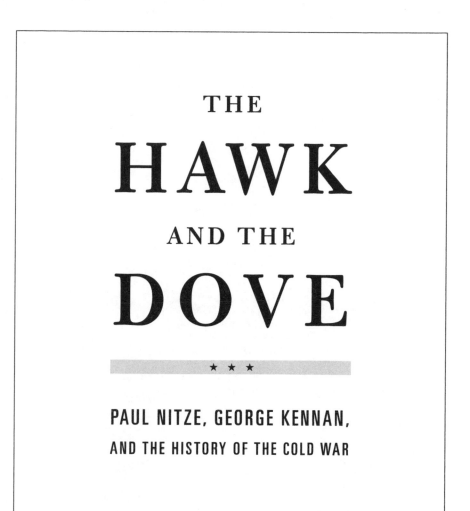

THE

HAWK

AND THE

DOVE

★ ★ ★

PAUL NITZE, GEORGE KENNAN,

AND THE HISTORY OF THE COLD WAR

NICHOLAS THOMPSON

HENRY HOLT AND COMPANY   NEW YORK

Henry Holt and Company, LLC
Publishers since 1866
175 Fifth Avenue
New York, New York 10010
www.henryholt.com

Henry Holt® and 🜨® are registered trademarks of
Henry Holt and Company, LLC.

Library of Congress Cataloging-in-Publication Data
Thompson, Nicholas, 1975–
  The hawk and the dove : Paul Nitze, George Kennan, and the history of the Cold War
Nicholas Thompson.—1st ed.
    p.   cm.
  ISBN: 978-0-8050-8142-8
  1. Nitze, Paul H.   2. Kennan, George F. (George Frost), 1904–2005.   3. United
States—Foreign relations—1945–1989.   4. Cold War.   5. National security—United
States—History—20th century.   6. Anti-communist movements—United States—
History—20th century.   7. Ambassadors—United States—Biography.   8. United
States—Officials and employees—Biography.   I. Title.
  E744.T494 2009
  973.92—dc22   2009009225

Henry Holt books are available for special promotions and premiums.
For details contact: Director, Special Markets.

First Edition 2009

Designed by Kelly S. Too

Printed in the United States of America
1   3   5   7   9   10   8   6   4   2

To Danielle and Ellis

CONTENTS

THE HAWK AND THE DOVE

★ ★ ★

PROLOGUE

On February 17, 1984, Paul Nitze decided that the arms race could wait. For the past two and a half years, he had led the negotiations between the United States and the Soviet Union. But on this day, he left that grave work in the early afternoon to dress in black tie and hop on a train to Princeton, New Jersey.

He was heading north to attend the eightieth-birthday party of a man who was both a close friend and a bitter rival: George Kennan. Nitze had been Kennan's deputy on the State Department's Policy Planning Staff in the late 1940s, and the two had worked together on some of the most important issues the country ever faced. They tried to reverse the partition of Germany; they helped write the Marshall Plan; they advised Harry Truman on whether to build a hydrogen bomb. And then, for thirty-five years, they had disagreed profoundly on the direction the country should take. Even at this moment, each believed that the other's desired policies could lead the United States to the ultimate catastrophe.

Nitze arrived just in time to join the sixty other friends, colleagues, children, and grandchildren at the celebration. After dinner ended, he stood up slowly and raised his glass to give a toast. "Among those born after 1904, I know of no one who has been more fortunate in his bosses than have I," he said. He then listed a series of remarkable mentors and what he had learned from each of them.

Soon he turned to the real center of attention: the taller, thinner, balder man celebrating his birthday. Kennan had just published a long article in the *New Yorker* and was hard at work on his seventeenth book, this one about the Franco-Russian alliance of 1894. An immensely complicated individual, he was revered both as one of the men who had started the Cold War and as the one most determined to end it.

Nitze continued gracefully. "George Kennan taught us to approach the issues of policy, not just from the narrow immediate interest of the United States, but from a longer-range viewpoint that included the cultures and interests of others, including our opponents, and a proper regard for the opinions of mankind.

"George has, no doubt, often doubted the aptness of his pupil. But the warmth of his and Annelise's friendship for Phyllis and for me has never faltered," said Nitze, referring to his and Kennan's wives.

"I extend my appreciation, gratitude and thanks to George, who has been a teacher and an example for close to forty years."

The guests clinked their glasses and cheered. It was one of the tensest periods of the arms race: just three months ago, Nitze's arms talks had collapsed in a way that many people thought would invite war; one week ago, the KGB veteran who had been running the Soviet Union had died. But this was a moment for two old friends, not for the quiet but ever-present terror that colored these years.

Kennan rose to respond: the main lesson he had learned from Nitze, he said, was that, when one disagreed with government, "it may be best to soldier on, and to do what one can to make the things you believe in come out right."

That evening, another guest asked Nitze how he and Kennan had remained friends despite their vast differences on issues of national security. Nitze smiled and responded that he had never had any difference with George "except over matters of substance."

PAUL NITZE and George Kennan were the only two people to be deeply involved in American foreign policy from the outset of the Cold War until its end. They had come to prominence in the tumultuous days that followed the Second World War when Germany was divided and the Soviet Union turned from ally into enemy. They immersed themselves in the great questions and events to come: the Marshall Plan, Korea, the ever more dangerous arms race, Vietnam, détente, SALT, glasnost. They stepped offstage only when Germany reunited and the Soviet Union dissolved.

The two men were equally influential and equally important, yet vastly different. Nitze was the diligent insider, Kennan the wise outsider; Nitze the doer, Kennan the thinker. Kennan designed America's policy for the Cold War, and Nitze mastered it. With respect to America's ability to shape the world, Nitze was an idealist and Kennan a realist. In their old age, Nitze still wanted to win the Cold War, and Kennan wanted to be done with it. Their views overlapped at strange and crucial moments; but for most of their working lives, they disagreed profoundly. In the *New Yorker* article published just before his eightieth-birthday party, Kennan had indirectly criticized Nitze—who marked the piece up vigorously and also sent a letter to a mutual friend complaining that the argument showed a "complete separation from fact and logic."

Nitze was the hawk. When the United States and the Soviet Union built up their terrifying weapon stockpiles soon after World War II, he argued that the best way to avoid a nuclear clash was to prepare to win one. If you want peace, prepare for war. More than any other American, Nitze gave shape to the arms race. Kennan came up with the word *containment* that was used more than any other to describe America's Cold War policy. But he saw it as a political strategy for combating a political threat. Nitze defined the word the way it was really used: as a military strategy for combating a military threat.

Nitze's strengths were his organizational skills, his commitment to logic, and his endurance. Few people knew more about weaponry and few people were able to gain as many allies in different parts of Washington. He worked for, or consulted with, every president from FDR to George H. W. Bush. He even impressed his adversaries with his ability to absorb facts and make arguments about nuclear arms. "Nitze was a god," said Aleksandr Savelyev, one of his Soviet negotiating counterparts. "Just not our god."

Nitze never, however, learned how to manage his superiors: he ended up personally alienating six of those ten presidents. Fired, demoted, or forced to resign so many times that he lost count, Nitze never became either secretary of state or secretary of defense, although he often seemed to deserve both posts. Still, no failure or rejection ever made him sulk for long or disappear. "Presidents came and went. But every year there was Paul Nitze," said George Shultz, the secretary of state under Ronald Reagan.

Kennan was the dove. For forty years, he argued that America must end its dependence on nuclear weapons. If you want peace, act peacefully. During almost every military conflict from the Korean War through the Iraq War that began in 2003, he argued for forbearance.

Kennan was a brilliant writer: his histories earned the publishing world's highest prizes, and his memoirs offer one of the finest sketches of America in the first half of the twentieth century. He objected to the arms race—and NATO, the UN, the Korean War, the Eisenhower administration, the Vietnam War, the student movement of the 1960s, the Carter administration, the Reagan administration, and American policy at the very end of the Cold War—with an eloquence that even his steadfast enemies respected.

He also had an uncanny ability to predict many of the great events of his lifetime. When the Cold War was just beginning, he foresaw how it would end. He immediately understood that splitting Germany and creating NATO would harden the division of Europe. In 1949, he astutely predicted how the nuclear arms race would unfold. He foresaw the Sino-Soviet split and grasped, very early, the flaws in America's strategy in Vietnam.

These keen powers of perception, however, were married with profound vulnerability. Minor slights sent Kennan into deep despair. His last government job ended in failure when he resigned after a trivial setback. If Nitze treated wounds as scratches, Kennan felt scratches as wounds.

Neither of these idiosyncratic and original men conformed exactly to the hawk and dove labels, of course. Yes, Nitze drove the arms race. And he always believed that the Cold War was a series of moments of urgent peril in which the United States must display strength. But if he spent 90 percent of his career raising tensions, he spent the other 10 percent—the moments when actual conflict loomed and he was helping to shape the consequential decisions—lowering them. He tried to halt the Korean War and then helped stop it from spreading. He tried, early on, to extricate the United States from Vietnam. No one worked harder during the Reagan years to broker major arms deals with the Soviets.

Kennan, for his part, was a dove with hidden talons. He helped set up the CIA and later advised it. He worked closely with the FBI. His views on social issues and the value of democracy were those of a pterodactyl. Early on, he advocated standing up firmly to the Soviets. Though terrified of nuclear weapons, he took pride in not being a pacifist and he recommended declaring war against Iran after rioters seized the American embassy in 1979.

DESPITE THESE MANY differences, Kennan and Nitze were warm friends throughout the Cold War. And that lasting friendship has inspired this book.

Nitze was my grandfather, and I remember well his receipt of a letter in 1999 from his old colleague. Nitze was ninety-two years old then, Kennan ninety-five. I was a twenty-four-year-old journalist and had just moved to Washington, D.C. My grandfather was old and frail but, that November, we spent a lovely evening playing bridge and having dinner with friends of his. He, as always, dressed in a jacket and tie and enjoyed a glass or two of red wine. At some point during the evening, he said he wanted to read a letter.

On October 28, he had published an op-ed in the *New York Times* titled "A Threat Mostly to Ourselves," in which he declared that the United States had no more need for the arsenal he had spent his life building and studying. "I see no compelling reason why we should not unilaterally get rid of our nuclear weapons," Nitze wrote. "To maintain them is costly and adds nothing to our security."

The letter in response was equally simple and heartfelt. "Dear Paul: Warmest congratulations on your recent *New York Times* article, with every word of which I agree," wrote Kennan. "In the light of our long standing friendship and mutual respect, it is a source of deep satisfaction to me to find the two of us, at our advanced ages, in complete accord on questions that have meant so much to each of us, even when we did not fully agree, in times gone by."

Nitze smiled and laughed as he read it. Later, as we said good-bye, I remarked on the elegance of Kennan's prose. "Yes, George could always write brilliantly," reflected my grandfather, seeming to pause on the word "write" as if to suggest what it left out. "He really could."

His memory, already failing, would decline rapidly in the years ahead. I never talked in depth with him about Kennan, but I remembered that letter five years later, when both men died. Their passings came just six months apart, which seemed fitting. Soon thereafter, I began to investigate their lives and to attempt to discover how their contradictory influences shaped a struggle for the world. My research revealed two very different men who nonetheless shared a commitment to the United States and to their very different ways of serving it. As Alexander Bessmertnykh, a Soviet foreign minister who worked across from each of them at different points during the Cold War, said to me, "They both were great in their own gardens."

What follows is a story about friends, but not about friendship. The pair attended each other's birthday parties and family weddings. They often inspired or enraged each other with their ideas. But the letter in 1999 was a rare one. There are no piles of correspondence or transcripts of personal conversations. They were good friends but not best friends; perhaps if they had been closer, they would have fallen out.

They did, however, greatly respect each other and admire each other's seriousness of purpose, demeanor, and dedication. They realized they shared an uncommon endurance. They also shared a similar fate: neither reached his ultimate ambitions, while many lesser men reached the positions of influence to which they both aspired.

Most important, they represented two great strains of American thought during the second half of the twentieth century. And perhaps they realized something I came to believe as I worked on this book: one can understand much of the story of the United States during the Cold War by examining the often parallel, and sometimes perpendicular, lives of Paul Nitze and George Kennan.

1

★ ★ ★

NOW IS THE TIME TO LIVE

Surrounded by chaos, George Kennan remained calm. He stood on the balcony of the American embassy in Moscow, gazing down on the wild celebration below. Women in headscarves danced, screamed, and hugged one another. Men in big lumpy jackets raised their arms and passed each other through the air. Kennan's nine-year-old daughter, Joan, pranced about on the balcony, tossing candy down to the celebrants. Starved of sugar for the last few years, people lunged up to catch the Life Savers and Necco Wafers.

It was May 9, 1945, just after American and Soviet troops met in Berlin, together snuffing out the last noxious flames of Nazism. Four years before, invading German forces had pressed up against the very outskirts of Moscow. But the Red Army had held the city, and then gradually begun to push the Wehrmacht back. For the last two years, the Soviets had steadily marched west, with the government marking each victory by firing salutes over Moscow. The bigger the victory, the bigger the salvo. In recent months, Muscovites had followed their soldiers' progress by counting the shots exploding gloriously into the night sky.

As word of the capitulation spread, Soviet citizens had swarmed toward the American embassy, a five-story building just across Red Square from the Kremlin. By early morning on a cloudless day, thousands of people were standing out front, cheering. America had helped defeat the Germans and it had supplied wartime Russia with everything from Spam to Studebakers. "Now is the time to live," declared a Russian officer deep in the crowd. "Boy, oh boy," mused a young American corporal, "if I'd played post office every day until I got into the army, I wouldn't have been kissed as many times as I've been kissed today."

Amid the frenzy, Kennan remained more pensive than passionate. The door now opening led to a very uncertain future. Old Europe had dominated the world for centuries. Now, two countries from beyond Europe's borders—a former British colony separated by an ocean and a neighbor long considered backward—had joined hands at the center of the continent. From this moment on, everything began anew.

Kennan, a student of history, understood that the future depended on who won the peace, not only on who had won the war. The communists in Russia had been a small, isolated group of pamphleteers before grabbing power in the mayhem of 1917. "The aftermaths of wars are the decisive moments of foreign policy," he had written his sister two years earlier.

> It is here, in the fields of broken ice, that the lines are drawn which endure—depending on the wisdom with which they are selected— anywhere from a generation to a century. And it is naturally the victors to whom these opportunities present themselves. This is the second great chance we have had. We muffed the first. If we muff this, too, can we be sure that we will be given a third?

With the ambassador away, Kennan, the deputy chief of mission, was the most senior diplomat present. Terrified that the masses might carry him off on their shoulders or toss him in the air, he eventually began waving from the balcony. Then, as the crowd continued to surge and grow, he decided he really had to do something more. He walked downstairs and stepped gingerly out onto the pedestal of one of the great columns in front of the building.

FORTY-ONE YEARS OLD in the spring of 1945, George Frost Kennan stood about six feet tall. He dressed in a gray or black three-piece suit, wore a felt fedora, and stood straight. He had already lost much of his hair, which helped to give him a dignified and weathered look. When deep in contemplation, which was much of the time, he would draw his eyebrows together narrowly. The feature everyone noticed first was his eyes: a bright but pale blue—to many friends, an index of the intensity of the thought behind them.

He liked to take long walks through the countryside, and he liked to sketch, always in black and white, because he was colorblind. Everything in his life was ordered and neat: he kept every tool he owned in exactly the right place and always wrote his thank-you notes on Christmas Day. He enjoyed making things with his hands, and he loved telling stories to his daughter, Joan, the nine-year-old on the balcony. At night, he would regale her with tales about two pixies named Tim and Bell and their droopy-eared cocker spaniel, Uncle Zachariah. He made up these stories as he went, always ending in a way that made her want to hear more.

He felt deeply; he observed deeply; he saw every event as an opportunity to train his mind. Disciplined in the extreme, he believed that outward order, created by staying in control of his actions and his attire, could offset inner turmoil. And of the latter there was much. Kennan despaired for his country and for himself. To his friends, he appeared perpetually worried. Throughout his life, he kept a dark and somber diary, entering a world of literary self-flagellation even on days when he appeared cheery. When traveling alone, instead of calling ahead to find a good restaurant, he would wait until the last minute, rush out to the most miserable-looking place in the neighborhood, and then complain about the food.

Kennan felt an almost karmic connection to the Soviet Union. An older relative, also named George Kennan, had explored Russia in the late nineteenth century and written popular books criticizing the czardom and describing life in Siberia. The younger Kennan would often say that he felt like a reincarnation of the traveler: his birthday, he would point out, February 16, 1904, fell fifty-nine years to the day after his namesake's.

Soon after joining the Foreign Service, Kennan had begun to study the Soviet Union. He began working in the American embassy in Moscow when it opened in 1933, after the United States normalized relations with the Communist government. He stayed until 1937 and returned in 1944. He traveled extensively, studied the Soviet economy, and read much of Russia's classical literature. He started writing a book on Chekhov, though he never finished it. He spoke better formal Russian than Stalin, whose thick Georgian accent was hard for many Muscovites to understand.

Living abroad, Kennan missed the events that transformed America during his early adult years: the Great Depression, the New Deal, and the mobilization for World War II. His distance from his homeland was matched by his closeness to this new place. "As always Russia seems something poignantly familiar and significant to me—as though I had lived here in childhood, and I react intensely to everything I see and hear," he wrote upon his return to Moscow in 1944. "It gave me an indescribable sort of satisfaction to feel myself back again in the midst of these people— with their tremendous pulsating warmth and vitality. I sometimes feel that I would rather be sent to Siberia among them . . . than to live on Park Avenue among our own stuffy folk."

These warm feelings extended only to the people and the landscape, and only to the boundaries of Russia proper. For the Soviet government, and for communism, Kennan had nothing but contempt. Having worked as Ambassador Joseph Davies's interpreter during the purge trials of the 1930s, Stalin's first effort to exterminate everyone who might have ever had an independent or counterrevolutionary thought, Kennan saw through the dictator's madness and demonic suspicion. Stalin, in turn, was aware of the young American and his opinions.

During World War II, Kennan watched Moscow squeeze its supposed allies whenever it could. In the months leading up to the exultation in Red Square, he tried desperately to warn Washington that the Soviet Union was gobbling up eastern Europe and absorbing lands with every right to independence. Poland—an ally of the United States and Russia and an early victim of the Nazis—was a particular concern. Kennan was certain that the Soviet Union was behind the massacre of nearly five thousand Polish officers in the Katyn Forest early in the war. In 1944, the Soviets had refused to give aid after the Polish resistance rose up against the Germans in Warsaw; more frustratingly to Kennan, Moscow even refused to allow the United States the use of a base in Ukraine to help deliver arms to the resistance. It seemed clear to Kennan that Moscow intended to turn postwar Poland into a communist vassal state, not one run by democrats or friends of the West. "Soviet political aims in Europe are not, in the main, consistent with the happiness, prosperity or stability of international life on the rest of the continent," Kennan wrote his friend Charles Bohlen, then Franklin Roosevelt's interpreter, in January 1945.

No matter how anxious he felt as delight engulfed the Moscow streets on May 9, Kennan was still the ranking American in the capital. He had to respond to this outpouring somehow. He stood upon the pedestal: deeply hostile to the government, devoted to the people, and terrified that some epic clash was looming between a country he had learned to love and the country he served. The crowd quieted and looked up; his daughter stopped tossing the candy and peeked over at her father.

"Congratulations on the day of victory," shouted Kennan. "All honor to the Soviet allies." The crowd screamed riotously, and he darted back inside.

THAT SAME DAY, another fast-rising student of international affairs sat in his office in Grosvenor Square, London. He was exhausted, having spent the previous days racing around the German front. But the winding down of the war meant the acceleration of his job. And he would soon get an urgent message—to his mind, the best he could possibly receive.

Thirty-eight-year-old Paul Henry Nitze was one of the directors of the U.S. Strategic Bombing Survey, an organization charged with investigating the effectiveness of the Allied bombardment of German industry. Ground troops had dominated past wars, but many people believed that airpower would win the wars of the future. Nitze's job was to draw the strategic lessons from this conflict.

Nitze stood a wiry five foot nine and three-quarters. What everyone noticed first was his intensity: the pencil ripping through paper as he took notes, the constant motion, the desire to break every problem apart and reassemble it as a series of neatly ordered lists. He grasped concepts quickly; he gave orders well and carried them out exactly; he seemed to need little sleep. Even when ostensibly relaxing at home, he would stay up late talking, eating, and drinking but then get up at four A.M. to read. He delighted in the origin of his last name. "Nitze," he liked to assert, comes from the same root as the Greek word *nike*, "and the Greek word *nike* means 'victory.'"

He dressed with haste, but always in a fine suit and often in elegant suspenders. Although he was perpetually a bit rumpled, he gave the impression of a man with excellent taste who had more important things on his mind. (A burglar once cleaned out his closet and passed up everything else in the house.) When at home, he would begin his days by practicing Bach on the piano. After work, he would return and mix a martini for himself, judging the gin and vermouth ratio according to, he claimed, a finely calibrated sense of sound. He loved to meet new people. "PHN collects people," his wife wrote, "as some collect butterflies."

An economist by training, Nitze had spent the 1930s working as an investment banker (and learning that one can make money even when an economy collapses). He had moved from Wall Street to Washington as the Panzers rumbled through France in the early summer of 1940. He spent much of the next five years at the State Department, mainly working to obtain strategic minerals from South America. But in May 1945, as the cease-fire sounded, he was flying back and forth between London and the front lines, carrying a pistol. His noncombatant ID for that period shows a haggard figure, bow tie slightly askew.

He had come to the USSBS through a back door. In the fall of 1944, an old family friend, Colonel Guido Perera, mentioned that he was helping to start up this new organization. A few days later, Nitze got into a fierce argument with his boss at the Foreign Economic Administration, Leo Crowley, over a group of people Nitze had "borrowed" from elsewhere in the State Department to help on a project. The fight ended with Nitze resigning and Crowley hollering that if he quit now the younger man would never again work in a Democratic administration. Nitze strode out, hopped in a cab, and headed to Perera's USSBS offices at the Pentagon. As he liked to tell the story, he had another job within two hours of Crowley's threat.

Just as Russia had special meaning for Kennan, so did Germany for Nitze. Both his grandfathers had been born there, he learned the language as a child, and his parents identified strongly with its intellectual traditions and culture. The Nitzes had been in Germany when World War I broke out; seven-year-old Paul had watched from a hotel window in Munich while people lined the sides of the central road to cheer the first soldiers marching off to the front. His father pinned a small American flag on the boy's clothes so that no one would mistake him for a Brit. At fifteen, Paul worked in the engine room of a ship that traveled across the Atlantic to Germany. He returned in 1929, delightedly exploring Berlin and the countryside by bicycle with a new friend named Alexander Calder. In spring 1937, he had cruised through the country with his wife in a Ford Model T. As an adult, Nitze found much pleasure in Beethoven, Wagner, Goethe, and Hegel. The culture of the fallen Kaiser Reich was to be admired and honored, and his USSBS work was thus much more than a means to analyze the effects of the Allied bombing; it was part of a quest to understand what had deformed the country of his roots.

Nitze's job in early May of 1945 was to track down the surviving leaders of the Third Reich, particularly those who could assess the effectiveness of the air campaign. Nitze was coordinating a series of teams dashing about countrywide, measuring bomb crater depths and rounding up enemy technocrats. He would join his men for interrogations, when not journeying through the ruins himself, and then return to headquarters to report back.

And this day, as he worked in London, he got an urgent message. Two of his people poking through makeshift offices in northern Germany had found a door marked "Speer," gone inside, and waited. About an hour later, an elegant man walked in and declared that, yes, he was indeed Reichminister Albert Speer—the man known as Hitler's architect. Speer probably knew more than anyone else about what the raids had accomplished, and now he was in Nitze's hands.

ALBERT SPEER HAD JOINED the Nazis out of misplaced idealism and opportunism, not boiling hatred. An energetic young storm trooper, he caught Hitler's eye in 1933 and became the Führer's luncheon partner. From then on, each step forward meant one deeper into darkness. Soon he earned the task of designing the structures appropriate for a Thousand-Year Reich. His statues would out-tower the Statue of Liberty; his arches would dwarf the Arc de Triomphe; history, he hoped, would rank his buildings far above those of the pharaohs. His personality matched his creations: cold and technocratic, overwhelming and overbearing.

In 1942, Speer became the Reich's minister of armaments. For the next three years, he would maniacally, and brilliantly, manage steel shipments, railroad tracks, and components for V-2 missiles. As German production somehow kept going under the rain of bombs, Speer began to earn a reputation as a wartime genius: a master of detail who could somehow increase Germany's fighter aircraft production even after the Allies had destroyed all the plants along with the ball-bearing factories that fed them. Speer was a worthy enemy, the West decided. His black magic explained how Germany had resisted for so long.

But in May 1945, the towering enemy had crumbled. Hitler had spent most of the past year living in a damp underground bunker, receiving daily injections of sulfides and other toxins that he considered panaceas, even as they slowly mottled his skin and rotted his mind. As the Russians and Americans closed in, he demanded one last round of death, calling for the heads of his brother-in-law, his old surgeon, and other newfound "traitors." Then he put a pistol in his mouth while his wife of twenty-four hours poisoned herself next to him on their sofa.

With Hitler dead and the war over, Speer knew the role he would have to play to survive: the man of all-knowing competence. Germany was full of besotted men who had once held great power and who either defied their captors or were merely too hungover to be of much use as informants. The Allies could capture them, interrogate them, learn nothing, and have no reason to keep them alive. Speer would be affable, charming, and indispensable.

The interrogation took place in Glücksburg Castle, a beautiful moated Renaissance structure near the Danish frontier. Nitze and his colleagues, including the future UN ambassador George Ball and the future renowned writer on economics John Kenneth Galbraith, stayed on a boat in the harbor. They spent the mornings preparing questions and then arrived at the *Schloss* each afternoon around two. Speer would sit on a low settee, hands locked around one knee, in a small room furnished in red and gold brocade. As he listened to the questions, he would lean forward a bit. When answering, he would rock gently back and forth, always calm and confident. The one rational man in the utterly irrational system was telling his tale. Speer's insights and information were exactly what the Strategic Bombing Survey needed.

Commanding an awe-inspiring knowledge of the German war machine, he brought the whole dreaded system to life with detail. American bombs had been less effective than British bombs but more intelligently targeted. Attacks on basic infrastructure, such as chemical plants, had most worried Speer—worried him so much, indeed, that he argued against putting other targets underground. "I wanted to continue to offer you finished armaments production as a target so that you would not get the idea of destroying our industries producing basic materials which could only exist above ground."

He sounded at times like a coach who knew he outclassed the fellow on the other sideline and would have won if only he had better players. He never paused. He never evaded. He was never at a loss for words. He reviewed each American attack to explain why it had not done as much damage as it should have. "The second visible attempt at economic destruction was the attack on airframe production in February, 1944," he said during one session. "In this case it was a mistake on your part that you attacked the airframe production for so many months and not the production of motors." It was not long before the captured man began to cast a spell over his interrogators. Ball later recalled that Speer "evoked in us a sympathy of which we were all secretly ashamed."

One day, the survey investigators arrived to find Speer's secretary in tears. Her boss had technically been free, but that morning unknown men had seized him and taken him away. Perhaps they were remnants of the Gestapo? But, no: soon Speer arrived, calm as ever, to explain that another American intelligence unit had taken him, not realizing he was already working with the USSBS. "We were always having worse mix-ups than that under Hitler," he joked.

After more than a week of grueling discussion of German armaments, Nitze got a message from one of his superiors: "Paul, if you've got any further things you want to find out from Speer you'd better get him to-morrow." The day after that, Speer would be arrested. Nitze thought it over and decided he had enough dry details about Nazi factories.

The next afternoon, the team quizzed Speer about the inner workings of the Third Reich—the lives of Hitler, Göring, Himmler, and the rest of the Nazi high command. The story he told was astonishing. Germany had lost the war, Speer claimed, because the leaders were soft, drunken womanizers, entirely ignorant of the happenings on the front lines. Appropriately, their final crucial decisions were made inside an underground bunker where even the air had to be pumped in. Speer portrayed himself as the one countervailing force. He had not succumbed to greed during the glory days, or to vengefulness during Götterdämmerung. At the very end, he had countermanded Hitler's orders for a scorched-earth retreat—this, he claimed, he did out of loyalty to the German people and the German future, not disloyalty to the Führer. He had even returned to meet with Hitler in the bunker one last time, sneaking into Berlin as the rest of his former colleagues scattered.

The final interrogation ended at four-thirty A.M. The Americans told Speer to go home and get a good night's sleep. A couple of hours later, tanks rolled up to Glücksburg Castle and troops carrying submachine guns and hand grenades dashed in. "So now the end has come," Speer remarked, surrendering. "That's good. It was all only kind of an opera anyway."

★

GEORGE KENNAN KNEW Germany almost as well as Nitze did. He had grown up in Milwaukee, one of America's most Germanic cities, and lived briefly in the country at age eight. He learned the language, returned as a young Foreign Service officer, and then worked in Berlin after his first posting to Moscow. When the United States entered the war, he was serving in the American embassy in Berlin. When news of the bombing of Pearl Harbor came one night over shortwave radio, he helped burn all the embassy's codes and secret documents.

The Nazis soon rounded up Kennan and his colleagues and sent them for what turned out to be five months' internment in Bad Nauheim: a well-known spa with mineral springs, where FDR had summered in the 1890s; the Americans were confined in a rather pleasant place known as Jeschke's Grand Hotel. Kennan's friends there remembered him fondly for the historical lectures he gave and the way he negotiated with the German captors over subjects like rations and the loudness with which the Gestapo played Ping-Pong. He even played catcher on one of the pickup baseball teams. But the detainees were isolated; they were not contacted by their government and they had no idea when their imprisonment would end. Until his release in May 1942, Annelise Kennan did not know where her husband was.

With the war over, Kennan wanted to find the opposition figures he had met while in the country, particularly a man named Helmuth von Moltke. On May 10, the day after the outpouring in Red Square, Kennan wrote to a colleague in the Foreign Service inquiring about the whereabouts of his old friend.

The two first met, secretly, in 1940. Von Moltke, a member of Germany's greatest military family, had been reading *The Federalist Papers*. He told Kennan he was seeking guidance for how his country should reconstitute itself after it inevitably lost the war—a comforting thought for the American at a time when the Wehrmacht seemed invincible. The war had now ended as von Moltke had foreseen. But Kennan had had no news of the man himself since 1941. Now he sought not just a friend but confirmation that Nazism had not infected all of Germany and that wise men who had resisted Hitler from the beginning had survived.

The big question for Germany was what would come next. The country that had driven two world wars in the past thirty years had descended into chaos. Its neighbors wanted to loot it, to break it apart, or to do both. Many people thought Germany, or its culture, was fundamentally deformed. The U.S. government's Morgenthau Plan, which almost became official policy, called for "converting Germany into a country primarily agricultural and pastoral in its character."

Kennan, however, believed Germany needed U.S. aid and assistance; weak and abandoned, it would soon become a province of Moscow. The only solution was to divide the nation and try to make the western territories vigorous enough to resist Russian influence. A dismembered Germany, with the west as a buffer to the forces of totalitarianism, was preferable to a united Germany that could bring those forces to the North Sea.

To Kennan, this was just one of many lines that must be drawn through the map of Europe. The United States must split the world into "spheres of influence," he declared with resignation. We would maintain influence in western Europe; the Soviets could have eastern Europe. There was not much point in hoping for a belt of neutral countries down the middle of the continent: Russia would only gobble them up. "We should accept as an accomplished fact the complete partition of Germany along the line of the Russian zone of occupation," Kennan wrote.

Planning for the postwar world, of course, meant finding people who could run a respectable, competent western German government. And that was where von Moltke came in: he was the man who Kennan thought could best rule this new country.

Kennan's hopes were soon dashed. Von Moltke had survived the early years of the war, quietly hiding the depth of his opposition to Hitler even as he held secret meetings to plan for a post-Nazi Germany. But the Nazis had caught on and arrested him in January 1944. He had remained active in prison, smuggling out passionate letters about the future of Germany to his wife, Freya, who hid them in beehives in her garden. He survived a year, but the Allies did not defeat Germany fast enough. In January 1945, the "People's Court" of Nazi Germany condemned von Moltke to death.

His final letters describe the scene in vivid detail. He was like a journalist reporting his own execution, down to a sketch of where everyone at the trial sat. He was as cool as Speer, if in service to a greater cause. "My dear heart, first I must say that quite obviously the last 24 hours of a life are in no way different from any others. I always imagined that one would feel shock, that one would say to oneself: Now the sun sets for the last time for you," he wrote. "None of that is the case." He would go calmly, he said, feeling that God was on his side. His last letter read: "Only together do we constitute a human being. We are, as I wrote a few days ago, symbolically, created as one. That is true, literally true. Therefore, my love, I am certain that you will not lose me on this earth, not for a moment."

In May 1945, Kennan argued the case for von Moltke's promotion in a letter to a State Department colleague. "I can personally think of no one who would eventually make a better political leader for other Germans." Four months earlier, von Moltke had been hanged.

FOR ALL KENNAN's dismay over von Moltke, he had other priorities that spring than the matter of choosing a new ruler for Germany. He wished urgently to convince America to look realistically at the men now running the Soviet Union. In May 1945, he wrote a long memo that he would later consider one of the most important of his life. "Peace, like spring, has finally come to Russia," he began; but of those two arrivals, the change of seasons was "far the more noticeable on the Moscow scene."

Kennan was known inside the State Department as nothing more than a highly competent clerk, but he had enormous confidence in his ability to provide a map for a shattered world. He argued that one of Russia's greatest challenges would be managing all the territory it had acquired in the war. He loved to quote Edward Gibbon's line that "there is nothing more contrary to nature than the attempt to hold in obedience distant provinces," and he made that argument, and cited the scholar, here. Russia now was adding subjects from Estonia to East Prussia to the Kuril Islands at the same time that it was trying to extend its authority over nations long hostile, for example Poland and Hungary.

The trouble was linguistic and cultural. The people in these lands did not speak Russian and did not identify with the Russians. More broadly, Kennan correctly saw that the Soviets had transformed communism from a set of well-meaning principles into a rationale for totalitarianism. By 1945, Stalin had crushed the few ideals (and idealists) that Lenin had not liquidated. People would still do what the Kremlin asked, or commanded, them to do. But they would not do so because they believed that the doctrine preached in Moscow would make for a better world, or that Moscow even had that intention. The Soviet government, wrote Kennan, "has before its gates a submissive but no longer an inspired mass of followers." True in Moscow, that was even truer in the conquered territories.

The resulting strain on the Soviet empire, Kennan argued, would mean that Stalin would need Western assistance and cooperation. And here was his main point: Stalin knew exactly how to manipulate the United States. The Soviet Union was constantly leading America on, asking for one favor and then demanding two more. "They observe with gratification that in this way a great people can be led, like an ever-hopeful suitor, to perform one act of ingratiation after the other without ever reaching the goal which would satisfy its ardor and allay its generosity." When conflict came, Russia would simply call a summit, apologize, and announce that it was starting anew. America would acquiesce—until the next time Russia decided to stick its finger in the eye of its unwitting rival. Then the cycle would restart.

Kennan's memo ended in pained lament. A group of mendacious rulers crudely rationalizing their power by preaching a false ideology had clearly overreached. But the United States would need steady nerves and deep thinking to counter them. And success was not likely, he said, as long as Stalin treated America the way a farmer treats an ox with a rope through its nose: with occasional trepidation but an unwavering sense that he can move it wherever he wants.

Kennan's memo was forceful, beautifully written, and largely right—and it was ignored. He was just a cookie-pushing diplomat with a fondness for Gibbon (whom few people had read) and much venom toward Stalin (whom many people still admired). For nearly another year, the United States would trust and blithely negotiate with the man known to American tabloids as Uncle Joe. Kennan's time to influence the struggle between the two new superpowers had yet to come.

NITZE HAD HIS OWN problems with the USSR. He desperately wanted to capture key Germans before the Red Army did, and he sneaked around Flensburg, hoping the Soviets wouldn't be able to figure out who he was interviewing. In a letter home, he compared his operations to the plot of a spy novel.

He was more right than he knew. For while Nitze carefully locked his documents away, one of the Survey's assistants, Jürgen Kuczynski, was sending them off to the Soviets. Kuczynski had been spying for a decade and had even recruited Klaus Fuchs, the atomic scientist working in Britain who later gave the West's nuclear secrets to Stalin. Kuczynski had been careful over his long career and he fit in smoothly at the Strategic

Bombing Survey. Colleagues remember him as a quiet, elegant man who worked hard and was "easy to talk with." Meanwhile, though, he sent everything he could to Moscow: reports meant to be distributed only to fifteen people, starting with Dwight D. Eisenhower, quietly made it to Stalin.

Kuczynski's handler was his sister in England, then known as Ruth Brewer, one of the USSR's most important spies. Brewer was a housewife and mother who passed herself off as a persecuted Jewish refugee even as she worked toward becoming the first woman to be made an honorary colonel in the Red Army. A devout communist, she kept in contact with the Soviets through a radio transmitter whose components were hidden inside her children's teddy bears. Everything in her life was part of an act for the sake of the cause, even two of her three children. One was the result of her effort to create a cover story while spying on Japan; she conceived another with a man she married to get a British passport and residency.

Nitze knew nothing of what was going on behind his back, perhaps because he was exhausted, working seventeen hours a day, seven days a week, on detailed analyses of the bombings. The fatigue exhilarated him, though. "I have never felt better than I do at the moment," he wrote his mother. As would be true for the rest of his life, nothing cheered Nitze up like working hard on matters of consequence, and nothing would depress him so much as slacking off.

In mid-June, he won the chance to apply his energies to a problem that dealt with the future, not the past. He had traveled to Berlin in the hopes of meeting with Albert Speer's chief statistician when, one night, he received a cryptic message ordering him to the Frankfurt airport the following morning at six. Frankfurt was 120 miles away on bombed-out roads. He did not know where he was going or why. But he grabbed his driver and jeep, hurtled through the night, and arrived at the airfield fifteen minutes before the appointed time. Once there, Nitze got another brief order: he was flying to Washington to help organize the ongoing war with Japan.

FOR THREE AND HALF YEARS, the Japanese and the Americans had battled for the islands of the Pacific and the air above. By the spring of 1945, the United States had driven the Japanese back and begun a fierce bombing campaign against the home islands.

Nitze's job in Washington was to help draw plans for what everyone hoped would be the last stage of the war. Henry "Hap" Arnold, command-ing general of the U.S. Army Air Forces, believed that what the men in-volved in the Strategic Bombing Survey had learned from their analysis of the European air offensive could help the United States win without invad-ing Japan's densely populated, ferociously defended main archipelago.

Nitze got to work, convinced that Speer had taught him the most im-portant lesson of modern warfare: knock out the basic infrastructure. He stayed in the United States, furiously writing up lists of targets and pri-orities on long sheets of yellow paper. On the Fourth of July he took his pad to Jones Beach with his family, panicking after he left it behind while buying ice cream. Fortunately, no Japanese spies spirited it away from the drugstore before he realized his mistake.

Two weeks later, Nitze met with an army air forces planning group led by General Lauris Norstad to argue in favor of knocking out Japan's entire transportation system: its roads, bridges, and railroad tracks. America had already destroyed most of the enemy's shipping capacity; if the Japanese could not move materials around the country by land, Nitze argued, then neither could they build what they needed to fight back. Japan would, as he later said, "wither into surrender." But although oth-ers from the Strategic Bombing Survey backed Nitze up, the army air forces brass were not persuaded.

Since March, American planes had been dropping incendiary bombs on Japan's biggest cities, burning the wooden homes, offices, and factories. That strategy seemed to be working, Norstad's team argued. Nitze coun-tered that his plans were more efficient, as well as more humane. One of the generals at the meeting responded that the attacks on Germany had succeeded because the United States had targeted many different sectors. "Certainly the testimony of not only Mr. Speer but everyone else who had to do with the production effort in Germany," Nitze shot back, "is in di-rect opposition to this principle."

Nitze's advice was ignored, but that did not matter. Two days before his meeting with the planning group, a group of physicists had put on heavy welders' goggles to watch the most massive fireball in the history of mankind explode over Alamogordo, New Mexico. As the mushroom cloud went up, the director of the test, Kenneth Bainbridge, looked the physicist Robert Oppenheimer in the eyes and softly said, "Now we're all sons of bitches." Two weeks later, Norstad was choosing which cities to wipe off the map.

It was no longer of consequence whether America directed a fleet of aircraft to hit the ball-bearing plants, the railroads, or the cities. One plane, carrying one weapon, could destroy all of them and more. Nitze's plans and all of his hard-studied ideas about strategic bombing melted into obsolescence. New theories of offensive war would arise, but of a totally different nature. The most sudden of all new eras had begun.

2

CHARMING, WITTY, AND URBANE

O ne moves through life like someone moving with a lantern in a dark woods. A bit of the path ahead is illuminated, and a bit of the path behind," wrote George Kennan early in his memoirs. "We are, toward the end of our lives, such different people, so far removed from the childhood figures with whom our identity links us, that the bond to those figures, like that of nations to their obscure prehistoric origins, is almost irrelevant."

Almost, but not quite. The boy who sat alone and deep in thought in Milwaukee in 1910 could have traversed those woods by many different ways. But from the far side, the route he ultimately took looks fairly straight. The frail, elegant figure who in 2003 soberly predicted the tragedy to come in Iraq seems indissolubly tied to that child. Likewise, the ninety-one-year-old Paul Nitze, hobbling out onto the tennis court, where he would hit one ball and then rest for a minute on a chair he had set up on the baseline, seems inextricably connected to the young Paul Nitze, darting through the streets of Chicago's Hyde Park neighborhood.

The two men had plenty in common. They were nearly of an age: Kennan was born in 1904, Nitze in 1907. They spent their midwestern childhoods just ninety miles apart and attended the same summer camp—Camp Highlands, in northern Wisconsin—though not at the same time. Both traveled east for college (Kennan to Princeton, Nitze to Harvard). Both were too young to be drafted into World War I and too old to enlist in the fight against Hitler. Their rites of passage—journeys to Europe; love; first heartbreak; first job; marriage; success; failure; success again—came at similar times and in similar places.

But just as they were very different men, they were very different boys. Kennan never fit in; Nitze always did. Until he became a successful writer, Kennan was often short of money. Nitze was born with some, earned a lot, and married more. Kennan's recollections of youth are always about observations and feelings: what the young George thought when alone. Nitze's recollections are fables and adventures, populated by friends, criminals, and historical icons. In his memoirs, Nitze makes his youth sound like *The Adventures of Tom Sawyer*; Kennan's evokes *East of Eden*.

KENNAN'S LIFE BEGAN in tragedy. Two months after her only son's birth, Florence James Kennan died of a burst appendix. As the story was told, the doctors could have saved her, had they not refused to operate on a woman without her husband's consent—and Kossuth Kennan was out of town, fishing. His mother's death left George in the care of several aunts, three older sisters, and, later, an indifferent stepmother whom he would remember as a "highly nervous woman, thin and uncertain of herself . . . sort of a sissy." George's father, a quiet tax lawyer, seemed more like a grandfather, peacefully sitting in his chair reading the Bible. He never talked about George's mother. The only keepsake of her was a trunk on the third floor that held her clothes, her gloves, and long locks of chestnut-colored hair.

George's beloved sister Jeanette, two years older and his closest companion, would say that their mother's death scarred him. He admitted as much in later years, declaring that the event made him "in some way or another twisted." He was quiet and withdrawn; Jeanette remembered him as a boy staring endlessly into his soup. "George, stop thinking," his aunt once snapped.

It was, perhaps, appropriate that Kennan's childhood home provided little natural light. It had been built the wrong way around, so that the windows of the main room faced another house, while the side without windows fronted an open yard. George went to Milwaukee's Fourth Street School, across the street from the Schlitz Brewing Company, where one of his older classmates was Golda Mabovitch, later

Meir. Even at a young age, he displayed a talent with words, writing this poem when he was nine:

> I had a big cloth soldier
> just made for a little boy
> his arms and sword came off, you know
> but he is the funniest toy.
> He belonged to the German Army
> But that doesn't matter to me
> I brought him back to America
> Way across the sea.
> He can lift his feet right up to his eyes
> And up to his cap, that's more,
> He can't salute 'cause his arms are off
> And he could not salute before.

George skipped the eighth grade. Then his father packed him off to board at St. John's Military Academy, expecting the school to exert some stern masculine influence. The austere, regimented place did that and more. The other students beat him up, dropped snakes in his shirt, and stole the cookies that Jeanette sent. The discipline did not make him happy; he twice tried to run away, and the yearbook listed his pet peeve as "the universe." Nor did military school make him particularly tough. At Camp Highlands, his yearbook recorded him as a "quiet fellow," and his most memorable moment came when he got in a scuffle with another camper. The two were taken behind the dining hall where all the other campers massed to watch them slug it out, but the boys merely circled each other, neither one daring to throw a punch.

Not surprisingly, his unhappiness seeped into his poetry. At fifteen, he wrote:

> The net is drawn about him,
> he is now a misanthrope;
> all his friends they have forsook him;
> he'll do naught but grieve and mope.
> He's no longer independent
> he must follow certain rules;

he must set a fine "example"
to his happy fellow fools.

Most of the young men of St. John's headed off for West Point or other
military schools. Kennan, though, had learned about Princeton from
F. Scott Fitzgerald's *This Side of Paradise,* had applied, and had gotten in.
He spent his undergraduate years struggling to relate to others—perhaps
appropriately, given the famous remark by Fitzgerald's protagonist: "I
know myself, but that is all." Always short of money, Kennan could not
travel to New York with his friends or even buy tobacco for the pipe he
smoked because cigarettes cost too much. At one point, he could not
even afford a stamp for a letter to Jeanette.

At least once, though, he was caught up in typical college-years excitement. In a riotous 1922 letter to his sister, he described listening to a
Princeton-Chicago football game on a shortwave radio. When Princeton
won, George joined the celebration in the street. The next week, though,
he started to fret. "Last year I felt so lonely, the day of the Yale game, that I
tore loose after everybody had left on the train and I bummed my way up,
arriving just when the game started. It was all very well except that I did
not have a ticket, and late that night I got back to Princeton minus about
ten dollars and plus nothing, not even the sight of the game." Now he felt
even less hopeful that he would attend the big game. "We play Harvard
away, far away, several hundred miles, in fact, way off in Massachusetts."

But a few days later an angel appeared. Returning home from a pep
rally, Kennan found a note on his table telling him to report immediately
to the athletic association. He hustled over and was given a round-trip
fare on the Fall River boat line to Boston, a ticket to the game, and four
dollars' travel money. Some anonymous patron had smiled on him. "Now
do you wonder I bubble over?" he concluded the letter to his sister.

He seemed eventually to fit in and even entered an eating club, a key to
social success at Princeton. He became the club's assistant manager to pay
the fees. But that fleeting moment of social ease ended soon enough when
he decided that weakness had led him to join. The better course would be
to show internal strength and return to the wilderness with the unselected
rejects. Soon he would join them, sitting in a dining hall in total silence,
none wanting the others to think he could not bear the isolation.

★

NITZE'S MOTHER, ANINA Hilken Nitze, was a brilliant bon vivante. Famous men and women were her guests, and she shocked right-thinking people by smoking and arguing when she was supposed to be quietly keeping house. She befriended the dancer Isadora Duncan and once took out a mortgage to help raise bail for a client of her friend Clarence Darrow. She dressed her son properly, hiked up mountains with him, and showed him Europe. Paul Nitze would claim many decades later that she was "by far the greatest influence in my life." She showed "absolutely immense vitality and warmth and wit and energy, and loved me beyond any normal maternal love; it became overwhelming. At times, I wanted to get away from it. It was too intense in a way."

Paul's father provided order. William Albert Nitze was one of the country's great philologists. He taught at the University of Chicago for forty years, and a book he cowrote, *A History of French Literature,* was a classroom standard for decades. His *Arthurian Names in the Perceval of Chrétien de Troyes* was part of a renowned effort to trace the story of the Holy Grail through European literature. But he spent so much time in the ninth and tenth centuries that he often missed the twentieth. He worked in an office at home that he permitted no one else to enter: not his wife, not his children, not the woman who cleaned the rest of the house. His son remembered him scratching his pancakes and pouring syrup on his head. When he and Paul took walks, he sometimes entirely forgot the little boy beside him. When he did pay attention, it was often to correct. Nitze's own son recalls once hearing the sounds of plates shattering against the dining room wall as the two older men argued. Why? the boy asked his grandmother Anina. "They're arguing, and it's not that Paul's conclusion is wrong. It's that his argument is insufficiently closely reasoned to be worthy of the family honor."

Paul Nitze's best friend, Glenn Millikan, the son of a Nobel laureate in physics, lived across the street. The two boys converted a room in Nitze's house into a laboratory where they created a simple wire-telephone system to link their homes. They failed in their efforts to build a radio but had more luck with miniature bombs, which they set off all around the neighborhood. Tormented by other boys because of the elaborate Russian suits his mother made him wear—sent by her best friend, in Riga, and complete with patent leather belt and red short pants—Nitze joined a gang called the Scotti Brothers that controlled one of the neighborhood blocks. It was an early lesson in power relations: sign up with the strong kids and then no one else will knock you over. "You must have spent much of your youth fighting battles in defense of your sartorial virility, all to be blamed on our Mother," wrote his older sister, Elizabeth, six decades later.

At fifteen, Paul got a summer job working in the engine room of a ship traveling to Germany. It was his first experience with manual labor and real adventure, both of which he professed to love. Joseph Conrad, already Nitze's favorite writer, could have narrated the journey. The men he worked alongside were uniformly tough. "All of them had been in the war and nearly half of them had been prisoners of war," he wrote his mother. "The most interesting man was the fourth engineer, the engineer on my watch. He asked me to come and drink coffee with him after the night watch. We would sit for three-quarters of an hour while he would tell me stories of typhoons, smugglers, Siberia, Bucharest, Paris, India, China, in fact everything."

Still, Paul Nitze was not cut out for a career as Marlow or Nostromo. When he got back, his parents sent him off to Hotchkiss, an elite Connecticut boarding school where his most notable achievement was to start the "sequestration club." Hotchkiss banned sports for students who earned three demerits, forced them to touch the wall with their arms wherever they walked, and required them to run a three-mile course around the campus "triangle" every afternoon. When Nitze was sanctioned for visiting a nearby girls' school without permission, he responded by sending away to New York for little triangular medals bearing emblems of a man running. He gave them to the other sequestration club members, and all wore them with pride on their watch chains.

Paul was more than just a rogue, however. In a 1923 article for a school publication, he appeared to be both a dreamer and a rationalist.

If one looks at the stars for any length of time, they invariably fill one with a sense of awe and wonder. They seem so far distant, so unchangeable, and so vast that in comparison, we seem puny. Think of the vast multitude of stars, of their tremendous size, of their inconceivable age, and of the possibility of life on some of their planets. All these thoughts have but one effect, to make one feel quite insignificant. One thinks, in a universe of such immensity, what difference can the actions of a single human being make in the period of a lifetime?

If, however, we keep in mind the fact that for us the world is every-

thing and that each one of us is the center of his small universe, we realize that we are not such an unimportant thing after all. . . . Each one of
us has been entrusted with one life to do with as he thinks best. If he
makes the most of his life, he may accomplish things which will not only
bring him his reward but which will give an infinite amount of happiness and comfort to the rest of the world.

Finishing Hotchkiss, Nitze headed off to Harvard. Ambitious and
clever, he nonetheless had no immediate path to social success. He was not
an impressive athlete and, as the son of a professor, he did not have quite
enough polish or social status for any of Harvard's elite "final clubs."

Not a man to dine alone, Nitze enlisted a friend from the freshman
crew team, Freddie Winthrop. His ancestors having helped found Massachusetts in the 1630s, Freddie was a shoo-in for the most prestigious of
all the final clubs, the Porcellian. (Theodore Roosevelt had been admitted
but not so his cousin Franklin—a rejection FDR described to a friend as
one of the most bitter of his life.) When Winthrop was asked to join, he
declared that he would do so only if Nitze was invited too. The tactic succeeded, and the professor's son joined an exclusive network. At one dinner of members and alums, for instance, Nitze ate with a group that
included Leverett Saltonstall (a future U.S. senator), Nicholas Longworth
(House Speaker), Richard Whitney (president of the New York Stock Exchange), and a new recruit named Joe Alsop.

Nitze drank martinis with his fellow club member Charles "Chip"
Bohlen and kept a bottle of rum in his room's chimney. Members adhered
to the club's motto, *Dum vivimus vivamus* ("While we live, let's *live*") and
paid no attention to Prohibition. Nitze started writing home on Porc sta-
tionery, and not to recount his studies. In one letter, he describes hiding a
car by shoveling snow over it until it disappeared. In another, he and a
couple of friends dress up as nurses and have a baby-carriage race up and
down Massachusetts Avenue. "We were the darndest looking bunch of idi-
ots I have ever seen." They also got drunk, hurled one another into the river,
and tossed each other about in blankets. "The week has been a total loss as
far as studies go. And I am afraid the next couple weeks will also be."

After a terrible academic performance during his sophomore year,
Nitze buckled down—more or less. He worked hard enough as a senior
to graduate, and to earn a summa grade on his thesis, but in the process
he drove himself to exhaustion and then came down with hepatitis.

When he felt well again he got roaring drunk to celebrate the end of exams and took a bet that he and a friend could not canoe from Boston to New York City. Nitze spent the next eight days eating canned beans and paddling. Having won the bet, he decided to celebrate at yet another party in North Easton, Massachusetts, where he entered a sixty-yard dash, made it for thirty yards, and then collapsed. This time the hepatitis nearly killed him. He spent the next six months recovering, much of it at the house of a friend whose mother read Trollope aloud to the convalescent. "I am also feeling so sorry for you and Dr. Nitze," wrote a friend to his mother, apparently thinking that Paul was done for.

GEORGE KENNAN AND PAUL NITZE would not meet for some years, but their paths crossed in the late 1920s. Kennan had finished college and joined the Foreign Service, which sent him to study Russian at the University of Berlin. He found the city gloomy and unappealing—haunted, he wrote, by "the unfulfilled pretensions of a bygone day." The social life was empty. "Now in the high-ceilinged dining room, where Prussian officers once clicked polished heels on the polished floor, only a few dour foreigners eat their hurried meals in depressed silence."

Kennan was lonesome and reflective.

In the freshness of the morning, I walk on damp paths, along the sides of a quiet, tree-lined canal. Ripples murmur placidly against stone embankments. An occasional barge, with its cargo of yellow bricks, moves unhurriedly under the bridges while the restless traffic pours overhead. Watching those slow-moving barges and the shimmering reflections of the trees in the water, I can almost feel again the spirit of the day when the world had time to dream and consider. But then, I turn up into the roar of the Potsdamerstrasse; the mood is ruined, and the twentieth century is on me again.

Nitze ended up in Berlin at about the same time, but he certainly was neither dour, hurried, depressed, nor silent. Having decided to work in finance, he had convinced a firm to send him to Europe to analyze the German economy. When he arrived in Berlin, he quickly befriended Alexander Calder, who was making wire sculptures, including one considered quite scandalous that would produce the figure of a Christ child if you dropped a French coin into it. The two moved in together at the Pension Naumann, a place described as "glorious" by Nitze. "Frau Naumann was a very jolly old lady and her idea to take care of the needs of the clients was to have three large carafes on the dining room table filled with vodka, and one with white wine and one with red wine at every meal including breakfast."

Nitze and Calder arranged a "traveling circus" of friends who all bought bicycles and traversed Germany and then Holland, drinking, cavorting, and acting like puppies at a picnic. Back in Berlin, Nitze embraced upper-class German social life, toured factories, met leading businessmen, and traveled with a labor union official based at the University of Berlin. Through a friend at the Rot-Weiss Tennis Club, Nitze also became the temporary assistant manager of the star player Helen Wills Moody. Berlin, he recalled, "was full of life." He passed through Paris too: romping, partying, falling in and out of love. "Five people came within an ace of having nervous breakdowns and nothing happened. I could write five volumes on it and still not make heads or tails out of it," he wrote home. "I wouldn't have traded those three weeks for an ordinary lifetime."

Another friend, the artist Isamu Noguchi, would later say, "I didn't think Paul was going to make much of himself in life." Nitze responded, "I didn't think Noguchi was going to make much of *himself*."

IN THE LATE 1920s, Kennan fell in love with a woman named Eleanor Hard, the affluent, outgoing, and socially in-demand daughter of a respected Washington journalist. Kennan had had little experience with women and less experience with power. He did not love Eleanor deeply, but he loved the idea of who he could become if he married her. "I perceived in Washington, for the first time, that I could beat the people I had always envied at their own game. I saw I could become both respected and powerful,—that I, too, might someday make the very pillars of the State Department tremble, as I walked through the ringing corridors."

The two became engaged. But Eleanor soured on the relationship, and her father had never taken to Kennan at all. Soon the wedding was off. Eleanor did not even return the ring Kennan had given her, which had belonged to his mother. "Go back to your teacups and fancy pants and safe obscurity," William Hard told the younger man.

Kennan wrote Jeanette soon after the breakup and declared the debacle a learning experience. He would have to plot a new life course, far from his dream of the State Department's inner councils but much happier. "I will probably never be vastly admired; I shall never achieve much personal dignity; my wife, if I ever have one, will doubtless be in no sense ideal and will be generally spoken of as an impossible person. Far from becoming wealthy, I will probably effectively lose what money I have." But he would be independent. "Between 9 to 4, I belong to [the government] body and soul. I am an efficient consular officer of the United States during those hours, and I am reconciled to rendering in this manner unto Caesar all those things which are Caesar's. But when the last visa applicant has left, and the accounts are done, and door of the Consulate closes behind me, I am George Kennan, and if the government doesn't like it, it can whistle long and hard."

Kennan's pessimism about his prospects in marriage was belied when he fell for a quiet, beautiful Norwegian woman named Annelise Sorensen. They met in Berlin, through a friend of Kennan's who had married her cousin. "She is simply phenomenally sweet and unspoiled. I can't say enough for her. She has one of the most happy, unexacting dispositions in the world. She combines a childlike simplicity and sincerity and gaiety with a very mature common sense. She has enough dignity and discretion to be an ambassadress, and not a trace of conceit. Everybody loves her," he wrote Jeanette. "Even the German minister's wife, who hates me like poison, just melts when she sees her or talks about her." He summed up, "She was simply born a lady and I hope that I'll be a good enough husband not to spoil her." George and Annelise married in 1931; they stayed together until he died, seventy-four years later.

NITZE'S FIRST SERIOUS girlfriend, Mary Ames, was born into the prominent Massachusetts family that made the shovels used to build the Union Pacific Railroad. The two began to date during his Harvard years and were brought closer together by the most horrible moment in Nitze's youth.

Driving in his 1917 Pierce-Arrow from the Ameses' house in downtown Boston on the night of November 23, 1928, with Mary in the front seat, Nitze crossed Beacon Street from Charlesgate West. Suddenly they saw two people walking arm in arm; Nitze slammed on the brakes, but not in time. He jumped out, pulled the two into his car, and raced to the hospital. The man's leg was fractured. The woman, Victoria Stuart, was badly wounded; she died a few hours later.

Nitze was shaken by the accident and then by the suit brought against him by the families of the victims—a legal case that dominated his letters home for the next few months. He ended up paying lump sums of several thousand dollars to the man and to Stuart's estate, an arrangement his lawyer thought much safer than going to trial. "I am convinced there was no good ground for a conviction, yet juries are so swayed by prejudice that the fact that a Harvard student in the company of young people of means and social position, on their way to a Back Bay party, [became] involved in a motor accident, might easily lead to conviction."

Nitze kept his cool and acted wisely. Friends complimented his composure. His actions seemed to make Ames fall more deeply in love. Referencing his solo involvement in the suit, she wrote, "I can't bear the idea of you all alone out there—having to face everything yourself. But darling—know you are strong and you have proved that to us already." In another letter, she lamented, "You say I never tell you anything—I don't—it's time—last night I wanted to tell you I loved you. That I would marry you. But I could not. . . . You have so terribly much ahead of you—you are so far above me in every way—I didn't think I could make you happy—would help you—I haven't enough to give—I'm so young—and spoiled. . . . But I love you Paul—I do—I know I do now."

Nitze, however, was less smitten. At one point, he told Ames that she was lazy, thoughtless, and self-indulgent. Soon after he graduated, they broke off the relationship, and Nitze headed to Europe.

A few years later, though, he met a woman he considered his equal in strength and wit: Phyllis Pratt, the glamorous daughter of Ruth Baker Pratt, one of the country's first congresswomen. At one of his first appearances at her house, Paul, twenty-five years old and somewhat impertinent, got in a fierce argument over the causes of the Great Depression—with the governor of the Bank of England. Afterward, Pratt asked her daughter, "You are not interested in that young man, are you?"

"Perhaps," said Phyllis.

"I am going upstairs to be sick," responded Pratt.

She came down though soon afterward. "If you are interested in him, I'll change my mind. I love you, Phyllis, and if you are serious, I'll consider him a son of mine."

Neither Nitze nor his family had any hesitation. "Prepare yourself for the good news," he wrote his mother. "Phyllis Pratt seems to think that she can bear to see my sour face across the breakfast table for years to come and what's more enjoy it. . . . Come East soon and see the paragon. Your son has really done a master stroke."

At their fiftieth wedding anniversary, Nitze would reflect on a conversation that he and Phyllis had soon before they became engaged. He was driving her home along the East River and they parked to talk about whether they should spend their lives together. Nitze declared that he loved Phyllis beyond measure, but said he simply was not ready for marriage. He was too nervous, high-strung, ambitious, and temperamental. He was too interested in a career. But Phyllis said he had it all wrong. "I had arrogantly assumed it would all depend on me; if we got married it would depend on both of us. She was sure it would succeed."

He and Phyllis were married until she died, fifty-five years later.

IN HIS LATE twenties, Kennan's career in the Foreign Service began to soar. By his estimation, he earned promotions faster than anyone in his class. While serving in Moscow from 1933 until 1937, he made close friends inside the American embassy and in other European missions. He worked hard, mostly reporting back home on the Moscow political scene, and enjoyed life and debate with his friends. "Most of us look back on those days, I suppose, as the high point of life—the high point at least in comradeship, in gaiety, in intensity of experience." His daughter would later compare his experiences in those years to a "first love."

He left Moscow once in 1935, having become terribly ill three days after the murder of Sergey Kirov, a friend and rival of Stalin's. Kennan spent several months in an Austrian sanitarium. As was often the case with him, he may have stayed in his sickbed longer than necessary. In later years, he would confess to his daughter that he found nurses strikingly comforting—and alluring, too. He surmised that this was because of his absent mother and because of the female nurses who had been such a large source of what comfort he was given in his childhood.

After his stint in Moscow, Kennan returned to the United States for a year and worked on the Russia desk of the State Department. In September 1938, he was sent to Prague, a capital firmly in the sights of a Nazi government now beginning to make territorial demands upon its weaker neighbors. On his third or fourth day at the legation, a gorgeous woman with long golden hair stormed in. Why wasn't America doing anything for the hundreds of thousands of Czechs fleeing the Germans? she demanded. Kennan murmured that he could do nothing and wrote her off as an ill-informed do-gooder. Unknown then, the woman, Martha Gellhorn, soon made something of herself, both as one of Ernest Hemingway's wives and as one of the century's great war correspondents and letter writers.

Not long after his encounter with Gellhorn, Kennan had the irritating task of having to arrange for a visit by the son of America's well-connected ambassador in London. Kennan found the request ludicrous and the timing absurd. But he reluctantly and diligently took the son around. Years later, that young man, John Fitzgerald Kennedy, would make something of himself too.

In mid-March 1939, Hitler's army marched in. As the Germans approached, Kennan thought about an obsession of his: good form. By looking correct and bearing oneself in the proper manner, he believed, one could hide, perhaps even diminish, all sorts of inner turmoil. The morning the Nazis rolled into Prague, Kennan made sure to shave extra carefully, so as not to give the impression of someone harried by Hitler's triumph. Kennan maintained that kind of veneer throughout his life. Friends and colleagues would long note his fine sense of self-control and his extraordinary discipline. But underneath were stormy seas.

For example, three years after the Nazis arrived in Prague, during his internment in Bad Nauheim, Kennan confided to his diary that his fits of depression brought him closer to understanding reality than when he felt contentment. "There is only one solution. You have come to this conclusion over and over again. It is to abandon hope, to acknowledge one's self as old and beyond these things. My God, man, you are no youngster any more. What do you expect?"

The next day, his despair increased.

What do I actually want in life? Which is within the conceivable realm of possibility? For myself I would wish (1) a happy, beloved personal life, and (2) work which I consider positive. The first of these is out of the question because of the tragedy that has occurred. The second is out of the question largely because I am an American. If a people were only deluded you might do something with it. But when it is biologically undermined and demoralized, there is no future for it—regardless of the outcome of the war—but to suffer the consequences of its deficiencies. . . .

The only solution then, personally, is gardening, or the sort of a glorified gardening called gentlemanly farming—that is the perhaps the only form of playing with toys which is not ridiculous in elderly men. And it gives me a chance to acquit our responsibilities toward at least a small section of that earth which—in the mean—we men have so abominably misused and disfigured. . . .

Why in the name of God, must I be pursued by misfortune in this relentless way? . . . I cannot face these people now. I am burning inside with rage and humiliation. To think that I, George Kennan, should be in the position of having to conceal anything. If I go away then and lead a normal life, and the thing later comes out, I have made myself a double hypocrite. I should have to withdraw from them anyway. Then I should rather do it now and anticipate them.

In a moment of weakness, he had sinned and done something so heinous he could not even name it in his diary, and something he would never speak or write about publicly. But the nature of his self-approbation points to marital infidelity. And two people close to him confirmed that the event causing so much anguish was an affair with another detainee.

PAUL NITZE'S PROFESSIONAL CAREER began with a lesson about discipline. Recently graduated from Harvard, Nitze walked into the office of Clarence Dillon, the head of the powerful Wall Street firm Dillon Read, bearing a letter of recommendation from a family friend. Within "about five seconds," he wrote home, Dillon had figured him out. He was a young man floating on a cloud of self-confidence: the oldest son in a line of oldest sons dating back to the sixteenth century, who had rarely applied himself.

Dillon pointed to a spreadsheet lying in the office. "You see what I have in front of me?" he said. He was reviewing the fiftieth draft of a bond advertisement. "The most competent lawyers and accountants in New York have gone over this word by word, comma by comma, figure by figure," Dillon said. "And you know what I am doing? I am going through this to see whether the arithmetic is correct, whether the grammar is correct."

Lesson number one: pay attention to detail. Lesson number two: you will mean nothing to me until you have actually done something.

Still, Dillon saw promise in the young man, so he invited him to lunch with one of his vice presidents, a thirty-seven-year-old former naval aviator named James Forrestal. The two were trying to map out a merger that would create the most powerful bank in the country. "It was an extraordinary experience," Nitze wrote home. "I left feeling very small and ineffectual. Forrestal impressed me as being very keen and forceful. A much finer specimen than anything I have seen for a long time."

Dillon hired Nitze a few months later, right before the stock market crash that helped trigger the Great Depression. Nitze did apply himself, and he climbed fast. He was not a complete success, though. As with his investments throughout his life, Nitze lost big nearly as often as he won. For three years, he said, he became a "nonperson" in the eyes of Dillon after losing $1.5 million of the firm's money in a failed effort to take over a utility company.

Nevertheless, a decade after joining Dillon Read, Nitze had earned a reputation as one of Wall Street's ablest young men. He was again close to Dillon and he had become a confidant of Forrestal. But maybe his conversion from dilettante to executive had come too fast; at age thirty, he was tired of finance and convinced that he should do something he considered more important.

Nitze also knew that he had not lived up to his father's expectations. William A. Nitze always wanted his only son to be smarter, more intellectually distinguished, and more bookish—perhaps a professor of Romance languages. He thought a career in business was a step down for the family. Writing home, Paul frequently boasted about what he had read. He was always seeking a certain respect, and he knew he would not win it with a job as what the old man called a "money-lender." Years later, he would complain that no one had ever had a more demanding father.

But his father's example also haunted him in a negative way. Privately, he considered the great scholar a partial failure. William Nitze and his University of Chicago colleagues were, Paul recalled, "the most admirable group of men one could imagine." But, he added, "they were having no impact upon the things that were going on in the world that seemed to me to be the most tragic and important."

In 1937, just before the economy plummeted again, Nitze left investment banking to spend a year taking graduate classes at Harvard in philosophy and sociology. But it did not work. He could not find the answers in stock tables, and he could not find them in a deep analysis of Spengler.

He started his own firm: Paul H. Nitze and Company was a modest success, but running it was stressful, and he soon returned to Dillon Read. "It was kind of exciting working on [my] own," he would later recall, "but your judgment is better and you can do it better if you associate with a group."

He kept thinking he had more important work to do than finance. Then, one day, James Forrestal, who had become the firm's president, gave Nitze exactly that opportunity. On June 22, 1940, as France began its surrender to Germany, FDR asked Forrestal to join the government as an administrative assistant. Forrestal had worked closely with Nitze in their years together at Dillon Read and he sent a cable immediately to the young man, who was then negotiating a deal in Louisiana. "Be in Washington Monday morning. Forrestal."

Nitze bolted to the capital. His destiny was at last apparent: he would find his identity in service to his country. There remained just one obstacle to overcome: a black sheep in the family who would complicate Nitze's ambition at several more points throughout his career.

AT AROUND ONE A.M. on July 30, 1916, a fire broke out aboard a barge moored at Black Tom Island, in New York harbor. An hour later, the barge's entire cargo of munitions blew up. More explosions followed. The ground shook as though in an earthquake; a fireball filled the sky. Nearly every window in Jersey City blew out; the streets of Manhattan's financial district were filled with glass. Even the windows of the New York Public Library, three and a half miles uptown, shattered. "City Is Terror Stricken," declared the *New York Times.*

Five nights later, at the top of the Hotel Astor in midtown Manhattan, a stout, burly man walked up to a smaller, mustachioed fellow and triumphantly said: "How about that bonfire?" The smaller man asked for details on who had planted the explosives. "It's better if you don't know too much," replied the other. The smaller man signaled his agreement and quietly handed over two $1,000 bills.

The conspirator making the payment was Paul Hilken, Paul Nitze's uncle and the man for whom he was named. Hilken's role in the sabotage of the munitions barge was to funnel cash from German intelligence operatives to the men who had pulled off the job. The aim of the conspiracy was to thwart U.S. arms shipments to Britain.

For years, Hilken kept his role secret, continuing his career as a successful Baltimore businessman. But in 1928 he decided to come clean, after being persuaded to do so by lawyers working a case brought against the government of Germany by American companies whose property had been destroyed in the blast. The lawyers had learned of suspicions of his role in the attack, tracked him down, and promised him that there would be no legal consequences for speaking out. Hilken's ties to Germany had dissipated over the years and he agreed. At first, the results were disastrous. Hilken tried to prove that the German government had supported the conspiracy, but he lacked proof. Germany won an early round in the international court adjudicating the dispute. The press denounced Hilken as both the traitor he admitted to being and the liar he appeared to be.

On Christmas Eve of 1930, however, Hilken was rummaging in his ex-wife's attic, looking for a place to hide presents for his daughter in the house he had lived in thirteen years earlier. He found a small hidden door that revealed a long-forgotten wooden box. In it were a number of old magazines that revealed the particulars of the conspiracy: the key messages had been written in lemon juice on their pages.

To read the messages, one had to take a hot iron to the paper, scorching the lemon juice and turning it brown. Four-digit numbers split up some sentences; Hilken remembered that dropping the first digit and reading the last three in reverse revealed a page number. The decoder would turn to that page, hold it up to the light, and look for pinpricks in particular letters. The pinpricked letters would then spell out a name to be inserted in place of the four-digit number. Hilken now had documentary proof of his own involvement as well as that of his co-conspirators'.

At first, the encoded messages were denounced as forgeries, but Hilken eventually persuaded the courts of their authenticity. Then, in 1939, twenty-three years after the barge exploded, and thanks to the long hard work of the prosecutor, John McCloy, a conspiracy was proven. The court ordered Germany to pay the United States $50 million.

The verdict vindicated Hilken but did not restore his good name. The next year, when his nephew headed to Washington, the FBI began an intensive investigation of his background. Not only had Paul Nitze's uncle organized sabotage on behalf of Germany, but Nitze himself had also reportedly exclaimed at a dinner party in 1940 that he would rather live under Hitler's Reich than the British Empire. The investigation was long and it was thorough. Meanwhile, Nitze could not be put on the government payroll: he began his career working for Forrestal on a Dillon Read salary.

Eventually, Nitze was cleared. He had made foolish comments about Germany—perhaps out of ignorance, or perhaps as part of his penchant for contrarian argument—but nearly everyone interviewed described his loyalty as unquestionable. His mentor played a particular role. "Forrestal indicated that he had known Nitze for many years and considered him one hundred percent American and neither pro-German nor pro-Nazi," read the report.

Nitze could finally become an official employee of the U.S. government. He also now had an extensive FBI file, full of details of his uncle's sins and the bureau's unfounded suspicions that his mother was a Nazi supporter as well. His enemies would circulate this material repeatedly through the coming decades.

KENNAN, TOO, HAD a skeleton in his filing cabinet: an essay he wrote while in a very dark mood.

His problem was intellectual, and it stemmed from his disorientation upon returning to the United States in 1937 after nearly a decade abroad. He felt alienated in a land that had transformed itself culturally, economically, and politically since his departure. The quiet Midwest of his childhood seemed to be vanishing. Political bosses and ethnic lobbies dominated Capitol Hill during the fierce congressional election campaign of 1938. Not for the last time, Kennan felt like a man without a country.

He was working in Washington and living in Alexandria, a city he detested as full of "filling stations, advertising signboards, hot-dog stands, junked automobiles and trailer-camps. . . . Dirt, heat, rats and decay: that was Alexandria in the summer." As he saw it, the United States had lost its independent spirit. Advertisers had turned people into dupes; modern magazines, movies, and fiction were turning minds to mush. Even American agriculture was broken.

Brooding in this foul mood in the summer heat, he wrote an essay he called "The Prerequisites." American democracy and culture had fundamental flaws, he asserted. Government had to solve them, but could do so only by changing its entire nature. "The only solution to the problem lies along a road which very few Americans are willing to contemplate: along the road which leads through constitutional change to the authoritarian state."

Kennan was no doubt influenced by his experiences in Austria in 1935, a country whose authoritarian rulers he considered completely benign. The same could happen here, he thought, and it might even represent what the authors of the Constitution would want if confronted by America's current disarray. He did not want a dictatorship but, in full misanthrope mode, he declared that this dreadful country needed the firm hands of a group of young, dedicated, organized, and highly educated men. The new order would deny suffrage to immigrants, women, and blacks. Clear-sighted white men would make decisions wisely and quickly for the general good.

How would this group of elites come to power? Kennan did not say, but he was confident it could happen. He mentioned violent insurrection, only to declare it probably unnecessary. "If the present degeneration of American political life continues, it is more probable that power will eventually drop like a ripe apple."

Fortunately, the apple did not drop. And fortunately for Kennan, no one saw the essay for decades. He never finished it, let alone sought to publish it. It gathered dust in his files for decades until C. Ben Wright, an enterprising doctoral student, dug it up in the mid-1970s, much to Kennan's embarrassment. By then, it had become a relic: the youthful ravings, produced during a very dark and long-ago moment, of a man who had long since made his reputation.

IN LATE OCTOBER 1943, Kennan was on the final leg of the arduous five-day journey from Portugal to Washington, sitting in the dining car of a train headed south from New York to the capital.

He did not know what awaited him there. As chargé d'affaires in the American embassy in Lisbon, Kennan had been negotiating over U.S. access to the Azores islands, an ideal mid-Atlantic base. Kennan thought, as he usually did, that the U.S. government had handled the talks crudely and disrespectfully, so he had discarded his negotiating orders and given the Portuguese prime minister assurances that America had no intention of seizing the islands. After this act of insubordination, Kennan received a note summoning him home immediately. He feared a severe governmental reprimand.

As Kennan pondered his fate, another well-tailored young man approached him. Paul Nitze was always looking for conversation, whether in a Berlin guesthouse or a Washington-bound train. He found something compelling about Kennan and sat down across from him in the dining car. The pair started talking and Kennan told a story about a party he had attended where one of the guests, shooting rockets off on a hot, dry day, had started a fire that nearly burned up the land nearby. Kennan had organized a bucket brigade to put out the conflagration. "He found the episode hilarious," Nitze recalled.

The junior man no doubt found it hilarious too. It was his kind of stunt. Every Fourth of July for decades, Nitze would host fireworks parties, inviting hundreds of guests to his Maryland farm. One specialty was a firework that looked like an American flag.

The two talked about politics in southern Europe and the dangers of Soviet communism. Nitze found his partner "charming, witty, and urbane." At Union Station, they shook hands and parted ways. Nitze went back to the State Department to continue his wartime economics work. Kennan, hoping to rescue his career, hustled into a meeting with the secretary of war and the Joint Chiefs of Staff. He then met with the president, who found the young diplomat brilliant and fully persuasive. Instead of being fired, Kennan returned to Portugal with a letter of presidential support. Less than a year later, the Azores would provide a critical wartime base for the Allies.

Kennan spent the rest of the war abroad and at its end stood over the Victory Day celebration in Red Square. Nitze ended up in Glücksburg Castle and then on Jones Beach, trying to write up his plans for a bombing campaign against Japan. The two did not meet again for several years, but they remembered each other's names.

3

★ ★ ★

A STRANGE INTENSITY,
A STRANGE BEAUTY

The morning of August 6, 1945, was calm in Hiroshima. "The hour was early; the morning still, warm, and beautiful. Shimmering leaves, reflecting sunlight from a cloudless sky, made a pleasant contrast with shadows in my garden," recalled Michihiko Hachiya, the director of the Hiroshima Communications Hospital.

It was the doctor's last thought in an era of a certain kind of innocence. Forty years earlier, Einstein had shown on paper that matter was equivalent to energy. At 8:15 A.M. the *Enola Gay* passed overhead, opened its bomb bay doors, and demonstrated that equation in a horrible way.

"Suddenly, a strong flash of light startled me—and then another," Hachiya remembered. "The view where a moment before had been so bright and sunny was now dark and hazy. Through swirling dust I could barely discern a wooden column that had supported one corner of my house. It was leaning crazily and the roof sagged dangerously. . . . To my surprise I discovered that I was completely naked. How odd! Where were my drawers and undershirt? What had happened?"

Hachiya was one of the lucky ones. America had stolen fire from the gods and kept the news secret until that clear Monday morning. A few people in Washington had briefly discussed warning the Japanese of the power of this new weapon, or perhaps inviting their leaders to watch a demonstration. But to Harry Truman, the decision to drop the bomb on Hachiya and his neighbors was an easy one. Truman felt he had to act fast. America was winning the war against Japan, slowly gaining territory and closing in on the home islands. But Japan was holding on, and victory might require a massive invasion. The bomb might end the war quickly and save huge numbers of American lives.

On August 8, two days after the Hiroshima explosion and one before Nagasaki met its terrible fate, Stalin called to the Kremlin George Kennan and Ambassador Averell Harriman. The Soviets were in, he told them. Red Army troops were now surging toward the eastern enemy.

Harriman began the conversation by explaining how pleased he was to learn of the rekindled alliance. This was an exaggeration. The Soviets were entering the battle far later than America had hoped, and the United States wanted to limit the credit Moscow could claim for defeating Japan.

Stalin knew the American was being insincere. But he also knew what the war had required of his country. The streets of Leningrad had filled with the frozen and the starved before the United States even entered the fight. What did it matter if his country was attacking Japan a little late? So he responded to Harriman with his own string of platitudes.

Harriman then moved to the big topic: how did Stalin think the Japanese would respond to the new weapon? Stalin knew far more about the atomic bomb than his interlocutors suspected he did. In 1942, a Soviet physicist notified him of the suspicious fact that articles on nuclear physics had stopped appearing in British and American scientific journals. More directly, at least two spies had been passing top-secret information to Moscow: George Koval, an electrical engineer whose treachery did not become public until sixty years after the war, and Klaus Fuchs, the nuclear scientist originally recruited by Ruth Brewer.

Stalin predicted Japan's reaction fairly well. Many leaders there wanted to change governments and put into place a regime more likely to end the war, he said. The atomic bomb might give them that excuse.

Hinting at his frustration that his country had not developed the weapon first, he called the bomb "a very difficult problem to work out." The Soviets had tried to make one but had failed, and they had found a factory showing that the Germans had worked on it too. Had they succeeded, Stalin said, Hitler would never have surrendered.

Harriman declared that the bomb could have peaceful uses. Yes, said Stalin—it could mean "the end of war and aggressors"—but "the secret would have to be well kept." Harriman agreed and, making an argument that would reappear throughout the Cold War, repeated that the bomb could help keep the peace. "Unquestionably," replied Stalin.

With that, Harriman and Kennan returned to the American embassy, where Harriman fired off a cable to tell Truman that Russia had entered the war.

Stalin already had a team trying to split the atom. But until Hiroshima, he had not realized the monumental strategic power the weapon would confer. Soon after the Americans left the Kremlin, the generalissimo told his men that equilibrium had been broken. Within two weeks, he had ordered a crash atomic development program and put his most ruthless lieutenant, Lavrenti Beria, in charge. The arms race had begun.

PAUL NITZE HAD a Wall Street instinct for sniffing out information that had been kept from him. He had helped organize mineral procurement for the war effort—tracking down substances no one had heard of from countries no one had visited for purposes no one could talk about—and he had noted that the U.S. government needed a lot of unusual materials, such as mercury flasks and beryllium. He had even heard about an inquiry by the vice president to identify all the world's sources of uranium. By the summer of 1945 he knew something was going on. A friend who worked as a mining engineer told Nitze he knew that America was building a massive new bomb with all these materials—but he did not think it would work.

It did work, of course, and the day after Hiroshima the leaders of the Strategic Bombing Survey began to discuss their urgent new task: measuring the weapon's effect. One week later Japan surrendered; a couple of weeks after that, Nitze was flying across the Pacific.

Moved by the land's beauty, he felt a deep animus toward its people. Their nation had dropped five-hundred-pound bombs on the sleeping sailors at Pearl Harbor, deified kamikaze pilots, and refused to surrender until well after the war was lost. "This was the most beautiful country I'd ever seen . . . populated by the most hateful of all people on earth," he would write later.

After paying his respects to Douglas MacArthur, the American supreme commander overseeing the occupation, Nitze began planning a trip to Hiroshima. He sent his top assistant to try to find a building that the survey could acquire for a base. The aide returned and told him,

"There is nothing there to requisition." For the first time, Nitze had a real sense of the damage done. The team was eventually stationed on ships lying off Hiroshima and Nagasaki.

To many, the weapon seemed almost supernatural. Rumors flew among survivors that the bomb would give off deadly poisons for the next seven years. Robert Oppenheimer would later remember himself quoting from the Bhagavad-Gita when he learned that the first test had succeeded: "Now I am become Death, the destroyer of worlds." Even President Truman had invoked God when announcing the strike on Hiroshima. "It is an awful responsibility which has come to us. We thank God that it has come to us, instead of to our enemies; and we pray that He may guide us to use it in His ways and for His purposes."

But Nitze saw the atom bomb as just another weapon, something he and his colleagues could analyze acutely but calmly. Yes, it was epically powerful. But we could think about it, discuss it, include it in plans. "With weapons of that size," Nitze wrote, "the effects were not infinite: they were finite." His report for the survey, published in the summer of 1946, declared that people should strip their "minds of any lingering prejudice that the atomic bomb is supernatural or incomprehensible in its operation." The report then went on to explain, clearly and concisely, that the bomb worked by loosing three forces—pressure, heat, and radiation—the first two of which were also produced by other bombs.

Nitze's goal, he said, was to put calipers on the destruction and on the recovery. He was struck by how fast the railroads in Nagasaki had recovered, and how buildings made of reinforced concrete survived the bombing and "rose impressively from the ashes." Years later, he would remember a story of a train passing through Hiroshima when the bomb fell. People sitting near open windows were not cut by flying glass, but they died of radiation exposure. People sitting by closed windows were bloodied by the glass, but protected from the radiation.

Nitze's report came out in the summer of 1946, two months before John Hersey's famous essay about the bomb. The USSBS paper appeared in thick government binders. Hersey's "Hiroshima" appeared in an issue of the *New Yorker* devoted entirely to his reporting. The goals of the two documents differed as much as their presentation.

Here, for example, is how the USSBS described the defense offered by clothing:

Flash burns were largely confined to exposed areas of the body, but on occasion would occur through varying thicknesses of clothing. . . . One woman was burned over the shoulder except for a T-shaped area about one-fourth inch in breadth; the T-shaped area corresponded to an increased thickness of the clothing from the seam of the garment. Other people were burned through a single thickness of kimono but were unscathed or only lightly affected underneath the lapel.

Here is Hersey:

The eyebrows of some were burned off and skin hung from their faces and hands. Others, because of pain, held their arms up as if carrying something in both hands. Some were vomiting as they walked. Many were naked or in shreds of clothing. On some undressed bodies, the burns had made patterns—of undershirt straps and suspenders and, on the skin of some women (since white repelled the heat from the bomb and dark clothes absorbed it and conducted it to the skin), the shapes of flowers they had had on their kimonos.

Despite the cool tone of the report, the images of Hiroshima stuck with Nitze. He would almost never talk about the terrible things he had seen, except on a few occasions when challenged by people who said he did not understand what nuclear war was like. Then, he could get tense and emotional, replying, in effect: Why, yes, actually I'm one of the few people who really does understand. And toward the end of his life, his memories of the horrors began to bubble out. He would talk about what he'd seen back then, even as his conscious awareness of the present faded.

HARRY TRUMAN WAS CONFLICTED in his thinking about Joseph Stalin in the fall of 1945. Before his improbable arrival in the White House, the Missourian had shown a streak of knee-jerk pro-American fire, famously proclaiming on the Senate floor in 1941, "If we see that Germany is winning we ought to help Russia and if Russia is winning we ought to help Germany, and that way let them kill as many as possible." But with responsibility came ambivalence. "I like Stalin," he wrote home to his wife, soon after becoming president. "He is straightforward. Knows what he wants and will compromise when he can't get it."

It was a measured reaction to an enigmatic man. Most Americans now think of Stalin as the merciless tyrant he was. But he was also curious, highly intelligent, and sensitive. As a young man, he was a poet, a singer, and a voracious reader. He memorized works by Gogol and Chekhov, while amusing himself with Thackeray, Balzac, and Plato. At seminary, he would sneak in worldly texts and read by candlelight, sometimes hiding books in stacks of firewood. He studied Esperanto intensively when he thought it the likely language of the future. "He didn't just read books," said a friend. "He ate them."

He had a lovely voice and often sang at weddings. Much of his poetry described the beauties of nature. It was so accomplished that Prince Ilia Chavchavadze, a prominent Georgian poet, published five poems by the impressive "young man with the burning eyes." One early poem ended with a declaration that in becoming learned he could help others:

> While the joyful nightingale
> With a gentle voice was saying—
> "Be full of blossom, oh lovely land
> Rejoice Iverians' country
> And you oh Georgian, by studying
> Bring joy to your motherland."

Poet or not, Stalin was always tough. He had grown up in Gori, a Georgian city that took pride in its tradition of no-holds-barred, full-on street fighting. His alcoholic father once thrashed him so hard that there was blood in his urine for days. But his mother pampered him and stood up for him. She ensured that one day he would be able to get out of Gori and leave his mark on the world.

Stalin started with crime, turned to politics, and eventually merged the two. Gradually, his soul turned entirely black. According to his daughter, Svetlana, everything changed in 1932 when her mother killed herself. To Svetlana, this act was a historic hinge, connecting the relatively peaceful late 1920s with the terrible purges of the 1930s. "She took what was good of him to the grave," Svetlana says. When Svetlana's older brother tried to commit suicide but misfired the gun, his father told him that he was good for nothing—not even a good shot.

By the time of the German invasion, Stalin had become the monster we now recall, even if he could still charm. He did not have a philosophical mind, but he had a sharp and quick one. Although he looked decrepit—five foot four, with discolored teeth, a withered arm, and a pockmarked face; Kennan called him "an old battle-scarred tiger"—he still seemed heroic and wise.

Even Dwight Eisenhower came somewhat under the tyrant's spell. Several days after the atomic bomb exploded in Hiroshima, the general joined Stalin in Red Square to watch a parade in the dictator's honor. The *New York Times* reported, without irony or skepticism, that Eisenhower watched as "hundreds of portraits of Premier Stalin in many native styles from the various republics moved with the procession. One great statue of him was placed in the square before him and became a heroic background for a dance avowal of devotion."

But Kennan was not charmed at all. He clearly perceived Stalin's demonic side. "His words were few. They generally sounded reasonable and sensible; indeed, often they were. An unforewarned visitor would never have guessed what depths of calculation, ambition, love of power, jealousy, cruelty, and sly vindictiveness lurked behind this unpretentious façade."

Kennan had seen the Soviets double-cross the United States repeatedly over the war's final months. He was frustrated by Washington's desire to maintain an illusory friendship with the Soviets, and pained by his masters' indifference to his missives on the need to treat Stalin severely. In late August 1945, he wrote to his friend and colleague Freeman "Doc" Matthews, declaring that he planned to resign from the Foreign Service. "I do hope that it will be possible for you to send a successor for me by the end of October at the latest. As a matter of fact, I would strongly recommend that you send two successors."

WHILE KENNAN FOUGHT over policy, Nitze embarked on a new investigation. His task had expanded beyond the bombing survey; he was also in charge of interviewing Japan's former leaders and establishing why the war had started and what they had thought as it progressed.

The most senior man he talked to was Prince Fumimaro Konoye, who had been prime minister in three different governments. His tenure in the first started just before Japan initiated full-scale aggression against China; his tenure in the last ended just before Japan struck the United States.

A man of contrasts, Konoye was both intimidating and weak. According to Japanese lore, he came from a family of divine descent, brought to earth by a deity sent down by the Sun Goddess. He was brilliant, learned, worldly. He translated and published Oscar Wilde's *The Soul of Man Under Socialism*. He sent his son to the Lawrenceville School and then Princeton. At the same time, though, he was nervous and vulnerable. He seemed to come down with a grave illness whenever a crisis hit.

Nitze began their interview with a straightforward question. When the war with America started, how long did Konoye think it would last, and how did the Japanese army think it would end? Konoye answered vaguely that he had not thought it would last long, and that he could not remember any exit strategy. Asked about army plans, Konoye claimed ignorance. Nitze grew frustrated and his questions became tense. "The impression we have gained so far is that you agreed to a declaration of war against the United States with no information at all as to how victory was to be achieved or as to how the war was to be brought to an end."

Neither tough nor friendly questioning elicited the information Nitze sought. Finally, he moved on to his other big question: how much had the nuclear bomb mattered? As before, Nitze spoke in a manner fit for an American courtroom.

Konoye struggled in response, sounding more like a broken man than a dishonest one. Speer had seen the interrogation by Nitze as an opportunity to match wits, to build his legacy, and possibly to save his life. Konoye had almost nothing precise to say.

"How much longer do you think the war might have continued had the atomic bomb not been dropped?"

"It is a little hard for me to figure that out."

"What would your best estimate be?"

"Probably it would have lasted all of this year . . . it is just a sort of general feeling, without much actual basis."

Both men left the interview frustrated. A few days afterward, Konoye's secretary showed up at Nitze's office with word that his boss wanted to make up for a poor performance. He handed Nitze the prince's private diary, including notes on events leading up to the start of the war.

Nitze was elated, believing that the diary capped an extremely thorough investigation. "If there are any unanswered questions about the war in the Pacific when we get through, it won't be for want of trying," he wrote his mother in December. "The boys know what happened to each ship, plane, shell, ton of coal, rodent, fly, open latrine, and house of prostitution during the course of the war."

Konoye's cooperation with Nitze did the prince no good, however. An American court indicted him for war crimes. The day before his arraignment, he invited a group of friends over for dinner and a talk. After they left, he asked for a copy of Oscar Wilde's prison letter, *De Profundis*, and retired to bed at around one A.M. He read the writer who had been so dear for so many years, underlining in red pencil several passages that had particular meaning to him. Among these was one that can be read as a final confession of his failure to alter the attitudes of other Japanese leaders about the war: "My ruin came not from too great individualism of life but from too little."

He dropped the book on the couch and then swallowed a lethal dose of poison.

ALTHOUGH KENNAN HAD declared his intention to resign, Matthews, along with another dear friend, Chip Bohlen, soon persuaded him that it was his patriotic duty to keep his post. He then quickly turned to the one thing he seemed always to love about embassy work: the opportunity to travel.

Early that September, he set out for Leningrad, a city he barely knew but to which he had a deep and emotional connection. He wandered the streets, observing people carefully. He noted the city's rhythms, its problems, and its passions. He walked past the Winter Palace and watched children bicycling. He sat on a bench near the Kazan Cathedral to see people boarding streetcars. He recalled that Leningrad was the city where Pushkin had written his masterworks and where nobles from the court of the czar had thrust Rasputin's body, already shot and poisoned, through the Neva River ice.

He wrote in his diary that he found it

a great, sad city, where the spark of human genius has always had to penetrate the darkness, the dampness, and the cold in order to make its light felt, and has acquired, for that very reason, a strange warmth, a strange intensity, a strange beauty. I know that in this city, where I have never lived, there had nevertheless been deposited by some strange quirk of fate—a previous life, perhaps?—a portion of my own capacity to feel and to love, a portion—in other words—of my own life; and that this is some-thing no American will ever understand and no Russian ever believe.

But Kennan was soon called back to Moscow. He still had a job to do in the embassy—including tasks he found wholly tiresome, such as serving as a factotum for men who knew vastly less about Russia than he did.

On September 14, 1945, he was told to arrange for a group of visiting congressmen to see Stalin and then to translate the exchange. He never liked this sort of setup—congressmen traveling abroad can display an un-fortunate combination of ignorance and entitlement—and things started going haywire early. According to Kennan's recollections, the delegation showed up at their rendezvous point both late and drunk. As they raced to the Kremlin in a pair of limousines, one member hooted, "What if I biff the old codger one in the nose?" Kennan later wrote: "My heart froze. I cannot recall what I said, but I am sure that never in my life did I speak with greater earnestness."

Fortunately, the congressmen all kept their hands in their pockets and the interview went smoothly: no one bloodied Stalin's nose, and no representative made his return in a flag-draped coffin. But another tedious political chore awaited: translating for the exceedingly deferen-tial Florida senator Claude Pepper. A member of the Senate Foreign Rela-tions Committee, Pepper asked Stalin about Soviet economic growth, the state of the Red Army, and how long the USSR planned to continue using German prisoners of war as laborers. Stalin gave wise, reasoned answers to all these questions. The Floridian then asked whether he knew that Americans still referred to him as Uncle Joe. Stalin said that he did not know what he had done to deserve the compliment.

Afterward, Pepper described the meeting in a *New York Times* piece filled with the sort of soft, fuzzy praise that later helped earn him the nickname Red Pepper. "The generalissimo is a realist, notwithstanding the fact that he is engaged in the mightiest effort ever made in a single nation to raise the standard of living of some 200,000,000 people." At the end of the meeting, Pepper had asked Stalin whether he would like to pass on any message to the United States. Why, yes, Stalin said. He would indeed. "Just judge the Soviet Union objectively. Do not either praise us or scold us. Just know us and judge us as we are."

Having offered those words of wisdom, Stalin walked over to Kennan and thanked him kindly for doing such a fine job of translating.

★

PAUL NITZE WALKED through the ruins of Hiroshima as the representative of a conqueror. The United States had won unequivocally, profoundly, and devastatingly. Only one nation had the ultimate weapon, and he was one of its emissaries.

But Nitze was not triumphant. The weapon was not a product of Yankee magic that no one else could replicate. And if others could make it, then they could use it. This led him to a question as dark as it was nerve-racking: what if the bomb was dropped *on* the United States, not *by* the United States?

Nitze's answer: if nothing changed, America would be devastated. A nuclear bomb would obliterate the center of Chicago, or San Francisco, or Washington, or New York, just as it had Hiroshima.

For Nitze, this was not a cause for paralysis, but a stimulus to try to change the odds. Nuclear weapons were just weapons. Man had created them, and man could limit their impact. Nitze had noticed that Nagasaki residents who reached bomb shelters had survived. What if the United States built a network of shelters? What if we designed more parks and rivers into our cities, places that could serve as firebreaks and escape routes? What if we made our buildings out of reinforced concrete? When he returned to the United States, Nitze tried to convince the city planner Robert Moses to require bomb shelters in all the big new buildings going up in New York City. The trip to Japan had opened Nitze's eyes, and he was beginning to sort through his responses to questions on which he would spend the next fifty years.

Kennan, too, was beginning to think through the implications of this new epoch. "It would be highly dangerous to our security if the Russians were to develop the use of atomic energy, or any other radical and far-reaching means of destruction," he declared in late September 1945. "There is nothing—I repeat nothing—in the history of the Soviet regime which could justify us in assuming that the men who are now in power in Russia, or even those who have chances of assuming power within the foreseeable future, would hesitate for a moment to apply this power against us if by doing so they thought that they might materially improve their own power position in the world." Kennan would later, forcefully, argue a different position. But he was resolute for now.

As that fall progressed, his mood darkened. Each diary entry showed a little more frustration than the last. He lashed out at Moscow's refusal to let American officials even talk to Russian citizens; he bemoaned a night spent listening to new Soviet records, declaring that "one of the fundamental facts about Soviet life [is] the excellence of that small part which is good and the extreme inferiority of that large part which is bad"; he squirmed through a talk by an American labor leader still in thrall to the Kremlin—"a sickening bit of bootlicking."

A week before Christmas, two old friends visited him: Bohlen and the British philosopher Isaiah Berlin. The three talked late into the night about the Russian threat and the tensions between socialism and capitalism. Kennan wrote that "Berlin, who is undoubtedly the best informed and most intelligent foreigner in Moscow . . . was firmly convinced that the Russians view a conflict with the western world as quite inevitable and that their whole policy is predicated on this prospect." Politics even infected Kennan's efforts at relaxation. A group of American military men stationed in Moscow formed a band called the Kremlin Crows, and Kennan, a good guitar player, would sometimes grab his instrument and sit in with them. But Moscow objected to the word "Kremlin" appearing in the name of an American band. The Crows had to paint over their drum kit and become the Purged Pigeons.

Kennan remained cheerful enough to organize the embassy Christmas carols as the season approached, inviting the staff up to his office, where he would pull out his guitar and play. But as the year turned, he feared that another war was coming to a weary world.

BUILT IN 1825, during the reign of Alexander I, Moscow's Bolshoi Theater premiered the works of Tchaikovsky and Rachmaninoff. Wagner conducted there. *Bolshoi* means "grand," and so the place is. A statue of four bronze horses drawing Apollo's chariot tops the theater. It was and is the center of Moscow's artistic life. And, on February 9, 1946, it became the center of much of the rest of the world's political life too.

That evening, Joseph Stalin entered the Bolshoi to the hysterical cheers of thousands of screaming Muscovites. When the squat, mustachioed leader strode on stage to give a much anticipated speech, everyone rose to chant: "Cheers for great Stalin!" "Long live great Stalin, hurrah!" "Cheers for our beloved Stalin!"

Stalin had written and edited the speech himself. He had even inserted the prescribed crowd prompts, such as "standing ovation," where he thought it appropriate. The evening was a preelection event, preparing the Soviet people to vote for members of the Supreme Soviet. Stalin, of course, did not need to ask his subjects for their votes.

Instead, he began in his thick Georgian accent by blaming the West for World War II, throwing out a classic canard of Marxist theory: the inevitability of capitalist warfare. Under capitalism, some countries get richer faster, which leads the poorer countries, and the ones with fewer natural resources, to take up arms. "The development of world capitalism in our times does not proceed smoothly and evenly, but through crises and catastrophic wars." Throughout the war, he had played up nationalist sentiments and addressed the people as "countrymen." Tonight they were just "comrades."

He then moved to praising the Soviet system and the people's courage through the long fight. After he declared that "the Red Army heroically withstood all the hardships of the war, utterly routed the armies of our enemies, and emerged from the war the victor," a voice in the crowd hollered, "Under Comrade Stalin's leadership!" Soon everyone in the audience was standing again and cheering.

Stalin then brought forth an array of statistics and plans, all meant to show that now was no time to relax. Toward the end of the speech, he uttered one of his most important, but also subtlest, lines: "I have no doubt that if we give our scientists proper assistance they will be able in the very near future not only to overtake but even outstrip the achievements of science beyond the borders of our country." It is likely that Stalin had just one scientific project in mind: the atomic bomb.

Stalin ended with some predictable propaganda about the election. But the message was clear: war was the locomotive of history. As his foreign minister Vyacheslav Molotov would later say, Stalin believed that "the First World War pulled one country out of capitalist slavery. The Second World War created a socialist system, the third will put an end to imperialism once and for all."

Waves of applause greeted the conclusion of the speech. "Cheers for the great leader of the peoples!" "Glory to great Stalin!" "Long live Comrade Stalin, the candidate of the entire people!" "Glory to the creator of all our victories, Comrade Stalin!" The speech was broadcast by radio across the Soviet Union, and tens of millions of copies were printed.

Stalin's words stirred the American embassy as well. Kennan wrote a memo summarizing the speech. Within a week, he got another request from Washington: "We should welcome receiving from you an interpretive analysis of what we may expect in the way of future implementation of [Stalin's] announced policies." It was an innocuous-sounding request, but an infuriating one too, coming after he had written so many memos on that very topic. Soon Kennan would begin the project that an embassy colleague later said would "both make and destroy him."

4

***

DECEIT, CORRUPTION, PENETRATION, SUBVERSION

Martha Mautner was working the last shift in the American embassy code room in Moscow on Friday, February 22, 1946. It was a bare and austere place, filled only with machinery. Polyfilm covered the windows, creating a low-tech defense against Soviet espionage attempts.

Mautner was alone in this bleak space as afternoon turned toward evening. It was George Washington's birthday, no one was around, and her eyes were on the clock. A vivacious twenty-two-year-old graduate of the Fletcher School of Law and Diplomacy, Mautner had joined the Foreign Service out of a determination to go abroad, see the world, and be a diplomat. And the best way for a woman to enter diplomacy, in those days, was to apply as a clerk. Mautner, whose academic specialties were political science and history, could barely type. So she found a copy of the typing-test paragraph for clerical applicants and went over it about 150 times, until she had reached the acceptable speed of thirty-five words a minute. Diligence paid off. Once hired, she was put on a track that eventually led her to diplomatic postings in Germany and Russia, and then an intelligence analyst slot back in Washington.

The clock struck five, and then six. Mautner's shift was almost over. She was thinking about her date that evening with a young, handsome Swedish diplomat. The two planned to meet up and then head to a dance party at his embassy. Uncertain he was the right man for her, she knew she could find another if things did not work out. Beautiful, young, smart—and working in a diplomatic corps where men vastly outnumbered women—Mautner could pretty much take her pick.

It was nearly seven, and Mautner was ready to bolt, when the tall figure of George Kennan appeared at the code room door. A cold, sinus problems, fever, and a toothache had laid him up for the past several days. He had last been seen upstairs, dictating to his secretary from a couch. But now he was standing before Mautner, holding a thick stack of white papers. He had an important and urgent telegram. It had to go to America, and it had to go now. He handed the stack to Mautner and told her to type it in and send it.

She looked with frustration at the first page and its ominous opening sentence: "Answer to Dept's 284, Feb 3 [13] involves questions so intricate, so delicate, so strange to our form of thought, and so important to analysis of our international environment that I cannot compress answers into single brief message without yielding to what I feel would be dangerous degree of over-simplification."

The State Department had asked Kennan to sum up the current situation with Moscow, to analyze Stalin's speech at the Bolshoi, and to explain why the Soviets were not going to join the World Bank or the International Monetary Fund. For three years, Kennan had sent telegrams warning of Moscow's hostility. He had been lambasting, haranguing, cajoling, arguing, and pontificating. But each quick memo describing Stalinist malfeasance had slipped into the quiet river of unread documents flowing through Washington. Now Kennan's masters had asked him to let loose, and he had obliged. His work combined the weight and breadth of any essay with the clipped urgency of a telegram—and he wanted it sent.

Mautner respected and liked Kennan. But she was also a little bored by him. Besides, she had a date to get to, and sending this document would take hours. She gave it a quick scan, quickly got the gist of it, and handed it back. "Does it really have to go out tonight?" she asked. "You've said all this before."

But Kennan insisted. Maybe the message was not new, but this version was important. Most likely, no one would read it. And most likely, anyone who did would not care. But Kennan had poured into it his anger, his wisdom, and his knowledge of history. He would be damned if this chipper young woman with her Swedish paramour would come between his 5,300 words and Washington. "They've asked for it," he said to her. "And now they are going to get it."

Mautner looked at the clock again, reluctantly took the telegram from Kennan, and headed toward the machine.

THE TELEGRAM WENT out at nine P.M., marked secret. Kennan went to bed, Mautner went late to her dance, and what became known as the Long Telegram began its journey into Cold War mythology.

Soon after the document's arrival, a colleague of Kennan's distributed it throughout the State Department and then rerouted it to every American embassy in the world, declaring it a brilliant work with which he was "absolutely enthralled." Averell Harriman passed a copy to Secretary of the Navy James Forrestal, who passed copies to hundreds of colleagues. The secretary of state read it. The president read it. Soviet spies in Washington read it.

The telegram sought to answer a question flummoxing Washington: why was the United States unable to find a policy toward the Soviets that worked? Washington was used to the traditional pattern of diplomacy and physics: action, reaction; action, reaction. But with Moscow the pattern broke. The Soviets seemed intent on quietly, but aggressively, trying to expand their territory and their influence, no matter whether the United States played nice or acted stern. The department was "floundering about, looking for new intellectual moorings," a State Department official, Louis Halle, wrote later. By February 1946, frustration had yielded to alarm: the latest crises were the Soviet refusals to join the Bretton Woods Agreements, to leave Iran, or to respect the independence of Turkey.

To Kennan, every action by the Soviet Union made a perverse sense. Soviet hostility was not a function of U.S. policy; Russian history and psychology predetermined it. "Originally, this was insecurity of a peaceful agricultural people trying to live on vast exposed plain in neighborhood of fierce nomadic people," Kennan wrote in the abbreviated style of a telegram. "To this was added, as Russia came into contact with economically advanced West, fear of more competent, more powerful, more highly organized societies."

Now, in 1946, this traditional anxiety had another burden: justifying Marxist dogma. The men in the Kremlin did not really believe in Marxism. But it was the "fig leaf of their moral and intellectual respectability." In Kennan's view, Stalin and his lieutenants operated a thuggish police state.

Denial of that fact required that the Soviet leadership pretend to be something else, and Marxist revolutionary doctrine was a plausible cover. So the regime had to keep preaching the inevitability of conflict with the imperialists. Otherwise, "they would stand before history, at best, as only the last of that long succession of cruel and wasteful Russian rulers who have relentlessly forced country on to ever new heights of military power in order to guarantee external security of their internally weak regimes."

Throw all these factors together—traditional insecurity, tyranny, and the rhetoric of Marxism-Leninism—and Soviet policy made sense. No matter what America did or said, the Kremlin would respond by trying to undermine the United States. "We have here," proclaimed the Long Telegram's most quoted sentence, "a political force committed fanatically to the belief that with U.S. there can be no permanent modus vivendi, that it is desirable and necessary that the internal harmony of our society be disrupted, our traditional way of life be destroyed, the international authority of our state be broken, if Soviet power is to be secure."

Kennan structured his telegram in five parts. The first two described Moscow's hostile rhetoric and its deep chauvinist roots; the next two described how the Kremlin would try to undermine America, openly and then subtly; the last, in a manner befitting a preacher, offered a solution for combating the Soviet threat, concluding with a vague call for national unity and moral uplift. "Problem is within our power to solve—and that without recourse to any general military conflict."

The memo's strengths were its timing and its style. Beautifully written, Kennan's analysis was built on a deep understanding of Russia. It showed courage and provided clarity. It put the blame on Moscow, not Washington. "Kennan tied everything together, wrapped it together in a neat package, and put a red bow around it," said George Elsey, an aide to Harry Truman.

Unsurprisingly, given that it was a cri de coeur, the Long Telegram did have logical shortcomings, in particular its depiction of the Kremlin as both supremely canny and hopelessly deluded. According to Kennan, the same government that had the power to undermine the West in dozens of tricky ways was incapable of receiving or processing objective information about the world. The Russians had the intent and the capability to penetrate everything from the "liberal magazines" to "women's organizations" to unsupportive governments like "Switzerland, Portugal" to "police apparatus of foreign countries." Yet Soviet leaders had no idea how any of these organizations functioned. "I for one am reluctant to believe that Stalin himself receives anything like an objective picture of outside world."

But these criticisms were raised only in later years. At the time, what mattered was that a brilliant writer with deep knowledge of Russia was declaring that the Soviet Union was a steadfast enemy of the United States. ⁊

IN SCIENCE, a single paper can transform someone's reputation. That almost never happens in diplomacy, but it happened with the Long Telegram. When George Kennan ambled into the embassy code room to torment Mautner with his clutch of papers, perhaps a couple hundred people knew his name. Almost immediately, he was transformed into the diplomatic legend he would remain for the rest of his life.

"If none of my previous literary efforts had seemed to evoke even the faintest tinkle from the bell at which they were aimed, this one, to my astonishment, struck it squarely and sent it vibrating with a resonance that was not to die down for many months," he wrote in his memoirs. "My reputation was made. My voice now carried."

The secret was timing. America had given Stalin a long leash for six months after the war ended. But he had stretched that leash to snap up swaths of territory in central Europe, and now he was gnawing at Turkey and Iran. Just two weeks after the Long Telegram, Winston Churchill spoke in the gymnasium at Westminster College in Fulton, Missouri, and employed a metaphor based on the device used to prevent fires from spreading from stage to audience in old European theaters: "From Stettin in the Baltic to Trieste in the Adriatic an iron curtain has descended across the Continent."

A few Americans still argued that their nation's harsh rhetoric had created Soviet intransigence. Henry Wallace, who had served as Franklin Roosevelt's vice president before Truman, urged that the United States give assurances that it was not trying to form an anti-Soviet bloc—a steel curtain blocking light from the other side of the European window. Using a back channel through the Soviet secret service, Wallace had also offered to help Stalin as an "agent of influence" in the United States and had declared that he was "fighting for Truman's soul."

Kennan considered Wallace's ideas preposterous. After hearing the former vice president quoted on the BBC, he sent out a memo even harsher than the Long Telegram.

> Some of us [at the embassy] have tried to conceive the measures our country would have to take if it really wished to pursue, at all costs, goal of disarming Soviet suspicions. We have come to conclusion that nothing short of complete disarmament, delivery of our air and naval forces to Russia and resigning of powers of government to American Communists would even dent this problem; and even then we believe—this is not facetious—that Moscow would smell a trap.

Two weeks after sending the Long Telegram, Kennan used his new-found influence to press for promotion and reassignment; otherwise, he threatened, he would resign. A new job quickly opened: deputy commandant for foreign affairs at the National War College, a new institution set up for the education of mid-level military men and Foreign Service officers. Founded partly on Forrestal's initiative, the War College would give Kennan a base from which to educate the military, the State Department, and the public about the impending threat. In April, Kennan, aged forty-two, began the long journey home.

He moved into a large house overlooking the Washington channel of the Potomac. From his office, he could gaze out and see both the Pentagon and the Capitol. The job would provide an excellent opportunity for a man who had lived abroad for nineteen of the past twenty years to renew his knowledge of his own country. In the summer of 1946, he embarked on a national speaking tour. He then gave a series of thirteen lectures at the War College upon his return.

Kennan's thesis in these lectures was that the United States needed to find a midpoint between war and peace and that it should bring to bear economic, political, and psychological "measures short of war." The Soviet Union's goal was to increase its power, and America needed to push back wherever possible. The Soviets did not want war; they wanted a victory by steady accumulation. A partial list of the actions of which they were capable included "persuasion, intimidation, deceit, corruption, penetration, subversion, horsetrading, bluffing, psychological pressure, economic pressure, seduction, blackmail, theft, fraud."

The United States, Kennan argued, had to fight back in similar ways, though perhaps not drawing on that entire list. If communists appeared ready to take power in Italy or France, we had to thwart them. We had to send aid to nations at risk, and we had to publicize our efforts. To counter subversion in Greece, America needed "about three ships all painted white with 'Aid to Greece' on the sides, and to have the first bags of wheat driven up to Athens in an American jeep with a Hollywood blonde on the radiator."

We needed craftier intelligence agencies and better ways of countering Soviet propaganda. We had to recognize that war would lead to apocalypse, and that peace was a chimera. "Perhaps the whole idea of world peace has been a premature, unworkable grandiose form of daydreaming," he wrote. "Perhaps we should have held up as our goal: 'Peace if possible, and insofar as it affects our interests.'"

At no point, of course, should the United States actually try to overthrow or change the Soviet order. Any such attempt would only rally people around it and, besides, we had no idea what would rise in its stead. Stopping Soviet expansion would suffice. As Kennan put it in one of his speeches: "The problem of meeting the Kremlin in international affairs therefore boils down to this: Its inherent expansive tendencies must be firmly contained at all times by counter-pressure which makes it constantly evident that attempts to break through this containment would be detrimental to *Soviet* interests."

Kennan gave his lectures in an academic setting and with a suitable scholarly air. He quoted Gibbon, explained the minutiae of the Soviet political system, and told funny stories about diplomats in the time of Peter the Great. But he did not try to place his ideas in the context of anyone else's arguments. As would be the case throughout his career, Kennan cited not a single contemporary or recent political thinker. He had synthesized everything in his own mind.

Although he did not discuss nuclear weapons, they profoundly affected his thinking. He kept a diary that year of every book and paper he read, and it's packed with works by the new breed of nuclear theorists: for example, *The Absolute Weapon,* a collection edited by his War College colleague Bernard Brodie, which included the essays "International Control of Atomic Weapons," by William Fox, and "The Atomic Bomb in Soviet-American Relations," by Arnold Wolfers. The weapon also influenced his notion that we needed to engage the Soviets in small ways so that we would not have to fight them in a big way. In his notes from an essay he read on Clausewitz, he wrote, "Does not significance of atomic weapons

mean that, if we are to avoid mutual destruction, we must revert to strategic political thinking of XVIII century? Total destruction of enemy's
forces can no longer be our objective."

Kennan did not confine himself to strategic theory. His lectures also
showed a man angered at American democracy, and sometimes even at
the idea of democracy itself. "I believe that there can be far greater con-
centration of authority within the operating branches of our government without detriment to the essentials of democracy." Alexander
Hamilton was right to argue "that a dangerous ambition more often
lurks behind the specious mask of zeal for the rights of the people, than
under the forbidding appearances of zeal for the firmness and efficiency
of government." In one talk, Kennan declared that "there is a little bit of
the totalitarian buried somewhere, way down deep, in each and every
one of us."

These social reflections, however, attracted little attention. People listened to his political analysis. And, once again, James Forrestal was there
at the crucial moment.

The navy secretary attended many of Kennan's lectures and grew in-
creasingly impressed. He asked Kennan to write a paper for him about the
Soviet threat, following up on the arguments made at the War College.
Kennan obliged, and Forrestal sent that paper around town too.

More important, Kennan turned the paper into a talk at the Council
on Foreign Relations. Afterward, Hamilton Fish Armstrong, the editor
of *Foreign Affairs,* asked Kennan whether he might be willing to publish
it in the magazine. Kennan said yes. But, wary of making grand public
statements as a second-tier State Department employee, he asked that
the journal identify him only as "X."

WASHINGTON IN 1946 was a time and place to make careers and reputa-
tions. Among the men elected to Congress for their first terms that autumn
were John F. Kennedy, Richard Nixon, and Joseph McCarthy. National
policy was like a cauldron of molten wax, waiting for people to stamp it
into shape.

Paul Nitze was the right age, and in the right place, having returned
to Washington to work on his USSBS report. But he was floundering, and
frustrated, too, that no one wanted to read this magnum opus. The Strategic Bombing Survey's summary report on the Pacific War was his Long

Telegram, the document he had thrown himself into—the document he thought explained the future by dissecting the past. It explained the war; it explained the atomic bomb; it laid out future roles for the several armed services. But he could not get it into print. He tried desperately to get it, or a part of it, run in *Reader's Digest*. He sent it to almost everyone he knew in Washington, enclosing fresh packs of salmon with some of the letters. He mailed it to every member of Congress.

But few wrote back and none appeared to have actually read the text. The newspapers gave the report only casual treatment. Nitze's two supervisors, the men who had hired him and directed the project, did not even seem to care. The one thoughtful response in Nitze's files likely compounded his frustrations. "I am deeply distressed at the casual treatment this report got in the press," wrote the Harvard law professor W. Barton Leach in a long, praiseful letter. Leach added that he feared that "your work will have been wasted."

One year after the war, few people wanted to revisit the planning for the Battle of Leyte Gulf. The only interest in Nitze's report seemed to come from the navy and the army air forces. And they were not seeking to learn from it. They wanted to use it or to discredit it.

The services knew that a massive military reorganization would follow the war, and each was set on staking its budgetary claims. That branch to which the public gave the most credit for victory would get the largest share of congressional outlays and the most power. As a result, each tried desperately to control the Strategic Bombing Survey, and Nitze spent much of his time diving under his desk to avoid friendly fire.

The worst attacks came from the navy. Rear Admiral Ralph Ofstie described Nitze's exposition as "a vicious and deliberate attempt to discredit the entire naval service" that he had read with "complete revulsion." In sum, Ofstie declared the report "wholly biased, false in great part," and "of no apparent value to other than self-seeking individuals." Nitze recognized that this drama arose from bureaucratic politics, and it's no surprise that the military brass would never awe him again. Throughout his career, he would respect smart generals, but he did not quiver just because someone had stars on his shoulders. And he did not trust the service secretaries to tell him exactly what weaponry they needed; he always did his own research.

Ultimately, the navy survived the reorganization and Ofstie's blast was forgotten. But a second controversy—one that went unnoticed at

the time of publication—turned out to be of more historical consequence. The debate was spurred by Nitze's answer to one of the key
questions of the report: had the atomic bomb helped to end the war?

Nitze's answer was a firm no. "Based on a detailed investigation of all
the facts, and supported by the testimony of the surviving Japanese leaders involved, it is the Survey's opinion that certainly prior to 31 December 1945, and in all probability prior to 1 November 1945, Japan would
have surrendered even if the atomic bombs had not been dropped, even if
Russia had not entered the war, and even if no invasion had been planned
or contemplated."

The conclusion was presumptuous ("based on a detailed investigation
of all the facts") and not merited by the evidence. If anything, the preponderance of Japanese leaders interviewed by the Survey believed the
opposite—including Prince Konoye. Japan was politically chaotic in 1945,
with groups of disillusioned civilians struggling against the military. Some
diplomats had been waving the white flag for months, but, before the
atomic bombs dropped, plenty of generals and admirals had declared
their firm intention to fight until the last kamikaze crashed into the last
destroyer.

The confidence with which Nitze expressed his view reveals a man
who could let his conclusions outrun his facts. He had come to Japan
certain that the war had been winnable without the atomic bomb, particularly if the United States followed his bombing plans. And his argument fit the thesis that the bomb was just another weapon—one that did
not even tip the scales of the war—not an overwhelming force.

The necessity of the destruction of Hiroshima and Nagasaki became
one of the great debates of World War II historiography, and Nitze's report got the readership he sought—long past the expiration date on his
salmon packs. But here he did not stand with his usual allies; over the
years, those citing him included left-wing historians ranging from Howard Zinn to Ward Churchill. What better support could there be for the
proposition that the bombings were unnecessary than the conclusion of
a government-sanctioned report written by a hawk like Paul Nitze?

ALTHOUGH HE WAS NOW IN DEMAND, Kennan still had not decided to
spend his career in the Washington hurly-burly. He had always wanted to

write weighty books: he had histories planned, and he still thought of finishing his biography of Chekhov. His months at the National War College had also given him his first real chance to spend time at the farm he had purchased in 1942 in East Berlin, Pennsylvania. (The location would cause trouble once, when a State Department friend terrified his secretary with a note saying Kennan was "leaving for East Berlin.") Kennan liked dealing with rainwater tanks, fixing fences, and working on the chicken house. To the slight irritation of some of his friends, he also considered all of the above to be excellent weekend activities for guests.

Kennan imagined several possible professional futures. Should he do intelligence work? Should he become a professor, publishing scholarly tomes on the current Soviet Union, the past Russian empire, or the United States? Should he try to get a job in university or foundation administration? Or should he ditch his training and head either to Wall Street or off into the fields? In early 1946, Kennan sat down with his diary to lay out a matrix of everything he could do with his life.

	REQUIREMENTS OF FAMILY	OPPORTUNITIES FOR QUIET AND DETACHMENT	MORALS AND INDEPENDENCE	OPPORTUNITIES FOR CONTRIBUTION TO THOUGHT	TRAVEL	PART TIME IN COUNTRY	INCOME
INTELLIGENCE	X				X	X	
ACADEMIC— SOVIET	X	X	X	X		X	X
ACADEMIC— RUSSIAN	X	X	X			X	
ACADEMIC—US	X	X	X	X		X	X
ACADEMIC ADMINISTRATION	X					X	X
FOUNDATION WORK	X				X	X	X
BUSINESS	X						X
FARMING		X	X	X		X	

The grid did not include a column about the possibility of meeting or working with interesting people, and nothing about opportunities for advancement or further fame. A return to diplomacy was also out. Kennan mainly wanted time alone with his thoughts and his family. The grid, in fact, made a pretty good case for becoming an academic. But then a better opportunity came knocking—one that had not been on the chart at all.

5

AVOID TRIVIA

Paul Nitze hustled down the hallways of the State Department. The most admired man in America had requested his presence and had a furious question to ask: "Who authorized you to tell a predecessor of mine as secretary of state that he was a crook?"

The man asking was General George C. Marshall, the former chief of staff of the army. In late 1946, Nitze had moved from the USSBS to State's Office of International Trade Policy. Soon thereafter, Marshall had become head of the department.

Marshall generally did not need to raise his voice. Marked for greatness at an early age, he stood straight and acted straighter. When he was a young soldier, his commanding officer was asked in a performance review, "Would you desire to have him under your immediate command in peace and war?" The response: "Yes, but I would prefer to serve *under his command.*" *Time* magazine named him Man of the Year in 1943 and again in 1947.

After the war, Marshall had hoped to retire. But Truman tapped him to try to mediate a peace in China and then to run the State Department. That was how he ended up with a nervous Paul Nitze standing before him, trying to justify his criticism of a Liberian business deal proposed by former secretary Edward Stettinius.

"But what he proposes to do is crooked!" Nitze hollered back, growing angry.

Marshall's response would forever endear him to Nitze. Instead of demanding a retraction, he decided to research the issue. And then, having investigated, Marshall agreed. Stettinius had been out of line.

It was a minor incident, but a telling one. Marshall respected and listened to his younger subordinates, and he seemed to care only about the national interest. His charges viewed him as an utterly incorruptible gentleman, indifferent to the mass media and totally loyal to the men and women with whom he worked. Nitze would later describe his mentor as someone who had inspired his life in public service. Marshall's "understanding of and love for the democratic institutions of this country . . . was something I hadn't run into amongst the Wall Street operators who were fully engrossed in the petty magnification of I."

Chip Bohlen, who became Marshall's personal assistant at the State Department, felt the same way. "I have never gone in for hero worship, but of all the men I have been associated with, including presidents, George Catlett Marshall is at the top of the list."

And there was a third youngster who would learn at Marshall's feet that year: George Kennan, the man Marshall selected to sit in the office next to him and serve as his chief of policy planning—a job that called only for someone who would constantly reappraise America's grand strategy. It was the perfect spot for Kennan, and one well worth the return from his farm. When he asked his new boss for advice, Marshall offered one sentence that would stick: "Avoid trivia."

Kennan set about assembling his staff, and one man who seemed like a pretty good fit was a sharp young economist whom he had met on a train a few years back. According to an oral history that Nitze gave in later years, Kennan brought the idea of making him the deputy of the staff to Dean Acheson. "George, you don't want that fellow," said the undersecretary of state, who had known Nitze in his Dillon Read days. "That fellow's a Wall Street operator. You want some deep thinkers."

IN THE LAST days of 1946, a high-pressure area had begun forming around the Arctic Circle. As the new year came, the weather system moved south, eventually taking up what seemed like permanent residency above England. Europe had nearly destroyed itself in six years of war, and now the skies seemed eager to finish the job, striking the continent with the worst winter since 1880. Snow piled twenty feet high in

Britain. The Thames froze. Berlin hospitals treated nearly twenty thousand people for frostbite. It snowed in Saint-Tropez.

A hungry continent quickly began descending into famine. In the British zone of Germany, average daily caloric consumption dropped from an already dangerously low 1,500 in 1946 to 1,050 in the early days of 1947. Reports of cannibalism started coming in to aid agencies. "We are threatened," said the French minister of national economy, "with total economic and financial catastrophe."

With weakness came despair and disorder. In late February, Britain told the United States that it must cut off its aid to the embattled Greek government, struggling against a communist insurgency. Turkey, the British said, would also soon be on its own. The world's most powerful empire for the past 150 years was contracting.

The United States suddenly had several choices to make. First and most urgently, must it bail out the two Aegean nations? A high-level group including Kennan met at the State Department the night that the news came in of Britain's withdrawal of support. The planners quickly decided to send arms and aid. That move likely saved Greece from the insurgents, and it led to one of Stalin's many tactical pullbacks of the early Cold War.

Soon another battle raged: should the United States make it a principle to intervene in support of democracy? Here, Kennan was deeply skeptical. Declare that you will backstop every government facing a communist attack, and you will soon have a line of ambassadors with their hands out proclaiming that they have found some nasty Marxists hiding in the bushes. Announcing universal principles made no sense, either. The United States should fight communists in places crucial to its interests and where it had a reasonable chance of success (like Greece). It should ignore them where intervention appeared hopeless (like China) or in nations of peripheral geopolitical significance (like Guatemala).

Kennan had little influence on the debate. Soon Harry Truman would stand before Congress to declare: "At the present moment in world history nearly every nation must choose between alternative ways of life." Our enemies had wrought havoc in Greece, and now insurgents threatened that country with "terrorist activities." His voice sounded like that of a grandfather reading a bedtime story. But his words were as dramatic as the delivery was plain. "It must be the policy of the United States to support free peoples who are resisting attempted subjugation by armed minorities or by outside pressures." That idea would be named the Truman Doctrine.

Kennan cringed. Linguistic precision mattered greatly to him, and this speech was sloppy. We just could not, and should not, resist communism everywhere. In the 1946 essay "Politics and the English Language," George Orwell had included "democracy" and "freedom" on his list of meaningless words that are "often used in a consciously dishonest way." Kennan agreed. He was convinced that other nations would respond cynically to Truman's words, using trumped-up campaigns in the cause of "freedom" as a means to extract resources from America.

Nitze, however, was delighted by Truman's tough stance. Yes, he declared in his memoirs, the speech might have sounded as if the United States "was embarking on a world crusade." But we were not actually going to begin a crusade for freedom—and we did not. Truman was a man "with courage and guts" who deserved credit for understanding that the United States had to pick up the full burden "of leadership for the Free World, no matter [what] that required." To Nitze, the words did not matter as much as the climate of opinion they created.

As would be the case throughout the Cold War, Kennan cared deeply about principles and patterns, and he placed no intrinsic value on idealistic statements about the importance of freedom or any other vague cause. The United States probably would not live up to the expressed high standards, and others would treat the pronouncements cynically anyway. He also had no patience for people who preached, or assumed, American infallibility.

Nitze, however, believed in the power of American idealism and example. The United States was the greatest country on earth, and it should not shy away from using its power to improve the rest of the world. Equally important, America had been tested by the crisis in the Mediterranean and responded immediately in the appropriate way. For Nitze, that was good enough.

EVEN AS THEY DIFFERED on the Truman Doctrine, Kennan and Nitze agreed on perhaps the one question even more pressing in the spring of 1947 than the insurrection in Greece: should the United States bail out Western Europe? To both, the answer was a resounding yes.

Nitze was one of the first government officials to recognize the scope of Europe's economic woes. He had long discussions in late 1946 with the head of the Bank of Sweden, Dag Hammarskjöld, whose country was buying so much from the United States that it was running out of dollars. That same problem spread through Europe. That winter, Nitze told Will Clayton, the undersecretary of state for economic affairs, that the United States could solve the problem only if it sent Europe $5 billion a year for the next five years.

Failure, Nitze believed, would mean much more than just economic crisis in Sweden. In early March, he received a copy of a secret memo that Forrestal had written and sent to the White House counsel Clark Clifford. It envisioned a war between Soviet and American economic systems as fierce and consequential as the conflict the world had just come through. "The present danger which this country faces is at least as great as the danger which we faced during the war with Germany and Japan," Forrestal wrote. "Briefly stated, it is the very real danger that this country, as we know it, may cease to exist." The United States needed to prove that capitalism worked better than communism. The country had products—free markets and democracy—that the world was not buying. America needed "an all-out effort on a world-wide basis" to persuade other nations of the virtues of capitalism.

Kennan hardly needed convincing of these exigencies. He had written in the Long Telegram that "communism is like malignant parasite, which feeds only on diseased tissue." Now he, too, would campaign for the United States to aid Europe, which had survived the severe winter only at great cost to its people's health and prosperity. In the first official Policy Planning Staff recommendation, written in May 1947, Kennan declared that Western Europe's economic malaise was the most pressing and urgent issue facing the State Department. He described in detail a massive aid program—and then passed his plan to Marshall.

TWO WEEKS LATER, on the afternoon of June 5, 1947, Marshall, dressed in a plain gray suit, stood on a dais at Harvard University in front of fifteen thousand people and observed how wonderful everything seemed: the elm trees around him; the perfect, sunny skies; the students, bursting with promise and confidence, being graduated from this marvelous university and about to become America's elite. Then, reading his prepared speech in a quiet, monotonous voice, he told them the world was going to hell.

War had devastated Europe and gutted its industry. City dwellers had no money to buy goods. Without customers, farmers had little reason to plow their soil. Governments did not have the dollars to break the cycle. The United States had to step in, or "hunger, poverty, desperation, and chaos" beckoned.

Bohlen wrote most of the speech, but he based it on memos written by Kennan, who deserves credit for several crucial ideas. To begin with, the United States should rehabilitate, not relieve. The initiative and planning, however, should come from Europe. The European nations would tell us what they needed, and we would send it. If they organized the program and believed they had control over it, they would do a better job of protecting it. Kennan always distrusted the capacity of one nation truly to understand the needs of another, and he doubted his country's capacities as much as he believed in his own. Our struggle against evil did not make us infinitely good or wise. In his Policy Planning Staff paper, Kennan had written: "It would be neither fitting nor efficacious for this Government to undertake to draw up unilaterally . . . a program designed to place [Western] Europe on its feet economically. This is the business of the Europeans." Marshall inserted those words directly into his speech.

Kennan also argued, successfully, that Germany should play a part in the plan: "To talk about the recovery of Europe and to oppose the recovery of Germany is nonsense. People can have both or they can have neither." He well remembered the disastrous divisions of the continent in the aftermath of World War I.

But how far did Europe extend? The day after delivering the speech, Marshall looked over at Kennan and Bohlen at a State Department staff meeting and asked whether the Soviets would accept if we asked them to join. No one in the room wanted such participation. The Soviets would surely try to undermine the process, and it was hard to imagine Congress sending money to Moscow. No one, though, wanted it to look as if America had stiff-armed the Soviets and divided Europe. Kennan's advice: play it straight and offer to include the USSR. In the best-case scenario, Stalin would reject an agreement fairly proffered. Invitations are daily dropped in the mail that the sender hopes the recipient will decline—but rarely are the stakes so high.

At first, the plan confused the Soviets. They initially considered joining, but a month after the speech, as the nations of Europe met in Paris to discuss the U.S. proposal, Moscow realized it had its leg in a snare. The plan was an effort to integrate the economies of Europe and draw them closer to the United States, and it was pulling Soviet clients like Czecho-slovakia, Romania, and Poland westward. Stalin suddenly demanded that the East European nations withdraw from the conference—and thus he guaranteed that Moscow would earn the blame for any line drawn through the center of Europe. Kennan's gamble had worked.

Kennan had traveled to Paris and participated heavily in the talks there, transitioning from just a planner and a thinker, at least temporar-ily, into a man of action. The next question he would have to deal with was what the plan would actually include. In mid-July, Kennan wrote a memo noting the absence of specific proposals concerning exactly what aid would go where. It began: "Marshall 'plan.' We have no plan."

Kennan would have to figure out the details, and then to help get them through Congress. At this critical moment, he acquired an important colleague, one who labored hard and offered an entirely complementary set of skills. For the first time, George Kennan found himself working with Paul Nitze.

Almost simultaneously, Kennan's life was transformed for the second time in eighteen months. A year and a half earlier, he had been an anony-mous bureaucrat. The Long Telegram had made him known within the government; now another article would make him known to the world. George Kennan was about to become a prophet.

"THE POLITICAL PERSONALITY of Soviet power as we know it today is the product of ideology and circumstances." So began, innocently enough, the article bylined "X" and titled "The Sources of Soviet Conduct" in the July 1947 issue of *Foreign Affairs*. The State Department had stamped through Kennan's request to publish this anonymous piece, which seemed unlikely to be widely read.

But then the *New York Times* wrote about the essay, *Newsweek* quoted it, and *Reader's Digest* and *Life* excerpted it. Arthur Krock, a columnist for the *Times,* had seen a draft on Forrestal's desk a few months previ-ously. He recognized the prose style and the argument. Soon Kennan was unmasked and the article was everywhere. The evasive byline only made it that much more intriguing. A month after it ran, Kennan was no longer "X." He was one of *U.S. News & World Report*'s People of the Week.

Like the Long Telegram, the X article began with a long analysis of Soviet thought and motivations. When Lenin seized power in 1917, ideology and history taught him that menacing capitalists would set out to destroy his new government. This fear led to the creation of a dictatorship hostile to the outside world. Since then, communism's promise of perfection and liberation had obviously failed. Why? An unsleeping array of external enemies endlessly sabotaging Soviet success served nicely as an explanation.

Kennan argued that this paranoid view of the West was not going to change. Without the menace of a great external power, the whole logic of the system would collapse, exposing the leaders as frauds. So they would keep poking, haranguing, and double-crossing America. The Soviet Union was like "a persistent toy automobile wound up and headed in a given direction"; "a fluid stream which moves constantly, wherever it is permitted to move, toward a given goal"; and, invoking a famous advertisement, "the white dog before the phonograph" that hears "only the 'master's voice.'"

The United States thus would never be able to persuade the Soviet Union—whether toy, stream, or hound—through logic. We would have to block it, divert it, or maybe even grab its collar. In the most famous sentence Kennan ever wrote, he declared: "The main element of any United States policy toward the Soviet Union must be that of a long-term, patient but firm and vigilant containment of Russian expansive tendencies." And, one paragraph later: "Soviet pressure against the free institutions of the Western world is something that can be contained by the adroit and vigilant application of counterforce at a series of constantly shifting geographical and political points."

Although the Soviet Union was the prime threat to American society, Kennan argued that we did not have to defeat it. We just had to outlast it. The government was a weak "crust" and communism held inside itself "the seeds of its own decay." The United States should refrain from provoking Moscow, whether through confrontation or histrionics. Patience and containment would lead to success. Eventually, "Soviet Russia might be changed overnight from one of the strongest to one of the weakest and most pitiable of national societies."

Kennan surely felt a surge of excitement as the news stories about his article began to appear. A measure of fame came for his family, too. Friends of his daughter Grace at Radcliffe started referring to her as "Miss X." But any frisson that came with the celebrity turned to terror when George Marshall summoned his junior planner into the secretary's office, arched his eyebrows, and asked about the essay. It was his belief that "planners don't talk"—and they particularly don't make grand pronouncements on policy toward the USSR—so why was the head of his planning staff all over the press? Kennan explained that the results were not at all what he had intended, and that he had cleared the paper through the proper channels. Marshall dismissed him, apparently satisfied.

That brush fire extinguished, Kennan turned to a more lasting problem. The article had given currency to a word—"containment"—that quickly earned the label of "doctrine." But Kennan had not defined "containment," and each passing day seemed to give it a sharper, more militaristic edge. *Reader's Digest*, for example, spun the academic title of Kennan's article into "The Only Way to Deal with Russia." Then, through creative cutting and pasting, it turned the original first paragraph, about the complexities of the Soviet Union, into one that made it seem that the Soviets were itching to "overthrow" us.

Banned from commenting publicly, Kennan watched his cautious and deliberate utterances spinning away from him. Later, he wrote that he felt "like one who has inadvertently loosened a large boulder from the top of a cliff and now helplessly witnesses its path of destruction in the valley below, shuddering and wincing at each successive glimpse of disaster."

He would have shuddered more if he knew how the article was going over in Moscow. According to Georgi Kornienko, who helped translate "The Sources of Soviet Conduct" for Stalin, when a copy was prepared for the tyrant, "containment" was rendered not as the accurate *sderzhivanie*, but as *udushenie*. "strangulation."

AS THE BOULDER careened out of Kennan's control, one powerful hand reached out to give it a particularly hearty thrust. Walter Lippmann, arguably the country's most influential columnist, read the article while summering on Mount Desert Island, Maine, and retreated into his little office in the spruce woods to respond with vigor. He devoted fourteen consecutive installments of his column, "Today and Tomorrow," to a critique of X. Harper & Brothers soon published the essays in a book titled *The Cold War*, which in turn gave the forty-year conflict its name.

Lippmann knew Kennan slightly—the two had met the previous spring and agreeably discussed aid to Europe—but he knew Kennan's editor, Hamilton Fish Armstrong, quite well. Best friends for years, Armstrong and Lippmann had once dined together weekly at New York's

Century Club and talked on the phone every day. Friends referred to them as Damon and Pythias.

That would change into something more like Beowulf and Grendel in the late 1930s when Lippmann began an affair with, and then married, Armstrong's wife, Helen. The two men never spoke again, and Armstrong banned Lippmann's name from *Foreign Affairs*. After Armstrong's death, in 1973, his second wife delivered to Helen a packet of four love letters, three unopened, from Lippmann. Armstrong had learned about the affair when he intercepted them decades before. "I read only the first three lines of one of these," said his note to Helen.

In later years, Kennan would ascribe some of Lippmann's acrimony in the fourteen columns to the bad blood with Armstrong. As the columns appeared, Kennan read them with "bewilderment and frustration," watching as "they held against me so many views with which I profoundly agreed."

Lippmann declared that the article was a deliberate, well-vetted policy announcement, and he wrote with the passion of a man trying to save his country from folly, not just as a man peeved at a fellow mandarin. He began by assailing Kennan's suggestion that seeds of decay were sprouting in the USSR and that we needed only to wait. "Do we dare to assume, as we enter the arena and get set to run the race, that the Soviet Union will break its leg while the United States grows a pair of wings to speed it on its way?"

But Lippmann's larger point was that a policy of containment meant letting the enemy choose the battlefields of the future. The United States would have constantly to respond, and always on Soviet terms. This inevitably meant overstretch. Lippmann lumped the X article together with the Truman Doctrine, declaring that the two "must in practice mean inexorably an unending intervention in all the countries that are supposed to 'contain' the Soviet Union."

Finally, Lippmann declared that the State Department was divided between officials who wanted America to follow the dangerous, aggressive, entangling policy of containment and those who preferred the sensible "Marshall line," in which we would aid and respect other nations. Mr. X, of course, was the point man for the former group.

Kennan fumed. He had opposed the Truman Doctrine and had written much of the Marshall Plan. Now Lippmann was suggesting that the article's author supported the Truman Doctrine and opposed the philosophy behind the Marshall Plan. Kennan wanted to respond, but the secretary of state had requested his silence. Lippmann's monologue would continue unchallenged.

To Kennan, the fundamental problem was that Lippmann had interpreted containment as primarily a military doctrine, so that containing the Soviets at a given point meant drawing the sword. Kennan saw containment as political, and he drafted a letter to the columnist arguing that point. Containment meant propaganda and aid, not pistols and tanks. He did not want the U.S. armed forces committed in Greece, Iran, and Turkey where the Soviets were exercising overt or covert pressure. The Soviets were making "first and foremost a political attack. Their spearheads are the local communists. And the counter-weapon that can beat them is the vigor and soundness of political life in the victim countries."

Kennan did not send the letter. Two years later, though, he learned that Lippmann was going to be on the same New York–to–Washington train and (after being briefed and assisted by an aid) he presented the columnist with a long monologue on the topic. It was one of many times throughout his career that Kennan would find himself arguing that the meaning of containment had slipped away from his original intent.

THE MARSHALL PLAN was in dire trouble entering 1948. A confident Republican Party, enjoying its first congressional majority in almost two decades, was not going to accede easily to a proposal coming from the Truman administration. Young men who had risked their lives to save Europe once did not want to give up their paychecks to save it again. According to a report issued later that year by New York congressman John Taber, chairman of the House Appropriations Committee, much of the aid the United States had already sent abroad since World War II had been wasted.

Kennan knew that the Marshall Plan was imperiled, but he could not stomach testifying on Capitol Hill. In January 1948, he described for his diary a ferocious argument with the columnist Joe Alsop about whether the diplomat had a duty to speak up. "I pointed out that personally I had entered a profession which I thought had to do with the representation of United States interests vis-à-vis foreign governments . . . that my specialty was defense of U.S. interests against others, not against our own

representatives." The attitude was a long-standing part of Kennan's character. He loved, and excelled at, solitary efforts: writing books and memos,
giving speeches, talking on the radio. He quivered when it came time
to interact.

Paul Nitze had no such qualms. The previous summer, he had worked
with Kennan to outline the plan. Afterward, he had transferred into a
small, intensely dedicated group reporting to the undersecretary of state
for economic affairs, Will Clayton. Early on, two of Nitze's superiors collapsed from exhaustion, leaving him as one of the most senior economists
on the plan. Nitze borrowed all the proto-computers from Prudential Life
Insurance and began calculating what exactly each European nation
needed. "It really has become a nine ring circus requiring almost factory
assembly line techniques to get the work done," he wrote home.

Nitze's job was to become a master of charts. He lovingly ported
around huge stacks of paper showing precisely what we were sending
where. How much cotton yarn, rubber, eggs, potash, nitrogen fertilizer,
zinc, freight cars, eggs, rice, and pig iron should we move abroad? How
much to Portugal and how much to Germany? When would it arrive
and how much would it cost? Nitze marked his documents in pencil and
checked the figures against his own addition. He was working for the
capitalists, but it almost seemed like the job of a centralized planner.
"He is young, able and a hard worker," wrote Clayton. "Moreover he
knows more about the Marshall Plan than perhaps any other individual
around here."

Soon Nitze was defending the Marshall Plan in press conferences, of
which he wrote, "I know of no more concentrated form of mental exercise." Next, he served as the aide-de-camp for higher-level administration officials at hearings and prepared documents for Congress. "I don't
mind congressional hearings, in fact I rather like them," he wrote, exactly
one week after Kennan's argument with Alsop. During one marathon
session working over a weekend, a future member of Truman's Policy
Planning Staff (Charles Burton Marshall) swung a chair at a legendary
Harvard professor (William Yandell Elliott) while Nitze and America's
future top delegate to the United Nations (Ernest Gross) looked on.

Arthur Vandenberg, a Republican who was likely the plan's hinge
supporter in Congress, declared it "backed by more hard work and careful research than almost any other bill to come before Congress." But hard
work does not guarantee success; for a while, Nitze thought the plan

doomed. It eventually passed, but then came another challenge: hearings in April 1948 in front of Taber's committee over how to appropriate the aid.

Taber had his knives out for Nitze. A few weeks before the hearings began, an ally of his called the FBI and asked for "any derogatory information" on Nitze. The congressman, apparently, was worried that Nitze was in line for a promotion that would give the State Department more power over the program, while leaving Congress with less. The ally of Taber, whose name is crossed out in the memo, added "that he felt Nitze's parents were Communists."

When the hearings began, Taber declared that he wanted Nitze to justify every single commodity the United States sent abroad, starting with goods going to Austria. When they got to pulses, or beans, Taber exclaimed: "Pulses are things you can raise pretty readily and easily on a small acreage. Do you have anyone who knows about that?" Taber moved on. "You have coffee in here. Why do you have coffee going to these people?"

"Coffee is one of the things that is in great demand in these countries," Nitze responded vaguely.

"They did not have any in 1946–47 or 1947–48, did they?"

"I believe not."

Eventually, Taber exploded and told Nitze that he was wasting the committee's time. He needed someone with answers.

Nitze responded that he could have the answers if allowed to bring in expert witnesses, for example specialists in Austrian agriculture. But Taber, who seemed intent on stalling the plan and embarrassing the witness, would have none of that. He stood up and went into an adjacent room to telephone an old colleague and friend, Undersecretary of State Robert Lovett.

Taber began the conversation by berating Nitze: this Harvard-educated banker did not know anything about agriculture, Taber told Lovett. Nitze had never grown pulses, and he had not visited Austria to examine them. As Nitze later retold it, Lovett let Taber blow off steam and then asked, "How many rivets are there in a B-29 wing?" Taber snapped back that Lovett would of course know more about that since he had served as assistant secretary of war for air. "That's just the point," Lovett said. No one can know everything.

After half an hour, Taber came back to declare a retreat. "Mr. Nitze," he said, "you can call your experts. We'll adjourn the hearing now, and you have them here tomorrow morning."

The hearings went on for weeks; Nitze lost fifteen pounds in the process. But eventually Taber acquiesced. Pulses and coffee were soon steaming across the Atlantic. The Marshall Plan turned into one of America's greatest foreign policy triumphs: it helped save Europe both from starvation and from communism, creating a reservoir of goodwill that would last a generation. In its development and passage, Kennan and Nitze worked in tandem, each taking advantage of his strengths. Kennan had the big ideas and thought through the grand strategy; Nitze understood the economics and managed the fight.

6

★ ★ ★

ARCHITECT OF THE COLD WAR

Late one moonless night in October 1949, a boat called *The Stormie Seas* drew close in to the Albanian coast. Nine exiles grabbed guns and equipment and rowed ashore. They darted inland and eastward. After ten miles, they split up into two groups.

The goal was counterrevolution. They were supposed to organize their old friends, make new ones, and begin building a resistance movement against the communists who had seized power during the chaos of World War II. The operation was secret, subversive, likely violent, and highly dangerous. It was also the most aggressive version of containment that George Kennan ever advocated.

Kennan had a long history with spying. During his first posting in Russia, in the 1930s, he had taken great pride in cultivating secret sources. When based in Lisbon, he specialized in intelligence work under diplomatic cover. "My real mission," he would say later, "was the coordination of American intelligence in Portugal." In early 1948, he had watched the United States and the just-formed CIA help swing an election in Italy away from the communists. By the middle of that year, Kennan had become a strong advocate of covert action. "He knew that there are things that you have to do in the dark nights and then reconcile yourself with God," said Walter Pozen, his son-in-law.

That May, Kennan wrote: "Political warfare is the logical application of Clausewitz's doctrine in time of peace." To stifle the spread of communism the United States should do anything in its power, from propaganda to economic aid to "such covert operations as clandestine support of 'friendly' foreign elements, 'black' psychological warfare and even encouragement of underground resistance in hostile states."

Kennan regretted that the United States lagged in black ops. "The creation, success, and survival of the British Empire has been due in part to the British understanding and application of the principles of political warfare. Lenin so synthesized the teachings of Marx and Clausewitz that the Kremlin's conduct of political warfare has become the most refined and effective of any in history." The United States had yet to figure it out: "We have been handicapped however by a popular attachment to the concept of a basic difference between peace and war."

He argued for a range of responses, all of which he considered political containment. The United States should fund and support refugee groups with their eyes on overthrowing communist regimes; it should secretly fund anticommunists in free countries. If the Kremlin seemed close to acquiring something, like a "Near Eastern oil installation," the United States should sabotage the asset. Kennan also urged the creation of an "Office of Policy Coordination" and spent much of the spring and early summer of 1948 working out the details. In one memo to Lovett, he declared: "Time is running out on us. If we are to engage effectively in intelligent, organized covert activities, appropriations must be obtained."

He wanted the Office of Policy Coordination to be small and to be managed by the State Department. He eventually conceded that the newly formed CIA could run it—with Kennan providing some oversight as an official representative of State. He put forward a list of six men who could lead the organization. His top choice, a handsome track star turned lawyer named Frank Wisner, got the job.

With the organization in place, Kennan and Wisner went to work. The first plan described in the files released decades later by the State Department was to send balloons over communist territory, scattering propaganda leaflets on the prevailing winds. Less dramatically, Kennan helped design the National Committee for a Free Europe, a CIA-organized group that created the pro-American Radio Free Europe, broadcasting into communist countries.

Kennan and Wisner also worked together around this time to import an ex-Nazi named Gustav Hilger to advise the U.S. government. Kennan had known Hilger in Moscow fifteen years before and considered him "the dean of all 'Russian experts' and the foremost diplomatic authority on the Soviet Union." In the meantime, however, Hilger's résumé had accumulated some nasty stains. Although he played no significant part in the Final Solution, he had spent the war working for the Reich's foreign minister, Joachim von Ribbentrop, and recently released documents now make it virtually certain that Hilger knew about the mass murders of Jews.

It is unclear whether Kennan had any inkling of Hilger's wartime activities, but he certainly took pleasure in Hilger's arrival and the two spent a weekend together soon afterward. According to a document released by the CIA in 2006, Kennan thanked Wisner in October 1948 for taking Hilger on at the OPC, and ended by praising Wisner for not only getting Hilger into the country but also sneaking his family out of the Soviet zone of East Germany. "Because the humane and decent thing is sometimes overlooked in the operations of our governmental bureaucracy, it may not be out of place for me to observe that I think you have done the right thing."

Kennan's relationship with Hilger caused him problems in the 1980s, when a historian named Christopher Simpson made it a centerpiece of his book *Blowback,* which savaged the postwar importation of Nazis to America. Some of Kennan's other plans exploded much sooner. It was not easy to manipulate elections, overthrow governments, and seize oil fields. Moreover, the KGB regularly skunked its American rivals. In 1949, this lesson was underlined in blood on the rocky shores of Albania. Kennan was directly involved in planning these early operations, and they went very badly.

The Albanian security machine had known about the landings in advance. Troops patrolled the coastlines, villagers had been warned, and hillside shepherds were on the lookout. Not long after the infiltrators split up, one group was ambushed. Three of the four men were killed and one disappeared. The other group of five trudged south through the mountains at night, hiding in caves during the day. They tried to communicate by radio, using a loud, forty-pound pedal-powered generator that they lugged through the forests. The police shot one of the group as they traversed a ravine. But thanks to luck and daring the four survivors somehow managed to safely retreat out of Albania.

For the next five years, Wisner and his colleagues continued to send refugees into the country. But "everyone was arrested when they arrived," says Frank Lindsay, a longtime friend of Kennan who was part of the early intelligence operations. Albanian troops intercepted newly arrived insurgents or were waiting when the latest round of rubber boats washed ashore. Some poor operatives parachuted straight into the hands of the police. Others survived only because they missed their intended landing spots.

The communists had thoroughly infiltrated Western planning. Double agents filled the refugee communities from which the CIA recruited; worse, the British liaison to the project was Kim Philby, a Soviet asset. The Americans totally trusted Philby, and he often knew more about operations than did Wisner. The KGB's understandable suspicion that so rich a source must actually be a triple agent only slightly limited the damage done.

Kennan watched with horror as the Albanian operation and many others ended in abject failure. The CIA, meanwhile, dealt with disaster by pressing deeper into the labyrinth of special ops. Suspicion grew, and in some cases bent toward fantasy. Maybe, Wisner thought, the Adriatic operation had failed because the Soviets had penetrated the agency with a telepathic ray. Soon the CIA was testing whether LSD could help it understand mind control, slipping the drug to men who came into the whorehouses it ran in San Francisco and New York and then watching through one-way mirrors. At its Addiction Research Center in Kentucky, the agency kept a group of subjects on the drug for seventy-seven consecutive days. Containment had turned into psychedelic chicanery. The weird part of the Cold War had fully begun.

IN ASSEMBLING HIS COVERT organization, Kennan turned to James Forrestal, his old ally and patron. Forrestal had helped organize the CIA actions during the Italian elections and he gave his blessing to Kennan's suggestions for developing a variety of covert operations.

Born in the Hudson Valley, in the town now called Beacon, Forrestal had worked his way into Princeton from a childhood of modest means. Afterward, he took a job on Wall Street, where he advanced quickly, eventually moving to Dillon Read. His unwavering attention to business carried him far and fast, but his family life paid a heavy price. Nitze recalled that when Forrestal planned an evening at the theater with his wife, a glamorous *Vogue* writer with a drinking problem, he would buy three tickets: one for her, one for him, and one for his assistant. If work kept him at the office, she would not sit alone. Nitze would sometimes deliver documents to Forrestal's residence on Beekman Place; he found the real estate impressive and the marriage disastrous.

Forrestal told Nitze that he had learned toughness from his home-town blacksmith. He did not like the veneer to be seen through. Nitze once walked in on Forrestal at Dillon Read and found him on the phone making a contribution to a charity in Beacon. "Forrestal was annoyed at my intrusion, probably because he wanted to protect the tough unbend-ing image that he thought enhanced his effectiveness."

Forrestal joined the government as a liaison between Franklin Roo-sevelt and the business world. Here too he rose steadily, from presidential assistant to undersecretary of the navy to secretary of the navy, to secre-tary of defense. Walk into the Pentagon today and his bust greets you, with its piercing eyes and the slightly off-center nose, broken during a boxing match. "He could have been cast as a moving picture star, a smarter and more sophisticated Humphrey Bogart," Nitze wrote in an unpublished recollection.

During and after World War II, Forrestal was deeply suspicious of Stalin. In the fall of 1945, he argued vehemently that we should not share our secrets with the Soviets, a moment some historians consider the first fateful break with Moscow. The distrust prompted him to circulate the Long Telegram, write the 1947 paper declaring that the Soviet Union threatened the very existence of the United States, and join Kennan in setting up a special department for dirty tricks. Forrestal was always seeking new ideas and new approaches to problems. "He felt that the established echelons of government needed constant jolting up," Kennan reflected in a 1962 letter.

In Kennan's view, at least, Forrestal ultimately went too far. He helped Kennan considerably in setting up the Office of Policy Coordination. But reflecting back decades later, Kennan would lament OPC's growth and blame the Pentagon for it. He wanted it small and elite; Forrestal and the Pentagon wanted black propaganda offices franchised in embassies worldwide. "There is no method, there is no way except the method of worry, of constant concern, and of unceasing energy that will give us our security," the defense secretary said in 1947.

The constant concern eventually devoured Forrestal: by the late 1940s, he had begun a slow-motion nervous breakdown. Isolated and profoundly alarmed, he saw demons everywhere. Nitze's sister once found him in the bushes near the Plaza Hotel in New York. She asked what he was doing. Watching people, he said. I am just watching people going about their business.

In March 1949, the president replaced Forrestal as secretary of defense. Soon, he had become completely paranoid. Zionists were trailing him and the Soviets had bugged beach umbrellas all over Miami. Early that spring, he was committed to the U.S. Naval Hospital in Bethesda, Maryland, where the doctors began treating him with psychotherapy and insulin injections. They considered, but rejected, using electroconvulsive therapy.

After Forrestal was committed, Kennan wrote to him, "I was shocked to learn from this morning's paper of your illness and I don't need to tell you that you have my best wishes for a speedy recovery." For Nitze, Forrestal's collapse was more personal. The two were similar in both superficial and profound respects. Both had gone from Dillon Read into government, where they became anti-Soviet hard-liners. They had similar taste and style. They worked feverishly and worried obsessively. Each wanted to be more of an intellectual. Each had fought the military bureaucracy and suffered brutally for it. Tellingly, Nitze wrote in his later years that Forrestal's madness was not surprising, given all the pressures he faced. Rather, "that he held out so long is notable."

Kennan, too, might have seen a reflection of part of himself in Forrestal; he described his friend in a 1962 letter in words equally applicable to their author. Forrestal "had, I thought something of the ambitious tightness of the parvenu. He smacked a bit of F. Scott Fitzgerald. There was lacking, it seemed to me, the relaxation and languor of the securely well-born." Both men brooded deeply. But for Kennan, brooding was its own cure. He took long walks alone and wrote dark letters to his friends, undoubtedly helping to exorcise his demons. Forrestal, with his need to maintain the veneer of total control, lacked that release.

Forrestal lasted six weeks in the hospital, until the night of Saturday, May 21, 1949. According to a report long kept secret, he spent most of the evening pacing. At 12:20, he got a cup of orange juice and said he was going to bed; at 12:35, he got up to grab a cup of coffee; ten minutes later, he was apparently asleep. At 1:30, he popped out of bed and the corpsman on duty asked if he wanted a sleeping pill. Forrestal said no, but the corpsman went to ask the doctor whether he could have one anyway. When he returned, Forrestal was gone.

Lower in the building, people heard a thud. Forrestal's body, dressed in pajamas, was found facedown on the asphalt and cinderblock ledge outside room 384. He had plummeted thirteen floors, bouncing off other ledges as he fell. His bathrobe sash was tied tight around his neck; upstairs, a razor blade was found near his slippers. He had tried to hang himself and then either jumped or fallen out the window. At some point that evening he had copied out lines from a translation of Sophocles' *Ajax*, where the Chorus laments, "Better to die, and sleep / The never-waking sleep, than linger on / And dare to live when the soul's life is gone."

After his mentor's death, Nitze clipped one article for his files: a piece by Senator Margaret Chase Smith, of Maine, that began: "There is great joy in the Kremlin. A great American is dead—the man that the Communists hated and feared the most, James Forrestal."

"He was an architect of the Cold War," wrote the historian Ronald Steel, "and a casualty of it."

THE COLD WAR always felt tense and uncertain, but 1948 seemed particularly perilous. The world was cleaving into communist and capitalist spheres. No one knew who would gain where. The West was still unsure whether the antidote of Marshall Plan aid would help France cure its communist infection. Communists supported by the Soviets overthrew the government of Czechoslovakia in February. In China, Mao's communists were beginning to gain substantial ground against Chiang Kai-shek. Communists almost won the Italian election in April. The civil war in Greece continued. In May, communists assassinated a minister in Athens and the pro-Western government declared martial law over the whole country. Then, in June, Stalin decided he would try to take the West's most valuable, and most exposed, piece off the board.

On June 24, the Soviets shut down the railroads and roads linking West Berlin with the rest of West Germany. There were technical difficulties, they claimed. The same day, they severed access by water. Soon, they had totally cut off ground-level routes to West Berlin.

The Allies, however, still held the airports, and even Stalin would not take the political risk of shooting down an unarmed plane loaded with food and coal—particularly not after the United States carefully leaked word that scores of bombers capable of dropping atomic weapons were on their way to Britain. Soon the humanitarian aid planes began to land,

and land, and land. The rescue, called the Berlin Airlift, turned into a stunning propaganda victory, with the Western allies showing that their generosity and ingenuity could keep a city alive.

But it also showed the Policy Planning Staff the peril of a divided Germany. And it terrified Kennan, who told friends he thought the president should call up the National Guard. In early August, Kennan and a group of colleagues began to think through a possible solution. The United States could not take East Germany, could not yield West Germany to the Russians, and did not seem able to share the country. What were we to do? Nitze, with his German expertise, joined Kennan for the deliberations.

For the first two weeks of August, Kennan, Nitze, and their colleagues struggled to draw up a workable plan. Kennan dominated the proceedings, but Nitze later recalled that the two men were of "the same mind." In the end, they came up with a dramatic and controversial solution: "the early abandonment of military government, establishment of a German government with real powers, and withdrawal of the occupying forces entirely."

The lines defining the new Europe were hardening. If Germany remained divided, went the argument, so would the whole continent. A long, bitter cold war would become inevitable. Everything east of Germany, including potentially pro-Western Czechoslovakia and Hungary, would find itself indefinitely leashed to Moscow. With extraordinary prescience, Kennan and his group argued:

> If we carry on along present lines, Germany must divide into eastern and western governments and western Europe must move toward a tight military alliance with this country which can only complicate the eventual integration of the satellites into a European community. From such a trend of developments, it would be hard—harder than it is now— to find "the road back" to a united and free Europe.

The proposal differed entirely from Kennan's prior position. Three years earlier, he had wanted to dismember Germany; now he wanted to unify it. What had changed? In a letter to Anders Stephanson, a perceptive biographer who questioned the turnaround, Kennan explained that he had lost faith in the possibility of a well-governed, federal, divided Germany. The crisis over Berlin also made him realize how grave a threat a divided country posed to that city he loved. Last, Kennan declared, he had simply not understood Germany in earlier years.

Kennan and Nitze had little success in converting the rest of the government. In fact, almost everyone opposed the plan to end the occupation. On the cover of the August 12 proposal, Undersecretary of State Robert Lovett wrote, "This needs much more discussion with the Secretary."

The plan nonetheless survived. After the improbable reelection of Harry Truman, Kennan presented a more finished version, christened "Program A." Then, in March 1949, he traveled to Germany, hoping to bring back information he could use to lobby for his plan.

It was an emotional journey. The prewar Germany of Kennan's memories was gone and the land lay devastated. He was most affected by Hamburg, which the Allies had obliterated in the summer of 1943. There he saw the destruction as a human tragedy so profound that it called into question the idea of a just war:

> Here, for the first time, I felt an unshakeable conviction that no momentary military advantage—even if such could have been calculated to exist—could have justified this stupendous, careless destruction of civilian life and of material values, built up laboriously by civilian hands over the course of centuries for purposes having nothing to do with war. . . . If the Western world was really going to make valid the pretense of a higher moral departure point—of great sympathy and understanding for the human being as God made him, as expressed not only in himself but in the things he had wrought and cared about—then it had to learn to fight its wars morally as well as militarily, or not fight them at all; for moral principles were part of its strength. Shorn of this strength, it was no longer itself; its victories were not real victories; and the best it would accomplish in the long run would be to pull down the temple over its head.

When Kennan returned to America, he deployed his favorite and most powerful instruments: his beloved secretary, Dorothy Hessman, and her typewriter. He dictated a long, passionate memo, restating his and Nitze's arguments from August in starker terms. In form, it resembled the Long Telegram or the X article. He began by describing the opacity of the situation—"the complexities of the German problem today are so terrific that the problem may be said to have its own dialectics"—and then its importance. "This is one of the moments, as Bismarck put it, when you can hear the garments of the Goddess of Time rustling through the course of events." Once again, Kennan sought to guide the reader through a mysterious labyrinth, and once again he had a firm counterconventional conclusion: we should let the German people run their own country.

He presented his argument in person to Dean Acheson, who had replaced Marshall as secretary of state in January. But Acheson was unconvinced. Opinion was building steadily against Program A. His Russian memos had made Kennan a sage, but his German memos made him a crank. The U.S. military opposed him. The rest of the State Department had little use for his argument. The Soviets seemed wholly disinclined to withdraw from the country that had destroyed so much of Russia during the war—and from whose mines, as we now know, the USSR was already extracting uranium used in its nuclear arsenal.

In the spring of 1949, Acheson, Kennan, and Nitze set off to Paris for a meeting of the Council of Foreign Ministers. On the agenda would be discussions with the Soviets about the fate of Germany and, potentially, another opportunity to make the case for Program A. But on the eve of their departure, James Reston of the *New York Times* published a story based on a leaked version of the proposal: "U.S. Plan Weighed: Big Three Would Withdraw to Ports in the North Under Proposal." The story credited the idea to Kennan.

Reston's piece killed any last hope for the plan. Program A was too bold an idea, presented too casually. The Europeans read the article with fury, envisioning a return to American isolationism. Omar Bradley, chairman of the Joint Chiefs of Staff, saw the plan as naïve. Lucius Clay, the American military commander in Germany, declared it close to capitulation. Acheson, who was already leaning strongly against Program A, repudiated it.

Crushed, Kennan wrote a grumpy memo to the secretary of state explaining how hard he had worked on the plan and how sensible he still thought it. Nitze, characteristically, let the news roll off his back. His job was to help Acheson get the best deals he could, even if the ideal plan was out. The Soviets were not going to accept the big idea, and the Allies hated it. Too bad. He could still work on smaller projects, such as how to increase trade between East and West Germany.

While in Paris, Kennan and Nitze received the devastating news of Forrestal's death. It was perhaps fitting that just as their old mentor left the scene, Kennan and Nitze had begun a subtle battle for influence over a new mentor. Forrestal had brought the two men to Washington; now each was important in his own right. And the person they needed to sway was the new secretary of state.

JAMES FORRESTAL SHARED Kennan's and Nitze's weaknesses. Dean Acheson shared the two men's strengths. He could write almost as brilliantly as Kennan and see nearly as far into the foreign policy future. He had Nitze's resilience and his understanding of power.

The son of an Episcopal bishop of Connecticut, Acheson had the classic upbringing of the WASP elite: Groton, Yale, Harvard Law. He had clerked for Justice Louis Brandeis, become a powerful lawyer, and been named an undersecretary of the Treasury. In 1945, Truman made him undersecretary of state. In 1946, he won the president's undying loyalty with a simple act of kindness. After the Republicans drubbed the Democrats at the polls, Truman's train pulled into Washington's Union Station. Only one man was there to meet him and cheer him up: Dean Acheson. Three years later, in appointing Acheson, Truman said: "Twenty guys would make a better secretary of state than you. But I don't know them. I know you."

Acheson even looked the part—or perhaps he gave the part the look. Ruggedly handsome, he was the answer to a tailor's prayer: he wore elegant suits, and his stern, proud face harbored the most famous mustache in Washington. "Though it once seemed to climb his cheeks, like a vine seeking sunlight, it now is comparatively self-controlled and at peace with itself, quietly aware of its responsibilities," wrote the New Yorker in a 1949 profile. The only feature slightly off the mark was his rather large nose. Years later, Nitze bought his wife a horse for her birthday that had a particularly grand proboscis. He invited his former chief to the stables and told him the horse's name: Mr. Acheson.

While he had the looks and résumé of a secretary of state, Acheson had the temper of a sailor. He would explode in fury in the office, and once he came close to punching a Republican senator during a committee hearing. His wit, too, was legendary. At the Paris meeting, Acheson told a Soviet representative that his proposal was "as full of propaganda as a dog is of fleas, though in this case it was all fleas and no dog."

The wit could cut, particularly when directed at his friends. Acheson once compared Kennan to "an old horse pulling a buggy over a bridge who would stop periodically to see if it was he who was making all the noise." After Acheson's death, Nitze tried to raise money for a chair to be named after him at the Johns Hopkins School for Advanced International Studies. "I couldn't find a soul who Acheson hadn't offended and who didn't resent this."

A late-budding cold warrior, Acheson trusted Stalin far longer than did Kennan or Nitze, and was more open in the conflict's early days to sharing nuclear technology with Russia. He cowrote the Acheson-Lilienthal Report in early 1946, calling for an international organization to take control of all fissile material and for the United States to share its nuclear technology with Moscow. But like so many other people in government, he came around. "The year 1946 was for the most part a year of learning that minds in the Kremlin worked very much as George F. Kennan had predicted they would," he wrote in his memoirs.

Intellectually, Acheson seemed closer to Kennan than to Nitze. They wrote some of the sharpest letters in Washington, and both were capable of thinking strategically. Kennan went out of his way to appeal to Acheson's intellectual side. Two weeks before Acheson's swearing in, Kennan sent him a long memo on the problems confronting them and the magnitude of the changes needed. It began, "I really have no enthusiasm for sharing with people I have known—Kerensky, Bruening, Dumba, or the King of Jugoslavia—the wretched consolation of having been particularly prominent among the parasites on the body of a dying social order, in the hours of its final agony."

Nitze never wrote a sentence that vivid in his life. Nor was he intellectually at Kennan's or Acheson's level. He had yet to attain real responsibility, or to have written anything that attracted the attention of the people who mattered. He was still only a numbers man, if a smart one. But his temperament suited Acheson. The secretary liked to quote Oliver Wendell Holmes's line that "man is born to act," a maxim that fit Nitze, even at this early stage.

Nitze would later describe Acheson's fascination with a book by Clarence Day that Holmes had given him, *This Simian World*. The author argued that people are just monkeys. Yes, we can think, and this separates us from other animals. But we are not going to find answers in the endless quest for truth. Instead, we should just accept who we are, do the best we can, and not try to live up to unreachable ideals and values. Reflecting on this book, Nitze recalled a palm reader he had seen in college. She "opened my hand and stared at it for five minutes, saying not a word. When she finally spoke, she said, 'I can say nothing about this man; he has a purely practical hand.' "

THE POLICY PLANNING Staff was the ideal environment for George Kennan. The offices were sparse: the conference room had one round table, scattered with ashtrays, and comfortable chairs. There were no in-boxes or out-boxes. On the walls hung two maps: one of the United States and one of the world. It was a place for Kennan to think and to hold forth. Sometimes, the rest of the staff would just sit and listen, with no one else uttering a word.

The place attracted brilliance. John Paton Davies, likely the wisest U.S. analyst of China in the middle of the century, worked there. Dorothy Fosdick, a speechwriter for (and lover of) Adlai Stevenson, joined, too—and would often find Kennan unloading his emotional burdens on her at lunchtime. She went on to write a well-respected book, *Common Sense and World Affairs,* and to serve as the top foreign policy adviser to Senator Henry "Scoop" Jackson from 1955 until 1983.

Kennan ran PPS for two and a half years, and for much of that time he got his way. His country pursued a policy of containment resembling the one he had advocated in the X article and his National War College lectures. The Marshall Plan; covert manipulation of the Italian election; non-combat support for the Greek struggle against communism; quiet establishment of the Office of Policy Coordination. Kennan believed that the world had five strategic centers—the United States, Great Britain, Germany and central Europe, the Soviet Union, and Japan—and he wanted four of them kept out of the hands of Moscow. In this he helped the United States succeed, particularly through his full-throttle intervention into policy toward Japan in 1947 and 1948. When it appeared that the United States might withdraw, Kennan insisted that the U. S. occupation still had essential work to do, and the rehabilitation of America's former enemy became, once again, a primary political goal. In Asia's other great power, Kennan helped limit American support for the corrupt Chinese Nationalists, preventing deep U.S. involvement in that nation's civil war.

Another central piece of his strategy was for the United States to pry apart the communist nations. Many people in America thought a red was a red. But Kennan knew the color came in different shades; in the X article, he had argued that exploiting those differences was essential to a truly political containment.

On June 30, 1948, a diplomatic communiqué came in to Kennan's office: the Cominform had expelled the Yugoslav Communist Party. Josip Tito, undeniably a communist, was now also undeniably on his own. Kennan was elated. According to Joseph Alsop, visiting for an interview as the news came in, Kennan grabbed his guitar and started strumming in excitement.

Within two days, Kennan had written a memo that would outline U.S. policy to come. The Balkan rift mattered immensely. "By this act, the aura of mystical omnipotence and infallibility which has surrounded the Kremlin power has been broken." But the United States must not offer too strong or too sudden an embrace. Doing so might strengthen Tito's enemies, and Yugoslavia was still an antagonistic and communist country. Kennan proposed a careful balance. The United States would patiently and gradually begin talking to Belgrade. Eventually we would offer trade concessions. Nothing would be done too fast, but nothing would be neglected. Kennan's advice was followed, and, partly because of the successful American maneuvering, Yugoslavia remained independent, leaving Stalin to obsess over how to assassinate his rival. It was one of Kennan's clearest successes.

Nonetheless, Kennan's overall influence was beginning to fade. He tried to stop the formation of the Atlantic military alliance, NATO, because he feared that, as with the formation of a West German government, it would solidify the division of Europe. As suggested by his criticism of the Truman Doctrine, he did not want the United States mucking around in parts of the world where he felt we had little at stake. On these grounds, he opposed the recognition of the state of Israel. He thought the UN hopeless. By the time of his Program A, he was becoming known as a figure like Justice Holmes: a man recognized mainly for his formidable dissents.

As Kennan lost influence, Nitze gained it. The two men agreed on much, but Nitze was in sync with the times, far more confident than Kennan in his country's ability to do good and far more willing to believe in the promise of international organizations. He supported the creation of NATO. He saw nothing wrong with the Truman Doctrine. He believed the UN could play a useful role in global affairs.

In the summer of 1949, Kennan brought Nitze on as his deputy at

PPS. Kennan had already decided he wanted to leave, and he was clearly entertaining the notion that Nitze might replace him. When the junior man showed up for his first day of work, on July 29, Kennan gave him his office and moved his own workspace into the conference room.

At first, Kennan still dominated the PPS meetings, and the relationship started as one of eager student and admired teacher. During an economic crisis in Britain late that summer, Kennan delegated Nitze to handle most of the talks with the British. At the end, Nitze came to him with a summary. Kennan recorded in his diary the great mirth he felt when he and Nitze revised the paper together, inserting paragraphs that Kennan had written about the crisis before the meeting even took place.

Acheson took PPS's advice seriously on nearly every issue and would often come in to preside, turning up on Wednesday afternoons to review big ideas. He maintained a strong affection for Kennan. At one point in Nitze's early days, it was insinuated that Kennan had leaked important information to a newspaper reporter. Kennan was mortified, but Acheson set him at ease with a charming note, saying not to worry about it. "No one can both know you and suspect you. And the rest don't matter. This is life in a disorderly democracy."

Nitze was excited but nervous about his new job. He wrote to his mother in August: "Washington is hot, damp and close to being unbearable. Congress is in a mean and discouraged mood, the world rocks and creaks, the Russians gloat over our problems and cleverly spread dissension amongst us and I am supposed to come up with good and workable ideas on all problems what-so-ever."

As suggested by that letter home, Nitze's career could still have gone off in any number of different directions. He was an economics expert, a German expert, and an all-around bright guy. But soon came the event that put him on the track he would follow for most of the rest of his career—and that brought him head-to-head with Kennan.

7

WHAT WE ARE ABOUT

On the morning of August 29, 1949, a tall Soviet physicist with a goatee that reached his upper chest snapped out an order and started a countdown. Igor Kurchatov had stopped shaving several years before, following a tradition of Roman emperors who had laid aside their razors during times of battle. Now he was completing a project begun during the last war—but aimed toward the next one.

Ten kilometers away from him, scientists had constructed a thirty-meter tower surrounded by a small city, complete with brick houses, bridges, and tunnels. It was a forsaken spot in a valley between two hills, barren except for the tanks and scattered railroad cars and a few animals, including two camels, in pens. Day was breaking after a cold and windy night. Minus thirty minutes. Minus ten minutes. Minus three. Thirty seconds; two; zero.

And then Kurchatov watched with pride as a white flame rose upward, vaporizing everything around. "The fireball, rising and revolving turned orange, red. Then dark streaks appeared. Streams of dust, fragments of brick and board were drawn into it, as into a funnel," wrote one of his deputies. "The atomic mushroom was blown away to the south, losing its outlines, and turning into the formless torn heap of clouds one might see after a gigantic fire."

"It worked," declared Kurchatov. He hopped in his car and roared off to ground zero. The Soviet Union had detonated its first atomic bomb.

The effort was classically Soviet, combining brilliant research, clever espionage, and hard labor—with much of the uranium mining done by prisoners. Lavrenti Beria gave Kurchatov a joyful hug and asked the scientist to name the bomb. "RDS-1," he replied—"RDS" being the abbreviation of a phrase translatable as "Russia did it on her own." America later nicknamed the bomb "Joe-1."

The news for Kurchatov was doubly good. The lead scientist on the project, he had proved essential in ending America's nuclear monopoly. The reward for success was a bonus, a ZIS-110 car, and a dacha in the Crimea. The penalty for failure? Quite possibly, execution.

Six days later, a specifically equipped American B-29 took off from Japan and headed north. It passed near the Kamchatka Peninsula, sucking in air samples through filters mounted atop the fuselage. Radiation was detected at levels too high to be natural. Soon, scientists testing rainwater had found radioactive sludge, and the air force was tracking a radioactive cloud. The Soviets had caught up; what had happened to Hiroshima and Nagasaki could now happen to Houston and New York.

Almost no one in the U.S. government had expected this so soon. Intelligence reports suggested that the Soviets were still several years from developing a working bomb. According to a State Department aide who worked on atomic energy, Gordon Arneson, we still assumed "that our vaunted industrial capacity and organization could not possibly be duplicated in performance by the Soviet Union, peopled as it was by wild-eyed bomb-throwing Bolsheviks and peasants, all thumbs." The biggest doubter was the most important. Truman had once asked Robert Oppenheimer, "When will the Russians be able to build the bomb?"

"I don't know," responded Oppenheimer.

"I know," said the president.

"When?"

"Never."

When Truman's top atomic adviser, David Lilienthal, came to break the news, the president was quietly and serenely reading the *Congressional Record*. Lilienthal's report left him seemingly nonchalant; we could not really be sure the Soviets had tested an atomic bomb, he said. Lilienthal, startled, replied that yes, we could be sure, very sure. Truman snapped, "Really?" and gave Lilienthal a sharp look. For months, he stubbornly maintained that the radioactivity might have come from an exploding nuclear reactor.

George Kennan, on the other hand, was wholly unsurprised. On September 13, 1949, he got preliminary word about the test. On September 19, a second scientific panel confirmed it. On September 21, Kennan had dinner at Nitze's house to discuss how to manage the story with the press.

They got along well that evening, sitting at a grand dining room table on a black and white marble floor. But that was the last time—or, to be precise, the last time for fifty years, one month, and two days—George Kennan and Paul Nitze would agree on the most important issue of the Cold War.

WHEN THE FIRST mushroom clouds rose over Hiroshima and Nagasaki, Kennan was not nearly as shaken as his statements of four years later suggest. Early on he was a nuclear hawk. In the fall of 1945, he argued that the United States should not share its weapons with the Soviet Union. In the summer of 1946, he lambasted Soviet proposals that the United States disarm. Moscow's goal was to reach the day when the Americans, handcuffed by international law and public opinion, "would be stripped of atomic weapons whereas Russia, having been secretly developing them behind the scenes, would be their sole possessor." Once that happened, the Soviet Union could "confidently risk an outbreak of war between the Soviet Union and the western powers." To prevent that, Kennan wrote, the United States should press for an international nuclear agreement, even as "we quietly and vigorously proceed to develop the U.S. capacity to absorb atomic attack and to effect instant retaliation."

Two years later, those talons and that beak had disappeared. Exposure to the destruction of Hamburg had shaken Kennan, and his extensive reading at the War College about nuclear theory had filled him with fear. "Our effort must therefore be to convince the Russians that it is in their interest to disarm themselves—by acceptance of an international atomic energy authority," he wrote in his diary in 1946. Slightly later, he wrote: "We must be like the porcupine who only gradually convinces the carnivorous beast of prey that he is not a fit object of attack."

But perhaps the most important transformative factor was his conviction that America had listened to his warnings about Stalin all too closely. A country that had been accepting and beneficent in 1945 had become truculent by 1949. Unrequited love had become unrepentant hatred.

By September 1949, Kennan was terrified not only by the weapon but by the way his country interpreted the USSR's success. His countrymen did not realize, he wrote in his diary, that what matters are *"intentions, rather than the *capabilities* of other nations."* As a result, the United States was "drifting toward a morbid preoccupation with the fact that the Russians conceivably *could* drop atomic bombs on this country."

Up to this point, Nitze and Kennan had sailed side by side. Now they started to tack apart. To Nitze, capabilities did matter, perhaps even more than intentions. A passive regime could turn hostile overnight. Weapons that did not seem menacing on Tuesday could look deadly dangerous by Wednesday. And what evidence was there to suggest that the Russians did not have designs on us, or at least on our allies in Western Europe? Ask the Poles, Hungarians, Czechs, Yugoslavs, East Germans, Romanians, and Bulgarians about Stalin's restraint.

Nor did the weapon itself spook Nitze. He had studied its effects in Japan, and he knew that the damage it caused was finite. He was also beginning to formulate an arms management thesis: even if you never used them, nuclear weapons gave you leverage. If the other side knew you would triumph in the ultimate battle, they would more likely accede in the smaller skirmishes. Whichever side most feared escalation would make the first concessions. The ability to blast the USSR might obtain better basing rights in Turkey. Nitze did not appear to worry about the hyperarming that such a doctrine would almost necessarily engender. After all, if the United States really did wave its nuclear sword to get basing rights from Istanbul, what might the Soviets do next except redouble their efforts to catch up?

That fall, the central question for the U.S. government quickly became whether to try to build a hydrogen bomb, a fearsome weapon that used fusion, not fission. Scientists had kicked the idea around for years, with little progress made. But the capacity for annihilation was tempting.

Truman set up a committee of three people to help him make the decision: Secretary of Defense Louis Johnson, Lilienthal, and Acheson. Johnson would surely be in favor of the H-bomb, and Lilienthal would surely oppose it. Acheson was the tiebreaker, and his mind was far from made up. Before choosing, he wanted to consult with his two top policy planners.

In the weeks following the successful Soviet test, Kennan and Nitze had separated, slowly but inexorably. On September 30, Kennan first complained to his diary about his colleague, noting Nitze's desire to use the news of Russia's atomic bomb to commence a full reappraisal of U.S. policy. "I face the work of these remaining months with neither enthusiasm nor with hope for achievement."

Later, Kennan sent Acheson a quick memo setting forth nine leading questions for the secretary to consider. After the first one—"Would the use of the super-bomb constitute a menace to civilization itself through the possibility that it would pollute the earth's atmosphere to a dangerous extent?"—Nitze scrawled "no" in the margin. He then handwrote in a tenth question, trying to draw Acheson in the other direction: Would we know if the Soviets were making a hydrogen bomb too?

As the two men debated, they packed their schedules with meetings with outside consultants. Among the experts they met were their scientific doppelgängers: Robert Oppenheimer and Edward Teller, two men whose relationship in many ways mirrored that between Kennan and Nitze—from appearance to personality to politics. But there was one hugely important difference: neither Kennan nor Nitze would ever try to end the other's career.

ROBERT OPPENHEIMER STOOD nearly six feet tall, weighed as little as 115 pounds, and seemed to have an IQ of twice that number. Born two months after Kennan, he was a brilliant theoretical physicist who pioneered work in black holes and quantum chemistry. He read eight languages, including Sanskrit, and once learned enough Dutch in six weeks to give a technical lecture in the language. Selected in 1942 to run the Manhattan Project, he became an icon when his team succeeded in building the atomic bomb in time to win the war. The cover of the first issue of *Physics Today* simply displayed Oppenheimer's signature porkpie hat.

As with Kennan, behind the brilliance lay an unsettled soul. Oppenheimer was withdrawn and occasionally depressed to the point of contemplating suicide. He was nearly thrown out of graduate school at Cambridge for, on one of his darker days, poisoning an apple and leaving it on his tutor's desk. He escaped partly through literature. Martin Sherwin and Kai Bird, his Pulitzer-winning biographers, suggest that reading Proust harmonized the psychological conflicts that so haunted his youth.

Oppenheimer, like Kennan, believed that discipline was more than just a method for achieving excellence. He believed it was good for the soul. And as with Kennan, these forces—the brilliance, the unease, the imagination, the drive—pushed him into a yearning to create a new way to organize the world. Kennan's youthful romance was with enlightened despotism. Oppenheimer's, much more fatefully, was with communism.

Four years younger than Oppenheimer, Edward Teller was bulkier and huskier, with dark raccoonlike eyebrows. Like an impressive number of the twentieth century's most brilliant scientists, he was a middle-class Hungarian Jewish immigrant to America. That youthful experience of revolution and counterrevolution seared him, just as it seared his contemporary Arthur Koestler. The writer would turn his experience into *Darkness at Noon*; Teller would turn his into a lifetime effort to counter communism through weaponry.

Teller was energetic and obsessive. He did not speak until he was three, and then in complete sentences. He described himself as choleric, and one of his colleagues called him the only monomaniac he knew with several manias. A friend remembered traveling with him one weekend. On the train ride back, Teller grew restless after having eschewed work for two days. "Have you got a problem for me to solve?" he kept insisting. His friend finally gave him one: arrange a chessboard with eight queens so none could take another. Teller thought briefly and then announced that he had solved it. "Do you have another problem for me?"

He left Hungary in 1926, came to the United States a decade later, and joined the Manhattan Project at the very outset. His experience there was not particularly successful or happy. He became so obsessed with the possibility of creating a weapon utilizing fusion that at one point he refused to work out the fission calculations that the team needed. Like Nitze, his skills lay less in grand thinking than in construction, details, and surveying what everyone else had published.

By the time of Hiroshima, both he and Oppenheimer had begun to wrestle with the ethics of their work. Not long after the explosion, Oppenheimer met with President Truman and solemnly said, "I feel I have blood on my hands." Truman declared the meeting over and later muttered: "Blood on his hands! Dammit, he hasn't half as much blood on his hands as I have. You just don't go around bellyaching about it."

Teller seemed to have internalized that advice. In July 1945, before the Alamogordo explosion, he had written a letter to a colleague that began,

"I have no hope of clearing my conscience. The things we are working on are so terrible that no amount of protesting or fiddling with politics will save our souls." But he also felt strongly that his responsibility was to keep doing his job. "The accident that we worked out this dreadful thing should not give us the responsibility of having a voice in how it is to be used. This responsibility must in the end be shifted to the people as a whole and that can be done only by making the facts known."

For the next four years, Oppenheimer would find himself pulled deeper into questions about the ethics of what he had done. Teller just charged ahead, trying to figure out the H-bomb. Right after the end of the war, he asked Oppenheimer for support, but the master of the Manhattan Project had made enough bombs. "I neither can nor will do so," Oppenheimer said. Teller still found ways to continue his research. As soon as he heard of the Joe-1 explosion, he called a colleague and suggested that now was the right time to push again for fusion. He offered a wager: he would be a prisoner of the Soviets within five years if the United States did not make the super bomb.

Oppenheimer's arguments against the bomb in the fall of 1949 were mainly moral and political: he contended, for example, that if we disarmed, the Soviets might follow our example. But when he met with Nitze and the PPS, he resorted to technical arguments. He did not think the bomb could work. Nor could an airplane deliver something that large: we would have to send it in by oxcart. If we did make the fusion bomb work, the Soviets would copy our methods.

The next day, Teller came in and took Nitze to the blackboard, where he diagrammed the forces and reactions that he said could constitute this terrible weapon. They talked physics for two hours; at the end, Nitze was awed and persuaded. A fusion bomb was possible. Nitze felt enlightened by Teller and frustrated by Oppenheimer, whose politics seemed to have interfered with his science. (Ironically, however, the design Teller mapped out for Nitze never actually worked. Teller only developed a feasible system two years later, in collaboration with Stanislaw Ulam.)

Nitze believed what he saw on the blackboard, and his logic flowed seamlessly from there. It would be best if no one had such weapons. But it would be worst if the Russians had them and we did not. Thus, if it was possible for us to build them, it was necessary. We had to "be there first, and not leave the world in a position where the Russians could dominate."

★

DECEMBER 1949 was the critical month. Kennan had isolated himself in his office in order to write. He felt the weight of the future bearing down on him, and his pen was the only means by which he could push it back.

Oppenheimer tried to save Kennan from himself, urging a struggle against the bureaucracy on every front. If Kennan went to the president with nothing but a master plan for international cooperation, he would fail. He had to fight for his small, short-term ideas. The president might accede to a moratorium on building the hydrogen bomb. Would not that be preferable to getting nothing at all?

The pragmatic approach fell flat. Kennan had long ago decided to take a sabbatical from the State Department at the beginning of the forthcoming year, and he was now writing like a man with one month to live. He had essentially decided to defend his position in the bureaucracy with a single weapon: his coming opus.

Nitze, in contrast, fought for the bomb by land, sea, and air. He joined the Atomic Working Group within the State Department. He lobbied Acheson. To opponents of the weapon he offered compromises, such as pairing the development of the fusion bomb with a strategic review. His thinking continued to evolve. His notes from this period show a man playing with hypotheticals and theories. He covered each page with neatly ordered lists and often extremely dense doodles that look a bit like those of a brooding Kandinsky acolyte.

At one point, he drafted a proposal to "limit all armaments"; it would have required a commitment that no more than 3 percent of national income go to military purposes, with specific mandated maximums of ten submarines, three aircraft carriers, and three battleships. But most of his notes and lists provided the basis for his arguments in favor of building the Super. "Real question is (1) whether our present stance re A bombs increases threat of war (2) or acts as preventative to war." Above that he wrote: "To live as free men or not at all. Test of will. Gotterdämmerung."

Kennan emerged from isolation deathly exhausted, with a seventy-nine-page treatise that he would call the most important paper of his life. The Kennans had just had their third child, and, soon after completing the first draft, he wrote to Acheson that he "was tempted, day before yesterday, to go into the baby's room and say: 'Go on, get up. You're going to work today. I'll get in the crib.'"

Brilliant and prescient, Kennan's paper was also distinctly peculiar. In most of his writings, he got immediately to the point. This one started with an eleven-page analysis of the UN's current position on atomic energy—a tangent to the current debate. Tellingly, the State Department's historical editors chose to exclude this preface from the relevant volume of *Foreign Relations of the United States*.

But Kennan did eventually open the throttle, moving from the dry tangent to a passionate appeal, calling upon Shakespeare and St. Paul. America, he argued, needed to take a strong, decisive step away from its obsession with the atomic bomb. Human power now exceeded human wisdom, and if these weapons had to exist, some international organization should control them. Anticipating forty years of debate, he advocated the virtues of declaring a policy of not using the weapons first. He worried about how the public would process the fact that "there are no issues which could justify mutual destruction." Much of his argument was psychological. The power of nuclear weapons stretched so far past the terrible ends of human imagination that we could not figure out how to set a rational policy around them. "I fear that the atomic weapon," he wrote, "will impede understanding of the things that are important to a clean, clear policy and will carry us toward the misuse and dissipation of our national strength."

For example, he explained that moving forward on this path would begin a resource-devouring arms race that would provoke an "inability to find adequate criteria for putting them into proper perspective alongside other government expenditures." In the end, "the effort to achieve security through the cultivation of weapons of mass destruction tends to carry the public mind ultimately toward a dim 'no man's land' of total confusion."

Nitze found Kennan's paper entirely unpersuasive. On his personal copy, Nitze marked the two passages above and put thick question marks in the margins next to them. Throughout the rest of the text, he scrawled question marks, rejections ("No!"), and occasional caustic responses such as "Misreading of what we are *about*." At the bottom of page one, as if to emphasize Kennan's position on the great debate, Nitze wrote "prohibition" and underlined it twice.

Nitze agreed that nuclear bombs were deadly dangerous and that the world would benefit if they did not exist. But exist they did. We could understand them, and we could set rational policy surrounding them, starting with research into the Super. Despite the disagreement, he was courteous to his colleague. "All of us who worked with him were absolutely devoted," he said.

Nitze wrote a memo beginning with one of his classic efforts to split a problem into component parts that he could then tame with numbers and letters. He began by declaring that "there are two important new facts dealt with in [Kennan's] paper and five interrelated problems." The most important of these problems was that the United States was dealing with the present. Kennan fretted about the future dangers of the weapon, but the present circumstances were so grave that the country had to deal with them immediately and could not cede even a temporary advantage to the Soviets. "The possibility that an incorrect decision as to stockpiling or use might at sometime in the future be made does not appear to warrant a further delay in initiating an accelerated program to test feasibility."

Nitze's final argument was even simpler. The Soviets were going to pursue testing, and since we could not afford to fall behind we must match them.

Over Christmas weekend, Acheson took versions of Nitze's and Kennan's memos home to think the matter over.

IN THE MIDDLE of the hydrogen bomb debate, Kennan began to sour on the prospect of Nitze replacing him. "The question must soon be faced as to who should succeed me," he wrote Bohlen, not adding that the choice of successor had been made long ago. "My own inclination would be to say that unless you yourself would feel like coming home . . . they should leave it vacant for a while."

Kennan could not undo the existing arrangement, however; in January, Acheson announced the new director of the Policy Planning staff. Nitze "is 42, studious, graying, tweedy, and shy," reported *U.S. News*, getting the first four of its five modifiers correct. "Mr. Nitze, his friends and associates say, is less articulate and less spectacular than Mr. Kennan. He is more a listener and less an expounder, more a judge and less a pleader," wrote the *Washington Star*. "Kennan's leadership of the Policy Planning Staff was a little like a gallant cavalry charge with George brandishing a saber in the lead, astride the most spirited horse in the regiment," said a friend of both men who was quoted in the story. "Nitze operates more like a chief of staff—or like the editor of a great research project. He presides, listens, and suggests. He organizes, deputizes, and supervises. He weighs, balances, analyzes, and sums up."

Nitze certainly knew the size of the shoes he had to fill. He wrote to a friend: "One who has worked as closely with George Kennan as I have and knows the greatness of his quality must feel inadequate, indeed, at the thought of stepping into his place." His mother took the news in stride. "Dearest Paul: Read this horoscope. You may still raise livestock and turnips."

Meanwhile, a decision on the Super still had to be made. Acheson had sided with Nitze, which meant that Truman's advisory panel was now in favor of the bomb, two votes to one. Just after noon on January 31, Acheson, Lilienthal, and Secretary of Defense Johnson marched over to the president's office to present their recommendations. As they made their way over, Truman was sorting through papers and chatting with one of his assistants. The president looked at the famous motto above his desk— "The buck stops here"—and started musing about his big decisions. He had cut off Lend-Lease aid after the war (a blooper); pursued the Truman Doctrine (good); led the Berlin Airlift (also good); and implemented the Marshall Plan ("a ten-strike"). His secretary came in and announced that the three men had arrived. Truman beckoned them in. Now it was time to make another momentous decision.

THE PRESIDENT of the United States began to speak:

> We have known for a long time that there were possibilities of developing a type of atomic weapon which would have almost unlimited destructive power, depending on the amount detonated.
>
> At my direction, this matter has been given the most careful study by competent organs of this Government. On the basis of their reports to me, I have decided, after grave deliberation and in full consciousness of the nature of the issues involved, that it is not in the national interest that we should proceed at this time to the development of this type of explosive.
>
> The American people view with abhorrence all weapons of mass destruction. It is a source of profound regret to us that failure to reach international agreement on atomic energy control has made it necessary for us to proceed with the production of atomic bombs. I hope that we

will never lose our balance by entering on a race for the development of weapons of pure mass destruction unless it is clear that our security will be materially served thereby, on balance. In the present instance, I do not find that to be the case.

Had Truman so spoken, he would have utterly changed the course of the arms race. But he did not. The preceding words come from a draft speech that Kennan had written in case his arguments had persuaded the president. They had not. No evidence exists that Truman read his paper, and the actual meeting at which the final decision about the hydrogen bomb was made lasted a mere seven minutes. For Acheson, Lilienthal, and Johnson, Truman had one question: "Can the Russians do it?" The answer came back: "Yes, they can."

"In that case," the president said, "we have no choice. We'll go ahead."

The press statement that followed was short and simple. "I have directed the Atomic Energy Commission to continue its work on all forms of atomic weapons, including the so-called hydrogen or super-bomb."

As we know now, Kennan accurately predicted what would come about if Nitze's arguments won the day: there was indeed a resource-devouring arms race. But Nitze may well have been perceptive, too, in his fear that, if Kennan's arguments won the day, the Soviets would soon be threatening America with an apocalyptic weapon. Andrei Sakharov, a Soviet physicist who played a crucial role in building their bomb, wrote in his memoirs: "Any American steps to suspend or permanently cancel the development of a thermonuclear weapon would have been judged as either a sly, deceptive move, or the manifestation of stupidity and weakness. In both cases the reaction would have been unambiguous—not to get caught in the trap and to take immediate advantage of the stupidity of the enemy."

DEFEATED AND DEPRESSED, Kennan departed in February 1950 on a long fact-finding trip to Latin America. Kennan had tired of Washington; Washington had tired of Kennan. But if the diplomat expected a tranquil journey, he did not get it. Communist students protested his arrival; on four occasions, he was burned in effigy. Outside his hotel room, a guard holding a sawed-off shotgun sat in a ballroom chair. "I began to feel like a hunted beast," he wrote in his diary.

Visiting Mexico City, he wrote that "the night is restless, uncertain.

Violence seems just around the corner. The city sleeps the uneasy sleep of the threatened animal; and its dreams are troubled." Venezuela was worse. The country was cursed by oil. Americans came in and extracted it while the local population did nothing. Hundreds of millions of dollars poured in, "a sort of ransom to the theory of state sovereignty and the principle of non-intervention which we had consented to adopt." The result of this foreign money was that the population "was being unquestionably debauched by a continued influx of material goods which it had not really earned." The result was "the accumulation of wealth and the decay of man." Signing off in his diary, he reported that "incidentally, all of nature in Venezuela was a bilious yellow brown."

He met with Latin America's leaders, including Argentina's Juan Perón, walked through its cities, and contemplated from his hotel balconies the effects of colonialism. The official report he wrote on his return described a continent, doomed by geography, whose culture had been sapped by Spanish conquerors. Something had broken the region's soul, creating a corrupt and perverse "Alice's Wonderland . . . where nothing is ever wholly finished because things are never more than symbols." As for politics, he recommended that the United States relax and keep its hands off. Yes, we should try to discourage communism. But hazy lines divided dictatorships and democracy on the continent. The proper response was a "relaxed equanimity" about "the problems of the future in an area where those problems will always be multitudinous, complex, and unpleasant." Acheson found the report so incendiary that he actively suppressed it. A decade later, he told the FBI that it would have set off riots all across Latin America if it had ever come to light.

Kennan returned via Miami and, in a rare expression of warm emotion, professed that he actually loved his country. Needing to change his ticket at the railroad station, he had to deal with a clerk in training. "Their attitude toward this work in hand was characterized by that relaxed, unemotional but utterly objective and self-respecting attitude which is the mark of our people." Contrasted with the chaos of Latin America, the performance pleased him. "I went out onto the station platform with a sense of deep gratitude and of happy acceptance of this American world, marked as it is by the mediocrity of all that is exalted, and the excellence of all that which is without pretense."

★

KENNAN HAD RIDDEN the State Department bull for three years, but now he was sliding off. Nitze, meanwhile, was becoming ever more comfortable on its back. His analysis was broadening, and his assessments were hardening. At a meeting in December, he had responded to a question from Kennan by saying that a full-scale Soviet attack was "a tertiary risk." A month and a half later, Nitze declared that the risk had gone up substantially since the fall. One week after that, he sent in his first big-ideas document, describing "recent Soviet moves." Moscow, he thought, was gaining confidence and considering an attack.

Acheson had become Congress's whipping boy after supporting the accused spy Alger Hiss at a press conference in February 1950. Nitze had tried desperately to stop Acheson from offering the rash defense but had failed. Now the secretary was "treated on Capitol Hill with less courtesy and with smaller regard for the rules of evidence than if he were a convicted horse thief," wrote Walter Lippmann. But Acheson had Truman's trust, and Nitze had Acheson's. The two met every morning and frequently lunched together at the Metropolitan Club. "He became a virtual alter ego of Acheson," wrote the secretary's biographer Robert Beisner. That February, Nitze began preparing the full strategic review that the president had ordered the State Department to undertake in response to the resolution of the hydrogen bomb debate.

Nitze worked on the document with his customary vigor. He organized a team from the Policy Planning Staff and they started to write as a group—a far different approach from Kennan's solo efforts. Nitze also managed the bureaucracy, most significantly in an effort to circumvent Secretary of Defense Louis Johnson, an inveterate budget cutter. Initially, both State and Defense had been charged with writing strategic reviews. But Nitze persuaded the key Pentagon representative to abandon his separate project and join the State team. More deviously, Nitze classified all the work as "top-secret—restricted data," meaning that he could limit access to documents to a small group of people who held "Q clearances." His estimates thus stayed far away from the Treasury and the Bureau of the Budget. Nitze calculated the cost of his proposal for a strategic overhaul, but he deliberately left out the total, knowing that the vast sum would put a bull's-eye on the document.

Nitze and his group worked at a conference table in the Policy Planning offices. He would lean forward, taking notes on his yellow pads and chopping his arms for emphasis. He was intense and logical. Like Kennan, he was beloved by the rest of the staff, but more for his passion than for his otherworldly wisdom. "For the past six weeks, I have been putting every ounce of energy that was in me into an attempt to resolve a most complex and difficult set of problems which have been plaguing the State Dept.," he wrote his parents. "I got through last Friday and felt about as energetic as a worn out dish rag."

The result was a document christened NSC-68 that Nitze would later claim as the most important of his life. It was stark, long, and passionate. The paper read like a manifesto, partly because that's what Truman wanted—according to his aide George Elsey, "he liked it with the bark off"—and partly because the Policy Planning Staff had plans to eventually release it to the public. The paper was so dramatic that, after reading it, one State Department official spent the whole next day at home weeping, distraught over what matters had come to.

The argument began with the claim that the world faced a battle between freedom and slavery, with the enslavers plotting to destroy the United States. We might have the upper hand now, but that would not last without a change in policies. As soon as the enslavers gained the atomic lead, they would be tempted to strike. Thus, America's survival depended on a rapid buildup of the armed forces. That was our only hope to "check and to roll back the Kremlin's drive for world domination."

Using a classic rhetorical trope, the paper consistently referred to "the Kremlin design." The Soviets had "designs," whereas we had "purposes." As Anders Stephanson has pointed out, the Declaration of Independence used this phrase—"a design to reduce them under absolute Despotism"— and FDR used it to describe the Nazis. NSC-68 uses the word in that way fifty times: "The design, therefore, calls for the complete subversion or forcible destruction . . ."; "the Kremlin's design for world domination"; "that evil design"; "Kremlin's design that where, with impunity, we can be insulted and made to suffer . . ."; "a more violent and ruthless prosecution of its design."

Though Nitze had no theological background, the document sounded biblical at times. The Soviets ascribe to "a new fanatic faith, anti-thetical to our own." The point was to "defend our way of life, for which as in the Declaration of Independence, 'with a firm reliance on the protection of Divine Providence, we mutually pledge to each other our lives, our Fortunes, and our sacred Honor.'" The Americans would respond to the Soviet threat with a program that "must light the path to peace."

Despite its militant tone, NSC-68 did not focus on nuclear arms. Building up a conventional military capability received much more attention. Yes, the United States needed atomic weapons, but it needed even more to have the capacity to thwart small Soviet operations wherever they might come. The paper's most controversial argument was that in almost all cases the ends justified the means. "The integrity of our system will not be jeopardized by any measures, covert or overt, violent or non-violent, which serve the purpose of frustrating the Kremlin design, nor does the necessity for conducting ourselves so as to affirm our values in actions as well as words forbid such measures."

NSC-68's most influential assertion may have been that the United States could afford a massive arms buildup. Few in government believed that the U.S. economy could invest nearly as much in weaponry as Nitze proposed. But the man from Wall Street had run the numbers and was certain the country could pay the bill.

Both in NSC-68 and in later interviews, Nitze claimed that he had based his arguments on a paper Kennan had written eighteen months prior, NSC-20/4. That document did indeed call for strong action against the Kremlin, and it did assert the need for a military buildup. But it focused more intently on political modes of containment, declaring that the USSR was "still seeking to achieve its aims primarily by political means."

This conflict between the political and the military was not the only difference between Nitze's opus and the version of containment pushed by Kennan. NSC-68 also rejected Kennan's recommendation that the United States adopt a policy of never using nuclear weapons before the Soviets did; it called for fighting communism worldwide, whereas Kennan had long urged America to confine itself to a few strategic regions. And Nitze's clear conviction was that the Soviet Union had intensely hostile plans for America. "With the preparation of NSC-68 I had nothing to do," wrote Kennan, ten years afterward. "I was disgusted about the assumptions concerning Soviet intentions."

Once NSC-68 was written, Nitze tried to sell it to Secretary of Defense Johnson—a man whom he described as "the only person that I've ever known who would rather lie than tell the truth even when it was to his disinterest to lie." The key meeting was scheduled for March 22.

At the appointed hour, Johnson strode into the State Department room and immediately declared that he had not read the paper, had not had time to read it, and would agree to nothing. Startled, Nitze nonetheless began to outline his team's proposal. "Johnson listened, chair tilted back, gazing at the ceiling, seemingly calm and attentive. Suddenly he lunged forward with a crash of chair legs on the floor and fist on the table," wrote Acheson in his memoirs. "No one, he shouted, was going to make arrangements for him to meet with another Cabinet officer and a roomful of people and be told what he was going to report to the president. Who authorized these meetings contrary to his orders? What was this paper, which he had never seen?" Johnson stalked out of the room. The meeting had lasted fourteen minutes.

Word of Johnson's outburst spread through the government, winning sympathy and support for Nitze's cause. Later that week, Johnson left for NATO meetings in Europe and the paper began to circulate through the State Department. By the time Johnson came back, he could do nothing to stop it. Soon the paper was heading for Harry Truman's desk. Concerned about costs, the president would not sign it immediately. But events soon forced his hand. And just by getting his document to the White House, Nitze had taken a big step in turning containment from a political doctrine into an undeniably military one.

Years later, a student sent Nitze a master's thesis arguing that Nitze had "militarized containment." On his copy, Nitze crossed out that line and carefully wrote in his own view of NSC-68's objective. "This paper *more realistically set forth the requirements necessary to assure success of* George Kennan's idea of containment."

AS NITZE STRUGGLED with the bureaucracy, Kennan returned from Latin America, packed up his State Department office, and headed to his farm. He was thinking and writing, blissfully distant from the emotional debate about the hydrogen bomb.

Not long after his departure, Kennan was on his way to buy some trees from a nursery when he found himself deep in reflection about the Policy Planning Staff's successes and failures. He decided to write some verse in honor of them. The result began: "Friends, teachers, pupils; toilers at the wheels;/Undaunted drones of the official hive,/In deep frustration doomed to strive." Its last lines expressed Kennan's hopes for his maligned hive mates:

Perhaps in moment unforeseen
The Great White Queen,

made fruitful by your seed,

may yet create

So dazzling and so beauteous a brood

That world will marvel, history admire.

And then the scorned, no-longer-wanted sire,

From bondage loosed, from travail freed

Basking beside the rays these progeny exude,

May find the warmth to which all souls aspire

in autumn late.

In an interview three decades later, Nitze delivered a genuine compliment, with just the faintest touch of the backhand: "It was one of the most beautiful [poems], you know, worthy of Shelley. George could have been a great poet."

Kennan even seemed to have learned from the battles of the previous fall. Giving the address at the Dartmouth commencement in early June, he said: "It is good to have real issues in life: to know what one really believes in; to have those things which one detests drawn off." Conflict could be useful, too. "When we look backward over the years, we do not regret either the pain or the laughter—either the anguish of struggle or the enjoyment of the good things of life. We regret only the empty moments, marked neither by anguish nor by happiness."

As June passed on, even Nitze found that he needed a quiet moment or two; he departed for some salmon fishing in New Brunswick. His family, the Upsalquitch River, and the fish would keep him company. He asked whether Kennan would come back in for a short spell and run the Policy Planning Staff in his absence.

The Nitzes' camp was fifteen miles from the nearest road, in a spot of almost total isolation. Each morning, they would head out in canoes, cast their lines, and reel in the plentiful fish. But one evening, Paul was sitting at an open fire at a remote pool upriver from the main campsite when a guide came hustling up. Urgent news had just come over the radio. North Korean divisions were streaming into South Korea. Nitze, looking grave, hustled his wife and children to the horse-drawn barge they had used to reach the camp. "We've got to get back."

The last six months had driven Kennan and Nitze apart. The most dangerous event since the end of the last world war was about to bring them back together.

8

CONFINED TO KOREA

Sunday, June 25, 1950, might have been the one day when George Kennan regretted not having a phone at his Pennsylvania farm. He went there to relax, to chop wood, and to sit with his sketch pad. He relished time away from the outside world, and he enjoyed a leisurely weekend before driving back to Washington with his family midafternoon. Arriving at about 4:30 P.M., he picked up his newspapers: "North Korean Forces Drive into South, Seoul Hears" screamed the *Washington Post*.

Fighting had started about twenty-four hours before, when North Korean tanks began surging south, quickly overrunning the outnumbered South Koreans near the border. Many had never seen tanks, and none had been taught how to stop them. Some men strapped explosive charges to their backs and dove under the treads; others attached TNT to the ends of poles and raced at the tanks like medieval jousters facing an industrial enemy. The South Korean army soon fell into frantic retreat, blowing up bridges as it went.

Immediately upon receiving the news, Kennan hurried to the State Department, arriving to find Acheson deep in discussion with a group of colleagues. Pushed by Dean Rusk, then assistant secretary of state for Far Eastern affairs, the group had decided the United States should fight under the UN flag, not just the Stars and Stripes. Kennan disagreed. He had always thought the UN strong on rosy ideals and weak on substance. But the department had made its choice. With the Russians boycotting the

UN at that moment, and thus incapable of voting, the resolution had already passed.

An hour and a half later, Acheson departed for the airport to meet Truman, returning from his own vacation in Missouri. The secretary promised Kennan an invitation to a planning dinner that evening with the president. But when Kennan was about to leave for the dinner, Acheson's assistant told him he was not on the list. Seats were limited and she could do nothing. Most likely because of a bureaucratic cross-up caused by his late arrival, the State Department's top Soviet expert was closed out. In his diary, Kennan cursed his lack of a phone. It might have cost him access to the crucial planning meeting. And it had certainly kept him out of the debate over whether to fight under the UN flag—a choice, he lamented, "I would probably have been able to talk them out of."

Japan had controlled Korea—and oppressed it—from 1910 to 1945. But after the Second World War, the victors had split the country along the 38th Parallel, which they assumed would be a temporary dividing line until the country could reunify. In the north, the Russians installed Kim Il Sung, a Red Army sniper during World War II whose love of communism was less fervent than his love of self. (By the end of his life, his destitute country had 34,000 monuments to him.) In the South, the Americans had installed Syngman Rhee, a devout Christian with a Ph.D. in politics from Princeton. A few years after dividing the nation, the two superpowers withdrew almost all of their troops.

Unbeknownst to the United States, Kim had been pestering Moscow for months, seeking permission to invade. Stalin, fearing a clash with the Americans, hesitated. Finally, after a top spy assured him that the United States would not respond, he relented. The United States had massively demobilized after World War II and it had not sent troops into China to stop Mao. Would it really defend South Korea? Stalin guessed no.

He was wrong, of course. Yes, Korea was a small country to which the United States had no deep cultural or historical ties. Yes, it would be difficult to defend. America's military strength lay in her air force and navy, but Korea would require ground troops. And, yes, intervention would be risky. The peninsula bordered both China and the Soviet Union; any war there could trigger Armageddon.

But Washington's response was close to unanimous. This was an unprovoked attack, in the middle of the night, on a client state—just the sort of "piecemeal aggression" that NSC-68 warned against. If we did not take a stand in Korea, the communists would soon close in elsewhere.

Within three days, American troops were heading toward Korea, and the Seventh Fleet was steaming into the Taiwan Strait to block a Chinese invasion of the island. The only question was how fiercely the United States would try to repulse the North Korean armor as it plowed relentlessly southward. At the Sunday evening planning dinner, Truman asked whether the American military could knock out Soviet bases in the Far East. The air force chief of staff responded that indeed it could be done—if we used A-bombs.

A MASTER at discerning Soviet intentions from the placement of subordinate clauses in propaganda leaflets, Kennan made it his first main task to closely monitor *Pravda* as well as Moscow's press releases for signs that the USSR might join the fight. In his diary on Thursday, he declared that the Soviets wanted "to keep out of this business themselves in every way but to embroil us to the maximum with their Korean and Chinese satellites."

Still, there was some chance of Russian involvement; Kennan began drafting a paper for the National Security Council about how the United States should respond to future Soviet military moves. He labored over it, sent it in, and then was hit by an unpleasant surprise. Paul Nitze had returned from his salmon pools and the secretary wanted a revision. Kennan felt uneasy. "My whole framework of thought," he confided to his diary, "was strange to Nitze."

It turned out, however, that Nitze's thinking on the war matched Kennan's. Just finished with NSC-68, Nitze worried that the U.S. military lacked the strength to win. "I was, frankly, I think, more concerned than almost anybody else by the decision to intervene," he recalled. More important, on the central issue that summer—whether the American counterattack should surge past the 38th Parallel, turning the war into one of regime change—he and Kennan agreed completely.

In early July, the war looked very grim. The North Korean tanks were still pummeling their southern adversaries, and they had few problems with the untrained and ill-prepared U.S. arrivals. The first confrontation went so badly that American troops ended it by throwing down their weapons and taking off their boots so they could retreat faster through the rice paddies. "Guys, sweat soaked, shitting in their pants, not even dropping them, moved like zombies," wrote one soldier. "I just sensed we were going to find another hill and be attacked, then find another hill and so forth, endlessly, forever."

Kennan and Nitze believed that the situation would reverse itself. The U.S. general in command, Douglas MacArthur, had a reputation for genius, and new troops were arriving every day. The army that had defeated the Japanese and helped vanquish the Wehrmacht would reemerge as a cohesive and powerful force. Throughout July and August, Kennan and Nitze argued together for moderation once the war's momentum turned.

As they and the rest of the Policy Planning Staff saw it, the choices Truman made would "determine whether hostilities can be confined to Korea or will spread so that the danger of a third world war is greatly increased." The Kremlin, they argued, would not stand for a Korea fully under American control. The 38th Parallel was the status quo ante bellum, and to move north of it could lead to armed conflict with the USSR or communist China.

In arguing for caution, Kennan and Nitze might as well have proposed painting a hammer and sickle on the Washington Monument. John Allison, director of the Office of Northeast Asian Affairs, offered Nitze an "emphatic dissent" and described the PPS position as one of "appeasement," the era's darkest word. John Foster Dulles, the Republican statesman brought in as a consultant to the State Department during the crisis, rebuked Nitze in starker terms. "If we have the opportunity to obliterate the line," he wrote of the 38th Parallel, "certainly we should do so."

Kennan and Nitze fought back: Nitze by trying to find compromises, Kennan through ever more heated memos. By late August, Kennan was distressed and angry; he wrote Acheson that "the course upon which we are today moving is one, as I see it, so little promising and so fraught with danger that I could not honestly urge you to continue to take responsibility for it."

The American leadership had not decided whether to stop at the 38th Parallel or to do what the public now seemed to want: turn the Korean conflict into a war of liberation and reunification. Kennan saw a yet more ominous possibility lurking. It might not even matter what policy advice the State Department offered: Douglas MacArthur, the commander in the field, might not take it. "By permitting General MacArthur to retain the wide and relatively uncontrolled latitude he has enjoyed in determining our policy in the north Asian and Western Pacific areas, we are tolerating a state of affairs in which we do not really have full control over the statements that are being made—and actions taken—in our name."

THROUGHOUT THE SUMMER, the two men followed the war through the cables they got, the meetings they attended, and the journalism of an unlikely war correspondent: Joseph Alsop, a gay aesthete with an encyclopedic knowledge of Bronze Age art. A close friend of both men, he was also a formidable reporter.

Born in 1910, Alsop came to Harvard a few years after Nitze. The two men were brothers at the Porcellian Club, drinking more than their share of hard liquor out of the club's delicate glasses. In the 1930s, Nitze partied at Alsop's family house in Avon, Connecticut, rolling dice on the floor late into the evenings. Joe "was the most civilized, joyous kind of person you could find," Nitze said.

Brilliant in conversation and in print, Alsop moved to New York after college and quickly made his mark as a journalist. When war came, he traded his pen for a pistol but was trapped in Hong Kong after the Japanese attacked Pearl Harbor. He might have gotten out, but the last seat on the last plane was taken by Chiang Kai-shek's sister-in-law for her large dog. Soon captured, Alsop was interned for months by the Japanese. Upon his release, he worked as an assistant to General Claire Chennault, helping to plan the air war in China.

When he came back to the States, he signed up his brother Stewart to cowrite a column for the *New York Herald Tribune*. He became one of the era's most important writers on American politics, often using Kennan and Nitze as sources. A great-nephew of Theodore Roosevelt, and later a close friend of Jacqueline Kennedy, he also had fastidious tastes. When in Paris, he avoided restaurants on the Champs Elysées, claiming that the Metro passing underneath stirred up the sediments in the wines.

Alsop was devoted to Kennan and Nitze, but they both exasperated him. "The trouble with you, Paul, is that you're just a bureaucrat," he repeated over and over one night while wildly drunk with Nitze at Martin's Tavern in Washington. After one dinner party at the columnist's house, Kennan was heading to his car when Alsop flung open his front doors and yelled, "You know, George, the problem with you is that you're a nineteenth-century man." Kennan turned around and countered, "No, I'm an eighteenth-century man." In his memoirs, Alsop described Kennan "as resembling the priestess on the tripod at the Greek oracle at Delphi who inhaled the sacred smoke and then held forth. For part of the time, the God spoke truth through her mouth; for part of the time her speech was sheer gabble. The trouble was you never knew which element in what she said came from the God." Kennan, he added, "has been more wrong than anyone else and more right than anyone else—and no one, including myself, has ever reliably deduced which was which at the moment of expression."

At the end of July 1950, Alsop decided he had to report the story of the Korean War firsthand. He flew to Tokyo, arriving just as the American troops received the order to "stand or die" at the perimeter around the southern port city of Pusan, the last stronghold held by the United States as its army had been pushed almost out of the country. As that battle raged, Alsop traveled nearby to the southeast Korean coast.

The first battle Alsop witnessed, an assault on the sea cliffs on the road to the city of Chinju in early August, went so well for the United States at first that men were quickly calling for bulldozers to cover the North Korean dead. But then the U.S. progress slowed and North Korean mortar fire, roadblocks, and snipers pinned down the unit he accompanied. It was only at nine P.M. on the second day that the Americans broke the communist resistance.

The war continued like this for a month, with the Americans slowly regaining ground. Alsop would cover forward combat for several days at a time, joining the men in the danger zones with a copy of Thucydides in his pocket. Then he would return to Tokyo to file his stories and get some rest.

Gradually, the war's tide turned and Alsop's dispatches became filled with recordings of triumph. "Beautiful, just beautiful," said a captain, staring out at hundreds of North Korean dead and wounded scattered through the rice paddies one morning. "I like going after them better than having them go after me," one soldier told Alsop at the end of August. In September 1950 came the boldest stroke of all, an amphibious assault on the west coast port of Inchon well beyond the current battle lines. Alsop knew of the coming attack, as, it seemed, did everyone else. Men in Tokyo referred to it as Operation Common Knowledge. Even Mao had learned of it, and he tried to warn Kim.

But Kim did not listen, the coast was undefended, and MacArthur's troops surged ashore, splitting the enemy forces in half and severing their supply lines. It was the most daring, most brilliant, and most successful American gambit of the war.

After Inchon, suddenly it was the North Koreans who were retreating, spilling in hopeless disorder back past the 38th Parallel. The Americans pursued. The men boasted that they would soon piss in the Yalu River dividing North Korea from China. Alsop cheered them on.

But a few voices still advised restraint. During the summer Kennan and Nitze had not wanted the United States to pass the 38th Parallel, and in the fall they thought no differently. "Your battle accounts were the best I have seen in our press. They were like Tolstoy's passages from *War and Peace*," wrote Kennan to Alsop in mid-October. "Like Tolstoy, you are an artist and should write about what you see and perceive rather than what you think. For the latter I have respect, too, but not as much."

MAGIC, MANY PEOPLE BELIEVED, graced General Douglas MacArthur. The son of a three-star general who had commanded troops in the Spanish-American War, Douglas learned to ride and shoot at about the same age he learned to walk. He led troops during the first three major wars of the twentieth century, earning and cultivating a legend in each. During the First World War, he led from the front, not the rear, as his men surged through northeast France toward Germany. He disciplined soldiers who did not wear gas masks, but strode about the lines with neither mask nor helmet. He carried only a riding crop. During the Second World War, against overwhelming odds, he slipped away in a small torpedo boat from Japanese troops and blockading vessels as they took the American bastion at Corregidor in 1942. Once, while he was touring the Korean battlefields by jeep with journalists, his group spotted several unidentified aircraft. Men dove for cover. Not MacArthur. Descending regally from the car, he stared at the sky until the planes disappeared. Bullets, it seemed, would not dare hit the man. "God, the man is great," said one of his top aides to a *Time* reporter. "The greatest man in history," an air force general added.

Neither Kennan nor Nitze agreed. Both had had personal experience of the general when he managed Japan after World War II, and both considered him stubborn, imperious, even egomaniacal. Kennan, who had met with him during his tenure as head of the Policy Planning Staff, compared consulting with MacArthur to "opening up communications and arranging the establishment of diplomatic relations with a hostile and suspicious foreign government."

By the start of the Korean War, Nitze firmly believed that MacArthur was unfit to exercise the UN command. Truman likely agreed. In his 1945 diary, the president described the general as "Mr. Prima Donna, Brass Hat, Five Star MacArthur." But MacArthur was too popular and too powerful to remove, and the success at Inchon made him close to unassailable.

But soon he began to blunder. He split the command of his pursuing forces, giving more power to one of his acolytes and less to one of the few independent thinkers on the ground. Even after hordes of Chinese crossed the border between North and South Korea for a quick late-October raid, MacArthur continued to surge confidently onward.

Disaster began to unfold. Acheson later recalled that everyone sat around watching "like paralyzed rabbits." The president and secretary of state were far too unpopular to challenge the iconic general, in particular because, technically, he reported to the United Nations, not the United States. Even George Marshall, now secretary of defense (and a longtime colleague and rival of MacArthur's), told the general to press ahead. "We want you to feel unhampered strategically and tactically to proceed north of the 38th Parallel." MacArthur did just that.

SOME SOLDIERS REMEMBER the music most. A bugle would sound from the north, then one from the west. A moment would pass, and another eerie tone would rise from the south. Seconds later, the Chinese were upon you.

From mid-October through late November, the Chinese had infiltrated hundreds of thousands of troops across the Yalu. They hid in mineshafts and tunnels, moving at night. They carried precooked rice and beans so they would not have to light fires detectable from the air. When they ran out of food, they lived off the land. On November 25, 1950, they launched a massive surprise attack.

Veterans of the long civil war against Chiang Kai-shek's Nationalists, the Chinese troops were neither well armed nor warmly clad. But they knew how to fight, and they used music to communicate, to rattle the Americans, and then to celebrate. One American soldier vividly recalled a Chinese attack coordinated by whistles. He and his men hid quietly up on higher ground and then watched as the Chinese called off the attack.

Three soldiers then pulled out flutes and began to play. The others rose from their hiding places in rocks and bushes and began to dance.

China's onslaught crushed the scattered and poorly organized Americans. Surprised, terrified, and outmaneuvered, the GIs quickly turned tail. Soon began the American military's longest-ever retreat.

Washington immediately grasped the scope of the disaster. Acheson was despondent; Truman rattled. Even MacArthur was humbled. Nitze saw the beginning of a clash of civilizations, in which the forces of slavery were pummeling those of freedom. He gave a speech declaring that "a failure to act prudently, and in time, might involve our nation in the greatest ordeal of its history."

On November 30, Truman publicly broached the possibility of the ultimate response at a press conference with more than two hundred reporters. The president stood erect, wearing a necktie with the image of Paul Bunyan. All went well at first as he dodged some questions and gave short clear answers to others. But then, asked about plans for responding to the current crisis, he said, "We will take whatever steps are necessary to meet the military situation."

Including the atomic bomb? "That would include every weapon that we have," answered Truman. "There has always been active consideration of its use."

Another reporter pressed the president further. "Did we understand you clearly that the use of the atomic bomb is under active consideration?"

"Always has been. It is one of our weapons," Truman said. "It's a matter that the military people will have to decide."

Nitze was sitting at his desk at the State Department when the phone rang. "My God, get over to the White House, there's a real problem!" The president's men had immediately realized the implications of Truman's statements. Not only were we threatening to nuke Korea, but control of the bomb would be in the hands of the military.

Horrified, Nitze suggested doctoring the transcript to make it read as if Truman had given himself, not MacArthur, final authority. That was a hopeless ploy. Everyone had heard exactly what the president had said. Truman would just have to backpedal and wait for the outrage to dissipate.

Nitze had long pondered a nuclear response in Korea. Because of his work on the Strategic Bombing Survey, he was among the small number of officials who understood how nuclear weapons worked; he also knew how few we had in our arsenal. In July, the PPS had written a paper arguing that we should use nuclear weapons in Korea only in the unlikely event that we were certain their use would save the lives of Americans, would not widen the conflict, and would not incite international outrage. He had revisited the issue in early November and concluded that launching atomic weapons would not end the war. Worse, it would align world opinion against us and, quite likely, bring the Soviets in. "The real question was whether the advantages would outweigh the disadvantages," he later recalled. And the answer was that they did not.

Nitze was a hawk when it came to stockpiling nuclear weapons, but not when it came to using them.

"WHY AREN'T YOU in Washington?"

It was Friday, December 1, and Chip Bohlen, calling from his post in Paris, wanted to speak with Kennan. The State Department needed a Soviet expert during the grave Korean crisis, and Kennan had retreated into his academic shelter at Princeton to begin a one-year sabbatical.

"I have not been asked to come," he replied simply.

"I am on the phone to implore you, for God's sake, to get on the train, go to Washington, and see Dean and Marshall."

Kennan would not budge, even as Bohlen explained how much respect Marshall had for him, and how bad the situation was. "I was down there about three weeks ago," Kennan said. "But I was quite aware that I was not being put into possession of all of the facts."

"We run from the left side to the right and go nowhere, as though we were in a canoe in the middle of a big stream," Bohlen replied. "I implore you to go down there. You can't lose and it will do no harm."

"I'll think seriously about it," Kennan said.

After mulling it over, he called Acheson's assistant and declared that, if wanted, he was ready to serve.

The next day, John Paton Davies of the Policy Planning Staff returned the call. Yes, Kennan's help was wanted, and, yes, Director Paul Nitze had authorized his former boss's return as a consultant. Kennan took the next train.

★

HIS SECOND DAY back at the department, Kennan stepped into Acheson's office in the evening, after almost everyone had left the building. The secretary, looking worn out and beaten down, welcomed the company and invited Kennan to come back to his house for dinner and to stay the night.

The two retreated to Georgetown where, with the maids out, Mrs. Acheson cooked up a simple meal. The secretary began by describing his problems, particularly the collapse in Korea and the intense criticism of him by congressmen who had never forgotten his defense of Hiss. Acheson pointed to a new portrait of himself that hung in the living room. He explained that the artist had said he was trying to convey Acheson's resilience under a crescendo of attacks. "The Secretary told this about himself in a humorous vein, and ironically," Kennan wrote in his diary. "But there was no question about how deeply he felt about this matter."

Before going to bed, Kennan wrote Acheson a note in longhand, which he left for the secretary in the morning.

> In international, as in private, life what counts most is not really what happens to someone but how he bears what happens to him. For this reason almost everything depends from here on out on the manner in which we Americans bear what is unquestionably a major failure and disaster to our national fortunes. If we accept it with candor, with dignity, and with resolve to absorb its lessons and to make it good by redoubled and determined effort—starting all over again, if necessary, along the pattern of Pearl Harbor—we need lose neither our self-confidence nor our allies nor our power for bargaining, eventually, with the Russians. But if we try to conceal from our own people or from our allies the full measure of our misfortune, or permit ourselves to seek relief in any reactions of bluster or petulance or hysteria, we can easily find this crisis resolving itself into an irreparable deterioration of our world position— and of our confidence in ourselves.

GRADUALLY, NEWS FROM THE BATTLEFIELD began to improve. The Chinese, it turned out, were not invincible. After nearly being run off the peninsula in December, America regained its composure and retook the positions it previously held. Kennan, seeing that the risk of an imprudent American departure had abated, returned to Princeton. Soon the war was stuck in a stalemate. But, unbeknownst to most Americans for many decades, a secret battle was going on that could easily have ignited catastrophe.

After the Inchon landing, North Korea had called the Soviets for help. "On behalf of the Workers' Party of Korea, we express to You, the liberator of the Korean people and the leader of the working peoples of the entire world, our profound gratitude," wrote Kim to Stalin on September 30. Kim admitted that the war was no longer going well. "We cannot help asking You to provide us with special assistance."

Stalin did not want a world war—but also he did not want a communist client to be defeated, and he certainly did not want American soldiers pissing in the Yalu. He had sent supplies, and Red Army experts had trained Korean troops. But he had not committed his own forces. With the North Koreans retreating, it seemed a good time to fulfill an old promise to send planes to back up the decrepit North Korean air force. MiGs would soon circle the skies above Pyongyang.

Stalin knew the risks. He ordered that the planes not take off from Soviet territory, and he had them all painted in Chinese or North Korean colors. Pilots disguised themselves in Chinese-like uniforms, complete with blue trousers and orange-red boots. The crews went without their identification papers, and records of deployment were doctored. But Stalin almost certainly realized that America would likely uncover the plot. "Our pilots' work in the skies over Pyongyang will inevitably be discovered by the U.S. troops right after the first air combat, because all the control and command over the combat in the air will be conducted by our pilots in the Russian language," wrote his defense minister during the planning stages.

In 1951, Soviet pilots began to engage in bitter combat with the Americans, who did indeed quickly discover that although they wore Chinese uniforms, they spoke Russian. It would be the only time during the Cold War when U.S. and Soviet troops fought each other head to head in a pitched battle.

Word of the Soviet involvement was sent to the Policy Planning Staff and Nitze was asked how the Truman administration should respond. His decision: suppress all evidence of Soviet involvement. One should not "point the finger of scorn at the Soviet Union unless one was prepared to do something about it. And we weren't prepared to do something about it," he later said. The Policy Planning Staff wrote a memo titled "Removing the Fig Leaf from the Hard Core of Soviet Responsibility." But Nitze decided to bury it; every single copy was destroyed. He emphatically did not want a wider war.

BUT ONE MAN DID: Douglas MacArthur. As winter turned toward spring, he disobeyed Truman in ever more outrageous ways. At one point, the National Security Agency intercepted messages from the Portuguese and Spanish embassies in Tokyo indicating that MacArthur had told them of plans to turn the battle into a war with the Chinese, ideally one that would restore Chiang Kai-shek to power in the mainland. The intercepts were passed to Nitze, among others, and then to the president. "Outright treachery," exclaimed Truman, slapping his desk in anger.

In late March, MacArthur sent a message along the same lines to Joe Martin, the Republican congressional leader. Martin read the message on the floor of the House on April 5. "This looks like the last straw. Rank insubordination," wrote Truman in his diary. The president, whose approval rating was 26 percent, had to fire the war icon. On April 10, 1951, Nitze helped write the order relieving MacArthur of his command. Outrage swept the country and thousands of angry telegrams poured into the White House. Acheson was burned in effigy, and the general returned home for congressional hearings on the war.

White House aides circulated a mock schedule for his appearance in Washington that included such events as "1:50 Burning of the Constitution. 1:55 Lynching of Secretary Acheson. 2:00 21-atomic-bomb salute." Kennan noted in his diary: "The papers today were full of MacArthur and Truman, and I was full of premonitions of trouble. It seemed to me that we were like a crowd of drunken men on a raft, squabbling and gabbing while we drifted to the brink of the falls."

But the furor soon died down, particularly after Secretary of State Acheson outwitted and outperformed the general in congressional hearings. And even as that testimony about the progress of the war continued, a more important conversation was getting under way: negotiations for an armistice.

ON THE LOVELY SPRING afternoon of May 2, 1951, the United Nations met at its temporary headquarters by Lake Success, Long Island, to discuss

Palestine. Afterward, two American delegates, Thomas Cory and Frank Corrigan, hitched a ride back to Manhattan with Jacob Malik, the Soviet representative to the UN, and his assistant Semen Tsarapkin. Riding in Malik's rather unproletarian Chrysler, the group began to chat about Korea. They heatedly disagreed about who had started the war, and who was more at fault that it continued. But Malik did hint that maybe the two sides ought to have an informal discussion about bringing peace to the region. Later Malik asked what had become of George Kennan, "the number one American expert on Russia."

After the car ride, Cory telephoned Nitze to relay what had happened. Nitze immediately told him to fly down to Washington and then they both met with Acheson. The three decided that the United States could not appear too eager to seek a cease-fire and should not approach the Soviets formally. Kennan, however, could be just the man to begin a back-channel conversation with Malik.

Kennan leaped at the chance to try to solve a problem in the manner he always thought best: quiet negotiation between two discreet men who were fluent in the same language. He immediately contacted Tsarapkin. "I am writing to ask you to be good enough to tell Mr. Malik (whom I know very slightly) that I think it would be useful from the standpoint of both our governments if he and I could meet and have a quiet talk some time in the near future." Tsarapkin was to get in touch with Kennan's secretary at Princeton. "It will be sufficient, in any reply to her, to refer to Mr. Malik as 'the gentleman Mr. Kennan has asked to see.'"

Three days later, he got a response.

Gentleman Mr. Kennan has asked to see could meet with Mr. Kennan on Thursday, May 31st at 3:00 p.m. at his villa outside of New York where he is now, according to the recommendations of his physician. Suppose the address of villa is known to Mr. Kennan. Otherwise it would be possible to get the address from the one to whom the letter of May 26 was sent.

Kennan and Malik spent two afternoons debating. Malik did not seem to want to reveal much about the Soviet position, and Kennan was acutely aware that he did not know everything about his own government's stance. But the two men communicated through subtlety and careful emphases here or there. When Malik declared that the Soviet government wanted peace "at the earliest possible moment," Kennan heard both a sign of hope and a warning. If the problems could not be resolved now, perhaps they would get worse. At the end of the second meeting, Kennan said that Malik was misguided in believing American policy to be driven by some Wall Street conspiracy. "You see our country," Kennan said, "as in a dream."

"No, this is not the dream," Malik replied. "This is the deepest reality."

More important than what Malik said, however, was what he did. A couple of weeks later, he announced publicly that he wanted to begin negotiations with the United States, taking as a starting point the idea that both sides would withdraw from the 38th Parallel. Talks began two weeks later and went on for two years.

Both sides suffered huge casualties as the negotiations dragged on, hung up primarily on the matter of how to repatriate prisoners of war. Should all prisoners be sent home, whether they wanted to return or not, as required by the Geneva Convention? Nitze—with his deep animosity toward communism—joined Bohlen in arguing that it was not worth ending the war sooner if the cost was forcing captured North Koreans to return home against their will.

Debate over the issue lasted through the rest of Truman's term, until Syngman Rhee resolved the impasse simply by opening the gates of all POW camps in South Korea. Soon armistice talks accelerated and a dividing line through Korea was drawn again—almost exactly where Malik suggested it, and just about where it had been when the war began.

9

★ ★ ★

THE FULL MERIDIAN
OF MY GLORY

In April 1951, George Kennan's diary took a very dark turn. "I should find it hard, even if fortune favored me, to adjust to the consciousness of the jeopardy in which I have placed the happiness of other people. And not being sure that the blow would not still fall, I would continue to feel myself half a murderer, to have horror of myself, and to place limitations, in my own mind, on my ability to be useful to anyone else in any personal intimacy."

In a few days, he would depart for Chicago to deliver a series of lectures on the history of American foreign policy. He was nervous about how he would behave, and if he could tame the furies inside. "Here—there will be all the things that are difficult for me: a strange city, a hotel, solitude, boredom, strange women, the sense of time fleeting, of time being wasted, of a life pulsating around me—a life unknown, untested, full of mystery—and yet not touched by myself."

When he arrived, he seemed calmer, but still troubled. "I have never been any good at training children or dogs; that is why I am no good at training myself."

The next day he wrote: "Lay down in my room, to rest for the lecture. When I try, as I did then, to bring the spirit to a state of complete repose, shutting out all effort and all seeking, I become aware of the remnants of anxieties and desires still surging and thrashing around, like waves in a swimming-pool when the last swimmer has left; and I realize in what a turmoil the pool of the soul usually is, and how long it must lie untroubled before the surface becomes calm and one can see the bottom."

He would later add: "If dislike for one's self were really, as the religious teachers claim, the beginning of virtue in the sight of the Lord, then I should be on the verge of saintliness."

Kennan did not explain where, specifically, the angst came from or what caused it. But misery often sharpened his mind. He wrote the Long Telegram while violently ill. (He "felt his mind functioned better when his body was in a horizontal position," said his longtime secretary Dorothy Hessman.) His seventy-nine-page essay about the hydrogen bomb came as he lost faith in his country to do the right thing, and in himself to have influence. He wrote his brilliant letter to Acheson when despondent about Korea. In the decades to come, almost all of his finest work would derive in some way from what he called the turmoil in the pool of the soul.

And this time it was no different. The six Chicago lectures in April 1951 were classics. He collected them in a book titled *American Diplomacy*, which would stay in print for thirty-five years and become a standard university text. From now on, he would have no need to doubt his ability to maintain a reputation—or a bank account.

The slim, crisp volume is generally described as a broadside against—in Kennan's own, uncharacteristically clunky, phrase—a "legalistic-moralistic" approach to international problems. The first word referred to his belief that international law, or organizations like the United Nations, could not resolve the world's woes. The second word pointed to America's tendency to sit in moral judgment over other nations.

To put it more simply, the book was a critique of American democracy and its influence on foreign policy. In the first five lectures, Kennan traced American decision making through major international events, running from the Spanish-American War of 1898 to World War II. In each case, Kennan asserted, American politicians had acted unwisely. They did not understand what other nations wanted, and they did not understand their own nation's actual points of leverage. In large part because of poor leadership, the public remained indifferent until war began, whereupon hysteria followed.

The latter problem particularly infuriated Kennan. A conflict between the United States and another power could suddenly seem like an urgent necessity, even if it had been deemed not worth a single American life the day before. He declared:

I sometimes wonder whether in this respect a democracy is not uncomfortably similar to one of those prehistoric monsters with a body as long as this room and a brain the size of a pin: he lies there in his comfortable primeval mud and pays little attention to his environment. He is slow to wrath—in fact, you practically have to whack his tail off to make him aware that his interests are being disturbed; but, once he grasps this, he lays about him with such blind determination that he not only destroys his adversary but largely wrecks his native habitat.

Kennan's solution was to put manacles on our international ambitions. America was going to remain a democracy, and he preferred no alternative on offer. But if that made wise action in foreign policy impossible, we ought to have a less confrontational policy. Instead of grandstanding, warring, and constantly meddling in countries and cultures we did not understand, we should have "an attitude of detachment and soberness and readiness to reserve judgment."

Political scientists would classify this viewpoint as "realism." It was not new to Kennan: he had long doubted America's ability to understand other nations and to act effectively in foreign affairs—with his doubts growing as his power receded. Until the very end of Kennan's life, restraint was one of the pillars of his political philosophy. With rare exceptions, he would advocate that the United States leave other countries alone. His view derived partly from a feeling that no country could have decisive influence on another and partly from a sense that his country in particular would have only a baleful impact.

Paul Nitze saw the world very differently. In NSC-68 he had described the United States as "the center of power in the free world," which "must organize and enlist the energies and resources of the free world in a positive program for peace which will frustrate the Kremlin design for world domination." He never used such purple language again. But throughout his life he would believe strongly that the United States was indispensable, fundamentally good, and fully capable of changing the world for the better.

AS KENNAN MADE the transition to permanent outsider, Nitze grew into his role as head of the Policy Planning Staff, enjoying what he would later call "the happiest and most productive days of my life." He worked closely with Acheson on matters ranging from the decision to let Germany re-arm to the reluctant choice to offer some aid to French troops in their war in Vietnam. He was powerful and influential, if also somewhat anon-ymous. The economist Thomas Schelling, a young official working on the Marshall Plan in Europe at the time, remembers hearing about a "Nitze plan" and assuming that "N.I.T.Z.E." was an acronym.

The years of 1951 and 1952 were relatively calm for the Truman ad-ministration. The immediate crises that followed World War II had ceased. Western Europe was not going to go communist and Germany was going to remain divided. The arms race had begun, and the Korean War was drawing to a close. The balance of power no longer seemed so precarious. But in winding down the era of colonial empires, World War II had caused ferment across the former subject nations from the Gold Coast to Indonesia. Eventually, those colonies all won independence, some professedly democratic and others communist. For the most part, however, they were nationalists. And for the most part America did not know how to respond.

Nitze's first important engagement with the Third World had to do with Iran, an oil-rich country close to Israel and sharing a border with the United States' biggest enemy. Right after World War II, Stalin had gazed at a map of his country pinned to a wall of his dacha. He commented favor-ably on the USSR's northern, eastern, and western boundaries, then pointed southward, toward Iran. "But here I don't like our border!" he exclaimed.

By 1951, Britain controlled most of the country's oil through the Anglo-Iranian Oil Company and through the UK's close relations with the ruling shah. That year, however, a fierce nationalist named Moham-med Mossadegh took power and declared that, henceforth, the Iranian state, not arrogant British executives, would run the wells. The move incited a boycott by global oil companies; without British technical skills, Iran's oil industry began to collapse. Nitze's job was to help nego-tiate a compromise that would get Britain involved and the oil flowing again. His first crucial assignment was to talk with the new Iranian premier when he visited New York for a United Nations meeting in October.

Nitze expected to meet a maniac. Mossadegh had a reputation as a strident anti-imperialist who often fainted dramatically on the floor of the Iranian parliament. He slept through cabinet meetings and wept while giving speeches. His skin was pasty, his nose long. His shoulders slumped so badly that one writer described him as resembling "a condemned man marching stoically toward execution." When he met Nitze, he claimed to be ill, so he was taken to the U.S. Naval Hospital in Bethesda. When Nitze returned to talk, Mossadegh was wearing a brown mohair dressing gown. He insisted on remaining supine on his hospital bed.

Nitze was nonetheless impressed. He found the leader sane, rational, and always in control of himself. Nitze and his colleague George McGhee sat at the foot of the bed and argued over the terms of a potential deal to restart the oil industry. Nitze had boned up on prices, currency rates, and marketing patterns. He played the bad cop, pushing Mossadegh on every issue. The prime minister parried back and even used a little anti-Semitism to goad Nitze: "You know, I'm beginning to suspect that your name is Levy."

Later, Nitze would drive out to Virginia with the prime minister for a day at McGhee's farm. When the two began arguing about politics, Nitze realized that he was dealing with an elitist. America dreaded that Mossadegh would Bolshevize his country; instead, he wanted to reform its political system so that only the literate could vote. In Nitze's view: "He was canny, witty, and hard to pin down, a shrewd and tricky politician, but in my view, far preferable to the Shah and his regime."

Nitze's other brief was to negotiate with the British, as well as with the American oil companies, which, Mossadegh insisted, should become part of a consortium. These talks continued, often secretly, throughout 1952. By December, Nitze thought he had a deal; he flew to London for some final negotiations. But news of his trip had broken to the media. Dozens of cameramen swarmed him at the London airport, and the papers were full of speculation. He dodged the brouhaha and continued the talks, quietly thrilled with the attention. "In England, I found I had become a famous, if mysterious, person," Nitze wrote home.

The deal soon fell apart. Mossadegh decided the terms were not right, and the Americans had other plans for him anyway. In November 1952, the CIA had begun quietly plotting his overthrow. The following summer, mysterious riots would begin in Tehran. The agency hired thugs to run through the streets chanting pro-Mossadegh slogans, smashing windows, and causing mayhem. Soon they were in the heart of Tehran, sawing and chiseling down a statue of the shah. Then, another group of hired operatives arrived to "save" the situation by organizing counterdemonstrations. Just as planned, chaos resulted, which the agency fed by hiring circus performers, weight lifters, and jugglers to parade through the center of the city proclaiming their love for the shah.

The madness that day in August 1953 did turn the public against Mossadegh, and men began to surge toward the premier's house. At the end of a bloody fight, Mossadegh, dressed in pajamas and holding a cane, surrendered. The shah was back in power.

Nitze did not like the outcome of the American subversion at all. Shah Reza Pahlavi was incompetent, corrupt, and weak. Supporting him was like taking out a long-term lease on a rotting building. For twenty-five years, Pahlavi maintained close relations with the United States, and with the American oil industry, until a revolution brought to power a regime far more reactionary and anti-American than Mossadegh's—and one that relentlessly exploited the story of his martyrdom.

Kennan drew a different lesson from the CIA's intervention. The United States had not merely supported the wrong leader; it should never have become involved. His political philosophy held that one country should be extremely cautious about involving itself in another—and acting covertly through the CIA made such action both more tempting and more dangerous. Worse, after the restoration of the shah and the CIA's other supposed successes of the 1950s, Third World governments for generations blamed the CIA for every bad thing that happened to them. Every coup, every financial crisis, every power outage would be perceived as the result of a scheme cooked up by trench-coated men in the Virginia suburbs. A quarter century after the meddling in Iran, Kennan called his role in setting up the CIA's covert operations "the greatest mistake I ever made."

IN THE SPRING and summer of 1952, as Nitze negotiated with Mossadegh, Kennan was involved in his own bit of espionage, though he did not know it at the time.

Freshly appointed ambassador to the Soviet Union, Kennan was alone in his study at the American embassy in Moscow, reading aloud scripts from Voice of America. ("Threats, bullying, trickery, treachery.") His absence from government had not lasted long. One year after the Kennan-Malik talks, President Truman had summoned back the Soviet expert and former PPS chief. ("These were the bludgeons used mercilessly by Stalin.")

Kennan's family had not arrived yet, and meanwhile, to sharpen his language skills, he was reading aloud the VOA scripts regularly sent to him. They would help him remember the latest vocabulary connected to his work. He read the VOA propaganda calmly and precisely, practicing intonation and accent. Recalling the incident years later, he did not note which scripts he read, but those published that spring ranged from political diatribes to songs written by prison laborers.

Kennan sat and practiced in the embassy, wholly unaware that the wooden Great Seal of the United States that hung on his wall harbored a radio transmitter. Somewhere in Moscow, a KGB man listened carefully, no doubt wondering why the American ambassador sat alone, denouncing the Soviet Union in Russian deep into the night.

("There are many animals which are infinitely more powerful than the Bolshevik cat. The yearning for freedom, the hatred for tyrants, the thirst for life, the awareness of right—all these are many times more powerful than Bolshevist tyranny. The main thing is the will to struggle.")

KENNAN HAD ARRIVED in Moscow full of confidence. He said at one point that he believed he had spent his whole career preparing for this job, and the early days exhilarated him. Moscow was mysterious and mesmerizing. He felt he understood the men in power there; surely they understood him, too. They would know he was neither an enemy nor an ignorant dupe. He could work back channels and speak Russian man-to-man. Truman was not running for reelection, which meant that a new administration would arrive in January. Perhaps he could whack some sense into a relationship gone entirely insane. Off the record, he told reporters just before departing that he believed he could warm the chill between the two nations.

He wanted discipline, and he wanted to make a good first impression on his hosts. When he learned, before arriving, that two embassy underlings, Malcolm Toon and Richard Davies, had argued in *Foreign Affairs* that the United States needed to move past containment and try to detach Eastern Europe from the Soviets, he had them shipped out immediately. "Get those scorpions off the premises," Toon remembers Kennan saying.

Kennan's balloon deflated fast. He received no instructions from Washington, and the Soviet government showed no enthusiasm for conversation, in Russian or in English. Even the Russians he remembered from his younger days at the embassy averted their eyes. One official he actually spoke with was a young man who dashed into the embassy and told the ambassador that he could eliminate the Soviet high command if just given guns and money. Kennan threw the fellow out, assuming it was a Soviet trap—a suspicion that his biographer John Lewis Gaddis would later confirm.

Soviet handlers tracked Kennan everywhere, even when he went swimming. Thugs prevented his toddler son from approaching Russian children. The constraints were maddening and were made more so to Kennan because he believed them the response to amateurish American spy efforts. His colleagues were obsessed with photographing and recording and in general deploying various espionage gadgets of "a childish and 'Boy Scout' nature." American intelligence operations were not garnering information; they were merely games that reduced Soviet respect for the U.S. mission.

With Kennan in place, Stalin even started a "hate America campaign," which filled Moscow with lurid propaganda. "Placards portraying hideous spiderlike characters in American military uniform, armed with spray guns and injection needles for bacteriological warfare, stared down at us from every fence throughout the city," Kennan wrote.

The atmosphere rattled Kennan; at one point, he requested and received cyanide capsules from the CIA. He told Gaddis he had requested them because he feared that he would be captured and "I would be asked—or put under torture—and asked to tell things which I didn't want to tell."

A quarter century later, Nitze would develop another theory. Hearing of his old friend's request for cyanide pills, Nitze decided to investigate. According to a memo that Nitze kept in his files, his inquiries revealed that a CIA official named Hugh Cumming "carried the pills to Kennan—supposedly he got in trouble with some 'dame' and thought the Russians might in some way publicize it. They did not 'and he's been grateful ever since.'"

IN MID-SEPTEMBER, about four months into his posting, Kennan departed Moscow for a brief trip to London, where he planned to give a speech advocating that the United States soften its Soviet policy. His flight had a planned stopover at Berlin's Tempelhof airport and, as they neared the city, Kennan pulled out a small notepad and jotted down answers to potential press questions. If asked, "Have you seen Stalin?" he would reply, "There has been no occasion for me to ask to be received by Premier Stalin." He ran through a series of other questions and then wrote a note to himself. "Don't be a boy and don't feed the little ego. Be deliberate. Learn not to mind pauses and silences. Expect the lonely and the boring. Get use[d] to it. Never be a raconteur unless you are desperate."

Unfortunately, he did not follow his own admonition. On the tarmac, a reporter asked if the embassy had many social contacts in Moscow. "Don't you know," asked Kennan, "how foreign diplomats live in Moscow?"

"No. How do they?"

"Well, I was interned here in Germany for several months during the last war. The treatment we receive in Moscow is just about like the treatment we internees received then."

Martha Mautner, who had transmitted the document that made Kennan's name, witnessed the act that now permanently blackened it. But she did not think the statement seemed so outrageous; she considered it, in fact, "obvious."

Moscow, however, disagreed—or at least it did not want the obvious declared. Stalin could not possibly allow the American ambassador to compare him to Hitler. Kennan was declared persona non grata and barred from returning to the country, even to pack. His wife would have to arrange for their belongings to be shipped home. And the Kennans would have to live at their farm in Pennsylvania: they had rented out the house in Princeton, expecting to be abroad for at least two years.

Kennan got the news in Geneva, where his daughter Joan was attending school. He went straight to a movie theater, one place he knew the media could not find him and where he could compose his thoughts. Later, reporters finally ran him down at his daughter's school and surrounded the campus. The director of the institution had to hustle Kennan out the back entrance.

He was now an international sensation. His oldest daughter, Grace, heard the news by way of a passing newsboy's holler: "Kennan kicked out of Moscow."

The former ambassador to the Soviet Union was despondent. He grabbed the same little notebook in which he had scrawled the advice for the press conference to write out a few lines from Shakespeare. "Nay then, farewell! / I have touched the highest point of all my greatness /

and, from that / full meridian of my glory / I haste now to my setting / I shall fall / like a bright exhalation in the evening / and no man see me more."

NITZE HAD GOTTEN the result he urged in NSC-68: with the Korean War, the United States massively increased its military spending. But that was not enough. For the rest of the Truman administration, he would push for more and then more again.

He was obsessed with what he called "the correlation of forces." One could calculate some fuzzy, but still definable, comparison of U.S. and Soviet strength. How many weapons did we have? Who were our allies? Who did the rest of the world think was gaining power?

This almost mathematical notion would become the centerpiece of Nitze's worldview for decades; he believed it the key to making sense of the Cold War. Any Soviet advantage would foster aggression on their part, and yielding on ours. An American lead meant stability. When talking about this topic, Nitze would often hark back to the Korean War, which he thought had come about because Moscow felt relatively strong. The world was like a giant chessboard and the correlation of forces revealed who had the strongest pieces in the most advantageous squares. The theory had a relentless logic that led to an exponential speeding of the arms race. If the Soviet Union was ahead, the United States had to redouble its efforts to catch up. If the United States were ahead, it should redouble its efforts to expand its lead.

For the next forty years, Nitze became something like a coach on the sidelines of a never-ending race, exhorting his athlete to run faster each time he completed a lap, whether ahead or behind. He wrote NSC-68 in the spring of 1950 because he feared we had fallen behind. One year later, he concluded that we had to accelerate our rearmament; the interval between our moment of weakness and our moment of strength was an opportune time for the Soviets to move. Six months after that, his message was the same: faster, faster! The next spring, with peace talks ongoing in Korea, Nitze worried that the Soviets might reduce world tensions, and thus persuade the "free world to let down its guard and neglect its armament effort." A few months later, he perceived that the U.S. position had improved. His recommendation was predictable: a big lead in the arms race would give the United States ever so much more leverage.

But what if our redoubled efforts inspired the Soviets to work harder, too? Then a constant redoubling of effort would start a mad dash to disaster. Nitze did not agree with that line of argument. The Soviets wanted to destroy us and were working as hard as possible to do so, independent of our actions. America was reacting to their hostility, not inspiring it.

Most Soviet experts disagreed. In the summer of 1950, Kennan wrote in his diary about how easy it was for people to think of Stalin as a simple ogre, rather than to try to understand his complicated mind. In the summer of 1951, Chip Bohlen blasted Nitze's latest call for rearmament. "My chief objection," he wrote Nitze, "is the presentation of the Soviet Union as a mechanical chess player engaged in the execution of a design fully prepared in advance with the ultimate goal of world domination."

Yes, Moscow was aggressive, Bohlen conceded. But not ineluctably. By acting cautiously during the Korean War, Moscow had shown it was not hell-bent on confrontation. "Soviet actions in Korea," he wrote, "underline the extraordinarily pragmatic and opportunistic nature of Soviet policy and the absence of any fidelity to a blueprint, or even design."

Nitze would have none of it, arguing that if his opponent agreed with his premises he must agree with his conclusions, too. Bohlen, Nitze said, believed that the Soviet Union was hostile and opportunistic. Accepting that, "it seems to me that the unavoidable conclusion is that the U.S.S.R. will exercise their capabilities at any time and place they conceive to be favorable."

The two men slugged away at each other in memos and meetings, wearying Acheson. Eventually the secretary stepped into the ring and raised Nitze's arm in the air. The long-running debate between the Soviet experts and the Policy Planning Staff was at a stage where, as a friend of his had said in another context, "you hold the sieve while I milk the barren heifer." As Acheson later recalled: "The way to peace and action required separating the chief contestants for a cooling-off period. Accordingly, one stayed in Washington [Nitze], one went to South America [Kennan], and the third to Europe [Bohlen]."

That victory won, Nitze continued to push U.S. rearmament ever forward. Soon he got definitive news on the great issue over which he and Kennan had split. Three years after Edward Teller's blackboard sketching, the United States exploded its first hydrogen bomb. At 7:14 on the morning of November 1, 1952, Elugelab was a pretty coral island in the Pacific, emptied of all human inhabitants. One minute later, it was a crater two hundred feet beneath the sea. The explosion vaporized birds flying within several miles of the island. If exploded in New York City, the bomb would have obliterated all five boroughs.

Kennan trembled. Nitze smiled. A few months earlier, he had written another memo arguing that the United States should press ahead with H-bomb testing. Negotiations with the Soviets would come to nothing unless the correlation of forces tilted America's way. Only when well ahead could the United States talk about slowing down.

AFTER HIS EJECTION from Moscow, Kennan briefly put his tail between his legs. He flew to London, where it's likely that the first American to greet him was Paul Nitze, who was in town working on his Iranian business. The ex-ambassador then stayed quietly in Europe for a while, under orders to spare the Democrats the political embarrassment of his return until after the election.

Kennan realized that he had little chance at getting a top job after the Republican Dwight D. Eisenhower won the election and promised to bring along the hawkish John Foster Dulles as secretary of state. Kennan's chances of getting any post at all vanished when he gave a speech in the middle of January 1953 to the Pennsylvania Bar Association arguing that it would be foolish for the United States to try to overthrow Stalin, a statement the press viewed as a direct repudiation of Eisenhower's pledge during the campaign to roll the Soviet Union back. The next day's *Washington Post* declared, "Dulles Policy 'Dangerous' Kennan Says."

According to Robert Bowie, who was about to replace Nitze as head of the Policy Planning Staff, "this did not endear Kennan to Dulles." FBI officials put a note in their files that Kennan had "murdered himself politically."

Indeed he had. Dulles barely listened to Kennan's apologies and made no effort to find him a new job. In mid-March, he finally summoned Kennan to Washington and told him that he could think of "no niche" for him.

Kennan would soon pack up his papers from the State Department, an institution for which he had worked his entire adult life. On his final day, he wrote in his diary: "Then I took the elevator down, as on a thousand other occasions, and suddenly there I was on the steps of the building, in the baking, glaring heat: a retired officer, a private citizen, after 27 years of official life. I was not unhappy."

SVETLANA ALLILUYEVA WAS BORN in Moscow in 1926, Joseph Stalin's third legitimate child and first daughter. She stayed close to her doting father until her teen years, but the relationship frayed badly in 1943 when she fell in love with a dashing Jewish filmmaker named Alexei Kapler. Thirty-eight years old, handsome, and worldly, he introduced her to poetry and to art. Her full brother, Vasily, always jealous because Svetlana was the favorite child, told their father about Kapler and claimed he had introduced the girl to something else as well. Stalin erupted. "Such a war going on, and [you're] spending the whole time [fornicating]!" he screamed at her.

The relationship was off; Kapler was soon exiled and then sent to the notorious Vorkuta labor camp, north of the Arctic Circle. "My father thought that I was his girl. He wanted me to be his, and to always be with him," Svetlana says now, adding that only then did she viscerally understand his power. "It was the first time as a grown woman that I realized that my father could send a person to prison."

In December 1952, three months after Kennan's ejection, she stopped by the Kremlin. Stalin was behaving erratically, and dangerously: purging his doctors and the secret service while preparing a massive anti-Semitic campaign. He had decreed a vast military mobilization, as well as a study of the possibility of invading Alaska. To his twenty-six-year-old daughter, though, he acted normally. She recalls that her father's face had turned slightly red and that he boasted excessively about having quit smoking. Otherwise, he seemed fine.

Three months later, Svetlana had a feeling that her father was calling for her. She tried to reach the Kremlin but was told she could not see him. Disconsolate, she visited a friend who tried to cheer her up by taking her to a movie. Unfortunately, the theater was playing an adaptation of *The Captain's Daughter*, in which a father is executed in battle soon after forbidding his daughter to marry the man she loves. Svetlana sobbed throughout the film. The next morning, men instructed her to head to her father's dacha immediately.

The day before, Stalin had suffered a stroke. One of his guards found him lying near the cot he often slept on, dressed in pajamas and a white undershirt. He had wet his pants and could not talk.

His terrified servants had been slow to act; eventually, they summoned the dictator's daughter and son, as well as the Kremlin high command. Stalin's regular physician was in prison and no one could find his medical records. Svetlana remembered a chaos of people running, doctors applying leeches to her father's head and neck, and a nearly blind nurse trying to give him insulin, unaware that she was about to push the broken glass ampule down his throat.

Conflicting emotions roiled Svetlana. Her father's face seemed beautiful as he lay there on his deathbed, and she loved him more tenderly than ever before. But she also knew some kind of deliverance was on its way. His death would lift a burden from her, from her country, and from everyone over whose life his shadow had passed.

The end came soon, but it was painful for all. "His face altered and became dark. His lips turned black and the features grew unrecognizable. The last hours were nothing but a slow strangulation," she recalled.

> At what seemed like the very last moment he suddenly opened his eyes and cast a glance over everyone in the room. It was a terrible glance, insane or perhaps angry and full of the fear of death. . . . He suddenly lifted his left hand as though he were pointing to something above and bringing down a curse on us all. The gesture was incomprehensible and full of menace, and no one could say to whom or at what it might be directed. The next moment, after a final effort, the spirit wrenched itself free of the flesh.

WITH THE DICTATOR'S DEATH, Washington saw an opening. Now might be the moment to start a war, to make peace, or to press for concessions.

Eisenhower's top advisers split into two camps. Some wanted to take immediate action and promote chaos in the Soviet Union. Bohlen, recently named Kennan's replacement as Moscow ambassador, and Nitze, still head of PPS, led another group. They wanted to move slowly, the better to take advantage of the internal Soviet strife that would take a few weeks or months to manifest itself. Nitze suggested that the United States wait for a short while and then press for a settlement in Korea. Perhaps the new Soviet leader would willingly agree, ending that war and driving a wedge between his country and the Chinese.

Eisenhower made a different choice. He wanted to give a big speech about peace. Nitze was ordered to assist the main drafters.

Now one of the highest-ranking remaining veterans of the Truman administration, Nitze appears to have approached the task a bit like a parent who wants to encourage his child's idealism, but does not want him to make an error. He helped craft the oratory, but he also worked to exclude specific proposals and concessions.

A few days before the speech, Nitze was summoned to the White House on a Sunday morning and directed to a meeting in the president's quarters on the second floor. Opening the wrong door, he found that there, indeed, was Eisenhower—in the middle of changing clothes and clad only in his undershorts. The error did not amuse the president. "Once you've seen a man in his BVDs," Nitze later said, "the awe recedes."

The final speech was beautiful and passionate—and, as Nitze wanted, largely free of detail. At worst, the struggle between the United States and the USSR would end in atomic war. As long as the conflict continued, Ike said, the best we could hope for would be "a life of perpetual fear and tension." The president noted that "the cost of one modern heavy bomber is this: a modern brick school in more than 30 cities. It is two electric power plants, each serving a town of 60,000 population. It is two fine, fully equipped hospitals. . . . This is not a way of life at all, in any true sense."

Eisenhower entitled the speech "The Chance for Peace," and he ended with a call for the United States and the Soviet Union to try to resolve their problems. Both countries had new leaders. Now was a time to end the madness.

Moscow responded encouragingly. *Pravda* criticized some of Eisenhower's premises and noted the lack of specifics. But it also reprinted the speech accurately and in full. This pleased Kennan, whose last major task before leaving the State Department was to help analyze the Soviet reaction. "The present Soviet leaders are definitely interested in pursuing with us the effort to solve some of the present international difficulties." Their essential message, Kennan wrote, was "Put out your feelers: we will respond."

It seemed like an opportunity for a new and better phase in the Cold War—but Kennan and Nitze would both have to watch from the outside. Dulles had already thrown Kennan out. Nitze would soon feel a hand on his back, pushing him toward the door.

Eisenhower and Dulles had no respect for Acheson and thus limited patience for his allies. First, they replaced Nitze as chair of the Policy Planning Staff with Robert Bowie. Then, as Nitze prepared to move into a lower-profile job in the Defense Department, the *Washington Times-Herald,* a paper closely aligned with Joseph McCarthy, published a short article describing him as "the latest Truman-Acheson lieutenant contemplated for retention in a powerful position under the Eisenhower Administration." A few days before, McCarthy himself had called the FBI and "asked that he be furnished any available information concerning an individual named Nitze."

Almost immediately, Nitze was out. He had hoped to spend the next eight years continuing his work from the inside and helping to shape Eisenhower's foreign policy. Now, like Kennan, he had no idea whether his career had just come to a close.

10

★ ★ ★

A FULLY CONVENTIONAL LIFE

Paul Nitze and George Kennan stumbled out of government into the wilderness of Eisenhower's America together. They had arrived in Washington as young men on the rise. They had helped repair and rebuild the world. They had expected to stay in the State Department. And now, neither man knew what to do.

Kennan was forty-nine, Nitze forty-six. Each had four children, two off at school and two still at home. Each had dreams of striking a match to his public life—Kennan by heading to Europe, Nitze by returning to Wall Street—but their families did not want to move. Each man felt that his best work was yet to come. But each feared his chance had already passed.

Each man also now owned a farm—Nitze's was in southern Maryland—to which he retreated and where he at first found bliss. "This period of unemployment has a great many virtues," wrote Nitze's wife in the summer of 1953. "Paul looks better than he has in fifteen years and is busy from sun-up till sun-down with farm chores."

Each also began to spend time at a summer home. Nitze chose Northeast Harbor, Maine, close to the Rockefellers, Lippmanns, and Fords. Days were spent on the tennis courts and the trails of Acadia National Park. Nights passed dining on lobster, drinking red wine, and playing bridge. Kennan retreated to the Norwegian coastal town where his wife's parents lived, and where few people spoke English. There he would sail his boat and sit quietly in solitude. He later wrote longingly of "the one meal a day, with unvarying boiled potatoes."

And each toyed with elective office. One night, the doorbell rang at Kennan's Princeton house. A Pennsylvania farmer had driven 150 miles to urge the former diplomat to run for Congress. Kennan had not registered with either political party and professed not to know the difference between them. He asked the man which he supported. "It turned out to be the Democrats. It would have made no difference to me had it been the other one."

A sense of civic duty trumped electoral disdain; Kennan filed formal papers to enter the race for Pennsylvania's Congressional 19th District. The party elders supported him, but not enough to clear the field. He would not only have to face a Republican; he would have to put the rest of his life, and his ability to earn money, on hold to campaign against other Democrats. Kennan decided that the job was not worth it unless he was appointed, so he dropped out. He was never the most likely of candidates. When Dean Acheson and Nitze heard about Kennan's interest in running for Congress, they both burst out laughing at the thought of their former colleague on the campaign trail. And when a young Massachusetts senator named John Kennedy learned of Kennan's decision not to run, he called a friend to crow about the failure of the wise man: even someone with that reputation for brilliance could not make it to first base in the complicated world of politics.

Nitze too decided to try his hand. He began making speeches, kissing babies, and giving money to local Maryland politicians. One day a top official from the state Democratic Party rang him up. Nitze's pulse quickened at the prospect of an important endorsement. But no: the man wanted to know whether Nitze's charismatic and gregarious wife had any interest in running for office. Jealous and surprised, Nitze snapped no, much to his later embarrassment and regret. He took it as a clear sign he should abandon his foray.

Instead of Capitol Hill, Kennan and Nitze each found something of a base in intelligence work. Both spent parts of the 1950s consulting for the CIA, with Kennan doing it for several years. But their real homes now were in academia. In an act of remarkable hubris and daring, Nitze and a cousin-in-law, Christian Herter, had founded the School of Advanced International Studies in 1943. Neither knew much about either education or international studies at the time. Born to a prominent family, and an aide to the U.S. delegation at the Versailles Peace Conference, Herter was nonetheless just a first-term congressman; Nitze had spent two years in the State Department and at the time was a mid-level bureaucrat dealing with minerals procurement. They both seemed closer to graduate students than to the founders of a school in a position to grant graduate degrees.

But impulse and vision triumphed over inexperience. In 1944, one year after the two kicked around the idea over coffee, the first students showed up for classes in a building on Florida Avenue in Washington. By 1950, the school had affiliated with Johns Hopkins. When Nitze left government, he began fund-raising and lecturing for SAIS. The school would grow and grow, becoming one of the country's most important schools of foreign policy study. Nitze would long use it as a base, and he considered its founding to be one of his life's great accomplishments.

Kennan, meanwhile, returned to the Institute for Advanced Study, which he had joined briefly before his appointment to Moscow. Run by Robert Oppenheimer, and only loosely affiliated with Princeton, IAS welcomed humanists and historians but was populated mainly by scientists and mathematicians. The aging Albert Einstein, with his frizzy white hair flowing, often walked with Kurt Gödel, black hair combed down. John von Neumann was busy building a supercomputer in the boiler-room basement.

What everyone had in common was intellectual rigor, or at least the appearance of it. Beth Straus, a friend of Kennan's, remembers once going to an IAS dinner party where she sat beside two scholars who spent the whole time conversing past her in Latin. There was some initial resistance to Kennan's appointment—von Neumann, for one, voted against it because the diplomat had not yet produced any scholarship of "exceptional character." But Oppenheimer pushed it through. Kennan had an office, a salary, and quiet if not peace.

Describing a day during his first summer out of Washington, he wrote in his diary: "Behind me, figuratively stretched 27 years of foreign service; and behind that an almost forgotten and seemingly irrelevant youth and boyhood. Ahead of me, figuratively, was only a great question mark: somewhere between 1 and 30 years to live, presumably, and for what? I was numb inside and had little zest for the question."

As the Eisenhower administration settled in, Nitze and Kennan found themselves in similar circumstances. But they were like two planets that orbit the same sun and somehow fall slightly out of sync—then spin endlessly away from each other.

DWIGHT EISENHOWER WON the presidency in 1952 while campaigning against the "negative, futile and immoral policy of 'containment,' which abandons countless human beings to a despotism and godless terrorism." Instead of containing Moscow, we would roll the communists back.

Publicly mild-mannered and always responsible, Eisenhower did not really want to provoke the Russian bear—nor was he keen, once in office, to overhaul policies that he had helped the Truman administration design and implement. Within a few months of arriving in Washington, he was burying his campaign platform in a cemetery at the farthest edge of town. It was the start of a grand tradition in Cold War politics. Each time the White House switched hands after eight years being led by one party, the new president reverted toward the policies of his predecessor that he had denounced on the stump. Eisenhower started the trend. Kennedy campaigned on closing a missile gap that actually favored us. Nixon said he had a plan for peace in Vietnam. Carter declared that he would fundamentally change the arms race.

To come up with a new overarching strategy, Eisenhower's top advisers decided in the spring of 1953 to begin a massive intellectual exercise. Dubbed the Solarium Project, after the White House sunroom where they conceived the idea, the plan was for three teams to present three different foreign policy strategies. Team A would argue for a continuation of containment. Team B would add a militaristic edge to containment: telling the Soviets that we would start a war if they crossed specific lines. Team C would argue for rolling the Soviets back.

The president summoned Kennan to run the first group. Nitze's name was at the top of the initial list of candidates to participate, but somewhere along the way it vanished. In later years, he would assert that he passed up the opportunity because he wanted a vacation. An Eisenhower biographer, Richard Immerman, offers the more likely explanation that the president, firmly committed to limiting military spending, deleted Nitze's name.

For Kennan, the Solarium Project was an opportunity for redemption. He worked hard with his team of six men throughout the early summer. Then, in mid-July, he got to stand at a podium and lay out a sweeping foreign policy before Eisenhower, Vice President Nixon, and Dulles.

He started with his thesis from the X article that time was on America's side. If the United States could maintain its power, eventually the Soviet Union would sink under its own weight. He then repudiated military aggression. Yes, we might need to resort to armed action from time to time, but rarely and locally. The Soviets were not likely to attack America now, and they would not likely do so as long as our policies remained steady and calm.

Kennan's most dramatic proposal was a recasting of his and Nitze's plan from the summer of 1948. Germany should be reunified, and American and Soviet troops withdrawn. In addition, he proposed overt and covert action to sow dissent in the Soviet Union and to build up indigenous forces in countries that the Soviets might target. If we moved wisely and cautiously, Moscow's clients might slowly move toward our side. Sudden moves would backfire.

It was perhaps the most thorough and consistent presentation of the strategy of containment that he had pushed for the last six years. In his memoirs, Kennan describes the meeting as a triumph and a vindication. "At my feet, in the first row, silent and humble but outwardly respectful, sat Foster Dulles, and allowed himself to be thus instructed. If he then, in March, had triumphed by disembarrassing himself of my person, I, in [July], had my revenge by saddling him, inescapably, with my policy."

But Kennan exaggerated. Eisenhower did settle on a policy of containment, but in a version that was very much of his own choosing. He agreed that the Soviet Union should be contained, not rolled back. But he also wanted American security to depend on nuclear forces, and he pointedly ignored Kennan's recommendation to seek German unification. The policy paper that came out of the Solarium Project declared that the United States must maintain "a strong military posture, with emphasis on the capability of inflicting massive retaliatory damage." Kennan had surely not saddled the administration, inescapably, with that phrase.

For the most part, Kennan was a scrupulous memoirist, rarely succumbing to the temptation to exaggerate his influence. But just this once he indulged in self-delusion.

"IN WHAT CONNECTION have you known Dr. Oppenheimer?"

It was early 1954, and the anticommunist right was seeking more victims. The Soviets appeared to be churning out ever larger missiles and, in view of the USSR's technological inferiority, someone's treachery must have played a part. So now Senator Joseph McCarthy's forces had their shotguns of insinuation aimed at the man most responsible for building the atomic bomb: Robert Oppenheimer. Called to the witness stand to defend him was George Kennan.

He entered a long, dark rectangular room in a building near the Washington Monument. Three judges sat behind a large mahogany table. When not testifying, Oppenheimer sat on a leather couch against one of the walls, smoking cigarettes or puffing on his pipe.

Oppenheimer was facing a panel from the Atomic Energy Commission seeking to establish whether he should lose his security clearance. Oppenheimer stood accused of befriending communists in the 1930s and 1940s, giving them money, and even once lying to protect someone who had approached him in 1943 about passing scientific information to the Soviets. The government had thoroughly investigated most of these charges before, and Oppenheimer had been cleared. But the environment in early 1954 was different. McCarthyism was at its apex; criticism of the arms race could be construed as disloyalty or worse.

Kennan spent some of his time on the stand disputing the specific charges—for example, reminding the committee that the Soviet Union had been an ally of the United States in the early 1940s. But his main argument was that Oppenheimer was a special person of unimpeachable integrity.

"I have the greatest respect for Dr. Oppenheimer's mind. I think it is one of the great minds of this generation of Americans. A mind like that is not without its implications."

"Without its what?"

"Implications for a man's general personality. . . . I suppose that you might just as well have asked Leonardo da Vinci to distort an anatomical drawing as that you should ask Robert Oppenheimer to speak responsibly to the sort of questions we were talking about and speak dishonestly."

Besides the specific allegations involving connections to communists, the panel's biggest concern was Oppenheimer's early opposition to rapid development of a hydrogen bomb. He had tried to persuade other scientists not to work on it, and he had spoken out eloquently against the arms race, declaring in 1953 that the United States and the Soviet Union "may be likened to two scorpions in a bottle, each capable of killing the other, but only at the risk of his own life."

Kennan was grilled repeatedly about what would have happened had the Soviets developed the hydrogen bomb first. Treading very carefully—perhaps for fear of inspiring a separate inquisition targeted at himself—Kennan asserted that a Soviet lead would not have mattered much. They did not view the world through the same prism of relative strength and would not have used their military leverage for political gain. Next he was asked repeatedly what would have happened if the Soviets had had the hydrogen bomb and we did not. The investigators pressed and pressed, trying to get Kennan to say that Oppenheimer's views had made America weak, or that Kennan himself would not have wanted someone who had once had communist ties to serve in the Moscow embassy or on the Policy Planning Staff.

Kennan would not bend. Perhaps Oppenheimer had made mistakes when young. But he had made up for them and was a man of such talents and accomplishments that it would be utter folly to penalize him for small, probably irrelevant, indiscretions years ago.

"I do feel this," Kennan replied, "that the really gifted and able people in government are perhaps less apt than the others to have had a fully conventional life."

His interrogators latched on to that answer. Their task, they argued, was just to determine loyalty, not ability. That being the case, what did it matter that Oppenheimer was a genius?

"It is simply that I sometimes think that the higher types of knowledge and wisdom do not often come without very considerable anguish and often a very considerable road of error. I think the church has known that. Had the church applied to St. Francis the criteria relating solely to his youth, it would not have been [possible] for him to be what he was later. In other words, I think very often it is in the life of the spirit; it is only the great sinners who become the great saints."

One of his questioners offered to summarize that complicated argument: "I think you stated in effect, or at least you implied that all gifted individuals were more or less screwballs."

Kennan had been eloquent and brilliant, but he had not spoken in language appropriate to the circumstances. If anything, Robert Oppenheimer was on trial for being too smart: a man who had learned to read Sanskrit while studying physics was just the kind of fellow McCarthy did not trust. And comparing him to Francis of Assisi, the patron saint of animals, was not going to help.

Several weeks of brutal questioning ensued; Edward Teller, called as a witness, turned against his old colleague. Eventually, the board rescinded Robert Oppenheimer's security clearance.

Kennan was crushed, as were many of his friends—including Joe Alsop, who yielded to no one in his enthusiasm for hydrogen bombs but knew an inquisition when he saw one. The investigators had wiretapped Oppenheimer, withheld crucial documents, and operated pretty much like a kangaroo court. Alsop wrote to one of the panel members, former army secretary Gordon Gray: "Since we have been friends, and since I intend to express my opinion to others, I must express it to you also. By a single foolish and ignoble act, you have canceled the entire debt that this country owes you."

AS THE UNITED STATES TURNED on one of its sages, the Soviet Union turned on one of its savages: Lavrenti Beria. Head of the Soviet secret police, Beria had appeared ebullient (and rather intoxicated) at the mysterious scene of the dictator's death. Stalin's daughter was not at all surprised when told through one of his servants that Beria had danced upon getting word that her father was dying.

Beria was a vile man who took pleasure from torturing and murdering his enemies and innocent citizens alike. He used to send his bodyguards to pull women off the streets for him to rape. At the end of his life, his office contained a blackjack, piles of women's underwear, sex toys, obscene letters, pornography, and eleven pairs of silk stockings. While she was alive, Stalin's wife banned the "dirty man" from their house. Nonetheless, the great dictator promoted Beria steadily. According to Svetlana Alliluyeva, this was because "Beria was very clever to find my father's weakness—he loved flattery, especially after mother criticized him so mercilessly." When Stalin died, Beria thought he had a clear path to ultimate power: but he failed to realize that he had neither allies nor protection. "Nobody was hated more than this man," Svetlana said.

With Stalin dead, Beria engaged in a brutal, but quiet, battle with three rivals for ultimate control over the country: Nikita Khrushchev, Georgy Malenkov, and Vyacheslav Molotov. All were skilled political fighters, and all agreed that Beria had to go. One of the central objections that they discussed was his apparent consideration of the creation of a single, neutral Germany, out of U.S. or Soviet control. In June, three months after Stalin's death, the secret police chief was arrested on charges of betraying the motherland. After being held and interrogated for six months, he found himself begging for his life to no avail, hands tied and a towel in his mouth, as a three-star general fired a pistol into his forehead. Few people grieved. According to Svetlana, the credit for Beria's arrest belonged to Khrushchev, and "for that act alone, he should have a monument built to him."

With Stalin and Beria both dead, Khrushchev slowly consolidated power. He took a hard line on Germany, but he also sought to calm the furies unleashed in Stalin's final days. One of his moves was to make the country easier for Americans to visit—and one American eager to have a look was Paul Nitze.

For ten days in the summer of 1955, Nitze and his family stayed as guests of Ambassador Bohlen. The Soviet capital was the dark, militaristic place he had expected, but, driving in from the airport, Nitze gasped at the poverty and the "drab and somber" state of the city. The country that could turn the United States into a smoldering wasteland could not pave its streets.

Nitze almost tripped one day on a pipe rising from the pavement, which he was told was a vent for an underground bomb shelter. Later he went to a meeting of the Supreme Soviet and watched Khrushchev deliver a speech. The audience, he recalled, nodded off whenever the leader spoke of a new era of smoother relations with the United States. But people perked up and cheered whenever he used the word *mir*. The term is generally translated as "peace"—Tolstoy's great novel is *Voyna i Mir*—but Bohlen told Nitze that in this context it meant something closer to subjugation under benevolent Soviet, socialist rule. People appeared to be cheering for a world under Soviet supremacy.

At the end of the visit, Nitze and his family flew to Leningrad. Along with his recollection of the flight attendant carrying vodka up to the captain, Nitze's most powerful memory of the city was probably of the evening he spent at the Astoria Hotel. A jazz band began to play beautifully near the dining hall. Will you dance with me? he asked his wife. No, she said, there is nobody else on the dance floor. He turned to his eldest daughter. Will you dance with me? She, too, refused.

The next day, Nitze learned how instinctively wise his wife and daughter had been. The Communist Party of Leningrad, he was told, had recently banned dancing. If he had headed out on the floor, the musicians would have had to stop.

This joyless country, Nitze thought, was not the kind of place where anyone should live.

AS THE 1950S PASSED, Nitze refined his arguments about the correlation of forces and the possibility of achieving long-term peace through short-term strength. Looked at one way, the future appeared hopeless. Surely, sooner or later, something would go catastrophically wrong. If there was a 2 percent chance of war each year, then there was a better than even chance that war would break out sometime in the next thirty-five years.

But, Nitze reasoned, what if we could make it through the next decade? That would reduce the odds for the following decade. Surviving that second decade would reduce the odds of war during the decade after that. By staying strong, the United States might survive long enough to knock the odds down to zero. When Joe Alsop suggested to Nitze privately that maybe the United States should wage a preventive war and get the whole thing over with, Nitze heatedly rejected the idea. "I want us to have the best radar net in the world, the most potent Strategic Air Command, the most advanced guided missiles, the most ghastly atomic weapons, the strongest and most prosperous allies, and everything else. If we have these things, we may well deter the enemy from war long enough for the whole relationship to pass into another historic phase."

If war did come, however, Nitze wanted the United States to know how to fight it. In a January 1956 article in *Foreign Affairs*, he expanded his long-developing argument that the United States could actually win a nuclear war. Of course, no one would win if both sides fired off all their weapons. But that would happen only if both sides acted irrationally. Why blast the other, if you knew you would only get it back harder in return?

If one assumed a certain amount of rationality, war would stop before total obliteration. In that case, the better prepared side would be "in a position to issue orders to the loser and the loser will have to obey them or face complete chaos or extinction." The greater the United States' advantage in nuclear weaponry, "the greater are our chances of seeing to it that nuclear war, if it does come, is fought rationally and that the resulting destruction is kept to the lowest levels feasible."

Some of the research contributing to the paper came from a study group that Nitze had helped to lead in the previous months at the Council on Foreign Relations. He and a group of other distinguished foreign policy thinkers would meet about once a month on East Sixty-eighth Street in New York for tea at 5:15, continue through dinner, and then wrap up around ten. At the first meeting, Nitze had floated the idea that the United States would not have to unleash its entire arsenal in a conflict; it could use "tactical atomic devices in a limited war."

Nitze elaborated the idea at early meetings. In response, the group's director, thirty-one-year-old Henry Kissinger, pointed out an obvious flaw: "Once a war becomes nuclear, it is much harder to set any effective limits."

But Kissinger ultimately overcame his own reservations and became a forceful proponent of the possibility of limited nuclear war. In due course, he used the group's notes as the basis for a sweeping book, *Nuclear Weapons and Foreign Policy*, published in 1957. Kissinger was clearly a man on the rise: he was already a lecturer at Harvard, and Nitze had inquired about trying to hire him for SAIS the year before. The book would elevate him to a new level.

The most remembered thesis of Kissinger's provocative and alarming work was that limited nuclear war was not only possible but in some cases desirable. "With proper tactics, nuclear war need not be as destructive as it appears when we think of it in terms of traditional warfare." Much as Nitze had done in *Foreign Affairs,* Kissinger argued that the United States could use nuclear bombs for other purposes than crushing an opponent; we could use them to push our adversary to the point where surrender appeared preferable to continued resistance.

Despite its dense prose, the book was selected by the Book-of-the-Month Club and ended up on the best-seller lists. Kissinger was the chaplain on the pirate ship, the man who could explain and rationalize all the sins committed by the United States when it made these terrible weapons. He seemed to have mapped a middle road between the permanent standoff that everyone hoped we had entered and the total obliteration that everyone feared.

Nitze hated the book. "There are several hundred passages in which either the facts or the logic seem doubtful, or at least unclear," he wrote in a review. He scoffed at Kissinger's math. He declared the conclusions oversimplified and Kissinger's discussion of limited nuclear war profoundly flawed. No doubt, he was also unhappy that a man sixteen years his junior had parlayed an argument about limited nuclear war into fame. Nitze may not have had a patent on the idea, but he had certainly pondered it longer than Kissinger had. The stage was being set for a more dramatic clash a generation hence.

Asked fifty years later whether jealousy might have motivated Nitze's critique, Kissinger said, "It's a rational conclusion."

THE LIFE of the scholar was not for Nitze. Kennan once proclaimed that writing history was "the common refuge of those who find themselves helpless in the face of the present." That was a condition in which Nitze rarely found himself.

In the spring of 1956, Nitze's love of the fray led him to jump into the campaign of Adlai Stevenson, the former Illinois governor who had lost to Eisenhower in 1952 and who hoped for better results this time. A longtime friend of Nitze's sister, Stevenson was too soft on Russia for Nitze's taste: one of his signature proposals was a ban on aboveground nuclear tests. But he was preferable to the Eisenhower-Nixon-Dulles ticket, and Nitze worked long hours through the summer, helping to prepare the Democratic Party platform.

Kennan did have the patience for history. In 1956 he published his first major work of scholarship: *Russia Leaves the War*, an account of American diplomacy between the Bolsheviks' seizure of power in November 1917 and their removal of Russia from the alliance fighting World War I the following March. It was a gripping, vivid account of ill-informed American diplomacy. Kennan packed it with detail—in part, he would later say, to impress fellow historians, around whom he felt insecure. No doubt with a sly smile as he typed, Kennan tucked in a thorough debunking of a book written by William Hard, father of the woman who had spurned him three decades before.

When *Russia Leaves the War* was finished, Kennan, too, began to turn his attention toward politics. He and Nitze had met in 1954 to chat about Stevenson. By the winter of 1956, Kennan had committed to supporting him, if grudgingly. "I admire Stevenson as a sensitive, intelligent, and valiant person," he wrote in his diary.

> I consider him the sort of man to whom the people of this country ought to entrust the administration of public affairs, and probably never will. Dulles, furthermore, has thrust me into a position where if I am to be an

adherent of either party it can only be the Democratic. But what sort of Democrat am I? So far as domestic affairs are concerned, I am much closer to the Republicans. I think the protection of the farmer is mostly a lot of nonsense. I wish there were much more of what we have become accustomed to call unemployment. The labor union involvement in this country strikes me as shortsighted, reactionary, and partially corrupt.

I ought in truth to have nothing to do with either political party. . . . I hold no iron-clad brief for unity. I am not sure that we would not be much better off without California and Texas and Florida. By shedding our Latin-American fringe, we might have preserved something like a north-European civilization in the remainder of the country.

Ambivalence about his candidate aside, Kennan, like Nitze, found himself drinking the intoxicating elixir of political campaigns. Soon, he started drafting speeches for Stevenson, and getting very favorable responses. "How I wish I could write with the facility and perception that you do!" Stevenson wrote. "I may be uttering some of your words in a speech one of these days, and I hope you will forgive me if you detect no by-line!" Eventually, word started to circulate that Kennan was on the short list to become secretary of state.

One day in August, Kennan was staying with his twenty-four-year-old daughter, Grace, at his sister's house in Chicago. The phone rang and a somewhat familiar voice came on the line: "This is Mr. Stevenson of Liberty, Illinois." Grace dutifully took a message for her father about a dinner invitation—and was thrilled when she found out exactly which Mr. Stevenson had been on the line. Father and daughter headed over to the candidate's white, wooden two-story house for dinner the night the Republican convention nominated Eisenhower for a second term. It was a lively evening, and the group kept the television on as Vice President Nixon gave his acceptance speech. When it came time for Eisenhower to talk, photographers showed up at Stevenson's house, eager to shoot him watching his rival. Kennan and his daughter meanwhile quickly moved into another room. Most aspiring secretaries of state would have knocked over the wine rack to get into that photograph. Kennan hid.

At the end of the evening, Stevenson walked the Kennans out to where they had parked behind the house. "There was a bright moon, and the fields were in mist, and looked like a sea. We both felt intensely sorry for him: he seemed so tired and harassed and worn, he had so few people to help him; and his whole equipment for going into this battle was so shabby compared with the vast, slick, well-heeled Eisenhower organization," recalled Kennan. "It is clear that regardless of the outcome of the election this country is still removed by decades, and by phases of vast suffering, from anything like enlightened government."

A few weeks later, Kennan wrote Nitze, expressing despair at the political party both men supported. "I found myself disgusted by everything about the Democratic convention except Stevenson himself."

IN FEBRUARY 1956, Nikita Khrushchev sent for Svetlana Alliluyeva. He had something he wanted her to read, something that might embarrass her. He handed her the text of a long speech he was soon to deliver at the Twentieth Congress of the Soviet Communist Party.

She read silently and calmly through the sweeping, bitter, and brutal denunciation of her father. It began with a critique of the cult of personality around Stalin, and then detailed the methods of a man attached to "repression and physical annihilation, not only against actual enemies, but also against individuals who had not committed any crimes."

Svetlana did not agree with all of it, but she knew it was mostly true. Making no objection, she handed the manuscript back to Khrushchev and his deputy, Anastas Mikoyan. "We thought you were going to cry," said Mikoyan.

Khrushchev delivered the speech in a closed session to Soviet delegates at the Congress. He spoke passionately for nearly four hours, and when he finished the silence was near total. The speech was a brave and dangerous move. He wanted to exorcise the demon of Stalin without destroying communism: yes, the past quarter century had brought pain and horror to nearly every Soviet family, but it was one man's fault, not the system's.

Khrushchev's harsh words spread. Party members passed a little red booklet with the text through the Soviet Union. Moscow's east European allies read it. Eventually the text ended up in the hands of Israeli intelligence, and from there it moved quickly: to the CIA, to the State Department, to the New York Times, which published a story about it in June.

The exorcism pleased many communists, who knew that Khrushchev had spoken the truth. But it riled others who knew all too well how much he had left out, including his own culpability in many of the crimes he denounced. That summer, people in Eastern Europe began debating the merits of communism with an openness unseen for the next thirty-three years. Was Khrushchev genuinely suggesting that different paths to socialism were possible? Eastern Europe would soon test the proposition.

Protests appeared in Poland in June, sparked by food shortages but also fueled by the new debate. In late October, students in Hungary began demanding economic reform, free speech, and limits to repression. Mass protests and riots broke out. On October 23, protesters tore down the statue of Stalin in central Budapest, leaving just a pair of empty boots—posthumous humiliation for a man sensitive about the size of his feet.

Kennan thought this could be the beginning of the fissure he had long believed would split the Soviet order. The empire was coming apart, just as he had predicted in the X article. Interviewed by Joe Alsop for the *Saturday Evening Post*, he sounded uncharacteristically enthusiastic.

When Alsop asked why his prophecy of an eventual breakaway from the Soviets by Eastern Europe was being so dramatically fulfilled, Kennan answered that the Soviet Union had always had a problem in the region. Its countries had enjoyed greater freedom and wealth than the Russians. Allowing that disparity to continue would cause severe difficulties at home. But reversing it would cause problems in the satellites. Second, Kennan said, "is the plain fact that the Soviet communist system is deeply wrong—wrong about human nature, wrong about how the world really works, wrong about the importance of moral forces, wrong in its whole outlook. For this reason, I have always doubted whether the Soviet system would ultimately survive in full totalitarian form, even in Russia itself."

It was possible, Kennan argued, that the Red Army would squelch the protests. But that would only slow, not stop, the fundamental changes ongoing. Kennan predicted that Khrushchev would eventually lose power and the whole system would open up. "I think that the recent developments in Poland and Hungary are bound, sooner or later—and I don't predict the timing—to mark the end of Moscow's abnormal power and domination throughout all of Eastern Europe." The Soviet leaders, he said, "never realized how terribly tightly the spring had been compressed and what impetus it would get if you loosened it a bit."

In answer to Alsop's question about American claims that the United States deserved some credit, Kennan told a Russian fable about a fly that spends a day riding on the nose of an ox. At the end of a hard day at the plow, the ox returns home and the fly proudly greets the village: "We've been plowing." America provided a useful example of how free people could live but had done nothing directly to help.

Kennan, usually so prescient, made two errors that were very rare for him: he was too optimistic, and he misjudged the Kremlin. Even before the interview appeared in print—headlined "The Soviet Will Never Recover"—tanks had rolled into Budapest. The Hungarians fought back as well as they could, hoping desperately that the United States would come to their aid. Teletype messages sent from within Hungary to the Associated Press in Vienna vividly recounted the destruction of the dream.

RUSSIAN GANGSTERS HAVE BETRAYED US; THEY ARE OPENING FIRE ON
    ALL OF BUDAPEST.
THE WHOLE PEOPLE ASK FOR HELP.
YOUNG PEOPLE ARE MAKING MOLOTOV COCKTAILS AND HAND
    GRENADES TO FIGHT THE TANKS. WE ARE QUIET NOT AFRAID.
THE FIGHTING IS VERY CLOSE NOW AND WE HAVEN'T ENOUGH TOMMY
    GUNS IN THE BUILDING.
WE NEED MORE. IT CAN'T BE ALLOWED THAT PEOPLE ATTACK TANKS
    WITH THEIR BARE HANDS.
GOODBYE FRIENDS. GOODBYE FRIENDS. GOD SAVE OUR SOULS. THE
    RUSSIANS ARE TOO NEAR.

The fighting ended quickly. Thousands were killed, a new government was installed, and hundreds of thousands fled. The ox was gored and the fly could do nothing but buzz manically and then drift away. Kennan, consulting with John Maury, head of Soviet operations for the CIA, had no solution. A sudden war in Egypt's Suez Canal surprised and distracted Eisenhower, with the British and French backing an Israeli attack on Egypt, which had nationalized the canal during the summer. No American troops would go to Budapest. Kennan, then fifty-two years old, was eighty-five when Eastern Europe opened again.

November 1956 was, for him, a month of triple defeat. Adlai Stevenson lost the election; the Hungarian freedom fighters lost their war; and Eisenhower undermined the British and the French in Suez by threatening to deny support for the pound sterling if the battle continued. To Kennan, the latter was an unconscionable betrayal of our oldest allies.

He wrote in his diary:

The events of these recent days have been so shattering that I am at a loss to know how to react to them, personally. . . . If war comes, as it probably will, I had best seek a military commission and serve wherever I am then asked to serve. I shall probably not survive it; one rarely really survives two world wars in responsible public service. Nor will it make much difference what I do; for a government so unable to use serious counsel in time of peace will scarcely be able to make better use of it in time of war. But by holding a commission I shall give my family a better break in a country which has no use for civilians in war time, and which prefers that people serve uselessly in uniform rather than that they serve usefully in civilian clothes.

IN EARLY 1957, the Kennans returned to Washington, moving temporarily into Nitze's house while the two men prepared to give back-to-back testimony to Congress on arms and Middle East policy. In a reprise of their agreement over Plan A in 1948, both suggested that the United States try to work out a proposal for demilitarizing central Europe. CBS Radio made a thirty-minute program using their presentations.

Gradually, however, another issue was gaining ever more prominence in the American mind: the nuclear arms race. The Soviets appeared to be constantly gaining, and in the summer of 1957 they would test their first intercontinental ballistic missile (ICBM). Worries about radiation and fallout continued to grow. In a British cartoon from the time, one wolf warns another not to chew on children's bones because they contain strontium-90.

Nitze, as ever, used the escalation as an excuse to rethink strategy. And the conclusion he reached was that atomic weapons were not just weapons with which to wage war, or even to deter it. They were devices that could give you leverage in any conflict. If a dispute arose over Madagascar (or Berlin), the side with more weapons would be able to dictate its terms. "The atomic queens may never be brought into play," he wrote, taking a metaphor from chess yet again. "But the position of the atomic queens may still have a decisive bearing on which side can safely advance a limited-war bishop or even a cold-war pawn."

In the summer and fall of 1957, Nitze got a chance to present his views in the halls of government instead of in the pages of *Foreign Affairs*. The Eisenhower administration had formed a committee of prominent outside consultants to evaluate plans for civil defense. Rowan Gaither, a founder of the RAND Corporation, headed it. Nitze, being well known as a critic of Eisenhower, was initially excluded. But the committee gradually expanded its mission, and it would soon expand its membership. In September, Nitze wrote Acheson that he was going to join in "yet another agonizing reappraisal of our budget and defense position" and that, miraculously, the White House had not stopped him.

Through force of personality, experience, and technical knowledge, Nitze soon became a central member of the Gaither committee. When it came time to write a final report, he took over.

He worked intensively through a number of drafts, one of which began by declaring that the report would mainly be concerned with how the United States could fight a limited nuclear war. In other handwritten notes, he fretted about the environmental impacts of any nuclear combat. At one point, he described a meeting discussing "lethal northern hemisphere contamination" and the power of weaponry that would create it. Below, he scribbled, "Is this right?" in pencil. And farther below, in pen: "I doubt if anyone knows."

Ultimately, Nitze and his colleagues ended up producing a document much like NSC-68. America, the committee wrote, was in peril. The Soviets were building their nuclear arsenal faster than we were, and our defenses were weak. If we did not act, then we would be "completely vulnerable" by 1959 to ICBM attack. But we could respond and, if the public were properly educated, we would. "The American people have always been ready to shoulder heavy costs for their defense when convinced of their necessity."

The United States not only needed to spend more, the report declared, it had to change its strategic direction toward what later became known as "counterforce." What mattered was whether America's arsenal was structured so it could withstand, and retaliate against, a surprise Soviet attack. At present, Nitze wrote, a few direct hits could knock out the Strategic Air Command. But we could survive if we dispersed our weapons and planes, housed many of them in hardened shelters, and figured out how to shoot down Soviet missiles. The report also argued the necessity of arming more submarines with nuclear weapons. Our enhanced ability to respond to a Soviet surprise attack would deter the Kremlin from launching one.

Surviving a Soviet attack also meant protecting people, and much of the report focused on civil defense. Building shelters was not enough; we must train people in how to survive, physically and psychologically, living underground. "It would symbolize our will to survive, and our understanding of our responsibilities in a nuclear age." The report did not mention it, but the government would soon construct a gigantic underground office complex in West Virginia, stocked with four photomurals showing the Capitol with appropriate seasonal foliage.

The report, nearly finished, gained new urgency when, on October 4, 1957, the Soviets launched the first satellite into orbit. Suddenly, an aluminum sphere from central Asia was circling the earth, twinkling like a star as it passed over America. The Soviet Union had beaten the United States into space. The governor of Michigan composed a poem to mark the moment: "Oh little Sputnik, flying high / With made-in-Moscow beep / You tell the world it's a Commie sky / and Uncle Sam's asleep."

One month later, on November 7, the Gaither committee presented its recommendations and analysis at the White House. They failed to impress Eisenhower. He did not want, he said, to turn his country into a "garrison state." Dulles was outraged, cutting off the presenters and expressing his strong opposition to the civil defense proposals.

Ten days later, Nitze wrote the secretary of state a blistering letter. Without a "much more vigorous defense program," as outlined in the Gaither Report, America faced the prospect of a Soviet attack that could "destroy the fabric of our society and ruin our nation." The secretary's policies, meanwhile, had failed and would lead us to "default on our obligations to ourselves, to all who have gone before us, and to the generations yet to come." Nitze ended the letter with a piece of astonishing boldness: "Finally, assuming that the immediate crisis is surmounted, I should ask you to consider, in the light of events in recent years, whether there is not some other prominent Republican disposed to exercise the responsibility of the office of Secretary of State."

Soon afterward, Nitze and several members of the committee met to discuss what to do next. Perhaps, someone suggested, they should leak the report—and apparently they did. Soon the *Washington Post* was sounding the alarm. "The still top-secret Gaither Report portrays a United States in the gravest danger in its history," began the author, Chalmers Roberts. The front-page piece detailed the report, the panel of distinguished men who had composed it, and Eisenhower's initial reluctance to support its conclusions. If Eisenhower had thought he could bury the findings, he was wrong.

When Nitze was preparing his memoirs, one of his collaborators asked whether he knew who had leaked the document. "I'd rather not comment," Nitze said. He then coyly added that a journalist like Chalmers Roberts "wouldn't report it unless he had gotten it from several sources."

IN MAY 1957, John F. Kennedy telephoned his friend Priscilla McMillan. "George Kennan is going to be furious," the young man said.

Kennedy had just learned that he had won the 1957 Pulitzer Prize for his book *Profiles in Courage,* and he assumed he had beaten out Kennan and *Russia Leaves the War.*

But both had won: Kennedy for biography and Kennan for history. *Russia Leaves the War* also won a National Book Award, the Bancroft Prize, and the Francis Parkman Prize for literary distinction in the writing of history. A rookie scholar, Kennan had hit a grand slam his first time up. His book was vivid and original—and readers had noticed.

"There is no means, other than the cultivation and dissemination of historical knowledge, by which a society can measure its own performance and correct its own mistakes," Kennan declared in his speech at the National Book Award ceremony. He also wrote, in a note with more than a slight personal touch, "Many a man has worn out the best years of his life in official endeavor, aware that his contemporaries will never fully understand the significance of what he has been doing, and cherishing no greater hope than that some day, when the entire record can be spread out, people will be sufficiently interested, and sufficiently dispassionate, to give him his due."

Kennan's next big task was to prepare a series of talks for BBC radio. He had accepted a one-year appointment to a special chair at Oxford and agreed to give the prestigious Reith Lectures, an honor bestowed in preceding years on Robert Oppenheimer, Bertrand Russell, and Arnold Toynbee. That summer, mulling the task, he wrote, "To be fully honest, I should give the lectures on 'Why there is no hope in the international situation.'" He then began to muse about his ideal agenda: merging the United States with Canada and Britain, eliminating Washington ("and very good riddance indeed"), creating a new capital near Windsor or Ottawa, and then splitting the new nation into four regions. This would be followed by population reduction, the banning of cars, and a touch of autarchy.

"The truth is that democracy in the Western world could be saved from itself only by 50 years of benevolent dictatorship which would, like a doctor, restore the patient to a reasonable state of origin and then put him on his own again," he wrote.

Recognizing his flight of fancy, he added: "How would all this sound on the BBC?"

KENNAN DID EVENTUALLY choose his topics, labor over the preparation, and complete the scripts. Beginning in October, soon after the launch of Sputnik, he entered a glass-lined room at the BBC offices for six consecutive Sunday nights and, for twenty-eight minutes, sat in a chair at a long table with a microphone in the middle and tried to explain the world.

His first two lectures were smart, well-reasoned calls for the West to look at Moscow more soberly. The Soviet Union's economic progress was not part of a zero-sum game. If the USSR got a dollar richer, it did not follow that the West was a dollar poorer. At the same time, communism had indeed warped the Russians' views of America. But that meant we should deal with them patiently and calmly. The West should neither rush to war nor look to quick summits to solve its problems.

Kennan's last two lectures were likewise uncontroversial. The United States should hesitate before offering foreign aid to any country and not let developing nations blackmail it by declaring that they would go communist if not paid off. A fixation on the strength of NATO should not be allowed to undermine the relationship with the Soviets.

But in the third lecture Kennan kicked over a beehive by revisiting German reunification. It was time, he said, for the West to start negotiating with Moscow for a mutual withdrawal from Germany in order to remove the Cold War's central source of tension. "No greater contribution can be made to world peace than the removal of the present deadlock over Germany," he said. He did not call for an immediate departure, but suggested the issue be seriously explored. Yes, Moscow would resist at first. But "until we stop pushing the Kremlin against a closed door, we shall never learn whether it would be prepared to go through an open one." Nitze, commenting on the speech, said it was essentially a recapitulation of Plan A.

Kennan's cool logic lapsed only in the fourth lecture. Here he turned to nuclear weapons, a topic that caused him at points to lose his sober tone. He began by savaging a straw man, describing what he asserted were the views of people like Nitze. "They evidently believe that if the Russians gain the slightest edge on us in the capacity to wreak massive destruction at long range, they will immediately use it, regardless of our capacity for retaliation; whereas, if we can only contrive to get a tiny bit ahead of the Russians, we shall in some ways have won; our salvation will be assured." He then shifted, more eloquently, into a denunciation of the sort of civil defense measures called for in the Gaither Report. "Are we to flee like haunted creatures from one defensive device to another, each more costly and humiliating than the one before . . . concerned only to prolong the length of our lives while sacrificing all the values for which it might be worthwhile to live?" He ended by proposing that the NATO countries defend themselves through paramilitary units—groups of men trained to act like the French Resistance (except more effectively) if the Soviet Union overran their countries.

The response to the lectures was extraordinary. Front-page news throughout Europe and America, they may have been the most listened-to political addresses ever broadcast. Afterward, 72 percent of people in Britain were familiar with Kennan's name. Many commentators responded with ferocious attacks. Virtually no one agreed with Kennan's call for paramilitary units, and he would later profess regret at ever having mentioned the idea. His call for German unification did not go over much better. Even Nitze disagreed, arguing that the time for such ideas had passed: the amputated western part of the nation was now part of NATO and central to Europe's security.

Kennan's punishment for proposing disengagement from Germany came swiftly, and the most hurtful blow came from his old boss. "I am told that the impression exists in Europe that the views expressed by Mr. George Kennan in his Reith Lectures, particularly that a proposal should be made for the withdrawal of American, British, and Russian troops from Europe, represent the views of the Democratic Party in the United States. Most categorically they do not," wrote Dean Acheson in a press release. "Mr. Kennan has never, in my judgment, grasped the realities of power relationships, but takes a rather mystical attitude toward them." In a later essay, Acheson described Kennan's idea as a "futile—and lethal—attempt to crawl back into the cocoon of history."

Acheson asked Nitze to join in the press statement, but Nitze declined. As he explained later, "I refused, saying I had served as Kennan's deputy, was close to him as a friend, and although I agreed with Acheson's criticism, I did not want to criticize [Kennan] in public."

After the lectures, Kennan had characteristically fallen ill. He learned about the Acheson broadside from a newspaper while he lay in bed at a Swiss ski resort. He spent much of the rest of the day wandering around in the snow. "I am now in the truest sense a voice crying in the wilderness; and never, I think, have I felt a greater sense of loneliness."

AS KENNAN ISOLATED himself, Nitze became increasingly embedded in the Washington elite. The contrast between the paths taken by the old friends came through during a meeting in 1958 of a Council on Foreign Relations study group on military strategy. Nitze helped guide the discussion, made quick but smart comments, and signed up to lead the session on how to maintain stability in the arms race. Kennan said nothing, and then interjected a long, passionate critique of the group's premises. The rest of the group responded by roundly attacking him.

In 1959, Nitze journeyed to Africa and then reported back to John F. Kennedy's Senate committee. He hosted parties, attended dinners, and befriended journalists. Each July 4, he invited what seemed like half the Democratic establishment, as well as most of the leadership of the CIA, to his Maryland farm. Cocktails flowed; fireworks exploded; guests ran footraces and played tennis. One year, Nitze dropped to the ground for a set of one-armed push-ups.

As the Eisenhower years wound down, Nitze would find his views ever more in demand. After Sputnik, America seemed weak and John Kennedy promised to close the "missile gap" with Moscow. The Democrats reasoned that they could win the election by blaming Ike and acting tough.

Nitze became a top adviser on foreign affairs to the Democratic presidential campaign. He knew that if the election of 1960 went his way, he could soon be back on the inside—a moment he had waited for through eight frustrating years. When a friend asked him how he was doing under Eisenhower, Nitze responded: "I have no problems that a little more responsibility wouldn't cure."

★ ★ ★

11

DEADLY SERIOUS EITHER WAY

Paul Nitze picked up the phone in the library of his Washington house and heard the nasal voice of the president-elect on the line. It was late 1960 and Kennedy was offering his adviser a choice among three jobs: deputy secretary of defense, national security adviser, and undersecretary of state for economic affairs. "How much time do I have?" Nitze asked. "Thirty seconds," replied Kennedy. Nitze picked defense.

It turned out to be a bad choice. Kennedy later appointed Robert McNamara, the president of Ford Motor Company, as secretary of defense. McNamara wanted to choose his own deputy, and he wanted an administrator. Nitze had a reputation as an ideas man. The White House revoked the original offer and Nitze was dropped down a level to serve as assistant secretary of defense for international security affairs (ISA).

Power in Washington usually relates inversely to length of title. But Nitze made his eight-word job influential. He brought on brilliant and energetic young deputies and created something like a Policy Planning Staff for the Pentagon. Their first topic was arms control. Were the two superpowers locked into a never-ending spiral, destined to compete forever over who could drop more kilotons of horror on more cities more quickly? Would other countries soon join the contest?

Nitze saw the job as an opportunity to think big, and one day in March he took out his pad and began to ponder these questions. He had spent years now on details, white papers, and theory. Now he actually had influence. The critic had become the artist, and there he sat: likely alone, likely looking out the window at his views of the Jefferson Memorial and the Washington Monument. The early days of Kennedy's administration were a time of profound hope and optimism about potential change. And Nitze wanted to do his part.

Reduction of arms an essential object for many reasons.
Arms themselves a primary independent source of tension . . .
Sad record of those who neglect to keep the peace . . .
Path, long, dangerous. Don't rely on gimmicks. . . .
How do we prevent a world explosion. . . . Aren't at a stage where we know, or others know, the two steps or ten.

KENNAN DID NOT lobby hard for a job in the new administration. He had not worked for the campaign but instead had spent the summer traveling through Europe, and only happened upon news of Kennedy's nomination while at a railroad station in Verona. In his diary that summer, he declared that his public life was dead and that he could conceive of no possible useful function in Washington. Even so, he was crushed when he was not summoned.

"It is now nearly two months since the election and I have heard literally nothing from anyone in Washington in or around the new administration," he wrote in January 1961. "Most of the senior appointments in the foreign affairs field have been made—and to a large extent to people whom I thought of as friends: Dean Rusk, Adlai Stevenson, Chester Bowles, Paul Nitze, Mac Bundy. There has been abundant newspaper speculation about Chip Bohlen's future job. Concerning myself, the press has not printed a single word."

He wrote to Walter Lippmann complaining about the lack of attention. "Had I taken a less prominent part, in recent years, in the public debates on questions of national policy, I could let this pass without drawing any drastic conclusions from it; but in the circumstances I can regard it only as a sign of deliberate repudiation."

A few days later, though, Kennan's mood brightened. The president had not forgotten him; in fact, he wanted to meet in a week. Soon Kennan was aboard Kennedy's plane, briefing him on the USSR. Three days after the inauguration—during which the president famously stood bareheaded in the cold and told people to ask what they could do for their country—Kennedy called Kennan from the White House. Which embassy would he like: Poland or Yugoslavia? The U.S. Foreign Service wanted him back. Soon Kennan was packing for Belgrade.

JOHN KENNEDY STRODE into office appearing youthful and brilliant. Within two months he merely looked young—and the man responsible for this change of fate was a dictator ninety miles from U.S. shores.

Fidel Castro had seized power in Cuba in 1959, and one of the administration's first goals was to oust him. The plan was to land a group of fourteen hundred CIA-trained Cuban exiles on the island. Surging inland from the Bay of Pigs, they would inspire the rest of the nation to rise up against Castro's rule.

On April 4, 1961, Kennedy met with his top advisers. The CIA organizers detailed the plan and then the president invited everyone to comment. One of the first to speak was William Fulbright, a senator from Arkansas who considered the Castro regime a "thorn in the flesh" but not a "dagger in the heart." He spoke passionately and eloquently about his moral qualms. Nitze sat back, increasingly irritated by the lecture. He had long ago made up his mind about the morality of covert action, and he had no qualms about seeking to bring down a communist dictatorship. He dismissed Fulbright. Partly out of pique at the sanctimony and bluster, Nitze voted for proceeding with the operation.

Two weeks later, the exiles landed. They were quickly surrounded and either captured or killed. The survivors were sent to a sports stadium, where Castro berated them for four days. With TV cameras rolling, they applauded the man they had come to overthrow.

At their meeting before the inauguration, Kennedy had asked Kennan, the Office of Policy Coordination cofounder, his opinion of an exile-led raid of Cuba. He responded that the idea was fine, as long as it worked. "Whatever you feel you have to do here, be sure that it is successful; because the worst thing is to undertake something of this sort and to undertake it unsuccessfully."

Another debacle soon followed. Kennedy and Khrushchev scheduled their first meeting for June in Vienna. Before the trip, the president asked Kennan's advice. He told Kennedy to set his expectations low. Kennedy's best hope, he said, was that the two would begin to create an environment of mutual trust.

Khrushchev, however, had other ideas. The night before the meeting, he met with his politburo and proclaimed that he was going to pummel the silver spoon–bred amateur. Mikoyan played the role of Kennan, urging the initiation of a reasonable dialogue. But Khrushchev snapped back. Kennedy was weak because of the Bay of Pigs, and he would take advantage of that fact.

"I heard you were a young and promising man," said Khrushchev in greeting Kennedy, and the discussion started amiably enough. But then Kennedy allowed himself to be trapped in a discussion of Marxist theory, territory Khrushchev knew well. He had an answer for everything Kennedy said, and he gradually wore the president down. He denounced imperialism and railed against the American presence in Berlin. In a passage edited out of the official transcripts, he even declared that if the United States wanted war, it would be best to do it now. Why wait until both sides had developed even nastier weapons?

Afterward, Kennedy had a meeting at the American embassy with James Reston of the *New York Times*. The blinds were drawn and the lights turned off so other journalists would not spot Reston and envy the scoop. When the president arrived, he walked over to the couch, flopped down, and pushed his hat over his eyes. "Pretty rough?" asked the reporter. "Roughest thing in my life," said Kennedy. For the first time, noted the British prime minister, Harold Macmillan, Kennedy had "met a man who was impervious to his charm."

The White House called Kennan in to read and analyze the transcripts. His verdict was not positive. Kennedy had failed to push back on obvious points. He had appeared like a "tongue-tied young man, not forceful, with no ideas of his own."

Nitze had been one of just a handful of American aides to travel with Kennedy to Vienna. Afterward, he was handed a summary of the conversation with Khrushchev. Kennedy's last point was that the United States "cannot accept Soviet view of inevitability of change toward communism." Nitze scribbled in an addition: "This would not be possible if there were a further shift in the balance of power to the Soviet side." In Nitze's view, the United States could not afford to give an inch—a proposition that would be tested very soon.

———— ★ ————

THE MAN WHO bested the Harvard-educated, Pulitzer Prize–winning John Kennedy was semiliterate. Born in 1894, Nikita Khrushchev had grown up a peasant in Ukraine, so poor that he spent much of his youth barefoot. As a child, he had attended school for a total of two years; he could barely read and could not write at all. According to Dmitrii Shepilov, Khrushchev's foreign minister from 1956 to 1957, the premier "signed his own name with difficulty, usually scrawling just the first [three] letters: 'Khr.' There his powers of penmanship stopped. His written decisions were communicated verbally to his assistants."

The grandson of a serf and the son of a coal miner, Khrushchev toiled as a young man in mines and factories. Always energetic and witty, he joined the Communist Party out of his belief in revolutionary justice. Eventually he became an organizer and, in due course, friends with Nadezhda Alliluyeva, who introduced him to her husband, Joseph Stalin. Khrushchev shot up in the party: among other accomplishments, he supervised the construction of the Moscow Metro and directed the defense of Ukraine against the Nazis. By the time of his mentor's death, he had risen almost to the top. A bit of scheming, and the liquidation of Beria, would put him there.

He was bald and shaped like a pear. Nitze called him an "ugly, little man," but he had a definite roly-poly charm. He drank heavily and governed by instinct and improvisation. He did not grieve over friends and colleagues sent to the gulag. But, unlike Stalin, he did not live for intrigue and revenge. He was not "sadistic," Kennan wrote, "just rough." He was emotional and human. Bombastic and mercurial, he had close friendships and deep insecurities. "He's either all the way up or all the way down," said his wife in 1959.

He spoke in metaphors, very coarse ones. At one point, he pulled aside Moscow's ambassador to Yugoslavia and declared that if you stripped the West German leader Konrad Adenauer naked and looked at him from behind, you'd see that Germany is divided in two parts. But if you looked at him from the front, you'd see that his view of the German question "never did stand up, doesn't stand up, and never will stand up."

Such anatomical metaphors were his strength. More than once, he declared that it was time to throw a hedgehog down the pants of Uncle Sam. And when he wanted to cause trouble in Germany, he declared:

"Berlin is the testicles of the West. Every time I want to make the West scream, I squeeze on Berlin."

After his meeting with Kennedy in Vienna, Khrushchev decided to do just that.

ON SUNDAY, AUGUST 13, 1961, Paul Nitze was playing tennis in Northeast Harbor, Maine. John Kennedy was sailing off Hyannis Port, Massachusetts. And East German police were stringing barbed wire along the twenty-seven-mile border between West Berlin and East Germany.

That morning, men holding submachine guns began patrolling the crossings. Police lined up across the Brandenburg Gate to block traffic. West Berliners watched with curiosity and then rage. Two days later, concrete barriers replaced the barbed wire. Soon a wall would replace the barriers. The iron curtain had become a physical reality.

In the weeks and months before the wall went up, about a thousand refugees a day had crossed from the communist East to the democratic West, seeking jobs, stability, and freedom. In early August, the number had shot even higher. One of Khrushchev's speechwriters joked that soon only the East German leader, Walter Ulbricht, would remain.

The exodus was humiliating and devastating for the communists. Many of the smartest and most talented East Germans were fleeing. Unable to admit that, the communists christened the barrier the "democratic anti-fascist protection wall." It was meant to stop invasion and the "perfidious, subversive aims" of the West.

The crisis over Berlin had been brewing for several years. On November 27, 1958, Khrushchev had given the United States six months to leave West Berlin. John Foster Dulles responded that he was not afraid. He was right for his nation—Khrushchev let the deadline pass—but not for himself. The secretary of state was stricken by a fast-moving abdominal cancer and buried in Arlington Cemetery on May 27, 1959.

Then, in June 1961, Khrushchev threatened to sign a separate peace treaty with East Germany before the end of the year. That move was expected to abrogate the post–World War II deal that gave the Western Allies access to West Berlin. The United States would then need to launch another airlift or save that democratic enclave by force.

One of Nitze's aides telephoned him in Maine with the news of the wall's construction. Nothing was happening in Washington, the aide said. "If nothing's going on in Washington, I'm coming back on the next plane because something should be," Nitze shot back.

Kennan happened to be there already. Just before the wall went up, he stopped by Arthur Schlesinger Jr.'s White House office. The situation in Berlin terrified him. "I am expendable, I have no further official career, and I am going to do everything I can to prevent a war," he explained. "I have children, and I do not propose to let the future of mankind be settled or ended by a group of men operating on the basis of limited perspectives and short-run calculations."

NITZE'S JOB upon his return was to perform exactly those short-run calculations. He was put in charge of a group that would map out a series of contingency plans for Berlin. If the Soviets did A, we would respond with B. That might lead to C, which would demand a response of D.

Nitze began with the premise that one could and should think through all the possible ways to use nuclear weapons. This line of reasoning, a continuation of his limited-war studies in the 1950s, also intersected with the increasingly popular field of mathematics known as game theory.

One reflexive response to the horror of nuclear weapons was to throw up one's hands. As Kennan implied to Schlesinger, to go near the things was to tempt the most horrible fate. The inverse was to declare that the United States would launch its whole arsenal at the beginning of any nuclear confrontation. By 1961 this idea had become codified in American strategic doctrine in what was known as SIOP-62. In response to a Soviet nuclear attack, or as a preemptive strike, the U.S. Strategic Air Command's first move was, essentially, to obliterate the Soviet Union. At the time of the Berlin crisis, this approach was official U.S. policy.

Nitze thought the doctrine rigid and dangerous; instead, he drew up a plan modeled on "flexible response." The central idea was one known to gangsters everywhere: if someone shouts at you, raise your fists; if your antagonist does the same, pull a knife; if he pulls a knife, pull a gun. Ideally, you can settle the dispute without any of the weapons actually being used.

Nitze recommended four steps if the Soviets isolated Berlin. Begin with a probe: send a platoon of troops to try to get through the blockade.

If they failed, squeeze the communists through "non-combatant activity," such as an economic embargo. If that failed, invade and bomb with conventional weapons. If even that failed to open up Berlin, launch the nukes. Nitze broke that last step into three further steps: a demonstration bomb, a small nuclear strike, and then a general nuclear strike that would destroy much of the USSR.

Nitze preached the idea of flexible response through the fall of 1961. In an early September speech reprinted in the *New York Times,* he warned the Soviets that we "have a tremendous variety of warheads which gives us the flexibility we require to conduct nuclear actions from the level of large-scale destruction down to mere demolition work." Later that month, he spoke extensively about one of the most complicated moves in the sequence: demonstrating that we would actually use nuclear weapons in a conflict. One way to do that was to drop a nuclear bomb on the Soviet Union, but in a place where it would cause little harm. According to the diary of Henry Brandon, a British journalist, in mid-September Nitze mentioned the possibility of setting off a bomb on Novaya Zemlya, an Arctic island that the USSR owned.

Unlike some proponents of nuclear game theory, Nitze did not seem enthusiastic about the possibility of testing his ideas. In a memo he wrote to himself during the crisis, he lamented Khrushchev's posturing about Armageddon. "I supervised the engineers in Hiroshima and Nagasaki. Have followed these studies since. What would happen to Russia [if we dropped nuclear weapons of] 1000 megatons, 7000, 10000, 20000. Easy to make such threats but dangerous. Could lead to point of no return."

On October 3, Nitze met in the White House Cabinet Room with a group that included the president and the secretaries of state and defense. They discussed the increasingly tense situation in Berlin. A central question was whether a limited nuclear strike would necessarily precipitate general nuclear war. "Do you think possible to use nukes without becoming gen[eral]. Would depend on situation at the time," Nitze wrote on his yellow pad. One of the group's most aggressive members was the normally steady secretary of state, Dean Rusk, whom Nitze records as saying that the United States should tell Moscow that we would risk destroying "Europe, U.S. & Russia." He called that "pulling down house, because the house is lost anyway." Kennedy did not offer opinions or issue orders. But his nerves were starting to fray: at one point, Nitze recorded, "pres[ident] banged desk."

Tensions continued to rise. A few days later, Nitze visited the Soviet embassy in Washington to discuss the crisis. It was not a pleasant conversation. The Soviet ambassador had proclaimed that his country could utterly destroy Germany within ten minutes. Nitze said that might be so, but it "would not protect Moscow or Leningrad."

Two days later, at eleven P.M. on October 10, the president and key members of his administration gathered again in the White House to discuss Nitze's contingency plans. They all agreed that the first three steps made sense: probe, then harass, then attack with conventional forces. But then the president asked whether it was possible to have a demonstration strike or a limited strike without massive strategic bombing and general nuclear war becoming certain.

Secretary of Defense McNamara said yes. On this night, however, Nitze disagreed. He now thought a limited strike, or a demonstration, "would greatly increase the temptation to the Soviets to initiate a strategic strike of their own." Because of that, we should "consider most seriously the option of an initial strategic strike of our own." If we did that, "we could in some real sense be victorious in the series of nuclear exchanges."

McNamara disagreed again. No one could win a nuclear war. Secretary of State Rusk, returning to his more traditional moderate position, added, "The first side to use nuclear weapons will carry a very grave responsibility and endure heavy consequences before the rest of the world." The meeting adjourned with no decision made.

Forty-five years later, it seems that Nitze's horrifying argument was correct. Asked about the incident, numerous Soviet military officials all uniformly responded that they would have responded massively to any American strike at all, whether in Novaya Zemlya or Moscow. "Our war plans assumed that full escalation would be automatic," said Vitalii Tsygichko, a longtime Soviet war planner.

MEANWHILE, KENNAN WAS ALSO ENGAGED in clandestine negotiations. As tensions mounted in the summer of 1961, he began quiet talks with the Soviet ambassador in Belgrade. Perhaps the two men, speaking alone together in Russian, could quietly create a useful back channel. The White House agreed. Soon, Kennan began slipping over to the Soviet ambassador's house, without telling the U.S. embassy staff. The two men would meet in the ambassador's living room, drink tea, and chat.

In September, Khrushchev declared that he thought the back channel was not working well enough. "Unfortunately, however, I see from the dispatches of our Ambassador that they are spending too much time in, figuratively speaking, sniffing each other." He respected Kennan but wanted the talks to move at a faster pace.

> I never met Mr. Kennan but, so far as I can judge by the press, he is, to my mind, a man with whom preparatory work could be done, and we would accordingly authorize our Ambassador. But evidently in that case our Ambassadors would have to be given firm instructions to start talks on concrete questions without needless procrastination and not merely indulge in tea-drinking, not walk round and about mooing at each other.

Firm instructions never came; Kennan was frustrated, too. He reported to the United States that he had told his negotiating partner it seemed the Soviets had no interest in peace. Then he decided the same thing about the U.S. government. Why had his country not offered Moscow some concrete proposals? "Unless the West shows some disposition to negotiate," he wrote, "the hard line is going to be pursued in Moscow not only to the very brink but to the full point of a world catastrophe."

His back channel was soon cut off.

FORTUNATELY FOR THE WORLD, Kennedy never had to choose between McNamara's view or Nitze's in the debate over nuclear war. By the night of October 10, Khrushchev, well aware of his relative weakness—and probably aware of the contingency plans through the work of a canny KGB agent in NATO—was searching for a way out of the confrontation. On October 17, he backed away from his ultimatum: he would not sign a peace treaty with East Germany before December 31, and he would not cut off access to Berlin. The crisis briefly spiked one week later when a minor border dispute put American and Soviet tanks nose to nose in Berlin. But the tension dissipated quickly. The city was to remain divided and peaceful for the rest of the Cold War.

With the Berlin crisis defused, the Kennedy administration turned to smaller, less pressing issues. In early November, Nitze met with the president again. The subject this time was a potential U.S. troop buildup in a small nation in Southeast Asia.

Vietnam had not seemed to matter much when Kennedy took office. A communist government in the northern half of the country had been trying unsuccessfully to unite the country for nearly a decade. Eisenhower had engaged in a limited way, sending arms, aid, and a few advisers to help the south. Kennedy kept to the same course at first. The country was distant and poor; more important, Kennedy had long argued that fighting communism in places like Southeast Asia required building strong, free societies, not just blasting the communists.

But the pressure to intervene mounted. Vietnam was one of the few hot spots on the globe and the northern guerrillas infiltrating the south gained strength late in the Eisenhower years. In the spring of 1961, Kennedy decided to ship more advisers and more money—and to study the possibility of sending in troops. In October, his favorite military adviser, General Maxwell Taylor, traveled to Vietnam to report on the situation. When he returned, the president and some of his top aides met to discuss the options. Nitze's handwritten notes likely represent the only record of this November 10 meeting.

McNamara declared, "We need troops," and Rusk followed up by saying that adding three thousand men would give the United States a chance to knock back the insurgency. The conversation turned to ways to make the ineffectual government of South Vietnam, run by Ngo Dinh Diem, "more palatable." But the discussion came back to troops, and here the president was firm. "Don't say we commit. Don't want to put troops in," reads Nitze's summary of his statements. "Proceed with caution. Not putting in combat troops."

At the end, the president agreed to offer Diem some technical assistance. He then suggested that we ask our allies to share even this burden. "Make it multilateral. They have the same commitment."

Gradually Kennedy's caution eroded. By the end of the year, the commander in chief had sent in pilots and special forces teams. Combat troops, and then more combat troops, eventually followed. Nitze's notes on the November meeting end with a fateful remark by Rusk: "Our prestige is already involved."

KENNAN'S TWO YEARS in Yugoslavia proved to be both the end of his diplomatic career and a microcosm of it. He began with great enthusiasm and promise. He displayed wisdom and foresight in analyzing and understanding a distant land few Americans had penetrated. But he never comprehended the basic workings of American politics, and from that came his undoing. Too fragile and easily hurt, he was like Chiron, the wise and immortal centaur of Greek mythology who is shot by an arrow and develops a wound that never heals. The posting ended in disappointment and melancholy.

Yugoslavia had been a fresh start for Kennan. He was returning to the Foreign Service and to power. He mused that, if the job worked out as expected, he could have the formal and pleasant official retirement that John Foster Dulles had denied him. Belgrade was no Moscow, but it was not Ouagadougou. Yugoslavia was the only country to have split from the Soviet bloc, and its leader, Josip Broz Tito, was a formidable man worthy of study. Having declared himself "very happy at this time to merge my views" with those of the Kennedy administration, Kennan left, via ocean liner, to assume his post in May 1961. Young Foreign Service officers were thrilled to have the great diplomat coming to their embassy. The local town council near Kennan's Pennsylvania farm proudly named a new fire truck after him.

Like many curious people arriving in foreign lands, he was overwhelmed by the smells, sounds, and history. He went horseback riding, took long walks through Belgrade, and rapidly gained fluency in the language. He explored the countryside, met the people, and pondered the past of this immensely diverse land. He would ask his staff to write up little historical papers, which they would then gather to discuss.

The ethnic tensions that would destroy Yugoslavia decades later were suppressed during Kennan's tour. Everyone treated him with respect and openness, whether shepherds in the hills of Montenegro or elderly men in the churchyards of central Serbia. His experience provided a wonderful contrast with his time in Moscow during Stalin's paranoid final days. After one memorable luncheon, he brought to the ambassador's residence a peasant from southern Serbia dressed in traditional attire, complete with fur hat and leather shoes with turned-up toes. The episode demonstrated one of Kennan's odder traits: at home, he looked down on the working class, on non-Protestant ethnic groups, and in general on people unlike him. In Russia and Yugoslavia, all these groups fascinated him.

Only a few months into his tenure, Kennan experienced his first setback. In 1959, Congress had passed the Captive Nations Resolution. It was nonbinding and unimportant—the sort of thing the Hill routinely produces whenever a situation is too complicated for real action. One week a year, the president was required to voice his support for the day when all the "captive nations of the world" would achieve freedom and independence. Congress had named the Socialist Federal Republic of Yugoslavia as a member of the great communist conspiracy, even though it had broken with the Soviets in 1948.

Kennan considered it bad form to be technically committed by a branch of his own government to the overthrow of the government of the country in which he served. He had high hopes that the Kennedy administration would end the useless ritual of Captive Nations Week. But that did not happen.

A few months later, it was Tito's turn to anger Kennan. The Yugoslav leader hosted a conference in Belgrade for nonaligned nations, meaning those tied neither to Moscow nor to Washington. The event took place in September 1961, just as Khrushchev decided to resume atmospheric nuclear testing after a two-year hiatus. That move angered most of the world, but Tito declared at the conference that he "understood" the choice. He also took the Soviet side in the debate over Berlin.

An outraged Kennan, feeling personally betrayed, denounced Tito in the press and in memos home. He declared that Khrushchev could have written parts of Tito's speech. Henceforth, he asserted, we could no longer consider Yugoslavia "entirely a friendly or neutral nation." Other embassy officials reported that the Yugoslavs thought Kennan was overreacting. One month after the conference, a U.S. official wrote back to Washington that the Yugoslav assistant foreign secretary "last night inquired laughingly, 'is the Ambassador still angry at us?'"

A year later, Kennan got his comeuppance. In the summer of 1962, Congress decided to revoke trade and aid privileges to Yugoslavia. Kennan thought the action shortsighted. Trade with Yugoslavia mattered little to the United States economically, but it was important for the Yugoslav economy. Why should we penalize the peasants making little baskets by hand to sell in American supermarkets? Kennan showed absolutely no awareness that his own overheated reaction to events in the fall had helped stir anti-Yugoslav sentiment at home. According to Lawrence Eagleburger, who later became secretary of state and was then a junior official in the embassy, "he didn't realize that if he burned the base of the ladder he was standing on, eventually it would come crashing down."

In July 1962, Kennan returned to the United States to lobby for a reversal of the trade bill. He went on TV. He worked the halls of Capitol Hill. His energy, however, could not compensate for his lack of tact. Instead of seeking compromise, Kennan seemed shrill and condescending. Just before arriving, he complained of the "appalling ignorance" of Congress. From Washington, he wrote a letter to the *New York Times*, proclaiming the trade issue an example of why Congress should not interfere in foreign questions. "The issue is whether the Executive Branch of the Government is to be allowed sufficient latitude to handle intelligently and effectively a delicate problem of international affairs." While presenting this argument, sure to unite the whole legislature against his suggestions, Kennan expounded on his own "most careful thought" and "considered judgment."

In late September, back in Belgrade, Kennan decided to ask Kennedy for help. He must have expected the phone conversation to go well, for he decided to use an open line, which he knew the Yugoslavs would be monitoring. To set up the call, he summoned his butler, a White Russian later revealed as an informant for the Yugoslav secret police. Even if he did not already know this for certain, Kennan was too savvy not to have suspected it at the time. Clearly, he wanted the Yugoslavs to know what he was about to do.

The president came on the line immediately. Good. This provided a demonstration of Kennan's standing.

The ambassador made his impassioned plea against the congressional provision. But President Kennedy was noncommittal, and he then transferred Kennan to the office of Congressman Wilbur Mills, one of the bill's chief advocates. Mills, too, came on the line quickly. But he was gruff, and he briskly dismissed both the ambassador and his arguments.

With that, Kennan had publicly demonstrated his passion—and his complete ineffectiveness. He had overreacted to Tito's sins, overreacted to Congress's follies, and then overestimated his own ability to resolve the crisis.

As Robert Cleveland, then one of Kennan's principal subordinates, put it: "He was a better writer than ambassador."

ON THE NIGHT of Monday, October 15, 1962, Nitze was attending a State Department dinner for the West German foreign minister. He spent much of the evening arguing with a German intelligence officer about Soviet plans to take the whole of Berlin. The German said Khrushchev had no such designs: the risk of war was too great. Nitze countered that the Soviet leader might provoke a crisis somewhere else to gain leverage in Berlin.

Secretary Rusk left the argument momentarily to take a call in another room. When he returned, Nitze noticed that his normally imperturbable face had turned pale. After a short while, Rusk asked Nitze to join him on a terrace looking out over the glittering lights of Washington. He had grim news. American spy planes had photographed Soviet offensive nuclear weapons in Cuba.

Secrecy was essential. Top officials would have to keep to their schedules to prevent journalists from sniffing out the crisis. The next day, as planned, Nitze flew to Knoxville to give an address on the now uncomfortably appropriate topic of civil defense. When he returned, he joined ExComm, President Kennedy's top advisory group. At some of these meetings, Nitze was the only one taking notes. These notes, including those of conversations not in range of the secret White House taping system, survived in his personal papers.

Everyone agreed that the missiles were dangerous and provocative. Khrushchev was in a position to both taunt and threaten the United States. The first question at that meeting was whether to strike immediately. Unprotected and not yet operational, the missiles made juicy targets.

But the United States did not know for sure how many weapons had arrived. The spy photographs had spotted some missiles, but the Cubans and Soviets could have hidden more. Nitze's notes reveal that the ExComm group believed that "63 boxes, not like any we have ever seen" had come in through Cuba's ports. Did they contain other missiles that would hurtle toward New York soon after American planes took out the photographed sites? Acknowledging the potential for a massive conflict, someone proposed that all American women and children be evacuated from communist nations bordering the Soviet Union.

Nitze floated the idea of an air strike in which the United States deliberately hit only offensive missiles, the ones set up to destroy America, while leaving the defensive missiles designed to protect Cuba from invaders. But then he added, "Can you stop after 50 sorties or 400 sorties without invasion"?

Nitze was arguing both sides of a debate he had been having off and on for six years. Could a limited war stay limited? Dean Acheson replied that the consequences were "deadly serious either way."

MOSCOW FELT a strong emotional attachment to Havana. Khrushchev had known little to nothing about Castro when he came to power. But the bald five-foot-three-inch Ukrainian and the bearded six-foot-four-inch Cuban bonded immediately. More important, Cuba was the first country where communism had flowered without requiring Moscow's fertilizer and shovels. Anastas Mikoyan had visited the island in 1960 and reported back enthusiastically on the revolutionaries. He would later tell Dean Rusk: "We have been waiting all our lives for a country to go Communist without the Red Army. It has happened in Cuba, and it makes us feel like boys again."

But Cuba, ninety miles off Florida, was a part of American mythology as well. Teddy Roosevelt had fought in its hills and Ernest Hemingway had drunk in its bars. Until 1959, when Castro swept down from the Sierra Maestra and into power, American businessmen held sway there. Of more immediate importance, the Kennedy brothers were personally tied to it by the humiliation at the Bay of Pigs and they sought revenge. In November 1961, Nitze had sat in on a meeting on clandestine sabotage operations there; "all plans vague, grandiose," he jotted. In January 1962, Robert Kennedy described overthrowing Castro as "the top priority in the U.S. government. All else is secondary. No time, money, effort, or manpower is to be spared."

That same month, Khrushchev had also given a speech about humiliation—his being the retreat in Berlin that fall. Vindication required brinkmanship, daring, and the amassing of strength. "We should increase the pressure, we must not doze off and, while growing, we should let the opponent feel the growth."

By the spring of 1962, Khrushchev had settled on the location for his next move. That summer, Soviet ships sailed across the Atlantic. Military gear was kept belowdecks; decoy agricultural gear, like tractors, was kept conspicuously above. Once the ships approached the outer range of U.S. air and sea surveillance, men were allowed on deck only at night and only in small groups. Few knew where they were going. Each ship carried a small sealed envelope that the senior troop commander, the ship's captain, and a KGB officer would open at an assigned spot in the Atlantic. Only then would they learn their destination.

IN THE MOST famous photograph of the ExComm meetings, Nitze sits in a big leather chair at the end of the table in the White House Cabinet Room. A portrait of George Washington hangs on the wall directly across from him, an emblem of the republic now suddenly so vulnerable. John Kennedy, two flags draped behind him, sits in the middle of the table to Nitze's right. Papers cover the table and Nitze leans slightly, but intensely, forward.

Early in the debate, it became clear that the president had two main options. An air strike could take out the Soviet weapons and set up an invasion to remove Castro. Alternatively, a naval blockade could turn back the remaining Soviet ships and signal how seriously America took the crisis.

The group was split, and so were its members. Early on, Robert Kennedy announced that his brother would launch no "Pearl Harbor." But Robert had his hawkish side too. "It would be better for our children and grandchildren if we decided to face the Soviet threat, stand up to it, and eliminate it, now," he said. Secretary of State Rusk stayed quiet much of the time. But Nitze's notes also record a moment when the secretary recalled a line of T. S. Eliot's about how the world will end. Instead of going "down with a whimper," Rusk said, it would be "maybe better to go down with a bang." Chip Bohlen, present at the early meetings, threw in a dictum of Lenin: "If you encounter mush, proceed. If you encounter steel, withdraw."

Nitze would later recall his most productive meeting during the crisis as one he had with U. Alexis Johnson, deputy undersecretary of state for political affairs, on the night of October 19. Tired of the back and forth in the ExComm meetings—which he later compared to "a sophomoric seminar"—he and Johnson constructed a to-do list. His notes from that night reveal a classic Nitze logic chain, full of bullet points and potential countermoves. How would the Soviets respond to the announcement of a U.S. blockade, and how should the United States respond to the response? In the end, the men decided that the two main options did not conflict. Everyone wanted to get the missiles out with minimum risk. First we should try a blockade. If that failed, we should order an air strike. If that failed, we should invade. In short, Nitze developed a strategy of controlled escalation, just as he had done during the Berlin crisis.

The next day, Kennedy came back from a campaign stop in Chicago and guided ExComm to consensus. The United States would implement the blockade.

Nitze agreed with the decision and wrote out his views in longhand that evening. He believed it made sense to "follow the blockade route," but after giving that two or three days, he wanted an air strike to "eliminate the main nuclear threat." A retaliatory attack by the Soviets was highly unlikely, he wrote, given that our air force was now on high alert.

If the Soviets did retaliate, Nitze believed the United States should escalate: from a nonnuclear invasion to a quick strike against Soviet territory to whatever it took to get rid of the missiles. "If we permit the Cuban missile affront to go unanswered in an effective way, I see no possibility of negotiating with Khrushchev except on his terms. In other words, I believe we will have accepted his version of communist co-existence."

Underneath, as though leaving a note for posterity, he wrote his name: "Paul H. Nitze."

ONE MAN IN THE UNITED STATES was not afraid of war: Air Force Chief of Staff Curtis LeMay. To President Kennedy, he called a blockade the equivalent of appeasement. "I just don't see any other solution except direct military intervention *right now*," he pronounced on Friday, October 19.

Men like LeMay created another grave worry for Kennedy: some over-enthusiastic brass hat could start the war on his own. The president fretted particularly about a set of American nuclear-armed Jupiter missiles on bases in Turkey. If the United States hit Cuba, the Soviets might hit the Turkish bases. Should that happen, Kennedy did not want a rogue commander starting Armageddon.

On Monday, October 22, at a meeting in the Cabinet Room, he interrupted a briefing that Nitze was giving on Berlin to ask him to order the Joint Chiefs to make this point particularly clear to personnel at the American bases.

As a frequent sparring partner of LeMay, Nitze must have understood Kennedy's concern. But he was nonetheless reluctant to carry out the order, and he pointed out that the chiefs would consider it redundant.

Everyone already knew that they could not shoot off nuclear weapons without a directive from the commander in chief.

That did not satisfy the president. He wanted the order reinforced. "Can we take care of that then, Paul? We need a new instruction out."

Nitze responded quietly and without enthusiasm. "All right. I'll go back and tell them." His voice made it clear that the chiefs would not be happy. Nitze trusted that commands and regulations would be followed. Procedures would remain orderly. Why offend someone's dignity by suggesting otherwise?

"They object to sending a new one out?" asked the president.

They object to sending out a new order because it, "to their view, compromises their standing instructions," Nitze responded.

Surely a message could be sent, argued National Security Adviser McGeorge Bundy and Rusk. Perhaps they could just say the president was directing attention to the issue again.

Nitze pushed back. "They said the orders are that *nothing* can go without a presidential order."

Kennedy was now frustrated. The men handling the missiles in Turkey did not know everything that he knew, and he did not want anyone there to "fire 'em off and think the United States is under attack. I don't think we ought to accept the Chiefs' word on that one, Paul."

Kennedy probably intended the use of Nitze's first name as a reproach. But Nitze stubbornly refused to yield and carry out the command. It was a strange and damaging moment for him: he just did not seem to understand that this was a moment for accepting orders, not for fighting back. "But surely these fellows are thoroughly indoctrinated not to fire. This is what McNamara and I went over . . . and they really are indoctrinated on this point."

"Well, let's do it again, Paul."

Finally, he relented. "I've got your point."

ON THE EVENING of Monday, October 22, John Kennedy appeared on television, calm but firm. "We will not prematurely or unnecessarily risk the costs of world-wide nuclear war in which even the fruits of victory would be ashes in our mouth—but neither will we shrink from that risk at any time it must be faced." As he spoke, nearly two hundred nuclear-armed planes dispersed through the night. The Strategic Air Command was following the longtime advice of Nitze and many others. If you might be hit soon, spread out.

Throughout the crisis, Nitze tried to remain focused on the tasks at hand. He had a small staff from ISA working around the clock for him, turning out position papers in between meetings. One of his aides, Daniel Ellsberg, spent some nights sleeping on Nitze's couch. In a note scribbled to himself the day of Kennedy's broadcast, Nitze jotted down: "In light of present stakes, minor issues really are minor, and that with respect to major issues there is no way of avoiding choices and accepting the substantial risks and costs involved."

The first major risk was that the Soviets would try to break the blockade. When ExComm met on October 24, Soviet ships and submarines were still, as far as they knew, speeding across the Atlantic. At one point the CIA director, John McCone, left the room to get the latest position update. Imagining the lead ship approaching, President Kennedy asked what would happen next, "If we have this confrontation and we sink this ship," and then the Soviets answered with some action against U.S. forces in Berlin.

Nitze responded that the logical response would be to shoot down Soviet planes over Berlin. If the Kremlin followed with a further escalation, the United States would have to decide whether to attack Soviet missile sites and bases.

As Nitze spoke, McCone returned. We now know that the Soviet ships had begun to retreat the day before, but he believed that they had just now stopped dead in the water or turned around. War had been avoided—at least for the moment.

The Soviets still had an array of threatening missiles in Cuba, and the United States had to get them out. The next day, Nitze had lunch with Secretary of Defense McNamara. It is not clear who suggested the idea, but Nitze's notes indicate that at least one of them was considering whether the United States should tempt the USSR into starting a war. "Escalate blockade / provoke an attack / direct an attack," read the notes.

AS NITZE AND THE REST of the high command in Washington debated their options, George Kennan was far away and entirely out of the loop. As the CIA planes snapped the photos that would start the conflict, he was taking a long, brooding walk around Belgrade, thinking about whether to resign in the wake of his failure in the trade debate. His wife urged him not to quit and he agreed to stay on at least a little while longer.

The next day, he drove to Italy for a vacation. During the first frantic meetings at the White House, he was in Bellagio, reading Serbian history and working on lectures about the Marquis de Custine, who wrote a famous account of his travels in nineteenth-century Russia. He heard about the Cuban Missile Crisis when the president appeared on television.

Soon Kennan was back in Belgrade, addressing the embassy staff and their spouses about the crisis. He gathered the group in a club room on the ground floor of the embassy and gave a talk that Eagleburger remembered as "brilliant" and a "tour de force."

"We are now in [the] most serious world crisis since 1939," he began. He then explained the history of the Monroe Doctrine—the position, first articulated during the presidency of James Monroe, that the United States should remain the master of its own hemisphere. He added that the Soviets should have known that the United States would retaliate when it discovered the missiles. As for Castro, Kennan had no sympathy. "One of the bloodiest dictatorships [the] world has seen in entire postwar period. Not for a moment can we concede it reflects feeling of Cuban people."

The ambassador was calm and reasoned. He explained the historical background of the missile crisis and gave a passionate defense of Kennedy's decision to act. He ended the talk by drawing parallels to the Nazis' entrance into the Rhineland in 1936.

THAT VERY DAY, Saturday, October 27, everything almost went to hell. Kennedy received a belligerent note from Khrushchev, who in turn received a belligerent letter from Castro. The Cuban leader had stayed up all night and decided that the USSR should respond to any American invasion by "liquidating such a danger forever." Cuba shot down a U.S. spy plane, killing its pilot. Another American plane strayed into Russian territory after getting lost over Alaska and was almost knocked down too. Nitze met at the office of Undersecretary of State George Ball again. His notes begin with Ball's grim summary: "Unless we can return to political arrangement we will all fry."

But on Sunday, Khrushchev decided to end the game of thermonuclear chicken. He had spent one night sleeping in his clothes and was as shaken as his opposite number. He had become convinced that the Americans actually were going to attack, and military and scientific advisers had briefed him on just how terrible a nuclear war would be. As he had done during the Berlin crisis, he decided to seek a way out.

He found one during a meeting that morning. Shortly before, without telling Nitze, or many of the other members of ExComm, Robert Kennedy met with the Soviet ambassador Anatoly Dobrynin and offered to withdraw the American missiles from Turkey in a few months if the Soviets would pull out of Cuba. (Like many in the Kennedy administration, Nitze did not learn about the trade for many years—and when he did, he was furious, both because he had been kept out of the loop and because he thought the quid pro quo unnecessary.) The attorney general told Dobrynin that their deal had to remain secret. He might run for president one day and did not want it known that he had compromised.

Khrushchev was presiding over a frantic and frazzled cabinet meeting when he received word from Dobrynin of the possible deal. Soon Radio Moscow broadcast the deep, sonorous voice of Yuri Levitan. "The Soviet government," declared the man who had announced the end of the Second World War, "has given a new order to dismantle the weapons . . . and to crate and return them to the Soviet Union."

Reflecting on the crisis years later, Nitze explained that the central lesson was the importance of the correlation of forces between the two superpowers. The crisis started because Khrushchev sought to increase the USSR's strength and it ended because he knew his country was weak.

To Kennan, the crisis was an anomaly. The correlation of forces had stopped mattering when both sides acquired the ability to annihilate each other. Appearing on *Meet the Press* ten months later, Kennan said: "Nothing that has gone on in the Soviet Union in the last two or three decades is as puzzling to me as the motives which caused Mr. Khrushchev to put these missiles into Cuba."

In retrospect, and thanks to recently revealed documents of Khrushchev's, we know Nitze was right about the correlation of forces. But what we now know casts grave doubt on his view that a limited war could have stayed limited. The United States had grossly underestimated the number of Soviet troops in Cuba, and Castro had no qualms about starting a war in which, at worst, he would die a martyr. Soviet missiles were aimed at American cities, not just at weapons silos. Most terrifyingly, at the time of the crisis, and for nearly forty years afterward, the United States had no idea that the Soviets had hidden scores of smaller nuclear weapons on the island. A U.S. invading force would almost certainly have met a nuclear response. Learning this, and learning of Castro's willingness to use the weapons, "sent a chill down my spine," wrote Robert McNamara in 2002.

FOR NITZE, the immediate consequence of the crisis was a push away from the Kennedys' inner circle. Many people gained the president's confidence during those thirteen days, but Nitze lost it. In a 1965 interview, Robert Kennedy would claim that Nitze had been too much of a hawk. That does not seem to have been the real problem. McGeorge Bundy was far more hawkish, and the Kennedy brothers' esteem for him rose.

More likely, Nitze's real problem was that he did not work well with the Kennedy team. He was slow to take orders; he was impatient with the way Robert and John Kennedy's minds worked. They wanted to discuss and to mull. Nitze wanted to press ahead and take action. Bundy was at least compatible with them stylistically.

The issue was not a new one. Nitze had never done the things that would have endeared him to the president. He did not go to parties at the Kennedy compound on Cape Cod or let Robert Kennedy's children throw him into their pool in Virginia—and he thought rather less of the people, like Robert McNamara, who did. Years later, talking about the Kennedys, he said, "I knew them all, and from time to time went to these things, but you know [my wife and I] don't like to become parts of somebody else's group."

Nitze's punishment was twofold. He immediately lost some of his influence. And then, when the Kennedys and their confidants provided journalists and others with accounts of the crisis, Nitze was portrayed as one of the men ever eager to get the country into war. As the tapes and his notes reveal, he was conflicted about whether to strike. But the classification of people into hawks and doves (or, essentially, good advisers and bad advisers) depended partly on their closeness to the Kennedys. Robert, the ardent hawk of the early days, became "a dove from the start," according to his biographer Arthur Schlesinger Jr. Nitze suffered the opposite fate.

Removed from the inner sanctum, Nitze returned to the big issues that had occupied him early in the administration. In February 1963, he proposed, in a memo titled "Basis for Substantive Negotiations with U.S.S.R.," that America agree to substantial arms reductions, limiting NATO and its communist counterpart, the Warsaw Pact, to a total of five hundred nuclear missiles each. Since the United States was well ahead in the metric, that part of the deal benefited Moscow. But in return, the Soviets would have to allow West Germany to absorb East Germany.

It was a bold and well-timed proposal. The missile crisis had spooked and matured Kennedy. In June, he would give an eloquent speech in Vienna calling for a reduction in Cold War tensions. Nitze's memo could have been a useful starting point. But no one noticed it; Nitze did not even mention it in his memoirs.

Just a month after he floated his peace plan, Deputy Defense Secretary Roswell Gilpatric announced that he would soon be leaving his post. By all rights—experience, knowledge, and the promise given during that half-minute phone call from the president—the job should have gone to Nitze. "Kennedy expected to name Nitze to Gilpatric's post in Pentagon," declared the *New York Times*. But it was not to be. In the fall of 1963, the secretary of the navy was caught in a financial scandal. Kennedy had to fire him fast, and he needed a replacement. He turned to Nitze, who had no particular ties to the navy and who considered the secretaryship a demotion. But Kennedy twisted his arm and promised a more suitable post within a year. Nitze had no choice but to say yes.

GEORGE KENNAN'S REPUTATION had taken a beating, too. He had turned the conflict over Yugoslavia's trade status into a battle royal. The issue was marginal to the U.S. economy, to the balance of power, and even to Tito. But Kennan had damaged the administration's relations with Congress over it. Carl Kaysen, a presidential aide, remembers Kennedy becoming agitated when talking about Kennan after the fight in the fall of 1962. "The man doesn't know what he's talking about," the president exclaimed.

In January 1963, Rusk summoned Kennan to Washington. The two talked about his future and agreed that he should resign. Two years was long enough for him to serve in the post. Kennan lobbied for a reversal of the trade bill one more time that month—he even paid a visit to Nitze at the Defense Department to plead the case—but the battle was lost. In the spring, news of Kennan's impending resignation leaked to the press. That summer, he came home.

Kennan harbored no ill will. He still found the young president both glamorous and wise. He recognized the difficulty of finding a way to smooth our terrible relations with Moscow. In the fall of 1963, he wrote to Kennedy: "I am full of admiration, both as a historian and as a person with diplomatic experience, for the manner in which you have addressed yourself to the problems of foreign policy with which I am familiar. I don't think we have seen a better standard of statesmanship in the White House in the present century."

He may have sent the letter partly out of self-interest. Rumors swirled that Rusk might soon be forced out, which would shake the apple tree and perhaps drop a new job into Kennan's lap. But the feelings expressed were most likely genuine. Kennedy had had a terrific year, starting with the Cuban Missile Crisis and building with his much lauded Vienna speech.

Kennan mailed the letter on October 22 and got a charming hand-written note back. Less than a month later, the president was assassinated in Dallas. His death sent Kennan into a mood of profound sadness; his secretary remembers him pacing somberly. The day after, he did something very uncharacteristic for George Kennan: he stayed home and just stared at the TV.

12

★ ★ ★

ABOUT 60/40

Paul Nitze made enemies almost as rapidly as he made friends. Always standing a little offstage, he carried an aura of mystery. To some, he was the dark, overbearing sage of nuclear warfare—the man with "dangerous capabilities," as one biography of him is titled. To others, he was a too-smooth appeaser, never more than a step away from selling America out. Never completely on anyone's team, he lacked any constituency to defend him.

In November 1963, he learned this lesson the hard way. The Senate Armed Services Committee was evaluating his fitness to serve as secretary of the navy. Several members of the committee decided he was too weak. Though he had a vaguely hard-line reputation inside the Kennedy administration, much of his most aggressive writing, for example NSC-68, remained classified. Scratch one of these Harvard types, the argument seemed to go, and you find a world federalist.

Three years before, in a speech at a national security gathering at the Asilomar Conference Center in Monterey, California, Nitze had committed what some considered an unforgivable sin. Asked to stimulate discussion, he had wandered down an elaborate intellectual path: layering questionable notion atop questionable notion and pressing on to what he called the "grand fallacy." It culminated in the proposition that the United States should hand over control of its nuclear weapons to the UN. The conference goers had raised their eyebrows and turned their attention to other matters. Nitze had slipped the speech into his filing cabinet and forgotten it. But with the hearings coming up, a young, ambitious first-term congressman named Donald Rumsfeld unearthed it. He saw a chance to score points with conservatives and skewer a sheep in wolf's clothing.

The text had circulated in the Senate and among conservative constituents. Now the senators were hammering Nitze over his conclusion. He was meekly, repetitively, and futilely claiming he had not really "proposed" a handover, he had just thrown out the idea for discussion. The argument wasn't working, in large part because the speech was so detailed it had obviously been thought through extensively. (Nitze took all arguments seriously, even when being deliberately counterintuitive.) "It would have been better if I said, 'I propose for your consideration,'" proclaimed Nitze after about a dozen questions along these lines.

"That isn't the way it reads," shot back Senator Harry Byrd of Virginia.

"I recognize that, Mr. Senator."

"Well, what reply shall I make to the Veterans of Foreign Wars if they send me a copy, which I know they will, of your exact language in which you say you propose—p-r-o-p-o-s-e?"

Nitze squirmed. His hard-liner friend Scoop Jackson, of Washington, tried to defend him by asking questions about just how much the military budget had expanded under Truman because of Nitze's work. But it did not seem to help. And then Strom Thurmond, the most formidable voice of the Old South, strode up.

The South Carolina senator was a man of prodigious energy, not always directed in the most admirable ways. In 1957, he spoke for more than twenty-four hours straight, filibustering a civil rights bill. In 1964, he literally wrestled a colleague down and pinned him to the floor in order to block quorum. As a young man, apparently believing that segregation stopped at sundown, Thurmond fathered a child with his black maid. A few years after the Nitze hearing, at age sixty-six, Thurmond would marry a twenty-three-year-old former Miss South Carolina. He would serve in the Senate past his hundredth birthday.

On this day, all of his energy and anger focused on Nitze.

"Mr. Chairman, has the witness been sworn?" thundered the senator as he took the floor and demanded, in a fierce insult, that Nitze take an oath to tell the truth. Those nominated for a post by the president are rarely asked to do so, particularly not in the middle of a hearing when taking the oath may seem to cast doubt on their previous, unsworn testimony.

Thurmond then began to take apart the Asilomar speech. He thought the conclusion was terrible, and that the premises included ideas disrespectful of the Senate. He demanded to know why Nitze did not think the United States could win a preemptive nuclear war. When another senator came to Nitze's defense, Thurmond snapped: "I am questioning the witness. The Senator from Ohio can look after his business, and I will question the witness right now."

Thurmond then argued that the Asilomar speech was not just an isolated thought experiment. The well-tailored former aide to Dean Acheson had long been a coward. The senator next pulled out a dovish conclusion reached by a panel at a conference Nitze had attended at the National Council of Churches in 1958. Did Nitze agree with that? If not, why had he not dissented? Thurmond also needled Nitze about his association with the Bilderberg Group, an organization of Western intellectuals that had, suspiciously, last met in Cannes, France.

The dismemberment was brutal and personal. But despite their ferocity and some unflattering press—"Nitze opposed in Navy job for alleged pacifist views," reported the *New York Times*—the Senate ultimately confirmed him.

Now the alleged pacifist could move into a job he did not want.

THE NAVY DID not want Nitze, either. He had not served in the military. He had sided with the air force while working on the Strategic Bombing Survey. He had never run a big organization. He was associated with the budget-cutting, sharp-tongued, domineering Robert McNamara. "The Navy is getting ready to receive one of the biggest brains in town—I suppose it will be a stimulating experience for both him and us," carped an unimpressed admiral.

Before long, Nitze began to win respect and friends. He was tough but not ruthless. He sacked an admiral who was undercutting him, earning points for courage, but made no ostentatious show of cleaning house. He figured out who the smartest brass were and befriended them. He particularly liked the chief of naval operations, David McDonald, and moved him to an office right next to the secretary's quarters. Gradually, word got around that Nitze was a terrific manager who could spot talent. One of the young men he brought on, Elmo "Bud" Zumwalt, eventually became one of Nitze's closest friends and went on to be chief of naval operations himself.

Nitze learned to love what the navy loved, and he became a navy man. If his eye was on his next promotion, he did not show it. Ambitious though he was, Nitze was still a worker bee. He wanted to improve the long-term health of the service, not just score a few quick political points. He overhauled the navy's system for tracking Soviet subs and he revamped the process of ship design. When he read a staff study suggesting that modular design could cut costs, he traveled abroad to examine commercial locations where the method was in use, organized a test run at a navy shipyard in Mississippi, and then spread the practice throughout the service.

He thrived on international intrigue, as when the navy had to retrieve an atomic bomb that a B-52 lost in the Mediterranean. He set up a special covert intelligence-gathering organization that would later be called Task Force 157. Details mattered, too. He spent hours trying to figure out whether ships should be coated with oil-based or rubber-based paint, and he wrote a letter of consolation to the quarterback Roger Staubach when Navy lost the 1964 football game against Army. "He was so damn smart. The last thing you wanted to do was to brief him on something. You made any mistake on your slides or your figures, he would catch you," says Admiral Bill Thompson, a close assistant.

Nitze had not wanted the job because he believed it would keep him out of the meetings where major decisions were made. "The service secretaries, well, they're just warts," Richard Nixon would say. "I like them as individuals, but they do not do important things." Indeed, Nitze was out of the inner circle for many of the crucial debates over Vietnam. But the work turned out to be both satisfying and useful. He mastered technical details that would serve him throughout his life and he proved that he could run a complex organization. Much later, he would say that the job he did not want became the best one he ever had.

As in every job he liked, he drove himself to exhaustion. At one point, he had to check himself into the National Naval Medical Center, in Bethesda, with a perforated ulcer. His dear friend Charles Burton Marshall visited and asked how on earth one perforates an ulcer.

"I've never said this before and I'll never say it again," replied Nitze. "But the answer is 'McNamara.'"

Nitze and his boss had never quite bonded. The two were technocratic wizards, but McNamara more so. He could crunch any set of numbers. He was the man, everyone said, that the computers try to imitate.

Nitze—older, but junior—oscillated between admiration and disdain. He could not but marvel at the new defense secretary's mind, and at how quickly a former car company executive could assimilate the details of missile systems. But the genius was partly an act, and Nitze saw through it. Lying in the hospital in Bethesda, Nitze claimed that McNamara's problem was his relentless need to prove his brilliance and decisiveness. He would demand papers for early the next morning, expect you to stay up all night preparing them, then cut you off halfway through your presentation. He would proclaim that you had now told him all he needed to know—maybe because you had, and maybe because he was so caught up in the image of mountain-climbing, decision-making, problem-solving Robert McNamara.

The life of America's dazzling (and very image-conscious) secretary of defense paralleled, in many ways, the story of mid-twentieth-century America. When fighting men were icons, McNamara was helping plan the air offensives of World War II. When businessmen were lionized, he rose to run the Ford Motor Company. When the Kennedy administration galloped in and created Camelot, he was one of its strongest and most commanding cavaliers. By 1964, people were talking of him as a potential vice president.

By the time Nitze was working himself to exhaustion at the navy, though, McNamara had invisibly but inescapably started to crack. Deep beneath the Nitze-like exterior lay a Kennan-esque internal turmoil. Tormented by the number of people who had died carrying out his orders, McNamara was beginning a slow-motion nervous breakdown. Rational decisions piled upon rational decisions were beginning to seem to have created something entirely irrational.

By mid-1965, the human computer was flummoxed by an unsolvable problem. We had to win in Vietnam, but the war was not winnable on any permissible terms. McNamara continued to attack the problem from every angle, but he was heading inevitably toward a crash.

IN HIS OLD AGE, Nitze would take pride in his efforts to stop the Vietnam War both early and late in the conflict. He was not as proud about the middle, when he missed his best opportunity to actually change things.

While serving at ISA from 1961 to 1963, he warned against military escalation. He had run Truman's Policy Planning Staff when Ho Chi Minh started driving the French out of the country. He had helped manage the long, slow Korean War. He knew Vietnam would not be an easy place to fight. As the United States stepped gingerly into battle, Nitze argued forcefully against sending in ground troops. We should fight solely from the air and the sea, he told McNamara. In one June 1964 memo, he told McNamara that we could win the war entirely with air and naval forces. If we did send in troops, Nitze warned, we would not be able to limit our commitment: it would be like trying to remain "a little bit pregnant." Nitze's younger son remembers his father disconsolate at a greasy spoon diner off a Maryland truck stop, in the summer of 1964, fretting about the war and our growing commitment. It was time to get out, he said.

But Lyndon Johnson, who had replaced Kennedy, did the opposite. Congress gave the White House authority to go to war in August 1964, after the real and imagined attacks on an American destroyer in the Gulf of Tonkin. In February 1965, the Vietcong struck the U.S. helicopter base in Pleiku, killing eight Americans and wounding 126. McGeorge Bundy, visiting the country, was shaken and angered by the bloodshed. In a famous memo to Johnson, he wrote that it was time to escalate our involvement and demonstrate American resolve. We might not win, but at least we would show the world how seriously we took the thwarting of communism. "Even if it fails, the policy will be worth it."

The United States did retaliate fiercely after Pleiku, and soon American planes were bombing North Vietnam. In March, U.S. Marines came ashore at Da Nang to protect American bases. Meanwhile, the United States continued to lose faith in the South Vietnamese government. It had undergone seven reorganizations in one year and was now led by Prime Minister Nguyen Cao Ky, a dandified aviator who liked to wear a black flying suit and a purple scarf, with ivory-handled revolvers at the ready. In his first high-level meeting with U.S. officials, he arrived in tight black pants and red socks. He looked, said one diplomat, like "a saxophone player in a second-rate night club." As in Korea a decade before, and Iraq four decades later, America would find itself disappointed with its allies and surprised at the strength of its opponents.

In June, Nitze visited the country. Marines under his direction were dying and he wanted to see the action firsthand. He landed on an aircraft carrier on the South China Sea and traveled by helicopter to see his people fighting in Da Nang. He then headed to Saigon, the capital, where the commanding general, William Westmoreland, offered heaps of precise estimates of enemy strength. Nitze thought these were bunkum. How could we possibly know exactly how many Vietcong were out there? Westmoreland got angry and demanded to know whether Nitze was accusing him of inflating enemy troop estimates. Nitze denied this. He just did not think the numbers could be that precise.

Returning depressed, Nitze went to see McNamara to tell him the war was going poorly. Westmoreland had recently asked President Johnson for 200,000 more men, but Nitze was convinced that even that many additional troops would not nearly do the job. McNamara asked whether he was recommending that the United States withdraw. Yes, Nitze said.

"If we withdraw from Vietnam, do you believe the Communists will test us in another location?" asked the secretary.

"Yes."

"Can you predict where?"

"No, I can't."

"Well," McNamara said, "under those circumstances, I take it you can't be at all certain that the difficulties of stopping them in the next area they may choose won't be greater than the difficulties of stopping them in South Vietnam."

"No, I can't."

"You offer no alternative," McNamara said, his eyes glazing over.

If he had lost the defense secretary, Nitze still had a chance to persuade the president. That July, a month after Nitze's return, Johnson set up a great debate, calling in advisers of all sorts and asking them whether he should send in the troops Westmoreland had requested. Undersecretary of State George Ball was energetically opposed. But almost everyone else was arguing in favor. Nitze got his chance on July 22, when Johnson met in the White House Cabinet Room with all the service secretaries, the Joint Chiefs of Staff, and several other top aides.

Nitze kept private notes of the wide-ranging meeting. McNamara was worried about the effect of an escalation on the U.S. economy and he wanted to know what we should do if Prime Minister Ky asked us to get out. If that happened, dominoes would clatter down and Southeast Asia would be "gone." Harold Brown, secretary of the air force, worried that "getting pushed out is worse than getting out." Johnson suggested that it might have been a "mistake two years ago to step up." But now, he asked, was victory in sight?

At one point, Johnson asked for Nitze's views, giving him his best chance to change the course of the war. Yes, escalation was likely. Yes, almost everyone in the room seemed to lean to one direction—but only slightly. If Nitze said no and made a strong case, maybe he could push the other service secretaries to do likewise. And if they turned, who knew what would happen next? The exact exchange was recounted in notes taken by Johnson's assistant Jack Valenti.

"Paul, what is your view?"

Nitze noted that the war was not going well, but that it might be possible to reverse this course by sending in more troops. If we acknowledged that we could not beat the Vietcong, and then we withdrew, the world would change and the balance of power with it.

"What are our chances of success?"

"If we want to turn the tide, by putting in more men, it would be about 60/40."

The president pushed ahead. "Would you send in more forces than Westmoreland requests?"

"Yes. Depends on how quickly they—"

"How many? 200 instead of 100?"

"Need another 100 in January."

"Can you do that?"

"Yes."

Nitze was on board. Later, thinking back on the meeting, Brown suggested that Johnson's goal "was to pin everyone down so that, if things went wrong, no one could say he overruled his advisers." If so, the president succeeded.

In his memoirs, Nitze quotes from Valenti's notes verbatim, with one damning exception. When asked by Johnson about the chances of success, he does not write that he answered 60 percent, but that he answered "40 percent."

KENNAN'S MOMENT to weigh in on the Vietnam War came in early 1966. Six months had passed since Nitze's fateful meeting with the president. Two hundred thousand American soldiers were now deployed in the country, and seventeen hundred had died in battle. The United States was now incontrovertibly at war.

Kennan had stayed in Princeton since leaving Belgrade, writing and researching. He confided to his diary that, despite loathing Lyndon Johnson, he would like to be summoned back to Washington. But the call never came.

Until now, Kennan had remained almost entirely silent about the war. He cautioned against the United States going into Vietnam in the late 1940s, and he had forecast disaster, in the mid-1950s, if we did so. As American troops began filtering in, he fretted to himself. The day after the raid in Pleiku and America's retaliatory strike, he wrote in his diary, "The provocation, admittedly, was great; but this bombing of points in Vietnam is a sort of petulant escapism, and will, I fear, lead to no good results." Kennan believed that the policy would fail, and it would not be worth it.

In February 1966, the Senate Foreign Relations Committee called Kennan to testify. That committee's chair, Senator William Fulbright of Arkansas, was an old friend of Kennan and a new critic of the war. He had organized all-day hearings that were to be broadcast live on national television.

Kennan's face and voice were ideal for congressional hearings televised in black and white. The pace suited him; he looked and sounded wise. This would be one of his very finest days.

A year and a half after the Gulf of Tonkin incident, Vietnam was still mysterious to many Americans. They were not sure where it was, or why we were there. If some worried that the United States might be making a mistake, they usually kept quiet. After all, good Americans stand behind their government in wartime. But then this wise and weathered man appeared before Congress. He dressed elegantly, spoke calmly, and understood communism. He did not wear his hair long or denounce America, as students around the country were beginning to do. Most important, he was slowly and calmly dismantling every argument in favor of this obscure, faraway entanglement.

He began by asserting that we had little to gain in this remote part of the world, about which we had traditionally cared little. Now, it was distracting us from vastly more serious matters, such as our relationship with the Soviets. The obscure but bloody fracas was turning people in places of true strategic importance, like Japan, against the United States. Given the recent suppression of a communist uprising and coup in Indonesia, America had little reason to fear dominoes toppling through the region. "There is more respect to be won in the opinion of this world by resolute and courageous liquidation of unsound positions than by the most stubborn pursuit of extravagant or unpromising objectives."

Kennan did not urge immediate withdrawal, which could only prove chaotic and possibly embarrassing. Instead, he wanted the United States to limit its engagement, defend specific enclaves, and wait for a moment when we could pull out more easily. He also wanted to impress upon the Senate a principle: he concluded his testimony by quoting John Quincy Adams. "[America] goes not abroad in search of monsters to destroy," said our sixth president. "She is the well-wisher to the freedom and independence of all. She is the champion and vindicator only of her own."

The questions from the committee began on a positive note. "Mr. Kennan, words simply fail me in expressing the degree to which this testimony of yours has moved me this morning," said Senator Wayne Morse of Oregon. "[It] is going to be referred to for generations to come." Morse then reminded everyone that Kennan was no peacenik. He was the only man in the room to have been thrown out of Moscow by Joseph Stalin.

But soon Kennan was hit with tough questions about how he believed we should withdraw. Slowly, he kept insisting. We could hold a position and wait until things looked up. But would that not make us look weak? Would it not give power and confidence to the communists in Laos, in Cambodia, in the Philippines? No, said Kennan firmly. Then he smartly appealed to America's sense of its strength. A withdrawal "would be a six-month sensation, but I daresay we would survive it in the end."

Senator Frank Lausche, of Ohio, demanded to know how the man who had formulated the containment doctrine had turned so clearly against containing these communists. "The situation has changed," responded Kennan. America did not have infinite resources and now needed to contain both the Soviet and the Chinese communists. If we could save Vietnam at little or no cost, fine. But we now knew this was impossible.

Most essential, Kennan said, was to follow the principle of prudence and wisdom: do what you can when you can. No one could predict exactly how the world would turn out. What mattered was that we stop wasting resources—physical, financial, and emotional. "Perhaps the most important thing a government such as ours can have, as it faces the long-term future of international relations, is the right principles rather than the gift of prophecy."

The only outright hostility was manifested at the end of the day, by Stuart Symington, of Missouri. Symington had just returned from Vietnam, and he made sure Kennan knew it—and that everyone else knew that Kennan had never been there. Every soldier he had talked to was happy that America had joined the battle; all were eager to help the poor Vietnamese, struggling against the vicious communist invaders. When Kennan said that he did not think it was feasible to hold free elections during a civil war, Symington shot back with something between a non sequitur and a churlish word game. "What kind of elections do you think we should have if we should not have free elections?"

The senator then described a village where the Vietcong had "beheaded the children of the chief first, then his wife, then the chief himself." Given that retreat would put our allies into such monstrous hands, he asked, "Morally, do you think we have the right to desert them by going into coastal enclaves?"

Kennan held steady under the barrage. "Senator, if their morale is so shaky that without an offensive strategy on our part they are simply going to give up the fight, I do not think they are worth helping anyway. And, as for the question of our having a moral obligation to them, they have had enormous help from us to date. I mean, goodness, they have had help in billions and billions of dollars. How many countries are you going to give such a claim on our resources and on our help? If they cannot really do the trick with this, I feel strongly that the trouble lies somewhere with them and not with us." As he did throughout the day, Kennan was acting like a man who wanted the best for America.

The testimony was a media sensation. NBC broadcast the entire day of hearings. When CBS elected to show *I Love Lucy* instead, the legendary news president Fred Friendly resigned in protest. Lyndon Johnson tried to deflect the power of the testimony, proclaiming, hollowly, that there was not that much distance between him and Kennan. The next day, McNamara and Nitze spent their morning meeting talking about all the reasons why the secretary of defense thought Kennan's positions were wrong.

Hundreds of letters came in to Kennan. The mailman arrived every day "hauling sacks like Santa Claus," recalled Kennan's secretary, and the vast majority offered praise, not coal. He heard from housewives, servicemen, steelworkers, professors, ministers, friends, friends of friends, musicians, Foreign Service officers, aspiring poets, former missionaries to China. One woman wrote that she had been ironing when the testimony began and become so engrossed that she burned the clothes. Some people urged him to run for the Senate or for president. "My faith in the leaders, not only political, of this country and its ability to survive with honor is renewed. Thank you, thank you, for your willingness to be heard, regardless of the consequences," wrote a woman in Claremont, California. "Thank you for telling how to help our country please continue," wired a woman from Plaistow, New Hampshire.

Some of the letters were long, others short. Some were chaotic, others simple and wise. Probably three quarters came from women. "Your testimony on Vietnam was magnificent," wrote the *New Yorker* writer Marya Mannes. "Not surprising, really, from a man who consistently makes more sense than anyone I know."

IT WAS THE MIDDLE of the night, probably two or three A.M., when the phone rang at the home of Kennan's secretary, Constance Goodman. On the line was Donald Jameson, a Russian expert for the CIA. "Something has come up," he said firmly. "I have to talk with Professor Kennan."

Soon Kennan was awakened at his Pennsylvania farm. Though sleepy and confused, he recognized the voice on the other end. But Jameson was cagey: "We have a tremendous defection here," was all that the spy would say.

It was early March 1967. Ten time zones away, in Delhi, India, a beautiful Russian woman had walked through the glass doors of the American embassy and declared that she was Svetlana Alliluyeva, the daughter of Stalin. "*The* Stalin?" queried one of the diplomats on duty. "Yes."

The story of the decision to defect to the West began in 1963, when Svetlana fell in love with an Indian living in Moscow named Brajesh Singh. The two met in a hospital. He had just had nasal polyps removed to alleviate his chronic breathing problems and had cotton tampons in his nostrils. She had just had her tonsils taken out. They began talking one day while sitting on a couch in the hallway. As they convalesced, they slowly fell for each other. To Svetlana, one of Singh's most endearing traits was that after she revealed her parentage, he never questioned her about it again.

In 1965, she registered in Moscow for a civil marriage with a foreigner. Soon thereafter, Premier Alexei Kosygin summoned her to the Kremlin. "What have you cooked up?" he demanded coldly, sitting in her father's office. "You, a young healthy woman, a sportswoman, couldn't you have found someone here, I mean someone young and strong? What do you want with this old sick Hindu? No, we are positively against it." The marriage registration was revoked; a year and a half later, Singh died—of a broken heart, in Svetlana's opinion. Enraged, she insisted on taking his ashes to India.

It was her first trip outside the Soviet Union, and after a few months away she decided she had had enough of being told what to do. "Every week there was a call for me to come back, to go back, to go back," she recalled. "And I got madder and madder."

The final step was impulsive. She had two children in Moscow, from two previous marriages, aged twenty-one and sixteen, and a bag full of Indian presents to bring home to them. She had spent her whole life in the Soviet Union and it was wrenching to consider leaving her children. But she was a woman who could fall in love quickly, with men and with ideas. At three in the afternoon on March 6, fourteen years and a day after her father's death, she lay in bed, thinking. She had dinner plans that night, and a flight home in two days. But she could not bear the thought of returning. Too many people had given her too many commands for too long. Three hours later, she had packed a suitcase, grabbed her passport, called a cab, and slipped out to the sidewalk outside of the Soviet residence. "Do you know the American embassy?" she asked the driver.

"Why, yes, it's next door."

The Americans took a statement and tried to verify that she was not an imposter, part of some sort of disinformation ploy. They called the CIA back in the United States, but the agency, despite its reputation for omniscience, did not even know that Stalin had had a daughter. Soon enough, however, it decided to take Svetlana at her word and to quickly spirit her away. That night, dressed in a green raincoat and dark sunglasses, she boarded the first flight out of Delhi, along with Robert Rayle of the CIA, and flew to Rome. From there, she went on March 12 to Switzerland.

Svetlana had always lived in her father's dark shadow. She was judged and treated as an extension of him. And now she had become a woman without a country. She was not sure where exactly she wanted to go—any English-speaking country would do. Her main goal was to publish a manuscript composed of letters about her life written to a friend of hers, a physicist named Fyodor Volkenstein. This was her chance to become her own woman and take possession of her own identity. The State Department sent Kennan a copy of the manuscript; Jameson urgently asked him to read it and fly to Geneva.

The press had heard the news of her defection and her destination. Now hundreds of reporters were after her. For several weeks, she moved about the country, hiding at a ski resort at first and then at a convent, where she read *Dr. Zhivago* and relaxed by a lake. The nuns told the one reporter who knocked on their door that, no, Svetlana was not there. "I had a feeling of wonder that I had escaped the Soviets!" she said. "This I will recall even when dead!"

Kennan met Svetlana at a small house in Bern on March 23 and immediately won her over by his bearing—and by the fact that he had clearly read the manuscript carefully and appreciated it. He explained that he would help find a publisher and secure an advance, which would provide her a means of surviving her new life. Stalin had left her no money, because he had none: that part of socialism, at least, he believed in. Rumors flew that Svetlana had come to Switzerland to draw stolen funds from her father's hidden accounts. In reality, she was both princess and pauper.

Kennan's first task was to persuade her to come to America; his next was to persuade America to welcome her. On April 21, 1967, a few weeks after they met, she boarded a flight from Zurich to New York. At Kennedy Airport, she bounded down the stairs of the plane into a throng of reporters. "Hello there, everybody," she declared gracefully. "I am very happy to be here." The *New York Times* published ten stories about her on the day after her arrival, including a statement from Kennan asking that America "rise above the outworn reflexes of the 'Cold War.'" Alliluyeva's defection did not mean that we had won some sort of victory, he said. We should "accept a human being in herself and not just as some sort of extension of her paternity and . . . concede to her the sort of fair chance that millions of other people, displaced by handicap or misfortune from their native countries, have been accorded by our society in earlier periods of our history."

Svetlana charmed everyone at first. To much of the country, she was a symbol of the superiority of the American way. She seemed to genuinely subscribe to what America believed about itself. To the hippies, she was a cool foreigner who did not dress pretentiously. The *New York Times* compared her to "a visiting queen from some small, friendly country." Chip

Bohlen met with her and wrote to Kennan expressing amazement at her "complete self-possession and control." When the CIA gave her an intelligence test, Rayle said, her score was "off the charts." She even earned the respect of Albert Paloesik, the private detective assigned to protect her, after she pulled a rose off her suit and placed it on his sun visor: "She's so nice, I'm almost beginning to like Russians."

It was the beginning of a long and emotionally intense relationship for Kennan, one that would last for decades to come.

13

★ ★ ★

THE OTHER SIDE OF
THE BARRICADES

On October 21, 1967, Paul Nitze looked down from the Pentagon roof. The grounds resembled an enormous beehive, every inch covered and everything buzzing. Tens of thousands of people had come to protest the war in Vietnam. Under flapping Vietcong flags, speakers railed against American aggression. Norman Mailer was taking notes for what would become *The Armies of the Night*. The crowd took a moment of silence to commemorate the recent death of Che Guevara. "Out demons, out! Out demons, out!" chanted the crowd, hoping to exorcise, or perhaps levitate, the Pentagon.

Federal marshals surrounded the Pentagon. Behind them was another line, this one of troops. Radicals tried to provoke the soldiers by tossing vegetables at them; women bared their breasts. A group of angry demonstrators stormed the front of the building, dashing up the steps, pressing forward against the marshals' swinging batons. Six got inside through a side ramp but were quickly ejected.

Nitze was finally deputy secretary of defense, a post for which he had yearned since Kennedy took office. But the promotion could not have come at a more difficult time. By now, the United States had fully Americanized the war in Vietnam and simultaneously created an explosive conflict at home. The protest this afternoon marked the beginning of a new kind of militant resistance to the war that had gone profoundly awry. Soon America's campuses and cities would start to burn.

Organizing an orderly defense of the Pentagon was one of Nitze's first tasks as deputy secretary. He was worried that the demonstrators would try to storm the building and that the guards would overreact. He fretted that radicals would self-immolate, as one protester had done in front of the building two years before. He and McNamara agreed that there should be a light ring of troops around the sprawling complex. Reinforcements would wait in the center courtyard, ready to spring out wherever needed. None of their rifles would be loaded.

The day was stressful, and protests continued throughout the cold night. Radicals and soldiers stared at each other, each seeing their own vision of human debasement. Inside the building, female secretaries on duty dreaded that the protesters would burst in and rape them. But when the protests ended the next morning, no one was dead either inside or outside the Pentagon—which had remained firmly on the ground. Nitze was relieved to be cleaning up beer cans, not bodies.

His interest in the protesters was rather more than casual. At about this time, Nitze became involved in a more secret undertaking. The goal, he recalled in his later years, "was to try and keep tabs on and undermine the radical anti-war movement." His partner, he claimed in a late oral history (as well as in several conversations at different times with his younger son), was Warren Christopher, later Bill Clinton's first secretary of state.

Warren Christopher and I share a curious past. We were appointed to this strange task force working against the radical anti-war movement in the late 60s. He had much more imagination and a more fertile mind in cooking up schemes to tie the other side in knots, to make fun of them, to get them ridiculed and generally to make a mess of the anti-war campaign. I was very proud of our success in that campaign but he found it inconvenient to acknowledge that he had ever had anything to do with it.

Christopher remembers that he helped to organize the defense of the Pentagon, which he describes in his memoirs. And he and Nitze were unquestionably at meetings where domestic intelligence procedures were reviewed, and both served on the Pentagon's secret "303 Committee," which oversaw covert operations. But Christopher says that he cannot recall at all working with Nitze on any secret countersubversion.

★

THEORETICALLY, GEORGE KENNAN was on the same side as the protesters. He, too, wanted to disengage America from South Vietnam; he, too, despised American consumerism.

But Kennan was a conservative, at least in the sense of being a traditionalist. He had a model for what a student should be. In the 1940s, he had proposed a Foreign Service school, with strict discipline and uniforms. Later he wrote that his ideal school would "take young men of high qualities of intellect and character, train them to great hardness of mind and body, to maturity and seriousness of purpose, and to a genuine understanding of our society with all its virtues and imperfections."

This was an aspect of Kennan's obsession with form, and of his bond with Nitze. No matter how much the two men disagreed, they had similar views about how civilized people should behave themselves. Nitze seemed like just the kind of person who could have emerged from Kennan's ideal school. The students with shaggy beards throwing tomatoes and shutting down buildings in the 1960s would have been expelled immediately.

Kennan considered the radicals of this new generation misguided, as well as illiterate, drug-addled, and unhygienic. Like most American reformers, he considered them lamentable moralizers too. He would rail privately against them to friends and then in speeches. Eventually, he took his critique to the pages of the *New York Times Magazine,* where he published an essay titled "Rebels Without a Program" in January 1968.

Writing in the voice of a stern elder, Kennan classified the rebels into two categories: militants and hippies. He found the first group "full of hatred and intolerance." They had an extraordinary certainty concerning their own rectitude and insight—a certainty neither earned nor learned and entirely out of place in a rapidly changing world.

For the hippies, Kennan's feeling was "one of pity, not unmixed, in some instances, with horror." Their greatest error was the belief that somehow, through passive stimuli, such as drugs, humans could release marvelous things from within themselves. "It is only through effort, through doing, through action—never through passive experiences—that man grows creatively." He foresaw nothing but despair for those who sought an unattainable absolute freedom, instead of seeking such freedom as is possible within certain boundaries and rules. Artists and philosophers have known for centuries that serious liberty can exist only within restrictions. So-called free love, for example, would do nothing but destroy the bonds between people. "Love—and by that I mean the receiving of love as well as the bestowal of it—is itself an obligation, and as such is incompatible with the quest for a perfect freedom."

Kennan was not just angry, or worried about the students for their own sake. He feared that their feelings and actions could lead to a societal breakdown. "There could be no greater illusion than the belief that one can treat one's parents unfeelingly and with contempt and yet expect that one's own children will some day treat one otherwise; for such people break the golden chain of affection that binds the generations and gives continuity and meaning to life."

Here Kennan spoke from experience and from a frustrating realization that the old proverb is true: the son is more like his friends than his father. Two of his children were just at this moment rebelling. Christopher, the Kennans' only son, had grown his hair long, wore sandals and tank tops, and had even pierced his ears. Worse, a graduate of Groton, he had transferred from Yale to Santa Cruz. The Kennans' youngest daughter, Wendy, now a teenager, was starting to walk around the house barefoot and becoming more interested in boys than in her schoolwork. The children alarmed their parents, so much so that Kennan and his wife cracked open Wendy's private diary. "I wonder whether his criticism of the students was really because of his frustrations with us," reflected Wendy four decades later. Joan, the second-eldest daughter, says that the children's rebellion, combined with the turmoil around the rest of the country, convinced Kennan "that the end of the world was near."

At the end of the essay, Kennan proclaimed that he saw in the student demonstrators the same forces that had brought totalitarianism upon so many other troubled countries. If necessary, he would put his body on the line to stop them: "People should bear in mind that if this—namely noise, violence and lawlessness—is the way they are going to put their case, then many of us who are no happier than they are about some of the policies that arouse their indignation will have no choice but to place ourselves on the other side of the barricades."

Hundreds of letters flowed in to the *New York Times,* most of them denouncing Kennan. He had struck a nerve, largely because of the style of his critique. The students were used to, and could handle, attacks from the right. They were also accustomed to arguing against liberals, many of whom longed for the students' respect. But Kennan did not care what the protesters thought of him. He simply told the students that they had absolutely everything backward. They were not ushering in a happy, colorful new world. They were the better-off kin of the Russian nihilists who had paved the way for Stalin.

Kennan expanded the essay, along with a selection of the letters, into a book. Norman Podhoretz, the conservative editor of *Commentary*, described it as written in "an old-fashioned voice: cultivated, gentlemanly, poised, self-assured. There is strength in it, there is serenity in it, there is solidity in it, there is authority in it—but not the kind of authority that can easily be associated with repressiveness."

Other intellectuals were less impressed. After Kennan—dressed in a gray suit and silk tie, with a gold watch chain hanging across his vest—spoke at a meeting of the International Association for Cultural Freedom, the playwright Lillian Hellman rose to defend the students. "God knows many of them are fools, and most of them will be sell-outs," she said. "But they're a better generation than we were." Nearly everyone at the meeting agreed. Student leaders, Zbigniew Brzezinski (then teaching at Columbia), and Martin Peretz (future publisher of the *New Republic*) denounced Kennan. Outside the meeting, students chanted. Perhaps the only person in agreement with the guest of dishonor was an FBI informant, carefully taking notes of the exchange.

The most elegant critique came from W. H. Auden. "There is no one in public life for whose integrity and wisdom I have greater respect than Mr. George Kennan," began the poet. Most of Kennan's essay he agreed with. But he took great exception to Kennan's assertion that the student protesters had made him question whether civil disobedience has any role in a democratic society. To oppose that principle, wrote Auden, "is to deny that human history owes anything to its martyrs."

KENNAN, NITZE, AND THE FBI were focusing on the wrong target. As America's youth burned their draft cards and smoked their peace pipes, the Soviet Union was undertaking one of the most damaging spy operations in U.S. history.

It started some time around the end of 1967 in front of a Zayre retail store in Alexandria, Virginia. "Hello, dear friend. Please do not turn around, but walk with me," said a tall Russian to an American who held a folded copy of *Time* magazine under his arm. The American was John

Walker, a navy warrant officer and communications specialist in dire need of cash. He had walked into the Soviet embassy two weeks earlier, offering to sell secrets. The day of his meeting in front of Zayre, he was discussing a contract and a shopping list of secrets that highlighted a document known as a keylist, which would describe the function of America' s KW-7 military encryption machine. No one could read messages sent out by the device unless they had both the keylist and a KW-7.

Walker soon stole and copied the document. In early January 1968, he stuffed it in the bottom of a bag of trash he dropped in a prearranged location in another Virginia suburb. Now, to decipher America's most secret naval communications, all the Soviets had to do was acquire one of the machines.

A couple of weeks later, on January 23, the U.S. intelligence-gathering ship *Pueblo* was idling in international waters off North Korea. On board was one of the top-secret encryption devices. All seemed quiet. Sailors chipped ice off the deck and read the NBA scores sent in from home. Suddenly, a North Korean warship appeared. Then two MiG fighters buzzed the ship and three more warships came into sight. After a brief firefight, the *Pueblo* surrendered: the first American ship captured during peacetime since 1807. North Korea held eighty hostages and some of the United States' most secret signals equipment.

Back at the Pentagon, Paul Nitze "sweated peach pits" as part of the early response team deciding whether to strike back quickly. Should the United States try to sink the North Korean squadron before it could get the *Pueblo* into harbor? The options were limited because some of the planes nearest, based in South Korea, were loaded only with nuclear weapons. Nitze and the rest of the group decided they could do nothing.

Nitze found the incident vexing for two reasons in particular. First, there had been questions beforehand about whether the *Pueblo*'s mission was safe, but Nitze had personally approved it. The navy wanted to go ahead; Nitze later said he did not want "to be throwing dirt in [their] eyes." Second, as a former navy secretary, he knew what losing the ship meant. His notes from the early meetings are full of concern about the KW-7. Even a glimpse of that marvelous device would help the Soviets. Had he known about Walker selling out the keylist, he would have sweated something worse than peach pits.

Ultimately, the seizure of the *Pueblo* and Walker's ongoing espionage enabled the Soviets to track the movements of the American fleet.

According to Pete Earley, a biographer of Walker, the betrayal ultimately allowed the Soviets to decipher "more than one million classified U.S. military messages."

ROBERT MCNAMARA MARCHED confidently into the Pentagon in 1961; seven
years later, he tumbled out, shattered. The day of his departure, Lyndon
Johnson got stuck in an elevator right before the farewell ceremony, the
microphone went dead, and it rained. Nitze stood beside the president and
the secretary as water accumulated on McNamara's famous eyeglasses. The
White House ceremony rendered McNamara speechless. "Mr. President,"
began the worn-out secretary, "I can't find words to say what lies in my
heart. I think I had better respond on another occasion."

McNamara had come to doubt the war and Johnson had come to
doubt McNamara. The human computer had feelings—and now they
were of guilt, remorse, and confusion. Johnson packed him off to run the
World Bank and called in a longtime friend, Clark Clifford, to be defense
secretary.

Once again, a president had passed over Nitze. *Time* had listed him as
one of the leading candidates for the job, even if "perhaps too old," at sixty.
Nitze, however, felt perfectly capable. "I am sorry that LBJ went further
and missed the opportunity so clearly before him," wrote Dean Acheson.
"I do hope you get a chance at a top job. . . . You are so damned good!"

But Johnson and Nitze had never really gotten along. After the Texan's
succession to the presidency in 1963, he had called Nitze in for a meeting.
The then navy secretary had prepared diligently. But Johnson asked no
questions. Instead, he made Nitze sit on a couch while he himself went
about his presidential business: placing phone calls, dictating to his secretary, watching the three televisions in his office. After several hours,
Nitze was allowed to leave. Reflecting on the odd encounter, he decided it
was a test: Johnson was trying to size him up and decide how loyal he
would be.

Johnson's biggest concern about Nitze was his supposed softness on
the war. According to George Elsey, at the time a special assistant to the
secretary of defense, "Clifford was acutely aware that Nitze was better
prepared to be secretary of defense than he was and that Paul really deserved the job. But he did not get it because LBJ was a little worried about
how tough a guy Nitze was."

Nitze was deeply disappointed at the snub; his wife gave him two singing canaries to console him. But Clifford was now his boss, and Nitze would do his best. As he left a press conference the day Clifford's appointment was announced, a reporter asked Nitze, "What are you going to do now?" "Going back to work," he responded.

His first task was to educate the new secretary on the status of the war, a job that began each morning at 8:30 when the two men would join a small group. Clifford would begin the meeting by saying, "Paul, you're on," whereupon Nitze would speak his mind, generally about Vietnam.

Clifford believed the war was absolutely winnable. He was, remembered Nitze, a "fire-breathing hawk." Nitze wanted to slow down and disengage. As he had consistently argued, the United States had to prioritize. Saving South Vietnam was not worth nothing, but it was not worth everything. A brutal Vietcong offensive during the Tet holidays in January had shown how strong the insurgency was. Nitze recommended halting our bombing and opening negotiations.

The big question facing the department was whether to accede to General William Westmoreland's request for 206,000 additional troops. Two weeks into Clifford's tenure, the Senate called for someone from the Pentagon to justify the contemplated buildup. Johnson thought Clifford too green to handle the job. Nitze would have to do it.

AT JUST THIS MOMENT, Kennan decided to involve himself in presidential politics for the first time since 1956. His candidate was Eugene McCarthy, the senior senator from Minnesota, who was running on a platform of peace in Vietnam. The preferred candidate of young left-wing idealists, McCarthy himself was a near analogue to Kennan. Soft-spoken and philosophical, McCarthy had studied in a monastery when younger. He took breaks from the campaign trail to read poetry. Like Kennan, he appeared frail but was physically strong. He had played semi-pro baseball and, after losing the election, would report ably on the World Series for *Life* magazine. Rather too obviously, he considered himself smarter than the journalists who covered him. He was a politician with a love for many things besides politics.

Kennan's support offered the campaign respectability and depth at a time when it looked hopeless. He gave his elegant endorsement on February 29, 1968, Robert McNamara's last day in office. He began with a long lament about the failures of America's Vietnam policy and the probability that nothing would change if Johnson ended up running against Richard Nixon, the likely Republican nominee. It was time, he declared, to "register an electoral protest." The *New York Review of Books* soon reprinted the speech. To Democratic intellectuals, Kennan's endorsement made McCarthy seem a bit less like an imposter.

An electoral protest was indeed registered. On March 12, McCarthy won 42 percent of the vote in the New Hampshire primary. Four days later, Robert Kennedy, sensing the president's vulnerability, declared his own candidacy. Johnson both despised and feared Kennedy. His nomination was now clearly in doubt.

THE DAY KENNEDY entered the race, Nitze wrote Johnson a letter. He had spent a sleepless night thinking about having to testify and decided he could not do it. He did not believe in the president's policy and could not bring himself to stand up for it in front of a Senate committee and millions of TV viewers. "I do not feel myself to be in a position properly to defend the Executive Branch in a debate before the Foreign Relations Committee," he wrote in a letter. He offered to resign if asked.

First thing in the morning, he showed the note to Clifford, who read it and said: "I had no idea you felt so strongly about this."

"Well, now you know."

Clifford agreed to pass the letter on to the president. He asked only that Nitze drop the offer to resign.

Johnson was furious. A few days later, he called his former mentor, Senator Richard Russell, of Georgia, and vented as the White House tape recorder ran. The only thing saving Nitze's skin was that he knew how to run the department and Clifford did not.

"You take Nitze," fumed the president. "Refused to testify on the MAP bill on the military assistance. Just said he didn't believe in the policy. Did not think we ought to be in Vietnam. Just wouldn't do it. Just insubordinate. Wrote me a letter."

"Well, I would have got him out of there the next day," said Russell.

"Well, I would, but Clifford said he just can't do it so quickly by himself . . ."

"Well, Clifford ought to know some good men he could bring in there."

"Well, there are, but it is a question of just how fast you disrupt them until he can kind of get his feet on the ground."

Clifford's on-the-job crash course in Vietnam policy turned him against the war—with Nitze's vehemence speeding the transition along. Between January and March of 1968, the percentage of Americans who approved of Johnson's handling of the war had plummeted, from 40 to 26. And now one of the most formidable lawyers in Washington was arguing the doves' case.

Not even Johnson could hold out against the pressure from both the public and his closest confidants. By the end of the month, he had announced the recall of General Westmoreland and declared that he would soon give a major speech on the war.

Nitze found the early drafts frustrating. He scrawled a memo to himself headed "Defects of old speech," noting that it was just "more of the same" with no reference to negotiations or de-escalation. But Johnson kept revising. Gradually, he came up with a speech that described a substantial de-escalation. Most important, the United States would not send 206,000 troops. It would send 13,500.

But the biggest surprise came at the end.

With American sons in the fields far away, with America's future under challenge right here at home, with our hopes and the world's hopes for peace in the balance every day, I do not believe that I should devote an hour or a day of my time to any personal partisan causes or to any duties other than the awesome duties of this office—the Presidency of your country.

Accordingly, I shall not seek, and I will not accept, the nomination of my party for another term as your President.

MANY PEOPLE'S FEELINGS about the Vietnam War seemed to travel on a long disassembly line heading in one direction: growing doubt, rejection, and then ever increasing disgust and opposition. George Kennan, Robert Kennedy, McGeorge Bundy, Robert McNamara, Stuart Symington, and Clark Clifford all took this journey. But, as so much of the country, and so many of his colleagues, flew past, Paul Nitze seemed to stay motionless. Eventually, the mere act of standing still turned him into, relatively speaking, a hawk.

During the last few months of Johnson's tenure, Nitze was certainly to the right of his immediate boss. By the fall of 1968, Clifford had decided that a peace agreement was necessary for moral reasons—and political ones too. In early September, Johnson called Clifford and declared that he wanted the secretary to devote the rest of his tenure to working out a peace deal, partly to stave off the future denunciations of Richard Nixon, who would likely be the next president. "I'd like to let Nitze run the Department," Johnson told Clifford. The secretary's job would be to "try to figure out things that A—will give us some hope of success, that B—will at least be treating the American people fair, and C—that we'll damn sure look good before an investigating committee in February when they say what in the hell did you do."

To Nitze, this attitude took things a step too far. Yes, peace was desirable. But certain prices were too high to pay, and one such price was leverage with Moscow. Clifford, he would later say, had become "an absolute incontinent cut-and-runner."

In mid-September, Clifford came to one of the 8:30 A.M. meetings and declared that he wanted to bring the Russians into settlement talks. The previous summer, the two sides had planned to engage in arms negotiation. But in August the Soviet Union invaded Czechoslovakia and crushed the nascent economic and political liberalization in that still communist country; negotiations were aborted. Now, Clifford was proposing a trade. If Czechoslovakia kept "quiet for a week" and Premier Kosygin pushed the Vietnamese to the negotiating table, the United States would reopen arms talks and stop bombing North Vietnam.

Nitze detonated. "It's asinine—it's 'pissing' away an advantage we have! It'll undo the North Atlantic alliance if LBJ gets into bed with Kosygin."

"C[lark] M[cAdams] C[lifford] grows irritated!" wrote the note taker. Nitze, the secretary pointed out, had long wanted the Soviets to help with the negotiations. Yes, said Nitze, but not now. The Soviets had made a terrible mistake by going into Czechoslovakia. World opinion was turning against them; other communist parties throughout the world were aghast. Why give any indication that we could countenance this outrage?

The secretary then declared, "I'm for anything that will get the president to stop the bombing!"

"No, I'm not!" Nitze countered. "Not if it means doing things contrary to our national interest! Wrecking NATO by playing footsie with Kosygin [would] do so!"

As the meeting wound down, Clifford scolded his deputy. "Do not deprecate the concept of finding the means of persuading the President to stop the bombing in the North and until we get it stopped we can't get anyplace. I'm ready to take risks elsewhere, anywhere!"

"Nitze explodes again," wrote the note taker. "I feel passionately," Nitze told Clifford, "not to jeopardize U.S. boys, ever, any time, any place and there is no need now to play into Soviet hands."

Eventually, Nitze's position won out. No arms negotiations took place that fall.

/

IN HIS ESSAY on the student protesters, Kennan declared that they might one day see him on the "other side of the barricades." In fact, he was already there. In the late 1960s, Kennan was actively working with the FBI, analyzing information sent to him about students and blacks who, as he saw it, threatened America.

It was a familiar role for Kennan. As a young Foreign Service officer in 1931, he had sent back to Washington a list of Americans residing in Moscow whom he considered possible communist sympathizers. While interned in Germany in 1942, according to his FBI file, he had reported back on seven fellow detainees "on whom there was some suspicion regarding their attitudes and loyalties." As director of the Policy Planning Staff, according to other bureau files, "he had a weekly session with the FBI liaison representative and briefed him on the inside story of the Department's activities. The Bureau in turn made available confidential information to him." In 1951, a top aide to the FBI director, J. Edgar Hoover, wrote, "You will recall that George F. Kennan has always been friendly to the Bureau, furnishing pertinent and helpful information when in the State Department, etc."

Kennan's contact in the bureau in the late 1960s and early 1970s was William C. Sullivan, an assistant to the director for investigations. They had first met in 1963 and quickly struck up a friendship. Sullivan was a witty and well-read man with advanced degrees in both law and education. He quoted Santayana and Socrates in his letters and sent Kennan copies of his erudite speeches (one example: "Communism and the American Negro"). Ultimately, Sullivan became the third-highest-ranking official in the bureau; the *New York Times* described him as the only liberal Democrat ever to break into Hoover's inner circle.

But Sullivan, like Kennan, did not take a liberal stance on all matters. He was in charge of the FBI's counterintelligence program, COINTEL-PRO, against groups it considered extremist in the late 1960s, and it was he who recommended bugging Martin Luther King Jr.'s hotel rooms. After the 1963 March on Washington, Sullivan had written a memo declaring that the bureau "must mark [King] now, if we have not done so before, as the most dangerous Negro of the future in this nation."

Like Kennan, Sullivan was extremely concerned about the student left. The two exchanged letters about the need to thwart the radicals, with Sullivan hinting of devious operations under way by his organization. By 1970, the Black Panther Party had become a focus of anxiety for both men and Sullivan frequently sent Kennan secret FBI files on Black Panther leaders. By 1971, Kennan had accumulated a large dossier, ranging from a collection of speeches by the Panthers' leader Stokely Carmichael to campus flyers with titles like "Honkie Pig Chairman of Afro-American Studies Program."

"I must say that I stand in amazement," Kennan wrote to Sullivan in response, "at the fact that an organization can publish materials of this nature and still be permitted to carry on openly, and apparently legally, in our country." Kennan suggested the speedy passage of laws to make this kind of speech illegal and to give the government maximum discretion in punishing it.

> Any effective action to deal with these seditious factions in our national life, many of which operate on the very borderline between what is proper and improper, tolerable and intolerable, will require a series of rapid and fine decisions which the Executive Branch of the government ought to be empowered to take on its own responsibility, and for which it ought to be answerable only to the voters at the next election but not to the press or even to the courts.

In 1971, Sullivan was dismissed after running afoul of Hoover. The journalist Robert Novak, a close friend and confidant, recalls that the next year Sullivan told him that someday Novak "probably would read about his death in some kind of accident but not to believe it. It would be murder." Gradually, Sullivan became a very public critic of the FBI: questioning Hoover's mental stability in the director's later years and airing some of the bureau's dirty secrets before congressional committees.

In November 1977, shortly before another scheduled appearance in front of a House committee, he was shot in the head while walking in the woods. The shooter, a young hunter, said that he thought he had seen a deer.

NITZE, NOW SIXTY-TWO, desperately wanted to stay in government when the Nixon administration moved in. Having worked for Truman, Kennedy, and Johnson, he knew he did not have a chance at a top job. But he told friends that he would willingly accept a significant demotion. When nothing appeared immediately, he began to scratch out a draft of a possible memoir, beginning with the question "Has my generation . . . anything of value to pass on to the next generation?"

The answer, of course, was yes. And Nitze started by explaining how he learned to love his country and see himself as an American. He had not considered himself a patriot when he worked on Wall Street. But this changed when he arrived in Washington, met George Marshall, and learned that making decisions for the good of one's country was "morally superior to what I had experienced before and also more effective."

Nitze did not have a chance to elaborate on those thoughts. The new secretary of defense was a former congressman named Melvin Laird who had dealt with Nitze before and considered him a "hell of a good guy." Wanting to find a place for him, Laird immediately called his friends on Capitol Hill to see whether Nitze could win confirmation to his old job running ISA. A firm answer came back from Barry Goldwater: no way. The Arizona senator believed, erroneously, that Nitze had been behind the famous "daisy ad" that Lyndon Johnson used against Goldwater during the 1964 presidential campaign—a spot showing a little girl counting daisy petals, followed by a mushroom cloud that implied that a vote for Goldwater was a vote for nuclear war.

The left shot down Laird's other idea: making Nitze ambassador to West Germany. This time the fusillade came from Senator William Fulbright, a leading critic of the war who believed that Nitze had lied to him in 1967 about the Gulf of Tonkin attack. The senator apparently agreed with Carl Marcy, chief of staff of the Senate Foreign Relations Committee, who wrote to Fulbright: "[You are going to be asked] if you have any objections to Paul Nitze being named Ambassador to Bonn. My comment is that Nitze is an 'imperialist' at heart, and would not be a good person to support U.S. troop withdrawals and, therefore, might be a good Ambassador to Mali or some other equivalent position—but not Bonn."

Twice rebuffed, Nitze came up with an alternative plan. In the spring of 1969, he started with Dean Acheson the Committee to Maintain a Prudent Defense Policy. The group was dedicated to protecting the funding for Safeguard, a system of missile defense designed to protect American ICBMs. As planned, radar would track incoming Soviet warheads and then Safeguard would fire up its own missiles to destroy them. Critics called it a waste; Nitze considered it a potentially useful line of defense against a Soviet first strike. Nitze's first task was to hire some interns and research assistants. On the basis of friends' recommendations, he settled on three promising young men—Richard Perle, Peter Wilson, and Paul Wolfowitz—with a fourth, Edward Luttwak, joining the staff soon after.

THE INTERNS WERE all unknown graduate students in their twenties who were connected to the nuclear strategist Albert Wohlstetter, a friend of Nitze's. Perle had dated Wohlstetter's daughter and then roomed with Luttwak at the London School of Economics. Wolfowitz and Wilson had studied under Wohlstetter. Nitze did not know much about them when they started: in a memo written before they began, he referred to Perle as "Pearl" and declared that he had hired "Jack Wolfowitz," actually his recruit's father.

But Nitze quickly got to know his charges and impressed them. Perle recalls: "I was blown away by the rigor of his thinking. I marveled at his ability to take a complicated issue and break it down. He also had extraordinary abilities as a raconteur."

None of the four interns had quite found his identity yet. Luttwak—a new visitor to America who had been born in Romania and grown up in Italy and England—says he spent much of the summer chasing girls and learning about Washington's social life. ("At most of the restaurants in those days, they served food that would be rejected by prisoners in Italy.") Wilson, smart and sincere, would tutor Luttwak on the workings of American politics. Perle was a doctoral student in the process of abandoning his dissertation. Wolfowitz was scrounging for money.

Nitze's work ethic inspired all of them. If a senator made a statement against the missile defense system at ten in the morning, Perle remembers, they would have a position paper circulating among their allies by noon. Their closest confidant was Dorothy Fosdick, Nitze's old friend from the Policy Planning Staff. Now she was helping the four plot strategy aimed at winning over swing senators in what she knew would be a close vote on whether to fund the system. Appraising the odds early on, the group counted forty-one senators opposed, forty in favor, and nineteen undecided. They assumed their work would be tough, because few members of Congress found the topic of defense engaging. "Psychologically I think it is easier to get people emotionally involved in things that are expressive of macho," said Nitze. "As far as macho is concerned, it is the offense which is most attractive; the defense suggests somebody that is sly, deceptive, dishonest."

If Nitze impressed the interns, they equally impressed him. They churned out complex and sophisticated papers, many anticipating the great debates about missile defense to come. When opponents argued, for example, that missile defense was futile—no defensive system could stop every missile, and a single hit on a city could have utterly devastating consequences—they countered that the goal of Safeguard was not to protect cities; it was to protect America's own missiles—a goal where 90 percent, or 50 percent, effectiveness could make a vast difference. When opponents suggested that we could obviate any need for missile defense by adopting a policy of "launch on warning"—firing our missiles when our radars picked up a Soviet attack—the quartet had a complex rebuttal. First, we would have to be sure that our radars had actually picked up missiles; second, we might not have enough time to launch, particularly if we double-checked to make sure we were not tracking geese; third, radiation from the incoming missiles could fry controls and prevent a launch.

The best argument, however, was that it's hard to bargain away a system one does not have. Negotiations would soon begin with the Soviets, who were already constructing a missile defense array of their own. If we cut ours, we would lose leverage. This was an argument greatly appreciated by the White House and the State Department, although the new national security adviser, Henry Kissinger, fretted in a phone call to Secretary of State William Rogers that a future job given to Nitze would be seen as "payoff for his ABM testimony."

Ultimately, Nitze's side won by one vote. More important, four smart young men had just had a tremendous learning experience. Wilson would go on to become a defense analyst at RAND. Luttwak would quickly become a well-known strategic analyst, earning fame when his book *Coup d'Etat: A Practical Handbook* was found on the desk of a general who had almost succeeded in seizing power in Morocco in 1971. Wolfowitz and Perle would find themselves at the conservative center of almost every major foreign-policy debate through the second Iraq war.

In the middle of the Safeguard debate, Laird called again. He had a job that Nitze could fill, one that did not require Senate confirmation: the post of a negotiator in what would be called the Strategic Arms Limitation Talks, or SALT. Moving back to the Pentagon, and a tiny windowless office, Nitze now had a chance to try to bargain away the system his charges were working so hard to save.

GEORGE KENNAN ALWAYS WANTED peace and quiet. When he got it, he used it to flagellate himself.

In the summer of 1968, as America convulsed and Soviet tanks rolled into Prague, Kennan sat on his boat, off the Norwegian coast, and brooded.

> The extreme unhappiness with which I confront the prospects of returning home arises not just from the hopeless profusion of my obligations and involvement but also from awareness of my own personal failings and the lack of success I have had in overcoming them. My congenital immaturity of bearing and conduct; my garrulousness; the difficulty I find rejecting hard liquor when it is offered to me as part of hospitality; the uncontrollable wandering eye—all these things are unworthy of the rest of me. They limit what I could make out of myself and what I could contribute in the final years of active life.

He then lamented how hard doing all that would be, but how necessary too. "What, after all, is the alternative? A long series of trivial gratifications, punctuated by moments of dull, frightening despair?"

His fears were personal, national, and global. His diary records dark dreams about losing his memory, a sense of profound helplessness over Vietnam, and a growing dread of nuclear calamity. The use of those dreadful weapons had become "in part a certainty and in the other part a near-certainty."

When he returned to the United States, he kept his distance from politics. He met in October with Edmund Muskie, the Democratic vice presidential candidate. But Kennan stayed off the campaign trail. "I thought that if any president were to appoint me to office later," he wrote in his diary, "my value to him and to the country would be greater if I were known to the public, and viewed by the public, as a non-partisan diplomat and academic person, rather than as someone to whom the president was in political debt."

This judgment proved correct. When Richard Nixon came into office, Kennan suddenly had access to the White House again. Kissinger admired Kennan's writing and thinking and called him in with some frequency.

Kennan was far from the most influential adviser, but in at least one instance he was the most perceptive. In the winter of 1969–1970, he told Kissinger that he had picked up a series of subtle signs that the administration was planning to open up relations with China. This was two years before the pair surprised the world with their triumphant accord with Mao Zedong.

AFTER BOUNDING DOWN the steps of her airplane at JFK, Svetlana had continued to charm. A few days after her arrival, she had given a live-broadcast press conference at the Plaza Hotel in New York. She came across as flirtatious, beautiful, and witty. Asked whether she would become an American citizen, she responded: "I think that before the marriage should be love. So if I love this country and this country will love me, then the marriage will be settled. But I cannot say now."

She spent the next few months living on Kennan's farm. He had left for a trip to Africa, but his daughter Joan had offered to help take care of Svetlana. So the former grand duchess of the Kremlin drove off to East Berlin, Pennsylvania, to spend a summer working on her memoirs, drinking peach schnapps, and living with a constantly changing mix of Kennan's children and grandchildren.

With Kennan's help, she had sold her memoirs for around $1.5 million and was wealthy for the first time in her life. But her relationship with America was not as happy as she might have wished. Knowing almost no one besides the Kennans, she suddenly had to deal with being a celebrity. "The public! There really is no such thing in the Soviet Union. There is no public opinion, no public information, no public reactions," she wrote. "Now I had to get accustomed to something I found very difficult: this new sensation of life as on a stage."

The KGB gave Svetlana the code name Kukushka—which means both "cuckoo bird" and "escaped convict"—and sent an agent to try to kidnap her. When the attempt failed, they began a disinformation campaign against her, claiming she was mentally unstable. The leader of Moscow's Russian Orthodox church likened Svetlana to Judas. "How can one combine affiliation with a religion which teaches selfless love to fellow humans, with unnatural desertion by a mother of her children, with betrayal of her country and desecration of it?" Her two children, still living in Moscow, denounced her as well, possibly after KGB prompting.

The KGB then tried, unsuccessfully, to win her back. Donald Jameson, Kennan's contact at the CIA, wrote to him about their efforts. "Two KGB officers in New York have mentioned her recently to contacts of theirs. In both cases, the content of their comments seemed to foreshadow an attempt to urge Svetlana to return to the Soviet Union for family reasons. Maybe some day they will learn that kind of entreaty is most effective when it precedes the shillelagh attack rather than follows it."

Any possibility of a willing return to Moscow ended one evening when Svetlana was alone at the farm with some of Kennan's young grandchildren and his seventeen-year-old son, Christopher. She called everyone together near a grill out on the veranda. The coals were still hot and she asked Christopher to run for some lighter fluid. "You are all present here to witness a solemn moment," she declared. "I am burning my Soviet passport in answer to lies and calumny." The passport flared up and Svetlana blew the ashes into the air.

When Kennan returned to the United States from Africa, he arranged for Svetlana to live temporarily in Princeton. They began to have tea and to dine together. He invited important friends over to meet her and helped her find an apartment to rent. They watched the 1968 election together. Throughout her life, Svetlana had befriended older men, and Kennan enjoyed the role of friend and guardian. Stalin had thrown him out of Moscow; now he was the protector of the tyrant's daughter.

But the friendship was not an easy one. Svetlana was impetuous—she bought the first house a real estate agent showed her, on the spot—and temperamental. By the fall of 1968, she was also beginning to believe that the lawyer whom Kennan had secured for her, Maurice Greenbaum, had served her rather poorly. She was particularly angry that the copyright for her first book was issued in her translator's name.

Eventually, the same impulsiveness that drove her from Moscow drove her from Princeton. While living in her new home, she began receiving letters from Olgivanna Lloyd Wright, widow of the famous architect and matriarch of the compound devoted to his memory, Taliesin West. Wright wanted Svetlana to come and visit. The letters were persistent and persuasive and eventually Svetlana gave in. She paid no heed when friends told her the place was "strange."

Wright, it turned out, believed that she had found the reincarnation of her own daughter, also named Svetlana, who had died in a car crash. Her hope was that this new Svetlana would replace the old one. She got just what she wanted when Svetlana fell immediately in love with Wesley Peters, the first Svetlana's widower, and married him within three weeks of her arrival.

But it did not take long for Svetlana, now forty-four, to realize that she could not tolerate life at the compound, where everyone was supposed to be totally subservient to Wright: to confess to her and to listen to her. A few months after the wedding, she wrote to Kennan, referring to him as her adoptive father, and said that she loved Wes but feared for her future. Olgivanna Wright seemed all too much like a man Svetlana had known and observed closely: Joseph Stalin. "I see [similarities] every day and every minute."

The breaking point occurred when Svetlana became pregnant. To Wright, this was an unpardonable sin. No children had been born into the community since Frank Lloyd Wright's death in 1959. His widow believed that a new soul would disrupt her communication with the dead.

Wright could not bring herself to confront Svetlana directly, so she telephoned Kennan and urged him to force Svetlana to have an abortion and put an end to "this folly." She harangued him for forty minutes as he politely tried to reason with her; she threatened to travel to Princeton to make the case personally. Eventually, Kennan was able to signal Annelise to pick up another phone and declare that he had a guest and must end the conversation.

Svetlana soon left Taliesin West and divorced Wes. She had gained a beloved daughter, lost most of her money to Wes and the compound, and realized that even America could make her feel like she was living under totalitarianism. She headed back to Princeton.

★ ★ ★

14

THIS DELEGATION IS A DISASTER

O

The 1970s were the decade when everyone in Washington learned the fateful acronyms. Our silos were stocked with ICBMs (intercontinental ballistic missiles) that were armed with MIRVs (multiple independently targetable reentry vehicles). If the Soviets attacked, our best bet would be to counter with SLBMs (submarine launched ballistic missiles) or, maybe one day, stop them with anti-ballistic missile (ABM) systems.

Nitze had helped coin the new vocabulary and now he would master it. He studied the weapons the way a monk studies Scripture. Every word, and every weapon, had meaning. World peace hinged on a stable relationship between the U.S. and Soviet arsenals, and that stability could hinge on apparently tiny details. If Moscow were allowed to build just a few more of *these,* with *those* components, and we did not counter with *this,* the Soviets might be tempted to start a war. He had begun his reflections on the balance of atomic weaponry in Hiroshima with the Strategic Bombing Survey and had continued them since. Both at the beginning and at the end of the decade, he knew more about nuclear weapons than almost any other man alive.

Nitze's fascinated immersion was matched by Kennan's willfully uncomprehending alienation. To him, the acronyms and the details were preposterous. What could one, or twenty, or a hundred more of these horrors possibly mean if we already had enough to turn the planet into Venus? In one sense, the stockpiles were all too real. In another sense, they were imaginary, for by tinkering with numbers and fretting over ratios, we created an illusion of control. The truth was that we had built something far too powerful for us to manage. Kennan did not reach back to Hiroshima; he reached back to his trip to Hamburg after World War II, when he concluded that no rational man could any longer countenance war on a grand scale, even with nonnuclear weapons.

These two men reached these opposed conclusions through temperament and experience. One boy had spent his youth building home telephone sets; the other had quietly written poetry. One came to trust and believe in the power of numbers, whether in the form of Clarence Dillon's financial charts or Albert Speer's lists of ball-bearing factories. The other believed that technology destroyed more than it created. One spent his life gaining confidence: he was unusually popular, generally the smartest man in the room, and always well off. From the death of his mother soon after birth, the other spent his life learning doubt—self-doubt as well as doubt in the wisdom of the men making decisions for the world. One man's career had led him to believe that the U.S. government, especially when he was involved, could make sound decisions. The other man felt that the U.S. government was all too likely to go astray. One believed he could answer the new epic questions; the other believed that nobody could do so, and that the ghastly weapons were now in the saddle and riding mankind.

The two men had agreed on a great deal in the previous twenty years— Korea, Eisenhower, and Vietnam. But by the end of the 1970s, when nuclear weapons haunted every element of America foreign policy, Nitze and Kennan seemed to agree on nothing. Now they truly became the hawk and the dove.

IN OCTOBER 1969, Richard Nixon and Henry Kissinger decided to fake the beginning of a nuclear war. Eighteen nuclear-armed B-52s soared off from the western United States toward the Soviet Union. For three days, they danced around enemy territory, taunting Soviet defenses and refueling in air. The pilots were ready to discharge their weapons on command. Neither they nor the Soviets knew what the mission was. It might be the beginning of the war to end it all—or it might be a game played by a power-drunk new president and national security adviser.

It was the latter. The point of this perilous exercise, which remained a secret for forty years, was to convince the Soviets that Nixon was a madman. If they did not push the North Vietnamese toward peace, or make concessions elsewhere, this president might darn well press the red button.

Paul Nitze would never know about the feint, but it was designed partly for his benefit. Two weeks after the bombers returned, he set out for Finland as part of the American delegation to the Strategic Arms Limitation Talks. After the humiliations in Berlin and Cuba, the Soviets had begun frantically building weapons. The Americans, worn out by Vietnam, had slowed. Now the two superpowers had roughly equal strength. The Soviets had bigger and more numerous missiles; the Americans had better and more accurate ones. The Soviets led in large land-based missiles; the Americans led in intermediate-range missiles, submarine-launched missiles, and bombers. The task of the next thirty months—during which the SALT talks rotated between Helsinki and Vienna—was to equilibrate the arsenals.

Thus began a long, grinding wrestling match. Each side sought a deal that provided it a significant advantage while appearing fair. Nitze, for example, spent much time early on trying to recenter the talks on the metric called throw weight. Instead of just counting missiles, Nitze argued, we should compare the heft of the weaponry each missile could carry over a particular range. Not incidentally, this approach took into account the lead the Soviets had in size but ignored the American lead in accuracy. Nitze was like an apple farmer telling a watermelon grower that produce should be taxed only on weight.

If the talks were akin to a wrestling match, both sides used more than a few illegal holds. According to Nitze, the Soviets rented an apartment in the building across from the American offices in Helsinki and tried to spy with high-powered cameras and eavesdropping devices. At night, the Soviets would try to get the Americans liquored up, in the hopes that their secrets would spill. But still there was fun and camaraderie. Alexei Obukhov, a young member of the Soviet delegation, remembers walking into a sauna to find Nitze sitting there with the heat blasting. The American treated him to a long discourse on the unpredictability of human life.

Each side had one major goal for the meetings. The United States wanted to shrink the Soviet arsenal. The USSR feared, and wanted to limit, American missile defense technology. Nitze wanted to fuse the two issues and make a grand deal. The Americans would scrap their defense projects and the Soviets would agree to stop building their giant missiles. But these hopes were sunk by the man Nitze considered the Iago of the negotiations: Henry Kissinger.

Though the two men admired each other's intellects, they had never quite made peace after their dispute surrounding Nitze's book review in 1957. The relationship was not improved when, at the very beginning of the talks, Nixon and Kissinger had pulled Nitze in for a private meeting and declared that they did not have confidence in the putative leader of the delegation, Gerard Smith. Would Nitze be willing to communicate with the White House via a back channel? Nitze declined the offer and later declared it unseemly.

If Nitze did not want to pass secret documents *to* Kissinger, he was not above passing on information *about* him. The prime recipient was the national security adviser's bureaucratic rival, Secretary of Defense Melvin Laird, to whom Nitze gave information from the confidential conversations that Kissinger was holding with the Soviet ambassador, Anatoly Dobrynin. In these talks, Nitze believed, Kissinger's technical ignorance, or his craving for political acclaim, had led to damaging mistakes. Kissinger, meanwhile, had little patience for Nitze's endless fine-grained distinctions. Discussing detailed negotiating instructions with Smith on a secure phone one day, Kissinger mentioned Nitze and then said "I have seen more Talmudic studies from Defense than I thought possible." In March 1971, Kissinger told Laird on the phone that "this delegation is a disaster."

The first big clash came in May 1971 when Nixon and Kissinger agreed to split the issues of missile defense and arms reductions. Instead of the trade Nitze sought, the United States and the Soviet Union would make a binding deal on ABM systems while reaching a merely temporary agreement on the size of strategic arsenals. Nitze was furious both at the deal and at the back channel used to get it done. It was, he thought, a political stunt.

Nixon would soon have his own reasons to be angry with Nitze. In June, the *New York Times* began publishing a long series of leaked Defense Department documents, soon to be known as the Pentagon Papers, which traced the decisions that led the United States into Vietnam. Enraged, Nixon demanded to know how the leaker, a former Nitze aide named Daniel Ellsberg, had managed to lay his hands on the papers. As the former deputy secretary of defense, Nitze was a suspect, for he was one of a very small handful of people with a copy of the study. Talking about the leak—and about the possibility that they could break into the National Archives to steal documents themselves—Nixon asked his aide John Ehrlichman, "What about Nitze?"

Ehrlichman responded, "He's a co-conspirator."

Nixon was surprised. "Paul Nitze is?"

"I'm quite sure. Quite sure he's the guy."

"Damn."

In reality, Nitze was completely innocent; Ehrlichman had almost certainly confused him with former assistant secretary of defense Paul Warnke, whose papers Ellsberg had actually used. It is not clear when exactly the president learned that Nitze had nothing to do with the leak.

THE SALT NEGOTIATIONS were slow, tedious, arduous work. The two sides debated the exact kinds of radar used in their ABM systems and the mechanics of their submarine engines. As usual, Nitze was in full command of the minutiae. "You've got to know your cavitation when you go talk to Nitze," proclaimed one overwhelmed aide, referring to the noise that a submarine's propeller makes.

Ultimately a deal was going to get done: 1972 was a presidential election year, so Nixon was eager to sign something. And Leonid Brezhnev, the Soviet premier, was already beginning to notice the strains caused by his country's buildup. In the spring of 1972, he raged at his hard-line defense minister, Andrei Grechko: "If we make no concessions, the nuclear arms race will go further. Can you give me, the commander-in-chief of armed forces, a firm guarantee that in such a situation we will get superiority over the United States and the correlation of forces will become more advantageous to us?" When Grechko mumbled back, Brezhnev slammed the argument shut. "Then what is wrong? Why should we continue to exhaust our economy, increase military expenses?"

The final agreement came in two parts. In what became known as the ABM Treaty, each side would limit itself to two missile defense systems. In what became known as the SALT I agreement, each side agreed not to begin the construction of any new ballistic missile launchers for the next five years. In May 1972, Nixon and Kissinger flew to Moscow for the signing ceremony and to wrap up a few last-minute differences.

Given the political benefits of the deal, the president and national security adviser wanted the SALT delegation to remain in Helsinki, out of the limelight. So during the final days and hours, when numerous small bargains were struck, the actual negotiators and experts were kept at a distance, contacted from time to time by telegram or telephone. At the last minute, Kissinger agreed to summon the delegation to Moscow for the formal photographs and the signing ceremony. But the call came so late that the logistics collapsed: Nitze nearly ended up stranded at the Moscow airport. He commandeered a car to the ambassador's residence but was almost thrown out because the guards did not recognize him. He had spent two years working on the two agreements. And just before they were signed, he felt as if his long-time rival was frittering away all his work while the Secret Service held him in a hammerlock, proclaiming that they had never heard of anyone named Paul Nitze.

He arrived at the ceremony at the last minute, but was left standing virtually alone in the hall after Nixon and Brezhnev suddenly departed with their entourages. Frustrated and angry, Nitze could think of nothing to do but wander back to the Rossiya Hotel. At 1:30 in the morning he ate a room-service steak and then he went to sleep.

"THERE WAS MORE RESPECT to be won by superior performance in the part of the underling than by mediocre performance in the role of the king."

Kennan spoke this sentence while describing the origins of his writing style. His prose, he declared, derived from that of European diplomats, composing in the courteous, mannered, and often histrionic fashion. That was a language, and an era, of suave ripostes and brisk bons mots. And, as with Shakespearean actors, the dignity gained rested on one's performance, not on how opulent a costume one wore.

But Kennan was likely making a larger point as well. The quotation comes from the speech he gave accepting the National Book Award for the first volume of his memoirs—a book that also won him his second Pulitzer Prize. Consciously or not, he was surely also describing the way people should assess his life. After all, by the standards of the era's memoirists, he was much more an underling than a king.

Kennan published his first volume of memoirs in 1967, the second in 1972. Drawing heavily on his diaries and archival research, both volumes offered a brilliant combination of careful history, luminous writing, and honest self-examination. The public loved the books, and critics declared that they belonged with *The Education of Henry Adams*. The accolades conferred stature. Before the memoirs were published, Kennan was a wise elder, the man who had framed the idea of containment and testified early against the Vietnam War. But he was also a disembodied voice. No one had written a biography of him, or even a serious magazine profile. Apart from close friends, few people even knew where he had grown up.

The memoirs added flesh. People learned just how right Kennan had been, and how often: he had seen through Stalin's purge trials when the American ambassador had been grotesquely taken in by Soviet propaganda; he had foreseen what the Soviets would do to Eastern Europe and what the arms race would do to America; he had predicted the course of events, and proposed the proper responses, in Japan, Korea, China. He came across as a historical sage at a time when the country needed sages. The second volume came out soon after David Halberstam's *The Best and the Brightest,* that saga of the cocky men who got Vietnam terribly wrong. Kennan's memoirs told the story of a sober man who had gotten much right.

Among the books' most striking elements was Kennan's honesty. He described himself as a mistake-prone and overmatched antihero. The first three adjectives attending his self-portrait were "thin," "tense," and "introverted." He had no hesitation in arguing that he would have been better suited to another century. He concluded by declaring himself satisfied with the life he had lived—sort of: he considered himself "no less fulfilled than most others."

As was always the case with Kennan, he combined endearing detachment with an emotional sensitivity that could turn humility and honesty into self-pity. He concluded the second volume, for example, with nearly twenty pages describing the justly obscure struggle in Yugoslavia over most-favored-nation trading status. Losing the battle, he wrote, "took the heart out of any further belief in the possible usefulness of a diplomatic career." Ronald Steel summed up the first volume as "the story of a sensitive, intelligent boy from Milwaukee, Wisconsin who goes off to Europe, where he gains fame, if not fortune, in the service of his country, and after many trials and tribulations discovers that nobody ever understood him."

The books transformed Kennan into a true public intellectual. After they came out, he was frequently invited to write for the *New York Re-*

view of Books. He served as president of the American Academy of Arts and Letters. More than a voice, he was now something closer to an icon.

But the accolades came along with less charitable whispers. If you read the books carefully, some people said, you would see that Kennan was anti-Semitic.

IN THE PASSAGE that caused Kennan the most grief, he described his umbrage in 1942 when the State Department almost gave priority for boarding a ship bound for America to Jewish refugees instead of to the diplomats interned in Bad Nauheim. "Half of us were to be left behind, in German custody, in order to free space on the exchange vessel for Jewish refugees. Why? Because individual congressmen, anxious to please individual constituents, were interested in bringing these refugees to the United States, and this—although the refugees were not citizens—was more important than what happened to us." Kennan did not know about the Holocaust in 1942. But he certainly knew about it twenty-five years later, when he wrote these lines.

That was not all. The first Jews to appear in Kennan's memoirs were sitting in a café in Latvia in 1932 "talk[ing] in tense low tones about the possibility of getting past the American immigration laws." The next was a man who came to the American chancery in Prague after the Germans occupied Czechoslovakia in 1939. "He paced wretchedly up and down in the anteroom, through the long morning hours. In the afternoon, he decided to face the music and go home." And so it went. The Jews in Kennan's writing almost all seem to be painted in dark, shadowy colors: their faces shaded, their lips turned down. Any white Christian from a northern climate was hardworking, noble, and admirable.

Kennan's generous assessments extended to the Germans he met in Berlin after the war began but before he was sent to Bad Nauheim. He describes drinking in a bar with a prostitute who packed parcels in a factory by day and sold herself at night, without telling her fiancé, a Luftwaffe pilot off in Poland. She was articulate, sympathetic, and creative. Finishing that scene, Kennan wrote, "It will be easily understood that in the face of such experiences it was hard for me, in the ensuing years, to go along with the devil-image American opinion invariably ascribes to its particular political opponent of the moment." However admirable this particular woman may have been, the impression left was nonetheless strange: how could he feel such deep springs of sympathy with the life of a hooker whose fiancé was slaughtering the civilians of Warsaw, while not feeling a pang for the lives of those trying to flee the gas chambers?

Kennan had a number of Jewish friends. He and Robert Oppenheimer adored each other. He was close to a Jewish son-in-law, Walter Pozen. His longtime literary agent, Harriet Wasserman, was Jewish, as was one of his dearest friends in Princeton, Harold Hochschild. He reacted angrily in later years to people who hinted that he felt such prejudices. But there is an undeniable pattern in his writing. The most extreme example of the attitude appears in a letter he wrote his sister in 1943, by which time he knew that Hitler was driving Jews into penniless exile, though he did not know about the mass murders.

> I can think of no more stupid or dangerous prejudices than that tacit rule which prevents the recognition or even mention of a Jewish problem in our country. The smugness which laughs off twenty centuries of experience of other peoples in their relations with the Jews is the surest guaranty that those experiences will be repeated, in all their degrading ugliness, in our own country. It also represents, after a fashion, a triumph for Hitler. . . . For if he has not yet forced us to adopt his solutions, he has forced us to flee to the other extreme and to blind ourselves to the problem. And that is the beginning of the same thing.
>
> The Jews, when congregated in large numbers within the body of a non-Oriental people, exhibit certain reactions which inevitably render them a social problem. This is not their fault. It is one of the workings of history. For it, they should neither be blamed nor punished.
>
> Wherever this situation is ignored by the political power, and wherever society finds itself bewildered with Jewish penetration, resentful of Jewish methods of competition and incapable of coping with Jewish pressure without altering its own rules of conduct, then feelings are aroused which are primitive and exceedingly unlovely.

Kennan had a strong tendency to see people as members of groups, to attribute certain attitudes and failings to those groups, and then to call for their isolation—for their own good, of course. "Again, with my proclivity for thinking the wrong things," he wrote his friend Marion Dönhoff in 1965, "I am bound to say I have a soft spot in my mind for *apartheid*—not as practiced in South Africa but as a concept. I would rather see the negroes advance to self-respect and self-realization as a racial community than to witness the agonizing and unsuccessful efforts now being made in this country to find a proper place for them." Throughout his life, he suggested that American blacks be given their own state. And he always expressed astonishment and admiration when he had a positive interaction with a black person—for example, when a black cabdriver rang his doorbell to return a forgotten umbrella.

Kennan indignantly denied being racist or an anti-Semite. In his view, he was just willing to speak truths about cultures and classes that others would not acknowledge. And he was civilized in his disdain. He was too much the gentleman to let his prejudice dominate his character.

Still, people who knew him well sensed something. Walter Pozen, who still admires Kennan greatly, measured his words when asked about his former father-in-law's feelings toward Jews. Kennan was full of ambiguities and complications, yes. When reminded of the passage in Kennan's memoirs about boarding the ship back to the United States, Pozen paused for a second and then became much more intense. "He was interned in Germany. He knew what was going on. And he never wrote a word about it; he never wrote a single word about it."

BOTH NIXON AND BREZHNEV fell from grace soon after signing the SALT I agreement, with the much photographed handshake between the two leaders signaling the apex of the era of détente. Both men had wanted to reduce tensions, and indeed they had made the previous three years perhaps the calmest of the Cold War. Now both were in trouble.

Brezhnev had started taking opiate-based sedatives after the crisis in Czechoslovakia in 1968 and his habit was getting worse. Right before the SALT summit, he had overdosed and ended up taking Kissinger on a wild car ride to shake off the grogginess. Nixon, meanwhile, had begun to assemble the scaffolding from which he would eventually hang. Two days after the signing ceremony, burglars broke into the headquarters of the Democratic National Committee in the Watergate Hotel. Three weeks later, they tried the stunt again. A security guard called the police, and that was the beginning of Nixon's end.

Détente took a harsh blow in October 1973, when the Arab powers attacked Israel on Yom Kippur. The Soviets knew about the attack ahead of time but had not told the Americans. Now, wrote Nitze, "it was evident that their commitment to détente was nil." During the crisis, a group that included Kissinger put the United States on the high state of nuclear alert called DEFCON 3 while Nixon was in a drunken stupor. Brezhnev dug deeper into his pill bottles.

As the leaders of the two superpowers self-medicated, and harmony between the two nations dissipated, Nitze was in Geneva, home base for the second round of SALT talks. The first agreement had temporarily slowed the arms race. Many hoped that a second would fundamentally reconfigure it.

George Kennan happened to be in town too, researching his classic *The Decline of Bismarck's European Order.* One night the Nitzes headed over to the Kennans' apartment for dinner. Annelise Kennan was cooking and, most likely, chatting with Phyllis Nitze, with whom she got along famously. Suddenly, George came into the room, in visible distress. He had just received a letter from the Institute for Advanced Study saying that his leave of absence was for a shorter period of time than he had assumed. Soon the Nitzes were not only helping the Kennans pack up, but also agreeing to take over the lease and move in.

As with SALT I, Nitze's primary concern during this round of negotiations was that the United States not allow the Soviets to extend or lock in their lead in heavy missiles. Particularly worrisome was the development of the SS-18, or "Satan," and the SS-19. Vastly larger than the biggest American missile, those weapons seemed designed for a surprise attack on the ICBMs buried in hardened silos in the Midwest. Nitze had always believed that the side with the heaviest, largest weapons would have an advantage at every level of conflict. Or, as he put it so often, the side with the best-positioned queens could take the other side's pawns.

Looking for a way to push the Soviets back, Nitze proposed an extremely bold step: a 40 percent reduction in the size of the nuclear arsenals held by each superpower. The United States and the Soviet Union were about equal now. Why not have an equal but smaller number of devices? The proposition had no takers.

Nitze became increasingly frustrated. Kissinger was, once again, trying to speed things up by holding back channel meetings and working around the delegation. He was also speaking much more harshly of Nitze in his private conversations. "You know the president doesn't like him," he told one of Nitze's supervisors at the Defense Department in early 1973.

The ill-feeling grew when Nitze met with the *New Yorker* journalist John Newhouse, whom Kissinger and his staff had quietly but intensively prepped while refusing him access to the delegation. During the interview, Nitze quickly deduced that Kissinger had given Newhouse piles of classified material—but only the documents that, in Nitze's view, made the national security adviser look good. Worse, Kissinger had given Newhouse recordings of conversations among a panel that discussed SALT strategy that Nitze did not even know had been taped. Nitze brought his concerns about Kissinger's indiscretions to the attention of the U.S. attorney general but did not receive a response.

Nitze made it known that he wanted out of the talks, and, in January 1974, James Schlesinger, the new secretary of defense, offered him his old job at ISA, where he could go back to thinking about broader policy questions. It was Nitze's fourth shot at that position—and his third rejection. Once again, Barry Goldwater did him in, this time by telling the White House that he might support Senate proceedings on presidential impeachment if Nitze got the ISA post. Robert Murphy, an old friend from the State Department, sent Nitze a note of condolence. "Many thanks for your commiseration over my elusive appointment to the ISA job," came the response. "Needless to say, I had no idea the matter would stir up such a hornets' nest, but then Washington is full of surprises, which is one reason it continues to be such a rich, exciting city."

Instead of moping, Nitze chose to kick over his own Washington hornets' nest a few months later. He offered his resignation to Schlesinger and to Nixon. Receiving no response, he announced that he was unilaterally terminating his own appointment and circulated a press release declaring that he had come to believe the SALT negotiations hopeless and possibly doomed by political posturing. No reasonable arms controls deals would be possible "until the Office of the Presidency has been restored to its principal function of upholding the Constitution and taking care of the fair execution of the laws."

Two weeks later, Nitze appeared at a closed hearing held by the Senate Armed Services Committee and offered withering criticism of SALT, Kissinger, and Nixon. He disclosed the existence of Kissinger's back channel, a revelation promptly leaked to the press. Not long afterward, in mid-June 1974, he stung his rival, now secretary of state. He quietly informed his old protégé Richard Perle about a small bit of careless wording in the SALT I treaty that could allow the Soviets to improve their nuclear submarine fleet. As Kissinger testified on Capitol Hill about his plans for the continuing negotiations, Perle's boss, Senator Scoop Jackson, fired off a technical question about submarines that arose from this wording and that Kissinger was not at that moment prepared to discuss. Afterward, Jackson headed for the television cameras to gloat. "It was a terrible scene," Perle remembers gleefully. "Kissinger was furious."

Kissinger did not know then about Nitze's responsibility for that particular shot. But he of course recognized the damage done by Nitze in the previous month, damage he would criticize harshly in his memoirs. That summer, Kissinger's aide Helmut Sonnenfeldt prepared a letter about Nitze's departure for his boss to sign. It was a formal, bureaucratic document. But Sonnenfeldt, who was very good at channeling his boss—and who added a note saying that Kissinger would personally want to review the document— wanted to make sure it was appropriately cool. Instead of is staff's proposed beginning—"It is with deep gratitude for your contributions over the past five years . . ."—Sonnenfeldt began with "It is in full recognition of your contributions . . ." A paragraph down, "dedication, great skill, and exceptional insight" became "great dedication, skill, and insight." The arms deal did not bear "the imprint of your abilities and energy." Instead, it bore "your contribution." The deal and Nitze's role, read the draft, "have truly earned you the gratitude of all your fellow citizens." Sonnenfeldt crossed out "truly."

IN EARLY DECEMBER 1975, the phone rang in the home of one of Nitze's best friends in Washington, Admiral Bud Zumwalt. An unfamiliar voice delivered a brief, hurried message: Henry Kissinger was soon going to hold a press conference to attack Zumwalt. A few days later, the secretary of state did just that: for a blistering ninety minutes, he angrily criticized Zumwalt's recent accusations, made before Congress, that Kissinger was allowing the Soviets to violate SALT.

Four months later, on Friday March 26, 1976, Zumwalt's phone rang again and a voice that sounded like that of his earlier caller said: "You should know that on at least two occasions recently Kissinger has said to Dobrynin 'an accident should happen to Admiral Zumwalt.'" The caller hung up.

Zumwalt did not know where the call came from or exactly what "an accident" meant. No direct evidence exists that it actually came from Kissinger's office or that Kissinger really spoke those threatening words. Kissinger, himself, dismisses the allegation. (Dobrynin was too frail to respond to a query in 2009 about the incident.) Still, Zumwalt passed his memo to Nitze, who would soon begin quietly describing Kissinger as a "traitor."

Nitze had met Zumwalt while serving under Kennedy at ISA. One day, he had given a speech at the National War College that he thought was exceptionally good. Afterward he was told that, yes, it was good. But a young man had given a yet better one the day before. Nitze found out that the fellow was named Zumwalt and soon hired him.

They both loved details as much as grand theories; they agreed on arms control, and they complemented each other. Nitze had never served in the military; Zumwalt had four stars. Each needed the other, and they pushed each other's careers. According to Melvin Laird, Nitze persuaded him in 1970 to pass over more experienced admirals and make Zumwalt the youngest chief of naval operations in history.

Zumwalt clashed with Kissinger from the very beginning. At one of their first meetings, Kissinger tried to encourage a back channel around Laird. Zumwalt declined the overture. In November 1970, they had a long talk on a train; Zumwalt noted several statements that infuriated him. "K. feels that U.S. has passed its historic high point like so many earlier civilizations. He believes U.S. is on the downhill . . . the American people have only themselves to blame because they lack stamina to stay the course against the Russians who are 'Sparta to our Athens.'"

One of Zumwalt's greatest accomplishments was the integration of what he called the "lily-white, racist Navy." As many of the top brass saw it, he worked far too fast; as some of the young people coming in saw it, he did not work fast enough. Racially tinged brawls broke out aboard two ships. Photographers caught sailors giving black power salutes. Nixon saw the image on the evening news and ordered Kissinger to call Zumwalt and demand that he immediately give the protesters dishonorable discharges. Zumwalt responded that doing so would be illegal: they had a right to court-martials. Angered, Kissinger called Laird and demanded that he fire Zumwalt. Laird shot back that if Kissinger wanted the chief of naval operations fired, he would have to do it himself.

Relations between the two men continued to deteriorate. During the 1973 Arab-Israeli war, Zumwalt became convinced that Kissinger was withholding supplies from Israel because he believed that a little bleeding would soften it up for his planned postwar diplomacy. After leaving the navy, Zumwalt decided to run for the Senate in Virginia on, essentially, a platform of more weapons and less Kissinger. In the spring of 1976, with the Senate race in full swing, he published a memoir that included his notes of Kissinger's harangue about Athens and Sparta on the back jacket. Kissinger denounced Zumwalt's "contemptible falsehoods."

The dark, anonymous phone call about Kissinger's supposed comment to Dobrynin came that week. And around the same time, another curious incident occurred.

Zumwalt's youngest daughter, Mouza, a junior in high school, was driving home from a friend's house when she noticed a car following her. She stepped on the accelerator but could not lose the tail. She made it home safely and ran inside screaming, "There's someone following me!" Zumwalt grabbed the keys to his car, raced outside, and cut off the tailing car as it turned around in a neighbor's driveway. What the hell is going on? demanded the tall, muscular admiral.

The driver mumbled that he worked for a security company and had noticed Mouza speeding. Zumwalt got his name and driver's license and called a friend, Jack Lawn, who ranked high at FBI headquarters. Lawn learned that the man was a government employee, though of what agency he was not sure. Eventually, the Zumwalts came to believe that Kissinger had ordered the man to follow Zumwalt's ethnically Russian wife, also named Mouza—possibly to find information with which to blackmail the admiral. Presumably he had made a mistake and followed the wrong person. Told three decades later about this account and the alleged conversation with Dobrynin, Kissinger called Zumwalt's stories false and paranoid.

KENNAN HAD NO SYMPATHY for connivers, schemers, or people who took risks with nuclear-armed B-52s. But Kissinger's policies matched Kennan's ideal as much as those of anyone who held high office during the Cold War. "Détente" meant something close to the political form of containment that Kennan had described in the late 1940s. Kennan's containment was designed in the wake of a mighty victory, whereas détente was the reaction to a stunning failure—but the ideas were symmetrical.

The point of détente was to fold the Soviet Union into the world system and stabilize its relations with the United States, not to roll the USSR back or to push Brezhnev out. By making peace with China, Nixon and

Paul Nitze in the 1940s. He spent his early years on Wall Street, often frustrated by the thought that he should be doing something more meaningful with his life. *(Author family photograph)*

George Kennan in 1941. A fast-rising star in the Foreign Service, he had until recently been stationed in Prague. The day the Nazis rolled into that city, he shaved extra carefully so as not to give the impression of someone harried by Hitler's triumph. *(Kennan family photograph, courtesy of Grace Warnecke)*

Nitze in 1925, when he was a hard-partying young man. "I didn't think Paul was going to make much of himself in life," his friend Isamu Noguchi said later. *(Author family photograph)*

The Kennan family in about 1916, when George was twelve. He is standing in the center, surrounded by his father, stepmother, half brother, and three sisters. *(Kennan family photograph, courtesy of Grace Warnecke)*

Joseph Stalin with his seven-year-old daughter Svetlana in 1933, one year after his wife's suicide. "She took what was good of him to the grave," Svetlana said. *(Getty Images)*

A British soldier is hoisted in the air on May 9, 1945, as a crowd in Moscow celebrates victory in World War II. As the celebrants danced, Kennan watched warily from the balcony of the American embassy in Red Square. *(Getty Images)*

Secretary of the Navy James Forrestal arriving at the White House in 1945. When asked by FDR to join the government in 1940, he immediately sent Nitze a memo, "Be in Washington Monday morning. Forrestal." *(Harry S. Truman Library)*

General George C. Marshall testifying before the Senate in 1948 in support of the Marshall Plan. "Like everyone else, I admired him and in a sense loved him," said Kennan. *(Getty Images)*

Secretary of State Dean Acheson in 1952. He was initially a mentor to both Nitze and Kennan. But, after Kennan's Reith Lectures in 1957, Acheson put out a statement saying that his former protégé had never "grasped the realities of power relationships." Nitze rejected Acheson's request to join in making the statement. *(Getty Images)*

Edward Teller, left, and Robert Oppenheimer, right. The careers, and personalities, of the two physicists closely paralleled those of Nitze and Kennan. *(Getty Images)*

Ambassador George Kennan arriving in Moscow in 1952 with his wife, Annelise; son, Christopher; and daughter, Wendy. *(Kennan family photograph, courtesy of Grace Warnecke)*

Charles Bohlen, left, with Secretary of State John Foster Dulles. Bohlen was a close friend of both Nitze's and Kennan's. Dulles was one of their main antagonists. *(Library of Congress)*

Nitze and his wife, Phyllis, in the mid-1950s. They were married for fifty-five years, until her death in 1987. *(Author family photograph)*

In October 1956, Hungarian demonstrators tore down a statue of Joseph Stalin. Kennan and many others thought the protests could signal the beginning of the end for communism. But the Soviets soon crushed the revolt. *(AP Images/ Arpad Hazafi)*

Men and women peer over the Berlin Wall in 1961. During the crisis that October, Nitze told the president that the United States "could in some real sense be victorious in the series of nuclear exchanges." *(Library of Congress)*

Secretary of Defense Robert McNamara and President John F. Kennedy in Hyannis Port, Massachusetts, in 1961. Nitze frequently clashed with McNamara and was uncomfortable with the defense secretary's efforts to insert himself in the president's social circle. *(AP Images)*

A U.S. patrol plane flies over a Soviet freighter during the Cuban Missile Crisis in 1962. Nitze was a close adviser to the president during this time, and many of the private notes he took during critical meetings survived in his papers. *(Getty Images)*

Cuban premier Fidel Castro, left, and Soviet premier Nikita Khrushchev in Moscow in 1963. Castro urged a nuclear strike during the Cuban Missile Crisis and, up until the 1980s, he would argue for unprovoked nuclear attacks on America. According to a top Soviet war planner, Moscow "had to actively disabuse him of this view by spelling out the ecological consequences for Cuba of a Soviet strike against the U.S." *(AP Images)*

Secretary of the Navy Nitze in Vietnam. A critic of the war for most of his time in government, he agreed with Lyndon Johnson's decision to escalate it in 1965. *(National Archives and Records Administration)*

Protests at the Pentagon in October 1967. Nitze helped organize the defense of the building and watched from the roof. He would later describe working with a group dedicated to using covert methods to undermine antiwar protesters. *(AP Images)*

Svetlana Alliluyeva, the daughter of Joseph Stalin, at a press conference in New York after arriving in April 1967. Kennan helped her to escape to the United States, and she and he would become close confidantes. "You are one of those—naturally by birth—great American idealists," she once wrote him. "[But] you constantly betray yourself." *(Corbis)*

George Kennan during congressional testimony he gave about the Vietnam War in 1966. "There is more respect to be won in the opinion of this world by resolute and courageous liquidation of unsound positions than by the most stubborn pursuit of extravagant or unpromising objectives." *(Library of Congress)*

President Lyndon B. Johnson addresses troops in South Vietnam in October 1967. Johnson considered firing Nitze after he refused to testify in front of Congress in favor of the president's position on the war. *(AP Images)*

President Richard Nixon speaks with National Security Adviser Henry Kissinger in Austria in May 1972, soon before the United States signed the SALT and ABM agreements. Nixon and Kissinger infuriated Nitze by forcing the SALT delegation to stay away from the final negotiations. *(Getty Images)*

Chief of naval operations, Admiral Elmo "Bud" Zumwalt, seated third from left, talking to American sailors in Japan in 1971. Zumwalt, who was responsible for integrating the U.S. Navy, was a close friend of Nitze's and a fierce rival of Kissinger's. *(Official U.S. Navy photograph, from the collections of the Naval Historical Center)*

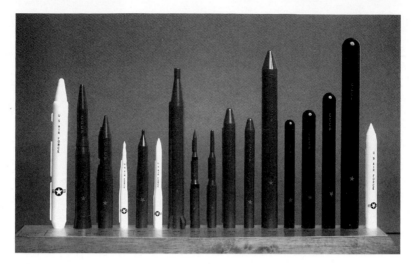

Models of Soviet and American weaponry similar to the ones that Nitze showed frequently at talks and presentations in the 1970s. The Soviet weapons were always represented as large and black, the American ones as small and white. *(Getty Images)*

Paul Warnke, at the microphone, after he was sworn in as head of the U.S. Arms Control and Disarmament Agency in March 1977, despite fierce and personal criticism by Nitze. President Jimmy Carter is to the right of Warnke. From left are Vice President Walter Mondale, Senator Thomas McIntyre (D-N.H.), Senator John Sparkman (D-Ala.), Senator Edmund Muskie (D-Maine), Senator Gary Hart (D-Colo.), Senator Alan Cranston (D-Calif.), Senator Hubert Humphrey (D-Minn.), and Secretary of State Cyrus Vance. *(AP Images)*

Nitze with his Soviet counterpart, Yuli Kvitsinsky, in 1981 during the INF negotiations. After formal talks got nowhere, the two men took an unauthorized walk in the woods and negotiated their own agreement. It was one of the most astonishing acts of insubordination in U.S.-Soviet diplomatic history. *(AP Images)*

Nitze in Reykjavík in 1986, with his head in his hands after staying up almost all night negotiating. He believed he had reached a major arms deal with his Soviet counterparts, only to see it collapse within hours. As he said later, "We tried, we tried. By God, we tried. And we almost did it." From left are Nitze, White House Chief of Staff Donald Regan, President Ronald Reagan, Secretary of State George Shultz, National Security Adviser John Poindexter, and Arms Control and Disarmament Agency head Kenneth Adelman. *(Ronald Reagan Presidential Library)*

George Kennan in the mid-1980s.

(Kennan family photograph, courtesy of Grace Warnecke)

Kissinger showed that they understood that communism comes in different forms and that different communist governments could be played against each other, a strategy for which Kennan had advocated passionately since the 1940s. Kissinger also talked about the need to move away from viewing the world as bipolar, and he considered the arms race merely one small part of the great competition with Moscow. America's military requirements, he said, were those of "sufficiency" in weaponry, not "superiority." Kennan agreed.

Kissinger, like Kennan, had little patience for vague and idealist calls for things such as human rights, particularly if they came at the cost of what they saw as more important issues. In a September 1973 phone conversation, the two men complained about all the attention given the Soviet dissidents Andrei Sakharov and Alexander Solzhenitsyn.

Kennan: "This is a hysteria of the western press."

Kissinger: "In total hypocrisy."

Kennan: "Not only that, but nothing as yet has actually happened to either [Sakharov] or [Solzhenitsyn]."

Kissinger: "Well you know what would have happened to them under Stalin."

Kennan: ". . . I don't think in any case that it's right for a great government such as ours to try to adjust its foreign policy in order to work internal changes in another country."

Kissinger: "Well, I'm so glad you are of that view."

The battle fought by Nitze and Zumwalt against Kissinger and Kennan was the familiar clash between idealism and realism. Zumwalt's Senate campaign was premised on the notion that Kissinger didn't appreciate America's greatness. To Zumwalt and Nitze, keeping the peace meant strengthening the United States and extending its reach across the world. Keeping the peace, to Kennan and Kissinger, meant remembering American fallibility and manipulating a careful "balance of power" among the United States, Europe, the Soviet Union, China, and Japan.

In 1974, a few weeks after Nitze had resigned and then sandbagged Kissinger on Capitol Hill, the secretary of state expressed his frustration over the arms competition. Fatigued after a summit in Moscow, he blurted out at a press conference: "What in the name of God is strategic superiority? What is the significance of it, politically, militarily, operationally, at these levels of numbers? What do you do with it?"

Nitze's sense of strategic superiority—were it to be wielded by Moscow—was grimly different. But a few months later, in an interview with the historian John Lewis Gaddis, Kennan declared that "Henry understands my views better than anyone at State ever has."

Kissinger returned the compliment three decades later. "I thought [Kennan] understood the political dynamics of the Soviet Union better than anyone else."

IF KENNAN was finally in tune with the people who ran the country, he had completely lost faith in the people who filled it. In the mid-1970s, he became a public prophet of civilization's decline.

The signal moment came in a 1976 interview in the magazine *Encounter* with George Urban, a broadcaster for Radio Free Europe. The conversation, which took up thirty-four of the magazine's pages, was intimate and pointed, made more so by Kennan's eloquence and precision. *Encounter* had a tiny circulation but it seemed as though everyone read this piece, including Paul Nitze.

Kennan began with a blunt and revealing self-description—"I am a strange mixture of a reactionary and a liberal"—and then proceeded to prove the point. "The industrial revolution itself was the source of most of the bewilderments and failures of the modern age," he said, describing himself as an eighteenth-century man. He followed with an echo of the X article, in which he had said that the Soviet Union held the seeds of its own destruction. The United States, too, now "bears the seeds of its own horrors: unbreathable air, undrinkable water, starvation."

Kennan seethed with loathing and contempt for the Soviet leadership. But he did not think they would attack the United States or use their weapons for blackmail. He also did not think them able to conquer and control Western Europe, much less the United States: they could barely administer their own homeland. What we needed now was to contain ourselves.

He argued that the United States ought to withdraw gradually from the far-flung corners of the globe. We should pump neither money nor rifles into Africa. We should recognize that the American experience is not universal and that we could best help others by minding our own business. "We have," Kennan said, "nothing to teach the world."

Throughout his career, two propositions had dueled in Kennan's thinking. The first was that America was pursuing the wrong policies—and should try to change them. The second was that the United States was incapable of following the right policies—and that it was hopeless to try to change them until the country's fundamental nature changed. Kennan never came down conclusively on either side. But from the 1940s on, as he became further and further removed from his days on the Policy Planning Staff, he seemed to draw closer to the latter proposition. By the time of this interview, he was almost committed to it.

Only by stepping back and taking a hard look at its own problems, he said, could the United States again become a force for good. Right now, the country was divided and confused and he could only see it reuniting "on a primitive level of slogans and jingoistic ideological inspiration." Where would that come from? The most likely source would be "a form of 'hurrah patriotism' which expresses itself in our country today in the programs of people like Admiral Zumwalt: mischievous ideas which would, if they were permitted to be put into action, lead to apocalyptic nuclear confrontation."

From this point in the interview on, Nitze filled his copy with annotations. The most caustic came when Kennan spoke of an experience from a sailing trip a few years back. "My family and I put in at a small Danish port which was having a youth festival. The place was swarming with hippies—motorbikes, girl-friends, drugs, pornography, drunkenness, noise—it was all there. I looked at this mob and thought how one company of robust Russian infantry would drive it out of town."

In the margins, Nitze scrawled: "He's on their side."

THAT WAS HARDLY TRUE, of course. During this very period, unbeknownst to Nitze, Kennan was engaged in a small but intense skirmish with the KGB. It started in August 1975, with a letter written by an American journalist in Moscow and passed to Kennan through the State Department's diplomatic pouch.

"Dear Mr. Kennan: I am writing on behalf of Joseph G. Alliluyev," it began, referring to the son Svetlana had abandoned nearly a decade before. Joseph "has asked that I get in touch with his mother regarding his desire to visit her in the U.S." He wanted to come on a three-month tourist visa and then to decide whether to stay in the West.

The writer needed to remain anonymous, both to protect himself from Soviet authorities and to protect his job as a journalist. "My company has strict prohibitions against its newsmen getting 'involved' in news events." The writer added that he would not give Kennan's name to Svetlana's son. "You are known—with no intentional allusions to your past—as 'Mr. X.'" The letter came with four pictures of Joseph to prove his identity.

Kennan took the letter and photograph over to Svetlana's house that afternoon. The proposal was too slippery and risky, they decided. It could easily be a trap. If Joseph wanted to communicate with his mother, he should do so openly. Kennan called Mark Garrison, the State Department official who had handed over the letter, and told him to pass a message to the journalist: Joseph's mother still loved him deeply. But if he wanted to come to America, he should send a letter by ordinary mail.

The journalist who sent the original message was an Associated Press reporter named George Krimsky. A Russian-speaker who had access to the dissident community, he had become friends with Joseph; he also saw the potential for a marvelous scoop. In return for his role as mediator, he wanted to be sure that he had exclusive access to the story of how Stalin's grandson defected to the West.

The affair had begun a few months before, in the spring of 1975, when a flamboyant young man named Alexander Kurpel had asked for a ride while Krimsky and his wife were leaving a restaurant. They began to chat; Kurpel explained that he was friends with Joseph and would happily introduce Krimsky to him. Soon, Krimsky found himself knocking on Joseph's apartment door and talking to him about his life as they walked through a Moscow park. During their second meeting, Joseph asked Krimsky to pass the message about a possible visit and defection to his mother.

Though Svetlana accepted Kennan's advice, it pained her. She had not seen her children in a decade and had suffered humiliation when they denounced her in public. This was an opportunity for reconciliation and vindication. But Kennan did not want to cause trouble, and he did not want to risk damaging relations between the United States and the Soviet Union.

On a brief visit to the United States, Krimsky phoned Kennan's house and explained that he was the journalist who had been in contact with Joseph Alliluyev. Annelise answered the phone and told him, firmly, that her husband wanted nothing to do with the matter. Krimsky then called Svetlana and arranged to meet her in New York. For all her emotional turmoil, she told him she believed that Kennan knew best. The risks of a visit were too great.

Back in Moscow, Krimsky went to see Joseph. The young man was nervous and twitchy. He pointed at the ceiling to indicate that the authorities had bugged his home. But he could deliver a brief message outside, away from the microphones: This all had to stop. The KGB had hauled him in and given him a message. They knew everything about his contacts with the West; if he continued, he would soon be exiled from Moscow. If he was lucky, he would find himself practicing medicine somewhere deep in Siberia.

Joseph was not harassed further, but the Soviets soon threw Krimsky out of Moscow. The official charges were preposterous; they revolved around the way he paid his housekeeper. The AP responded with outrage, declaring the move "just a pretext for getting rid of an aggressive, Russian-speaking reporter." *Time* added, "The real reason for Krimsky's expulsion was his coverage of the dissidents." The Carter administration expelled a Soviet reporter in retaliation. No one knew that Krimsky had tried to help the grandson of Joseph Stalin defect—a fact *Pravda* was unsurprisingly reluctant to reveal.

A few months after the expulsion, a rambling sixteen-page missive from Alexander Kurpel arrived at Svetlana's house. He wanted to tell her how much her son still loved her, how good a reporter George Krimsky was, and how he, Kurpel, could still be helpful. The letter was chaotic and at times delusional. Now certain that the whole episode had been a KGB ploy either to get her back to Moscow or to embarrass her son, Svetlana passed it on to Kennan.

He wrote her back, emphasizing that nothing but trouble awaited anyone who played this game. The episode was the second in which Kennan had been approached by someone in Moscow with an offer too good to be true (the first was the incident in which a young man had come to the embassy in 1952 with a plot to destroy the Soviet leadership). Both times he smelled a trap, and both times he was almost certainly right.

15

YOU CONSTANTLY BETRAY
YOURSELF

Paul Nitze spent the mid-1970s scaring the hell out of people. His message was simple and he took it everywhere: the Soviet Union had become a mortal threat, and the United States needed to get stronger fast. He hammered out papers and op-eds. He gave speeches, formed organizations, testified incessantly before Congress, harangued the president, consulted secretly, and appeared on TV. His hair was white now and he seemed always to stare intensely from behind his dark-rimmed glasses. He became a hero to some people and a dangerous villain to others. Now he was not just a man but the embodiment of a movement.

His main argument began with a hypothetical. Tensions could rise somewhere. Provoked, the rivals might begin threatening each other. What next? America had long counted on the strangely comforting doctrine of mutually assured destruction. Neither side would start the fight because both knew it would end in ashes. Even the most committed Soviet hard-liners knew that America could hit back three ways: with ICBMs fired from the battery of silos spread over the country; with bombers; and with nuclear-armed submarines. Knock out a leg of that triad and we would still have two devastating ways to strike back.

But then Nitze—with his charts, his legal pads, and his experience that dated back to Hiroshima—would say: Hold on. Let us imagine that the Soviets did strike. Their arsenal had become so powerful that they could launch an overwhelming salvo and destroy most of our ICBMs while crippling our bomber and submarine fleets. At the same time, they would crowd their people into their vast shelter system. The United States would still have a few ICBMs, nuclear-armed submarines, and bomb-carrying planes. But could we really retaliate in a meaningful way? The Soviet air defenses could shoot down many of our bombers, and submarine-launched missiles were notoriously inaccurate. America had designed its ICBMs for precision, not maximum destruction, so they would be particularly ineffective in this desperate scenario. Most important of all, if the United States hit back, the USSR would have enough weapons remaining to blast what was left of America into oblivion.

Nitze put the point plainly in an article titled "Deterring Our Deterrent," published in *Foreign Policy*. Henry Kissinger had declared that nuclear war was "unthinkable." Nitze argued the opposite: it had to be thought about. He backed up his position with graphics depicting the Soviets' superiority in throw weight and their ability to respond to an American strike. Nitze had no formal training in mathematics or science, but the paper had an air of technical expertise. "The crucial question," he declared, "is whether a future U.S. president should be left with only the option of deciding within minutes, or at most within two or three hours, to retaliate after a counterforce attack in a manner certain to result not only in military defeat for the United States but in wholly disproportionate and truly irremediable destruction to the American people."

The answer, of course, was no. And if the Soviets really believed they could force America into such a terrible corner—a shuddering president with his finger poised above the red button, choosing between total surrender and futile, genocide-inducing counterattack—then Moscow might just launch.

RICHARD NIXON RESIGNED the presidency three months after Nitze resigned from the SALT team. In came Gerald Ford, who was an improvement from Nitze's perspective—though not a big one. Ford kept Henry Kissinger in charge of foreign policy and did not seem to see the state of the arms race as one of urgent peril.

A few months into his tenure, Ford traveled to Vladivostok where he, Kissinger, and the Soviet leader, Leonid Brezhnev, worked out an accord in which the two adversaries pledged to equalize the total number of launchers and missiles with MIRV capabilities in their arsenals. The

United States agreed not to penalize the Soviets for having larger weapons; the Soviets agreed not to count the weapons held by America's NATO allies.

To many historians, this was a high point of Cold War harmony. Brezhnev fought desperately for a deal, fending off a seizure early in the talks and screaming at his defense minister that concessions must be made. On the final day, he grabbed Ford's hand, looked him in the eyes, and told him that they had an obligation to protect all mankind. Touched, Ford gave the Russian leader his brand-new Alaskan wolf-skin coat. Soon after the talks ended, Brezhnev collapsed completely; after his convalescence a few weeks later, he could barely read. "Brezhnev exhausted himself in the struggle for peace," recorded his close aide Anatoly Chernyaev in an October 1975 diary entry.

This all left Nitze cold. As far as he was concerned, America had been rolled again. The Vladivostok deal gave the Soviets a huge advantage in throw weight, leaving the U.S. arsenal in an inferior and thus threatened state.

In 1976, Nitze's old friend and fellow SALT opponent Scoop Jackson ran for president. But Jackson had lost four years before, and Nitze, not giving him much of a chance, decided to roll the dice on someone new: a peanut farmer, nuclear submarine engineer, and governor of Georgia named Jimmy Carter whose foreign policy views were all but unknown. Nitze sent Carter a big check and stamped a bumper sticker on his Mercedes. He had carefully worked through the politics of the race, determining that a fresh face would prosper in the post-Watergate, post-Vietnam, and mid-recession summer of 1976. Carter's naval background would also allow him to talk about peace while looking tough. Nitze figured that this was his last chance to get the cabinet position he had long coveted. And he knew that an early endorsement would improve his odds, since in some ways politics resembles finance. Payout is maximized if you invest early.

At the outset, the plan worked. Nitze offered advice to the campaign, and the candidate cited him in speeches. Nitze's goal seemed to be to convince Carter that, like Kennedy, he could win the presidency by being the Democrat who accused the Republicans of being soft.

In July, after wrapping up the nomination, Carter summoned Nitze, along with seven other leading Democratic foreign policy figures, to the house the governor had built for his mother in the pinewoods outside Plains, Georgia. Four of the guests were young up-and-comers; four were older men who had worked together in the Johnson administration and were now vying for the positions of secretary of state and defense: Nitze, Harold Brown, Cyrus Vance, and Paul Warnke.

Nitze was confident as the meeting approached. The morning of his trip to Georgia, he overslept and had to race to the airport at breakneck speed. Once in Atlanta, he and the other guests were put on a bus, given cold fried chicken, and driven three hours south to Plains. Nitze sat next to Brown and got in a fierce argument about American vulnerability as the Greyhound bounced along the Georgia roads.

The meeting convened in the living room, with everyone seated in a circle. Carter asked everyone their views on foreign policy and relations with the Soviets. When it came time for Nitze to speak, he pulled out a full presentation, along with charts. Gesticulating fiercely for effect, he spoke about America's vulnerability, Moscow's ICBM buildup, and Soviet civil defense. He was the most senior and experienced man in the room, and he played the part too aggressively. The others found the performance awkward, and neither Carter nor the other elder mandarins bought his argument.

Nitze, usually a gracious and socially skilled person, missed the mark not only in substance but also in tone. "He was a lion in a den of Daniels," recalled Walter Slocombe, one of the up-and-comers. Another of the young invitees, Barry Blechman, recalled that Nitze "was giving a presentation when the idea was to have a discussion." Nitze also forgot that he was talking to someone on the edge of the presidency. Throughout his career, young people would say that one of his great virtues was that he talked in the same hyperlogical way with everyone, whether an aide fresh out of graduate school, a peer, or a presidential candidate with a 25-point lead in the polls. Carter found the habit less endearing. "Nitze was typically know-it-all," the president recalled dismissively a decade later. "His own ideas were sacred to him. He didn't seem to listen to others, and he had a doomsday approach."

When Nitze returned home, he declared that everything had gone just as he had wanted. In reality, he had utterly blown it. Vance became secretary of state. Warnke became head of the Arms Control and Disarmament Agency as well as the lead SALT negotiator. Brown became secretary of defense. All the major spots were filled.

While reorganizing the department, Brown expressed an interest in bringing Nitze in as an undersecretary: despite their differences, the two men always held each other in high intellectual regard. But Carter had no interest in having Nitze anywhere in his administration: not in the cabinet, not in the Pentagon, not in the mailroom. Seven of the eight visitors to Plains that day received high posts. Nitze got nothing.

AT ALMOST EXACTLY the same time, George Kennan stumbled in almost exactly the same way. The stakes were lower, and the issue was in some ways the opposite. But in the summer of 1976, the intensifying national debate over nuclear weapons led Kennan to act in a decidedly indecorous and uncharacteristic way.

A thirty-two-year-old historian named C. Ben Wright provoked the tantrum. The author of a dissertation on Kennan, Wright had meticulously researched his subject's early ideas. Now he had written an article for *Slavic Review,* "Mr. 'X' and Containment," in which he argued that Kennan's initial conception of containment placed much more emphasis on armed force than the Kennan of the 1970s would have people believe.

Wright was an admirer. While researching a dissertation on U.S.-Canadian relations during World War II, he had read Kennan's memoirs. Inspired and awed, he changed the course of his studies.

Nonetheless, and despite Wright's respectful tone, this particular charge was an arrow aimed at Kennan's belly. Totally discomfited by America's arms buildup and worn down by the crude misconceptions that spurred the Vietnam War, Kennan wanted no ancestral responsibility for the state of American politics in 1976.

It was his term "containment" that had framed American policy for the past thirty years, but he had long distanced himself from the prevailing definition of that word by repeating vigorously the distinction that he had first firmly made in his unsent letter to Walter Lippmann twenty-eight years before. There was political containment—economic aid, diplomacy, building up morale, influencing elections (perhaps even covertly); and there was military containment—making big weapons, threatening others with them, and perhaps ultimately firing them off. He had urged using the broadest possible civil and political measures, but emphatically not more, and it was his life's regret that he had not made the distinction clearer in the article. Now the two concepts had blurred. Tellingly, in the latter decades of the Cold War, top Soviet officials translated "containment" with the same Russian word they used when translating "deterrence."

But Wright had scrutinized Kennan's writing and speeches between 1944 and 1947 and found evidence suggesting that he had not always opposed the application of some level of violence. Kennan had seemed at least partially convinced that thwarting Soviet expansion would require military strength and that a clash might be unavoidable. In a talk at the Air War College in 1947, he had told his audience: "With probably ten good hits with atomic bombs you could, without any great loss of life or loss of prestige or reputation of the United States as a well-meaning and humane people, practically cripple Russia's war-making potential." He was not advocating such a policy, but he was musing about the acceptability, under certain circumstances, of this startling strategic act. And three months earlier, during a study session at the Council on Foreign Relations, Kennan had suggested that America's then nuclear monopoly could supply political leverage over Moscow—very much the advantage Nitze was to continue pressing America to maintain.

The editor of *Slavic Review* sent Kennan an advance copy of the essay, to which he promptly responded with a private letter choked with rage, demanding that the quotations be removed. His ostensible concern was for security and protocol: Wright had found the Air War College transcript in a collection of personal papers that Kennan had given to the Princeton library and Kennan claimed that he did not recall receiving permission from the Air War College to declassify the talk. He demanded, too, the deletion of his remarks before the Council on Foreign Relations. "These discussions are confidential and the council would be deeply shocked, and very annoyed with me, if they were to be cited in print."

The editor of *Slavic Review* passed Kennan's letter to Wright, urging him to drop the offending passages. Wright refused. He noted that Kennan had not objected to other, less personally compromising, quotes that presented similar questions about their classification. He then contacted both the Air War College and the council and received explicit permission to use the quotes. The only person deeply shocked, and very annoyed, was George Kennan.

Wright's article appeared in the spring of 1976. It was smart and well reasoned, if not ultimately persuasive. Yes, Kennan was less pure than he claimed. But political containment was indeed the fulcrum of his

thinking throughout the 1940s. In the clearest test case—America's debate about how far to support its Greek clients during the civil war of the
late 1940s—Kennan had come down cleanly in favor of a political solution and against military commitment. Even during the controversial
discussion at the Council on Foreign Relations, Kennan emphasized
political resistance and made the same vague call for moral uplift with
which he ended the Long Telegram. "Mr. Kennan said that no 'get-tough
policy' was called for," recorded the council's note taker. "But rather that
we should take a dignified and self-assured position in the world. As
long as we show that our purposes are decent and that we have the courage to follow them through, the Russians will never challenge us."

Wright's piece was measured and calm. Kennan's rejoinder read like
something from the pen of Dean Acheson on a very angry day. "I stand, as
I see, exposed," Kennan began. "With merciless scalpel, and with abundant
use of scraps of language from my writings, Mr. Wright has stripped me of
my own pretenses and revealed me as the disguised militarist he considers
me to be." Kennan asserted that Wright had quoted him selectively—a
claim Wright obliterated in a follow-up response—and ended with a dark
and condescending admonition. The bending of language "presents, no
doubt, a powerful temptation for the younger scholar. But his mentors and
reviewers should warn him against it. It is too easy. Good history is not
written that way."

If the reply carried echoes of Acheson, Kennan's next move reeked of
Nixon. He pulled from the publicly open section of his papers in the
Princeton library the documents Wright had cited, along with several
others that were potentially explosive. These documents would remain
unavailable for thirty years.

Not surprisingly, the long-hidden papers include a few passages that
might have further tarred the image Kennan cultivated in the late
1970s. For example, at an October 1946 meeting of the Council on Foreign Relations, he contemplated atomic war and seemed to support
civil defense. "He felt that it was a mistake to assume, as was often
done, that Russia was necessarily less vulnerable than the United States
to atomic warfare," wrote the note taker, summarizing Kennan's argument that Russian industry was concentrated and thus exposed to attack. Kennan also appeared to advocate civil defense and said that we
should not "reject plans to make our cities less vulnerable [just] because

such plans can never attain perfection. He emphasized particularly the need of taking into consideration the possibilities of slum clearance and city planning."

Kennan was no militarist, then or later. But he was determined to prevent historians from uncovering anything that could be unfavorably interpreted or that might complicate his effort to distance himself from America's current militant posture—even if it meant sealing his own archive.

AS KENNAN TRIED to scrub away statements he wished he had never made, one of his closest friends decided to admonish him for things he had not done.

"I think I still should tell you something, what has been so many times on my lips, in these recent years," began Svetlana Alliluyeva in a letter that Kennan received soon after he read Wright's article. "[There is something] I always wanted to express to you (somehow, some time, in some possible way), I must put it in a very short simple message: Dear George you are unhappy—and this is very obvious—because you constantly betray yourself."

After leaving Taliesin West, Svetlana had spent four years in Princeton, near the Kennans and in constant touch with them; she even lived for a short spell in their house. But she grew restless, as she always did. She was bored living the sedentary, suburban life, and so she decided to pack up her daughter in 1976 and move west again, this time to California. "I do not miss Princeton. Last four years there proved to be not good times," she wrote to Annelise.

Safely out of the same city as Kennan, she now decided to be brutally frank; the letter she wrote was one of the most penetrating he ever received. Svetlana peeled back several layers of his personality, both praising and striking at the inner man.

You constantly do not allow yourself to be yourself.... You've put yourself—and all your life—into the pattern of (pardon me, please!) that deadly Presbyterian Righteousness which looks "good," only in pronouncements from the pulpit; which is based on human experiences of different era; different people; different social milieu, than yours.

> You are one of those—naturally by birth—great American idealists, to whom artists, Utopians and Politicians belonged just as well. People like Abraham Lincoln, Walt Whitman, Frank L. Wright (yes! yes! . . .), Thoreau, and many others—were born to be constantly misunderstood; to suffer through their lives of great discoveries, fighting with miserable middle-class mediocre mentality of their own compatriots, and of the rest of the world; people whose genius would be recognized too late.

Kennan's great mistake, she told him, had been to choose the wrong path in life. He might think himself born to be in politics. But no—he was a failure at such things.

> You are a writer. Not that academic type of historian who (no doubt about that!) collects awards every year from all important institutions of the world. Did these awards make you happier? . . . You could have written great number of books—of your own philosophy. It would be—by some—the most perfect, 100% American philosophy. . . . It was your own fault that you never allowed yourself to be what you are. To be what you've been born for.
>
> My dear George . . . I wish you not to be ever so frustrated, hopeless and sad about yourself. You could just allow yourself really the way of life you want it—in Scotland or elsewhere—where you could totally separate yourself from the killing vanity of [your home in Princeton]; from that depressing Norwegian narrow practicality; from constant calls from Washington, D.C. which only frustrate you, and remind you that you are a "retired ambassador."
>
> You do not need another award from some Historical Society. You have them all. One thing that would make you happy would be a book, where you could freely express yourself, your philosophy of history; your view of your own fellow Americans; your love to them all.

She advised him to move somewhere remote, abandon all other commitments, and spend his time thinking. "George, you deserve to be happy, you deserve more than anyone else to live your way. Then—and only then—you will be really giving others as much as you really can—and should."

★

PAUL NITZE HAD WORKED under every Democratic president since Roosevelt. But Carter stopped calling him after the debacle in Georgia. By the time the governor won a paper-thin victory over Gerald Ford, Nitze rightly feared that he would sit this administration out.

He was not one to put his tail between his legs, though. On November 5, 1976, three days after the election, he was back at it, browbeating a group of men and women who, he felt, underestimated the dangers facing the United States. This time, his victims were a team of young intelligence analysts sitting across a conference table in a meeting room on the seventh floor of CIA headquarters in Langley, Virginia.

Hard-liners had long believed that the CIA was underestimating Soviet strength, and they had pressured the Ford administration into appointing a panel of skeptics to evaluate the agency's work. Nitze was a key member of this so-called Team B, a group of elder statesmen and scholars led by the Harvard historian Richard Pipes. They had spent the late summer and early fall poring over raw intelligence as well as the CIA's annual National Intelligence Estimates (NIEs) of Soviet intentions and capabilities. They were specifically instructed not to make a so-called net assessment, a reevaluation of the entire balance of power with the Soviet Union. Instead, they worked through a set of detailed questions about Soviet intentions and arsenal composition. In October, Team B and Team A, which comprised the CIA experts, had exchanged drafts. Now the two teams were getting together to talk.

The meeting was a mismatch and a mauling. Early on, a young analyst named Ted Cherry began to argue that to understand Soviet military strength, one had to examine the entire strategic balance. As he talked, appearing overconfident and presumptuous to members of Team B, Nitze peered over his glasses and interjected in a withering tone, "You mean do a net assessment?"

"Cherry's mouth froze and he couldn't say anything," recalled Pipes. A long silence fell. Pipes eventually felt obliged to break in to limit the embarrassment. "It was a killer moment."

The older, more seasoned men continued to dominate the younger people. Team A had not prepared for a confrontation, which made the clash that much bloodier. "It was like Walt Whitman High versus the Redskins," one CIA analyst told the arms control specialist Anne Hessing Cahn. "We were overmatched," another said. "People like Nitze ate us for lunch."

After the meeting, the two teams retreated to their corners to revise their reports. Team B's second draft was a withering indictment of the CIA's understanding of the Soviets. Most important, they argued, Team A did not understand the way the Soviet leadership thought about nuclear war. The men in the Kremlin did not want such a destructive war, of course, but they knew it could happen, and they believed they could survive as victors.

After laying out that argument in great detail, the report followed with ten explicit and technical critiques of the assumptions used in the NIEs. Partly written by Nitze, this section alleged, for example, that the agency had underestimated the Soviet Union's civil defense efforts, its ability to track U.S. submarines, and the range of some of its bombers.

In December, both teams presented their final reports before the upper echelons of the agency and its new director, George H. W. Bush. By then, Team A's conclusions had shifted in the direction of Team B's—partly, according to one of the analysts who worked on the report, because they felt pressure from Bush to accede. Not long after the presentation at Langley, the full story of the Team B exercise appeared in the press. A firestorm immediately erupted.

Why, liberals asked, had there not been a Team C, filled with experienced people like George Kennan? Why had only hard-liners like Nitze received classified material? Soon congressional committees began investigating. Henry Kissinger gave a press conference in which he dismissed Team B and its assertion that the Soviet Union was achieving nuclear supremacy. People who claimed that, he said, "are not doing this country a service and not doing mankind a service."

The story behind the Team B exercise became downright mysterious a year later, when a boat washed ashore in the Chesapeake Bay. The boat belonged to John Paisley, the agency's designated liaison with Team B—and, according to his son, the man who originally leaked details of the exercise to the press. An expert on Soviet weaponry, he had handled such tasks as delivering classified material to Team B. And his empty boat was full of false identification documents and sophisticated radio gear. It also carried a briefcase full of (unclassified) documents relating to Team B.

A week later, a man's body was found floating in the bay, with a gunshot wound in the back of the head and diver's weights attached to the midsection. The police declared immediately that it was Paisley and that he must have committed suicide. But the body had decomposed beyond recognition and it appeared to be that of a man who had stood five feet, seven inches; Paisley was five eleven. If the body was his, and if he had done himself in, he had chosen an awkward method. Paisley was right-handed, but he would have had to have attached the weights, leaned over the side, and shot himself, execution style, through the left temple.

In the decades since the body's discovery, its identity has never been established. John Paisley was never heard from again.

A CENTRAL CLAIM of the Team B report—and of Nitze's many articles in the 1970s—was that the vigor with which the USSR was building its arsenal was an index of its malevolent intentions. Why would the Soviets be constructing so many heavy weapons, if not to put themselves in a position to threaten a devastating strike against the United States?

In retrospect, however, blackmail seems to have been fairly low on the Soviets' agenda. They were much more concerned to assuage their sense of technological inferiority, to prevent an American first strike, and to feed their sprawling military-industrial complex. The strongest evidence for this position comes from an extraordinary collection of interviews of twenty-two Soviet military planners and strategists commissioned by the Defense Department's Office of Net Assessment between 1990 and 1994 and long kept secret.

According to these interviews—the substance of which was confirmed by conversations in Moscow in 2009—weapons manufacturers drove decisions at least as much as the defense establishment and political leadership. According to the Defense Department interviews, a Soviet weapons manufacturer once came to Defense Minister Dmitri Ustinov to ask him to requisition a few dozen more missiles. "What will I do with them?" Ustinov asked, resisting the request. "But if you don't [order them], how will I feed the workers?" the manufacturer responded. Ustinov ordered the missiles built.

The military-industrial complex in the Soviet Union, it now appears, had even more power than its equivalent in the United States. At least the air force and navy—and Boeing and Lockheed—competed with each other. And they faced a constant (if quiet) chorus urging restraint. In Moscow, "everything was militarized," said Vitalii Tsygichko. "The whole country worked with weapons. We just had to keep feeding the machine. We couldn't stop it."

Team B was correct to assert that many Soviet leaders believed they could fight and win a nuclear war. Andrian Danilevich, one of the principal Soviet war planners, echoed the Team B report in a 1992 interview. "We considered that we held advantages in certain areas, such as throw-weight, land-based systems, in control systems, in silo protection, in number of weapons, so we thought we could win a nuclear war."

But the Soviets' war plans were entirely based on retaliation. They expected that America would start the war, and then that the Kremlin would respond massively. "We never had a single thought of a first strike against the U.S.," Danilevich reflected. "The doctrine was always very clear: we will always respond, but never initiate," Tsygichko said.

Perhaps the biggest flaw in Nitze's worldview at this time was his sense that the Kremlin's leaders were far less humane, and far less worried about nuclear war, than their American counterparts. The United States, he believed, would never launch a nuclear weapon, except as a last resort; the Soviets appeared much more ready to do so.

Recent interviews with Soviet war planners give a very different impression. And Danilevich, for example, offered a striking story demonstrating the point.

Some time in 1972, Brezhnev's defense advisers briefed him on the consequences of a massive out-of-the-blue nuclear strike by the United States. Eighty million Soviets would be dead; the armed forces would be reduced to a thousandth of their current strength; the European part of the Soviet Union would be laid waste by radiation. The country would be ruined, and yet the general secretary—assuming he had somehow survived—would have to respond.

The scenario "terrified" Brezhnev, according to Danilevich; what came next rattled the general secretary even more. As part of their presentation, Brezhnev's advisers staged a drill, during which he was to press a button that would launch three real ICBMs with dummy warheads. As the time came, Brezhnev was "visibly shaken and pale and his hand trembled." Standing next to Defense Minister Grechko, he asked, several times over, whether his next action would have any real-world consequences. "Andrei Antonovich, are you sure this is just an exercise?"

The Soviet leaders, it now seems, were human.

AS THE CARTER administration came in, Nitze decided to try a new approach to influencing policy: instead of just working the bureaucracy, he would rile up the public. With that object in mind, he sat down with friends in Washington's Metropolitan Club and created one of the oddest, and most successful, citizen-lobbying groups of the Cold War: the Committee on the Present Danger.

It made its public debut in November 1976, and it lived up to its name: its mission was to convince the public that there was a danger, and it really did run as a committee. Almost equal numbers of Republicans and Democrats filled its roster, from President Kennedy's secretary of state Dean Rusk to future president Ronald Reagan. Other members included Saul Bellow, Richard Perle, Richard Pipes, Norman Podhoretz, and Bud Zumwalt. Nitze served as chairman for policy studies. The committee did not have much money, in part because it refused to take a dime from defense contractors. "I have nothing to market but my reputation for probity," Nitze said then.

Three constituencies supplied most of the support: establishment hard-liners of the sort who, like Nitze, lunched frequently at the Metropolitan Club; conservative Jewish intellectuals, who until recently could not have gotten into the club; and John Birch conservatives, who would have wanted no part in it. The organization was a holding pen for the men and women later called neoconservatives. It provided one of the first opportunities for Scoop Jackson Democrats to bond with Barry Goldwater Republicans, helping to forge the coalition that would shape American politics for the next thirty years.

Nitze did not really care who was with him, or why. At this point in his life, the ends justified the means. He had become so fixated on convincing his country of the need for immediate action against Moscow that he would have worked with almost anyone. He had even reconciled with Henry Kissinger. He just wanted to win.

The committee's first fight occurred in the winter of 1977. The opponent was an old friend of Nitze's: Paul Warnke. The two Pauls had served together in the Johnson Defense Department and together had tried to slow the Vietnam War—Nitze, because he thought it was disadvantageous; Warnke, because he thought it wrong. In those days, they had found themselves in agreement—mostly. Leslie Gelb, a mutual friend and colleague, remembers sitting with them one day at the very end of the administration. Nitze had his feet on his desk and was drawing on a giant cigar. "It was a foot long, and he was puffing up so much smoke that he could barely be seen." They were drafting a speech and Nitze was unhappy with Warnke's suggestions. "No, No. I don't want to say those things," he shouted. Warnke stood up from a chair in front of the desk and went to the window. "It's us and the world," Gelb remembers Nitze saying. "It's about who gets who first." For Gelb's benefit, Warnke held his hand up to his head dismissively, but Nitze looked up at just that moment and caught the gesture through the cigar smoke. "The expression on his face changed. Things were never the same after that."

Through the early 1970s, Nitze and Warnke still saw each other at parties, and they remained publicly amicable. Warnke became a high-powered Washington attorney, forming Clifford & Warnke with Nitze's old boss. But then in the spring of 1975, Warnke published a piece in *Foreign Policy* entitled "Apes on a Treadmill." The striking central metaphor was a response to the argument that this country was losing a nuclear arms "race." In Warnke's view, we were actually "jogging in tandem on a treadmill to nowhere." Two years later, Warnke's argument had seeped into elite thinking and Carter offered him the leadership positions at the Arms Control and Disarmament Agency (ACDA) and the SALT talks—positions for which Paul Nitze was extremely qualified.

The president had hoped for expedited approval of Warnke's nominations. But as soon as Nitze learned that, he laid his body across the tracks. He sent a letter to the chair of the Senate Foreign Relations Committee outlining his concerns and then called Scoop Jackson. There would be hearings, and there would be a showdown.

On February 9, 1977, Nitze stepped up for his first day of testimony. He was direct, but measured and calm. He took Warnke's ideas seriously. He said that he would support his former colleague if he was confirmed. He also declared that he wanted to stimulate a national debate about arms policy so that the Carter administration would not negotiate a deal that the Senate would later reject.

On February 28, he returned to the Hill, but this time he came in anger. Anonymous attacks on his earlier testimony had been circulating on Capitol Hill, and he had concluded that Warnke was dissembling in his testimony. Friends remember Nitze having an angry gleam in his eye in the days leading up to his return to Capitol Hill. "We're going to get him," he said. A passerby who happened to ride in an elevator with Nitze the day of the testimony remembers thinking that he seemed to be hyping himself up like a boxer as he got ready to walk into the hearing room.

On this day, Nitze's tone was fierce. "I think [Warnke] talks about numbers without knowing what the numbers mean." "I [don't] think his understanding runs deep enough to know what it is he wouldn't have an understanding about." "I think he has great ability at confusing people."

Eventually Nitze was pinned by one of his interlocutors, the liberal New Hampshire senator Thomas McIntyre.

The senator began by reminding those present that some senators had personally attacked Nitze during his navy confirmation hearings in 1963. Perhaps, McIntyre was suggesting, there was a certain irony to today's proceedings: this time Nitze was the predator, not the prey.

"Mr. Nitze, in your opening statement you stated that your disagreement with Mr. Warnke was not of a personal nature, because you both like and respect him."

"I didn't say that. I said I valued him as a former colleague."

"Well, if you valued him as a former colleague, it makes it pretty clear that you don't really basically object to Mr. Warnke's character."

"It does not. I said I have valued him. Frankly, I cannot understand the things he has been saying in the last few days. I do not think they are proper."

"Are you saying that you impugn his character as an American citizen?"

"If you force me to, I do."

"That is very interesting. Do you think that you are a better American than he is?"

"I really do."

It was a terrible moment for Nitze. He had lost his cool and attacked the patriotism of an honorable and intelligent former friend. Nitze was a fiendishly competitive and passionate man, but he was usually calm in tense situations. This time he lost it. And without a doubt, the explosion was sparked in part by his jealousy at Warnke's nomination and his pique at Carter for passing him over. Asked about the incident many years later, Harold Brown compared Nitze's behavior toward Warnke to Edward Teller's questioning of Oppenheimer's loyalty. "[Nitze] tended to look for fights with any superior who was in a job he thought he should have had," Brown added.

Nitze's description of the incident, in his memoirs, is perhaps the most tortured and absurd paragraph he ever wrote. "[McIntyre] asked me whether I thought I was a better American than Warnke. I hesitated to answer but finally said 'I really do.' What I meant to say was, 'I really do take exception to what I believe to be inconsistent and misleading testimony by Mr. Warnke.'"

Even Nitze's friends were furious at him. And Warnke never forgave him. Immediately after the hearings, he removed a photograph of Nitze that he had long kept on a wall of his house, inscribed "To my co-conspirator" in acknowledgment of their work together on Vietnam. From then on, Warnke's wife would be reluctant to remain in the same room as Nitze.

Knowing he had blundered badly, Nitze sent out the transcript of his opening remarks to a number of friends, including George Kennan. His hope, no doubt, was to show that his concerns had rested on substance, not mere animus. "Dear George," he wrote, "I know that you hold an opposing view, however, I do hope you will find the time to read the enclosed copy of my opening remarks. . . . With warm regards, Sincerely, Paul."

Kennan replied with one of the kindest letters Nitze ever received.

> Dear Paul,
>   We have our differences of outlook, which is not surprising; but you know, I am sure, that I have never questioned your complete sincerity and intellectual integrity; and that no differences of this nature affect in the slightest degree the confidence and affection I feel toward you as a friend.
>   Sincerely, George K.

EVERY FEW YEARS, Kennan announced to his close friends, his family, and his diary that he had had it. He would not speak out in public anymore. His voice was not wanted; no one comprehended him; he would always be misinterpreted. From now on, he would only write history. And for a short while he would keep his resolution. But soon enough the wounded recluse would be stirred by the yet deeper conviction of the soundness, and importance, of his views.

The spring of 1977 was just such a time. Kennan's generous letter about the Warnke hearings provided no hint of his profound anxiety. Nitze was alarmed, but Kennan was afraid—a very different thing. The fate of the world had never before seemed so precarious. The country now appeared to face "a real and crucial parting of the ways: one road leading to the total militarization of policy and an ultimate showdown on the basis of armed strength, the other to an effort to break out of the straightjacket of military rivalry." It seemed to Kennan to be "a case of 'speak now or forever hold thy peace.'" He decided to make one more cry for reason and understanding. A few months later, he published *The Cloud of Danger.*

With its sweeping statements about people, politics, and his philosophy, the book suggests that Kennan had taken Svetlana's bracing advice, at least in part. But it was not the masterpiece she had demanded. He claimed to have written it "in one breath," and it read that way—hurried, even deliberately aimed at alienating his readers. The dedication read: "To my wife, Annelise, whose lack of enthusiasm for this and my other excursions into the realm of public affairs has never detracted from the loyalty with which she supported these endeavors."

The Cloud of Danger began with a long, withering critique of the United States—starting with the Constitution. Recent blunders, like the war in Vietnam, were not just the fault of a few shortsighted men: they were the inevitable result of a flawed system that gave Congress far too much power. Coming after Vietnam and the heavy-handed Nixon administration, this was an odd complaint. Kennan seemed to have Claude Pepper in mind, not William Fulbright.

Having dismissed the nation's founding documents, he then turned on its personal habits. Cars were wicked and pernicious. We must reverse the industrial revolution. More centralized planning was required. The media needed a spanking. Labor unions must stop striking. He sounded like a grumpy uncle, denouncing his entire family from the living room rocker.

Having begun in a way sure to upset most of his readers, he then conducted a tour of international relations, stopping off at nearly every region of the world. In both form and content, *The Cloud of Danger* closely resembled a document he had written for the Policy Planning Staff in 1948, "Review of Current Trends: U.S. Foreign Policy." In both, Kennan broke the world into discrete chunks and then prescribed disengagement from all of them except Western Europe, Japan, and the Soviet Union. *The Cloud of Danger* is often distinguishable only by its slightly more worn-down tone. In 1948, he had written of Asia, "Our political philosophy and our patterns for living have very little applicability." In 1977, he wrote of South Asia, "Surely, if there are any peoples of which it may fairly be said that we have nothing to hope from them, it is the peoples of that unhappy region."

But there was one country toward which his attitudes had altered dramatically: the Soviet Union. In 1948, he had written that the men in the Kremlin

> are an able, shrewd and utterly ruthless group, absolutely devoid of respect for us or our institutions. They wish for nothing more than the destruction of our national strength. They operate through a political organization of unparalleled flexibility, discipline, cynicism, and toughness. They command the resources of one of the world's greatest industrial and agricultural nations.

In 1977: "The Soviet leadership must be seen, then, as an old and aging group of men, commanding—but also very deeply involved with—a vast and highly stable bureaucracy." They were aware of the economic and technological backwardness of their country.

> Even if the Soviet leaders had wistful ideas of pressing for some sort of a military contest or showdown with the West, they would not wish to proceed in this direction, or even to hasten the arrival of such a situation, until they had progressed much farther than is the case today in overcoming of these various inadequacies, inefficiencies, and elements of political vulnerability in the situation at home.

The discussion of the Soviet Union was the book's sharpest; Kennan began to sound reflective instead of reflexive. He argued that the United States should not hope for the collapse of the Brezhnev regime: what, after all, would take its place? He asked why hard-liners always declared that we should look at Soviet military capabilities, not their intentions. After all, they simultaneously declared that Moscow should believe in *our* benign intentions. He assailed the United States for not including our NATO allies when counting our arsenal size. "I see no reason to suppose that twenty-nine NATO divisions, eleven of them armored and several of them German, supported with nearly seven thousand of so-called tactical nuclear weapons, look to [Moscow] like the pitiable and hopelessly inferior force they are constantly depicted as being to the Western Europeans and American public."

James Reston called the book "very wise" in the *New York Times.*

Ronald Steel dubbed it "alternately irritating and sensible." Unhelpfully for Kennan, *Pravda* declared that his "views have substantially evolved in the direction of common sense."

After several years out of the spotlight, Kennan was once more a public, and polarizing, figure. Then, in November of that year, he gave one of the most controversial talks of his life. The setting was the Council on Foreign Relations.

Kennan began the speech simply enough, lamenting the "melancholy notoriety" of the X article, now thirty years old. Next, he recapitulated his arguments about the Soviet Union. The men in power were "ordinary" and "perhaps the most conservative ruling group to be found anywhere in the world." They were "suffering greatly under the financial burden" of their "bloated arsenal." He professed confusion at the logic motivating the opponents of détente. He did not specifically mention Nitze, but seemed to have him clearly in mind when he talked about "my friends" who seemed overagitated by the Soviets and who "lose themselves in the fantastic reaches of what I might call military mathematics."

Kennan proposed a gathering of men of goodwill and knowledge of the Soviet Union. They should lay aside their prejudices "and all the arguments about who could conceivably do what to whom if their intentions were the nastiest" and just talk. It would be a time for policy makers to listen humbly to people with experience in, and knowledge of, Moscow.

The legendary diplomat David Bruce and Nitze's confidant Charles Burton Marshall were both sitting near the front. After Kennan finished, Marshall leaned over to Bruce with a wry smile: "George didn't leave much doubt who should chair the council of elders." Bruce smiled broadly. Kennan appeared to be writing a job description that fitted only him—much as he had done in a policy planning paper in which he had suggested that the U.S. problems with Moscow could best be solved by an able diplomat fluent in Russian who also had knowledge of Russian history and culture.

The *Washington Post* reprinted the speech and Kennan soon faced attack from all sides. Richard Pipes, writing cogently and with an even temper in *Commentary,* noted that "a debate between two parties, one of which regards the military relationship as crucial to the understanding of the 'real nature and situation' of the Soviet Union, cannot begin by placing this topic out of bounds." Eugene Rostow, one of the founders of the Committee on the Present Danger, came in with a more personal critique, describing Kennan as "an impressionist, a poet, not an earthling." His "policy is old-fashioned nineteenth-century isolationism, diluted occasionally by flashes of nineteenth century irritation." In the *New Republic,* Henry Fairlie accused Kennan of "senility."

Nitze's typed copy of the speech is marked up throughout. He set a big question mark under the phrase "man of peace," which Kennan had used to describe Brezhnev. Later he underlined "total rejection and hostility from our side," "hard-line opposition," and "chauvinist rhetoric." In a marginal note toward the speech's end, Nitze appeared completely perplexed that Kennan would profess that "the uncertainties [the arms race] involves are rapidly growing beyond the power of either human mind or computer."

BY THE LATE 1970s, Kennan and Nitze had become the diplomatic equivalents of Larry Bird and Magic Johnson: competing icons who admired each other and who would be forever linked. Kennan had become a cochairman of the American Committee on East-West Accord, an organization dedicated to reducing tensions between the two superpowers. Nitze, still the face of the Committee on the Present Danger, was hard at work doing the opposite. Each man appeared on talk shows and before Congress. The old sages were cited in the papers with similar frequency. From the beginning of 1977 to the end of 1980, the *New York Times* and the *Washington Post* mentioned Kennan 102 times and Nitze 108. In May 1978, the *New York Times Magazine* placed the names of the two men on the cover, across from a picture of Brezhnev. "Can Carter Handle Him? Two Opposing Views." Nitze contributed an essay and Kennan gave a long interview. Kennan's answer to the question posed by the magazine was a hedged yes. Nitze's, of course, was no. In the photograph accompanying his article, his eyes were wide open and he seemed to be pointing at the photographer, apparently ready to jump out of the magazine onto a million breakfast tables in order to mobilize the nation against the Soviet threat.

The fundamental difference between Nitze and Kennan was grounded in two long-running disagreements. The first was whether the United States, or anyone, could handle nuclear weapons. Nitze had always believed the answer was yes, from the Strategic Bombing Survey, through his arguments over limited war, to today. Kennan, forever scarred by Hamburg, believed it was no. Nuclear weapons were far too dreadful to leave in any human hands.

The second disagreement was perhaps more important, and it came from their differing views of the United States. Nitze's goal was to make the U.S. arsenal more survivable. He wanted our nuclear stockpile to be harder to destroy and he wanted the Soviet arsenal to be less well equipped to launch a first strike. Both principles, he believed, served the cause of peace. The United States would never start a war, but the Soviets might. The whole point of Nitze's work was to make such an attack less likely to succeed and thus less tempting.

Kennan, by contrast, had never subscribed to Nitze's vision of American benevolence. He considered his country fully capable of starting a war, either through malice or through folly. As important, Nitze might believe that our arms buildup was merely defensive. But Moscow would not see it that way. Each weapon we added was one less city that could survive an American strike. Tensions would rise. And with everyone armed and on edge, a minor incident could initiate a massive conflict—as had happened with World War I.

Neither attacked the other personally in the *Times* articles. Nitze simply asserted that Kennan seemed to believe in "accommodation" and left the charge at that. Kennan did not invoke his former colleague's name, but he did engage in dismissive psychoanalysis. Asked why the hardliners were so worried about Moscow, he responded, "It sometimes seems to me that people have a need for the externalization of evil. They have the need to think that there is, somewhere, an enemy boundlessly evil, because this makes them feel boundlessly good." Kennan, perhaps fearing Nitze's teeth in his calf, tried very hard to depersonalize the disagreement. "I shall soon be seventy-five years of age," he wrote Reston in 1978. "My means and energies are obviously limited. For me to try to involve myself in public disputes with Paul Nitze and others would merely mean to get myself chewed up in controversy."

Privately, though, both men could let loose. Listening to the glowing introduction given to Kennan at a Colorado banquet in the spring of 1977, Nitze began to flex his cheek muscles and clench his fist. Swinging toward one of his neighbors, he "unleashed a tirade," wrote Strobe Talbott. "For more than thirty years Kennan had been idolized; he had been the darling of the intellectuals. It apparently made people of almost any ideological stripes feel virtuous to praise Kennan's supposed virtues as a sage and a statesman and someone who knew what the Russians were all about and how to deal with them. Well, Nitze was getting tired of it. Where had Kennan's way led? It had led into the current mess, into a world in which the United States was weak and almost willfully letting itself get weaker."

When Kennan was roused, his usual response was something closer to a pained lament. Speaking with his biographer John Lewis Gaddis, Kennan said:

> [Nitze] has the characteristic view of the military planner. . . . Who is the possible opponent against whom you're supposed to plan a war? What do we assume on his part? We assume that he wishes us everything evil. We don't inquire why he should wish this. But, to be safe, we assume that he wants to do anything evil to us that he can do. And, secondly, then, when we are faced with uncertainties about his military strength, about his capabilities, we take the worst case as the basis for our examination. These things, I suspect, enter into Paul's views.
>
> And you see, then, that one of the differences is that he is dealing with a fictitious and inhuman Soviet elite, whereas I am dealing with what I suspect to be, and think is likely to be, the real one.

Kennan had become close to Gaddis when the latter was working on *Strategies of Containment,* a book describing all the ways Kennan's views of containment had been modified (and distorted) by his successors. Kennan found it brilliant; Nitze considered it less so. Gaddis recalls fondly an episode when he and Nitze were supposed to appear in 1979 at a conference at the Wilson Center to discuss papers they both had written about NSC-68. At the last minute, an illness prevented Nitze from attending. But he sent along a note to the chair of the session and asked that it be read aloud. "Whatever Professor Gaddis says about NSC-68 will be wrong and should be disregarded," the note said in toto.

NITZE LIKED TO USE models to demonstrate Soviet military supremacy. He would carry around re-creations of Soviet ICBMs, ten inches long and black. The American models were five inches long and white. Sometimes, in speeches or meetings, he would arrange the black missiles to point upward while laying the white ones horizontal.

The models served his primary mission in the late 1970s—derailing the SALT II agreement. As in the past, Nitze's argument was that size did matter. Based on the Ford and Brezhnev deal of 1974, SALT II limited the two sides to an equal number of missiles and launchers. But it did not take into account throw weight. The Soviet Union would once again deploy a brute supremacy.

For the next five years, the two sides discussed the treaty, with Nitze fighting it all the way. He gave speeches and interviews. He prepared meticulous charts and studied the treaty until he knew it as well as anybody. He wrote an eighteen-part series for the Committee on the Present Danger eviscerating the proposals being negotiated.

Carter tried to stroke him at first. He called a meeting at the White House with the members of the Committee on the Present Danger in the summer of 1977, in the vain hope of winning their support. He did not succeed. As the president declared that the American public would not support a massive arsenal buildup, Nitze began to shake his head and mutter, "No, no, no."

"Paul," the president snapped, "would you please let me finish?" In June 1979, Carter and Brezhnev signed SALT II, and Nitze redoubled his efforts. He testified sharply on Capitol Hill, hoping to block Senate ratification. The administration knew who its biggest opponent was. "Paul Nitze is worth 100 bureaucrats," one Carter strategist told the *Washington Post* while glumly assessing the treaty's chances. If ratification were to fail, said the head of the pro-SALT group, that would be "because the administration didn't start early enough to counteract Paul Nitze and others." Carter did however have a plan. "Henry Kissinger we will have to stroke," said one Carter official, "Paul Nitze we will have to beat."

The battle raged through the summer. The administration needed two thirds of the Senate for ratification, meaning that Nitze and other opponents needed thirty-four supporters to block it. Everyone knew the vote would be tense and close, and Nitze was relentless: talking, testifying, writing, arguing. (Kennan, on the other hand, refused an invitation from the Senate to testify.)

By late August 1979, advocates of the treaty thought they had sufficient support and wanted to bring a vote to the Senate floor. But then Nitze pulled his most devious move yet.

One morning, a friend from the CIA came over for breakfast—a former station chief who was quite senior in the agency. The two men began to chat about the Soviets. The United States, Nitze said, was finally ready to recognize the Russian threat. All that was needed now was some incident that would energize people.

The agency man then mentioned that a Soviet brigade was still based in Cuba. After the 1962 missile crisis, about seventeen thousand Soviet troops had stayed to help train Castro's army. Over the years, most had left; that a few thousand remained would not have surprised anyone in Washington. But, the gentleman from Langley told Nitze, he had new information: the agency had photographs and other evidence to suggest that the brigade was training for combat, not just instructing Cubans. Nitze listened carefully, then waved the story off. Everyone knows that, he said. But then he paused and thought for a minute. Maybe not everyone knows that, he said. Maybe a few people have forgotten. Maybe it was time to remind them. Yes, this was definitely news that could be recycled.

The CIA official returned to his office and, aware that he acted with the blessing of one of the most influential men in Washington, quietly made sure the news got around. Soon an intelligence report that identified the brigade as a combat force began to circulate. Word also quickly reached newspapers and key members of the Senate.

Chaos soon followed. Frank Church, of the Senate Foreign Relations Committee, declared that the SALT II treaty could not pass unless the Soviets removed the brigade. Moscow protested that the troops had been there for a decade and a half, and that their mission had not changed. In fact, they considered the charge to be so bogus that the Soviet leadership concluded someone in the White House must have decided to pursue a new, harder policy.

Eventually the Carter administration withdrew the SALT II treaty. The final factor was the Soviet invasion of Afghanistan in December 1979. But the battle had been lost before that, and the Cuban brigade leak was a key factor. Ralph Earle, the administration's lead negotiator on the treaty, remembered the incident with horror. "It was so distorted and overplayed," he said, yet it ruined the treaty's prospects. It was the "banana peel," Earle said, upon which SALT II came crashing down.

The scuttling of the treaty was a defeat for arms control, and for détente too. One of Nitze's longtime Soviet counterparts, General Nikolai Detinov, the top aide to Ustinov, reflected thirty years later that the rejection of the treaty changed the tenor of the debate within the Soviet Union and made everyone in the leadership more tense. Had the Senate ratified the treaty in the summer of 1979, "we would not have gone into Afghanistan," Detinov asserted. In fact, he added, the derailing of the SALT II ratification meant the derailing of the best chance that the two sides had to find a peaceful way out of the arms race.

The failure of SALT II was also a bitter political loss for Carter. Nitze could not have been happier about that. As always, he was eager to get back in; if Carter lost the election of 1980, another high post might open up.

At seventy-three years old, Nitze knew he was running out of chances, so, as the new campaign got under way, he spread his bets. He talked extensively with people close to Ted Kennedy, who was then mounting a primary challenge to Carter. He gave money to the Republican candidate John Connally, a former governor of Texas. He offered to consult for the campaign of former congressman John Anderson. He corresponded with former CIA director George Bush.

Eventually he threw his support to a member of the Committee on the Present Danger who came once during the campaign to dine at his house: Ronald Reagan, the former governor of California and charming B movie star, seen by many ordinary Americans as not just a contender for the presidency but also a challenger to the whole Soviet system.

With Carter, Nitze had joined the campaign early and then blown it. With Reagan, he joined late, but then played his hand well. He awed the candidate with his technical grasp of weapons science, and he held a press conference in order to establish himself as a longtime Democrat who now thought the country should vote Republican.

In November, Reagan swept to victory. Nitze could smile at last: Carter and Warnke were gone; SALT II had been defeated; the United States would surely begin a massive rearmament. And, once again, Paul Nitze was likely to be a member of the nation's highest councils.

16

I AM WORRIED ABOUT
EVERYTHING

In July 1981, Nitze was relaxing, cigar in hand, in his Arlington office, gazing out the windows that looked over the Potomac and back toward Washington. Eugene Rostow, now running the Arms Control and Disarmament Agency, had just called with a question. Might Nitze be willing to lead the forthcoming intermediate-range nuclear weapons talks?

His secretary, Nancy Jenkins, was in the room and the two started to laugh. Nitze had played tough on the call: How much authority would he have? To whom would he be reporting? But he and Jenkins both knew this negotiating was an act. Nitze had been hoping for exactly this call since Ronald Reagan's inauguration six months earlier.

He had not gotten a job when Reagan arrived, languishing as friends and former protégés glided into power. He had hung his coat briefly at the CIA, his frequent employer of last resort. First, he had written a paper for Langley on political unrest in Poland; then he had led a task force examining how the Soviets perceived their own nuclear capabilities. It was marginally important work: appropriate, perhaps, for the average forty-year veteran of Washington who had been collecting Social Security for a decade.

But Paul Nitze was no average seventy-four-year-old. "His manner sparkled with a youthfulness that made colleagues forty years his junior seem tired and spent," wrote a colleague. He still got up at four in the morning to read, devouring books like Konrad Lorenz's *On Aggression*,

Robert Pirsig's *Zen and the Art of Motorcycle Maintenance,* and Douglas Hofstadter's *Gödel, Escher, Bach.* He had kept himself astonishingly fit for a man his age, and he was still a force on the slopes of Aspen Mountain and the clay courts of the Northeast Harbor Tennis Club, where he played with a group of men known as the "silver foxes" and teamed up with his grandchildren in "parent-child" tournaments. "I had a particular philosophy as to how to keep oneself healthy," he once said, "and that was not to do regular exercise of any kind, but to beat your body up at least once every two months. Go off and shoot quail, ski hard, play five sets of tennis a day, or do some outrageous thing that got your body used to adjusting to violent change. It was my theory that this was a better way of maintaining your health than regular exercise. People who did regular exercise got into a rut, and some strange thing would happen and they would get a heart attack."

He kept up that regimen through his eighth decade. Because of it—or perhaps in spite of it—he was still fit, and eager to put that fitness to professional work. Yes, the offer on the table was an arms control job under Rostow, who knew vastly less about arms control; yes, his title would rank him below Paul Wolfowitz and Richard Perle, who had been his interns at the Committee to Maintain a Prudent Defense Policy. But Nitze cared only about having another chance to set policy, at whatever level. And he knew that, once inside, he would find his way back to power. "Paul's position never limited his influence," reflected Harold Brown. "He was convinced that his power of intellect made up for his bureaucratic rank."

Nitze said later that at this moment he flashed back to the late spring of 1950. George Kennan had been out of the Policy Planning Staff for a few months; one day he came to lunch with Acheson and Nitze in the garden belonging to the secretary of state. The three sat down and Kennan said forlornly, "You know, when I left the Department, it never occurred to me that you two would make foreign policy without consulting me."

Now Nitze was in almost the same spot, with one big difference: he was going back in.

He laughed again, his eyes twinkled, and he stuck his tongue out ever so slightly, as he often did when acting sly or ironic. "I feel like George Kennan," he said to Jenkins.

★

SEVENTY-SIX YEARS OLD when Reagan took the oath of office, Kennan had a firm routine when at home in Princeton. He would get up around six-thirty or seven and pick up the papers at the front door (the *New York Times, Die Zeit,* and the *International Herald Tribune*). He would check the thermometer and walk back upstairs to shave. He would dress in a jacket and tie and head to breakfast: hot cereal on cold days, cold cereal on warm days. He would read the papers carefully, often growing frustrated at inaccurate reporting—or accurate reporting of what he considered government folly. Some days he would bicycle down to his office at the Institute for Advanced Study. Other days, he would stay at home and work in his study in the tower that rose above the servants' quarters, completely cut off from the rest of the house. In the evening, he would have a small glass of scotch, but never two. He would dine with Annelise, turn the thermostat down two degrees, and go to sleep.

At first, Kennan considered Reagan an improvement over the previous occupant of the White House. Carter had been loud when calm was required. "Never since World War II has there been so far-reaching a militarization of thought and discourse in the capital," Kennan had written in 1980. "An unsuspecting stranger, plunged into its midst, could only conclude that the last hope of peaceful, nonmilitary solutions had been exhausted." Carter had also been weak when strength was required. Kennan believed that a declaration of war would have been the proper response to the students who stormed the U.S. embassy in Tehran in November 1979 and took sixty-six Americans hostage. He would also have interned all Iranian officials in the United States.

The new men, however, were experienced and competent. Moreover, Reagan's hard-line reputation might present an unusual opportunity. A six-foot-one, strapping, horseback-riding former movie star might be able to propose a major arms deal without being attacked by Congress and the press as a weakling. A few weeks before the inauguration, Kennan wrote to the economist Walt Rostow, Eugene's brother, to suggest that the new administration pledge to reduce America's nuclear arsenal by 25 percent.

Kennan's enthusiasm for Reagan vanished fast. Compared with other movie cowboys, Reagan was outwardly more the brash Sundance than the measured Butch. His strategy for the Soviets? "We win. They lose." At his first press conference, Reagan demonized the Soviet leadership. "The only morality they recognize is what will further their cause, meaning they reserve unto themselves the right to commit any crime: to lie, to cheat, in order to attain that." Behind the scenes, Reagan was much less harsh. In April 1981, for example, he sent Brezhnev a long personal letter urging that the two sides make peace. But publicly, he seemed the kind of man who might have pleased Kennan in 1946 but who grated now.

Kennan quickly shifted from eager counselor to somber condemner, unafraid to say that he was afraid and that Reagan's first few months had provoked in him a pounding fear. As always, Kennan's passion inspired eloquence, a full measure of which he displayed in May 1981 when he gave a speech accepting the Albert Einstein Peace Prize.

"Adequate words are lacking to express the full seriousness of our present situation." Communication between the United States and the Soviet Union had broken down; arms stockpiles had become grotesque. "We have gone on piling weapon upon weapon, missile upon missile, new levels of destructiveness upon old ones. We have done this helplessly, almost involuntarily: like the victims of some sort of hypnotism, like men in a dream, like lemmings heading for the sea, like the children of Hamelin marching blindly along behind their Pied Piper."

He proposed "an immediate across-the-boards reduction by 50 percent" of nuclear stockpiles, followed by a further two-thirds cut in arsenal size. Yes, he admitted, the proposal would be difficult to carry out. But it was worth a try, because we had to believe in our duty: "not just to ourselves (for we are all going to die sooner or later) but . . . to our own kind, our duty to the continuity of the generations, our duty to the great experiment of civilized life on this rare and rich and marvelous planet."

The *Washington Post* ran a front-page story about the speech, followed two days later with a piece entitled "George Kennan's 30-Year Nightmare." Two days after that, the entire text of the speech appeared in the paper. James Reston of the *New York Times* praised the wise words coming from "probably our most distinguished and certainly our most articulate living diplomat." Activists passed around pamphlets with Kennan's words at peace rallies. The Albert Einstein Peace Prize Foundation started a campaign to get ten million signatures in support of Kennan's plan. Kennan later equated the response to that he received from the X article, the Reith Lectures, and his Vietnam testimony.

Support, and possibly even a signature, might have come from an unlikely quarter. The day after Kennan gave his speech, a senator asked Nitze what he thought of the idea. A 50 percent reduction could make sense, he responded. The key condition would be the inclusion of every factor, including throw weight. To eliminate half of the heaviest missiles on each side would indeed make the situation more stable.

THE FIRST THREE years of the Reagan administration were probably the most dangerous of the Cold War. The new occupants of the White House wanted to show Moscow that these were no longer the namby-pamby days of Vietnam retreat and Jimmy Carter malaise. In Reagan's view, Moscow was an evil empire and the contradiction-riddled, pseudo-Leninist monstrosity could be pushed into retreat by American energy, decency, and confidence.

T. K. Jones, Nitze's technical assistant and collaborator in many of his 1970s essays, declared that the United States could survive a nuclear conflict if people dug holes and hid in them. "If there are enough shovels around, everyone's going to make it." Asked in his confirmation hearings whether the United States could survive a nuclear war, Eugene Rostow noted that Japan "not only survived but flourished after the nuclear attack." He added that: "The human race is very resilient."

"Oh, the race is; but I asked if either country would survive," responded Senator Claiborne Pell.

"Well, there are ghoulish statistical calculations that are made about how many people would die in a nuclear exchange," Rostow answered. "Depending upon certain assumptions, some estimates predict that there would be 10 million casualties on one side and 100 million on another. But that is not the whole of the population." Rostow might well have been General Buck Turgidson in *Dr. Strangelove*: "I'm not saying we wouldn't get our hair mussed. But I do say, no more than 10 to 20 million killed, top, depending on the breaks."

Deeds followed the words. In small and large ways, American behavior toward the Soviets took on an edge. The Soviet ambassador, Anatoly Dobrynin, lost his private parking pass at the State Department. The navy secretary, John Lehman, began running exercises far closer to the Soviet coast than any of his predecessors had dared before. American troops swooped into tiny Grenada to free that nation from communism as part of Operation Urgent Fury.

Kennan was not amused. The rhetoric from Rostow and Jones was part of a "mad welter of calculations about who could take out whom, and how many millions might survive, and how we might hope to save our own poor skins by digging holes in the ground, and thus perhaps surviving into a world not worth surviving into." In June 1982, Carroll O'Connor, one of America's best-known actors—he played Archie Bunker in *All in the Family*—visited the Institute for Advanced Study. He saw Kennan, staring out the window and looking gloomily at the falling rain. "Are you worried about things?" asked O'Connor. "I am worried about everything," Kennan replied. After they had been chatting for a few minutes, Kennan asked, "Are you one of the new professors here?"

Moscow was even less amused. Hitler had taken the Soviet Union by surprise forty years ago, and the Kremlin feared the new American president might do the same. "The policy of the Reagan administration has to be seen as adventurous and serving the goal of world domination," Marshal Nikolai Ogarkov told a Warsaw Pact chiefs of staff meeting in September 1982. "In 1941, too, there were many among us who warned against war and many who did not believe a war was coming. Therefore, since the danger of war was not assessed correctly, we had to make many sacrifices. Thus the situation is not only very serious, but also very dangerous."

Driven partly by this fear, Moscow also took *Dr. Strangelove* a step further than Rostow had. During the early 1980s, the Soviet Union had extensive discussions about deploying a doomsday machine that would automatically direct full-scale retaliation for an American strike, even if everyone in the Kremlin were dead and all normal lines of communication severed.

These plans were abandoned in 1985 when the Soviets deployed a system known as Perimeter that would allow for semi-automatic response. The system centered upon hidden "command missiles" protected in heavily hardened silos designed to withstand extraordinary blasts as well as massive electromagnetic pulses. Each missile had the launch codes that could fire off a fleet of ground ICBMs targeted at American cities. The command missiles would soar above the radioactive ruins and send down low-frequency radio signals that would start the apocalyptic vengeance.

Who would issue the order to launch the command missiles? Someone high up in the Kremlin or military command could do so. But if everyone with authority was dead, the missiles could be launched on the order of some junior official in the command center—as long as three criteria had been met. Some top official, in a moment of crisis, would have had to have sent a signal to unlock the missiles; all communication with the military authorities would have to have ceased; and a network of sensors measuring data such as radiation and pressure would have had to determine that the Americans had really hit. In other words, if the Soviets expected the United States to attack soon, they would have had a nearly foolproof way to guarantee that they could strike back.

There was another danger that America did not know about at the time. In the early 1980s, Fidel Castro urged Moscow to launch a preemptive nuclear strike against the United States. According to Danilevich: "The [Soviet leadership] had to actively disabuse him of this view by spelling out the ecological consequences for Cuba of a Soviet strike against the U.S. This changed Castro's positions considerably."

IN THE SPRING of 1982, four of Nitze's former superiors gathered together to repudiate his current boss.

George Kennan, McGeorge Bundy, Robert McNamara, and Gerard Smith made up the quartet. Nitze had served under Bundy in the Kennedy White House and as deputy to the other three men—Kennan at PPS; McNamara at Defense; Smith on the SALT delegation.

The men published an essay in *Foreign Affairs* arguing that the United States should declare that it would use nuclear weapons only in retaliation and would never fire them first. The United States had not made this pledge before because of its fear that nothing else could stop the massive Red Army if its tanks started rolling toward Paris.

The four men had followed very different roads to the same point. Kennan had denounced "first use" in 1950 and could have written the paper at any time in the following three decades. He had not done so, as he told Gaddis in 1984, because "I realized that if I were to write about 'first use' people would say: what the hell does Kennan know about military matters." Smith was an establishment Republican—a Yale law school graduate and the first chairman of the Trilateral Commission. But the Republican Party was trading away people like him during the Reagan years (and receiving electoral dominance in the Sun Belt and South in return). Bundy and McNamara, the antiheroes of *The Best and the Brightest,* had retreated steadily from hawkish positions ever since their years as the confident faces of the Kennedy administration.

Kennan played a minor role in drafting the *Foreign Affairs* essay, and his absence showed. The prose was dense and hyperlogical—hallmarks of the writing of Bundy and McNamara. They argued that renunciation of first use would strengthen the American alliance with Western Europe, where peace movements and antinuclear parties were gaining power. It would reassure the Soviets and it would simplify American planning. If the United States had no first-use intention, it would not need so complex an arsenal.

One of Kennan's few specific contributions was to knock out a personal shot Bundy took at Nitze in one of the essay's drafts. "We could say simply," Kennan wrote, that we "'are deeply unimpressed by the argument, recently so eloquently advanced in Washington . . .' or something similar. Paul deserves the reproach, but this is not the place to administer it."

To maximize potential press coverage, the quartet kept the article secret until close to the publication date. To Kennan, this could "be the most important article that has appeared in *Foreign Affairs* since the last war." They had four big names and utter confidence in their argument. As Bundy told a *New York Times* reporter, "On this issue, if you haven't changed your mind, you haven't been using your mind."

Nitze, of course, had not changed his mind on this issue in thirty-five years. And he eagerly accepted when the White House asked him to write a response for the *New York Times* op-ed page.

But, like Kennan, he did not seem to want to criticize his former colleagues personally. His final draft critiqued the most technical aspects of the article but never mentioned any of the authors by name. Nitze could be blisteringly funny and cutting in private about his adversaries. He once said of Bundy, "Mac was a great success as the dean of the faculty of Harvard, a position in which no man of integrity could possibly succeed." But he had no interest in a personal and public row.

In the end, neither the article nor Nitze's rebuttal had much effect. A minor public outcry and a flurry of press attention for the four wise men was followed by silence. The Reagan administration was not going to change its positions.

Watching from Moscow, the Kremlin thought Reagan's silence ominous; they took it as yet another indicator that he might be planning a first strike. Tensions were high, said Viktor Koltunov, a Soviet arms negotiator and defense official, and announcing a policy of no first use could have substantially calmed them: "it would really have had a lot of impact."

★

WHEN NITZE STEPPED into his new job under Eugene Rostow, many considered him an unthinking nuke-lover. *Mother Jones* magazine anointed him a charter member of the "Holocaust Lobby." The historian Barbara Tuchman declared: "Let us acknowledge it: the American and Soviet Governments have no real desire to limit nuclear arms. . . . It is indicated on our side by the appointment as chief delegate to the Geneva talks of [one of] the high priests of the hardline, Paul Nitze. A rough equivalent would be putting Pope John Paul II in charge of abortion rights."

But people who knew Nitze well thought otherwise. Outside of government, he created stress; inside, he reduced it. The appointment was "a stroke of genius," Paul Warnke said. "[Nitze] will get this administration a deal whether it wants one or not." Richard Perle called his mentor "an inveterate problem solver."

The problem that urgently needed solution was the presence of Soviet SS-20s looming over Western Europe. Moscow had put the highly accurate, mobile, triple-warhead missiles in place in the 1970s, believing that they would provide an invaluable advantage if World War III should break out in the same region as World Wars I and II. The Soviets also had plans for "deep operations," in which Red Army tanks would race across Europe, split NATO, and reach the beaches of France within a week. The SS-20s were essential to accomplishing this objective. According to Danilevich, "the SS-20 was a breakthrough, unlike anything the Americans had. We were immediately able to hold all of Europe hostage."

The monopoly, however, did not last long. In 1979, the Carter administration announced plans to deploy 108 equivalently advanced missiles known as Pershing IIs to Western Europe, along with a larger number of ground-launch cruise missiles (GLCMs). They were scheduled to arrive in 1983. Nitze's job was to negotiate a treaty to limit (or eliminate) both the Soviet missiles already in place and the soon-to-arrive American missiles, which terrified the Soviets because of the speed with which they could reach Moscow.

The logic behind the negotiations was extremely complicated. How could we work a deal in which the United States would trade missiles that had not yet arrived in Europe for missiles that were already there? And when assessing arsenal size, how would we account for weapons held by the British and the French?

One Saturday, Richard Perle came into his Pentagon office to wrestle with the papers stacked on his desk. What possible deal would make sense? Perle thought, read, called in men to brief him, and then spent hours thinking. That evening he suddenly hatched the idea that would drive Nitze crazy for the next three years.

"It came so quickly it literally took his breath away," Perle wrote in an autobiographical novel that, he said in an interview, was entirely accurate in its description of this scene.

> Zero. That was it. Zero. Zero for both sides.
>
> Get rid of all of them—SS-20s, Pershing IIs, ground-launched cruise missiles, the whole lot.
>
> We will abandon our deployment if the Soviets give up theirs. Oh, it was perfect. It was fair. Balanced. Simple. Elegant. Obvious. Clean. Tidy. Neatly wrapped.
>
> How could they say no? How could *anyone* fail to say yes?

Of course, people would criticize Perle's deal: it was demonstrably to the United States' advantage, so the Soviets would never accept it. Perle's "zero option" asked the Soviets to give up missiles already in position for missiles on the assembly line. It was like asking a man to trade his house for a blueprint.

Reagan, however, loved the idea. When Nitze went off to Geneva to begin the talks, he had firm instructions: convince the Soviets to accept the zero option. Nothing else was acceptable.

THE INTERMEDIATE-RANGE NUCLEAR FORCES (INF) talks began on a gray, snowy day in late November 1981. Nitze's black limousine pulled up to the Soviet mission in Geneva; he stepped out and walked up toward the porch of the building. Another man in a gray suit stepped off the porch to say hello. This was Nitze's first encounter with Yuli Kvitsinsky, a man he would come to know quite well.

Kvitsinsky was an up-and-coming Soviet diplomat. Forty-five years old, he had served in the Soviet embassies in both East Berlin and Bonn. He spoke perfect English and German. He did not have Nitze's technical knowledge—no one did—but he matched him in stubbornness. Nitze described the talks in a letter to his sister. "In each session it will go through episodes of competition in wit and humor, calm dead serious-ness, oratory or at least attempts at eloquence, and at least on his part outrageous polemics which I choose to believe offer me fine opportunities for brilliant thrusts, rebuttals and repartee. But underlying it is a sense of deadly seriousness." Frustrated when the Soviets demanded additional concessions on a point he considered settled, Nitze exclaimed, "This horse has already been sold twice." Kvitsinsky, similarly sharp-tongued, once declared that the zero option was "like the hole in a donut."

The two sides grappled for months. During the days, they would argue; in the evenings, they would relax. Gradually, Nitze began to understand his Soviet counterparts better and better. Kvitsinsky's deputy, Nikolai Detinov, remembers long evening conversations with Nitze about the future of computer technology.

Still, Nitze would not budge from zero, and Kvitsinsky would not budge toward it. Meanwhile, protesters massed throughout Western Europe and in the United States, and scientists fretted about the possibility that a nuclear strike would shoot so much soot and smoke into the atmosphere that the world could enter into a period of prolonged winter and mass starvation. In June 1982, half a million people walked from the United Nations to Central Park to demand nuclear disarmament. A few days later, the Soviet foreign minister, Andrei Gromyko, gave a speech discussing the Soviet Union's declared policy of never using nuclear weapons first in a conflict.

Nitze had begun to worry intensely that deploying the Pershing II missiles could divide the United States and Europe. Most damaging, a coalition of working-class, environmental, and antinuclear politicians could bring down the pro-American government in West Germany. That summer, he clipped a newspaper column in which Joseph Kraft described a recent meeting with Helmut Schmidt, the West German chancellor. The Atlantic Alliance was safe, at least temporarily, Kraft wrote. But Schmidt did not believe in stubbornly sticking to zero-zero. He wanted a deal in which the United States would halt its deployments before the fall of 1983. Now was the perfect time, Kraft argued. Russia was bleeding itself in Afghanistan and had recently appeared timid. Gromyko's speech was a positive signal. "So the moment now seems opportune for a major American effort to engage the Russians, at the highest level, in a joint approach to the limitation of nuclear arms that everyone in the world now wants."

"Was Kraft correct," Nitze wrote in one of his notebooks. "If so . . . what is time deadline—Oct 83 or now[?]"

He decided the answer was now. So he carefully hinted to Kvitsinsky that the two of them might solve the problem if they could negotiate alone. Kvitsinsky was intrigued, and on the afternoon of July 16, 1982, the two men got into the Russian's Mercedes and drove to the crest of the Jura Mountains, which divide Switzerland from France. Kvitsinsky's chauffeur let them off and they began to walk along a country road, through mountain pastures, and onto a logging road, until they were walking into the woods. Nitze was wearing boots given to him in 1942—a year when the United States and the Soviet Union were still allies; perhaps, he told Kvitsinsky, the two of them could resolve the irresolvable, now that they were alone, far from the microphones, the politics, the KGB and the CIA, the protesters, the military, the journalists.

So there they were: two men walking down a path, trying to resolve the most vexing division between two giant nations with world-destroying missiles aimed at each other. And Paul Nitze was about to commit one of the most astonishing acts of insubordination in U.S.-Soviet history.

AT THE BEGINNING of the talks, Nitze had told his opposite number that he wanted to strike a deal. He was an old man; he could take risks. The only unacceptable outcome was no progress at all. Playing bridge in his later years, when he could no longer keep track of all that was going on, Nitze would often open with outrageously high bids—three hearts, or six clubs. He might not make the bid, but at least he would get to play the hand. This move in the Jura Mountains was more or less the same kind of gambit.

Nitze had worked out a plan in his own mind for resolving the INF impasse—a plan much more likely to be accepted than Perle's—and he explained it to Kvitsinsky as they walked. The Soviets did not want the Pershing IIs in Europe. Fair enough. But, in return, the United States needed a substantial reduction in SS-20s, and the United States also needed to deploy the less menacing GLCMs. If the Soviets agreed to the terms of Nitze's proposal, each side would end up with 225 warheads, though the Soviets' would be more powerful.

Kvitsinsky listened, pushed back on a few points, and questioned a few technicalities. The two men then sat on a log, making notes, as a drizzle started to fall. They agreed to take the deal back to their respective leaders. Kvitsinsky was initially quite excited; he told Nitze he would send a signal within a few days if he had gotten a positive reception in Moscow. Soon after the two men parted, Nitze returned to Washington, where he cautiously informed his colleagues that he had worked out a grand compromise on his own.

Nitze met first with National Security Adviser William Clark, who seemed receptive. Eugene Rostow supported the proposal, too. Then Nitze visited George Shultz, who had recently replaced Alexander Haig as secretary of state. They went to lunch in the secretary's private dining room on the eighth floor of the State Department; Shultz brought along the director of politico-military affairs, Richard Burt.

The meal started pleasantly enough. Burt remembers thinking that nothing important would come up. But then Nitze started to recount his walk with Kvitsinsky, and he described the proposed deal. As Nitze explained the complicated arguments in favor, Burt's jaw dropped. It was, he recalls, "the most flagrant disobedience toward negotiating instructions that I had ever heard."

After the lunch, Burt gave Shultz his very angry opinion. The deal was a disaster on the technicalities: the United States needed the Pershings, and our allies would go crazy if we did not deploy them. And it was a disaster in form: you cannot simply ignore what the rest of the government has carefully choreographed. Shultz nodded, sphinxlike.

Richard Perle was off at a conference in Aspen, having told his staff not to disturb him unless there was an absolute emergency. On the fourth day, he got a note from one of the employees at the resort where he was staying. "Call your office, ASAP."

Perle rang back and was greeted by an aide who conveyed the impression that something had gone terribly wrong, though not something he felt he could discuss over a phone line. "What's wrong? Tell me what you can," Perle said.

"I'm going to speak cryptically. There's been an event in the negotiations that you need to be aware of."

"Okay."

"It is a potentially new and strikingly different thing."

"Give me some details," Perle said.

"It has to do with our white-haired gentleman."

Soon the two were talking pay phone to pay phone, discussing Nitze's walk in the woods. "Damn," thought Perle at the end of the conversation. He would have to fly back to Washington to confront his old mentor.

For the next few weeks, Perle rallied his troops against Nitze, and against a proposal he called "an act of intellectual and political cowardice." He did not win the battle immediately, but gradually he helped convince President Reagan that the proposal was fundamentally flawed. The Pershings we would be giving up were "fast flyers," Perle pointed out. The GLCMs we would get to keep were "slow flyers." The syllogism appealed to Reagan, who liked his arguments packed in clear and simple metaphors.

Nitze had a chance to save the proposal at a meeting in the White House Situation Room on September 12, 1982. He argued that the deal he had worked out with Kvitsinsky was the one way out of a dangerous predicament. The president did not buy it. Why, he asked, did we have to give up our fast flyers? Because, Nitze said, we had not deployed anything yet: we could not honestly expect the Soviets to trade their houses for our blueprints. Reagan smiled with his customary aplomb and coolness. "Well, Paul," the president said, "you just tell the Soviets that you're working for one tough son-of-a-bitch."

Reagan allowed Nitze to keep open a secret negotiating channel (code-named "King") temporarily. But the channel would prove useless. Kvitsinsky's government had squashed the proposal even harder than Nitze's had.

When he returned to Moscow after his private talk with Nitze, Kvitsinsky presented the plan to Deputy Foreign Ministers Georgi Kornienko and Viktor Komplektov. They reacted harshly. The deal was a hoax. Nitze, the man the Soviets called Grandfather, merely wanted to swindle his counterpart. He did not truly want a deal; he just wanted to figure out what the Soviets would concede by pretending to make a real proposal and observing where the Soviets yielded. Kvitsinsky was instructed not even to respond to Nitze.

Nitze could not escape his past as a hard-liner. The Soviets did not know him well enough to understand that he genuinely sought an agreement. They knew only the Nitze of NSC-68 and of the Committee on the Present Danger. Twenty-five years later, Kvitsinsky said: "[My colleagues] depicted Nitze as a shrewd and dangerous American hawk who hated communists and the Soviet Union. Out of previous experience, the general attitude towards him in Moscow was persistently negative. That is why my confidential contacts with him were met with suspicion and the results of them considered rather a proof of Kvitsinsky's gullibility."

And so the two men trudged back to Geneva. When they met up again, both were bitter, tired, and convinced that there was now little chance of striking a deal. Why try again? The woods of the Jura Mountains had turned out to be a dangerous place.

THE PUBLIC DID NOT KNOW about Nitze and Kvitsinsky's démarche until January 1983, when the White House fired Eugene Rostow and someone on his staff leaked the details. Suddenly, on his seventy-sixth birthday, Nitze was on the front page of the *New York Times,* under the headline "U.S. Aide Reached Arms Agreement Later Ruled Out."

It looked, at first, like bad news for Nitze: his freelancing, and his failure, had been exposed. But then it became good news, very good news.

The story turned Nitze into a hero: he was the man who had tried to make peace. Reporters rushed to his office. Glasses clinked in his honor in Georgetown. The deep thinker from the Policy Planning Staff had returned, replacing the high priest of the hard line. The episode even turned into a play, a story about two peacemakers, titled *A Walk in the Woods.* The Europeans seemed pleased, too. Nitze's sister reported that Helmut Schmidt had told her: "Your brother is the only man in Washington who has the intelligence and experience to understand the present situation facing us all. If, and as long as, he remains head of the arms-negotiating talks without interference, I would put my life in his hands." Even discounted for political flattery and possible sisterly inflation, it was a high compliment.

But adulation did not equal influence. Nitze still could not get the rest of the Reagan administration to back away from its adamant support for zero-zero. As fall came around, and the missile deployment approached, Nitze made one more effort to strike a back-channel deal with Kvitsinsky. But the Soviet negotiator had little interest in returning to the woods.

As the deadline drew near, tensions rose everywhere. In early September 1983, a Korean airliner full of civilians, including an American congressman, drifted over Soviet airspace and was shot down by two air-to-air missiles. Before even determining that the USSR was responsible, the Reagan administration denounced the incident as an act of brutality. The Soviets, for their part, believed that flight 007 was part of a deliberate provocation. In early November, a Soviet spy picked up on a NATO training exercise known as Able Archer and reported that it was the beginning of an all-out launch.

In late November, the Pershings arrived in Germany and the Soviets walked out of the INF talks. The writer Günter Grass compared the arrival of the missiles to the Wannsee Conference, at which Hitler and his lieutenants planned the Final Solution. Others took a more sanguine view. "Mieux un Pershing dans votre jardin qu'un soldat russe sur votre femme," read graffiti scribbled in Paris: "Better a Pershing in your garden than a Russian soldier on your wife."

Nitze was crushed. Not only had he failed, he had earned the enmity of much of the Reagan administration. To this day, Richard Burt seethes when asked about the walk in the woods, declaring that it was all done for "vanity." It had taken years of careful negotiation to prepare the Pershing deployment. But Nitze "almost ran that baby off the tracks."

Still, Nitze was forever rational. Arms deals were not good or bad in and of themselves. The right deal—a deal whereby weapon stockpiles went down but the United States' relative power remained the same or increased—would make the world safer. The wrong deal would make it more dangerous. The only agreement he could have reached in Geneva, once the bargain with Kvitsinsky fell through, would have been a bad one; therefore, he should not regret its absence. "The most important method of preventing a nuclear war is by deterrence," he told *Der Spiegel* after the talks broke down. "That's what really counts. Arms control alone is not going to do it. Arms control can mitigate some of the dangers. It can mitigate the expenses. It can move toward all kinds of things, but it can't be counted on to prevent war."

AS THE GENEVA TALKS lumbered along, Kennan's mood moved from somber to stygian. Just before negotiations broke off, he published an essay in the *New Yorker*, "Breaking the Spell." He believed that relations between the United States and the Soviet Union had become "dreadful and dangerous." Everything he observed suggested that the two superpowers were embarked on "a march toward war—that and nothing else."

The blame lay partly with the long arm of the past: Russia had mistrusted the West for two hundred years. But more blame belonged with the Reagan administration. The Soviet leaders did "not want a major war," Kennan argued. It would not serve their interests in any way. But an American government "madly riveted to dreams of world conquest" might yet drive them into battle.

Only a truly massive arms deal could defer the march toward the precipice. He wanted grand compromises and big sacrifices. Perhaps the United States should just start reducing its arsenal. And he did not want intermediate missiles discussed one day and ICBMs the next. He wanted all the issues treated as a whole, not cut "up into a series of fragmentized technical talks . . . [run] by politically helpless experts." In essence, he wanted to start everything anew. "What is needed here is only the will—the courage, the boldness, the affirmation of life—to break the evil spell that the severed atom has cast upon us all; to declare our independence of the nightmare of nuclear danger; to turn our hearts and minds to better things."

This was exactly the viewpoint that Nitze denounced to *Der Spiegel*. And not surprisingly, Nitze thought the *New Yorker* piece was mush. Writing to Louis Halle, an old friend and colleague from the Policy Planning Staff, he declared that Kennan was correct in his description of the problem. Civility had indeed broken down and the situation was indeed dangerous. But America was not to blame: Moscow was. He also could agree that Moscow did not want a major war. But that was only true in the sense that an aggressor, as Clausewitz said, would always prefer to enter your country unopposed. Moscow was wholly prepared to instigate a series of small wars, and it was confident that the militarily inferior United States would not interfere with those plans.

Nitze had even less patience for Kennan's technical recommendations. "George . . . mentions the field of arms control, which I will skip on the grounds that, at least from my point of view, he knows nothing about it." And he did not like Kennan's solemn tone. "Finally, all this is to be accepted despite its complete separation from fact and logic because George has had fifty-five years of experience dealing with the Russians."

But if Kennan's fifty-five years of experience had not given him perfect insight, Nitze's ten days in the Soviet Union during the Eisenhower administration seemed to have forever confused him. Tripping on an air vent for a bomb shelter in 1955 had helped convince him that the Soviet Union had massive civil defense efforts, which it did not. More important, Nitze endlessly recycled his recollection of Chip Bohlen telling him that the Russian word *mir* meant both peace and a world in which the Soviets ruled. He would often cite this tidbit in op-eds and speeches. To Nitze, this was the key to understanding the Soviet worldview—and he never paused to ask whether an ancient, linguistic idiosyncrasy could really define a country.

Kvitsinsky himself cited Nitze's obsession with the meaning of *mir* as a cause of his misunderstanding of the USSR. "Being a man of integrity and high education, Nitze had nevertheless some strange ideas about Russian history, civilization and intentions of Soviet leadership," Kvitsinsky said. "For example he suspected Russians of everlasting intentions to dominate the world because Russian for 'peace' and 'world' is the same word 'mir.' So (argued he) Russians when demanding peace in their statements actually were meaning subjugation of the world."

AFTER SEVERAL YEARS during which they did not write, Svetlana sent Kennan an angry letter in the fall of 1982, blaming him for her struggles, financial and otherwise. She had gone bankrupt and she was enraged at the school system in which her twelve-year-old daughter, Olga, was enrolled. She and Olga moved to London to start fresh. But the English schools were no better. Unhappy and anxious, she vented at her former protector. He, after all, had convinced her to settle in America.

He replied in measured tones and graceful words:

Dear Svetlana:

I am not going to argue with you about the past. I am sorry, of course, that you look back on it with such bitterness and are unable to understand that a number of people, including myself, did the best we could for you. . . . You know that you have only my most fervent good wishes for your own well-being, and Olga's. I wish some day you could find the peace and happiness life has thus far so largely denied you.

Unappeased, she wrote back:

There is a PATTERN in your dealings with people, George: 1/ you get interested and involved. 2/ people begin to listen to you, because you can provide leadership and advise. 3/ people begin to depend on you and need you. 4/ at this point you abandon them, because you are tired, bored, in a bad mood, etc etc. You have done that with Gene McCarthy Campaign; with George McGovern Campaign; you are doing it now with the Peace & Disarmament Movement (while they just need you MOST, to lead!); and you have done that to me.

Kennan did not write back, and she eventually calmed down. As before, a short period without communication would convince her that she needed Kennan's friendship. In the summer of 1983, she sent him a letter about her fears of nuclear calamity. "OH, HOW I WOULD LOVE to live under a government which does not possess atom bombs and does not threaten anyone."

By the time the missiles arrived in Germany, she was nearly without hope and she was eager for the help of her old friend.

> I do not know any OTHER time when a real threat to the world existence had been so strong and so dangerous. . . . George, you are a great peacemaker, and known for that. . . . PLEASE DO SOMETHING. RIGHT NOW. SOMETHING. REALLY BIG. . . . The world is hanging over an abyss. Time is running out.

Kennan wrote back, despondent.

> It is true that [my recent] statements have received a great deal of publicity and that there are now many thousands of people in this country who listen with respect to what I have to say and who look to me to take some sort of leadership in the effort to ward off the great dangers that seem to be advancing upon us. My difficulty, as you correctly recognized in your letter, is that while I could, perhaps, talk usefully with the Party leadership in the Soviet Union (if not with the military one), I cannot talk that way, and I know of no one who could, with my own government.

George Kennan was also anxious and unhappy—and as the world seemed to edge closer to cataclysm he saw no way to help prevent it. On the verge of his eightieth birthday, George Kennan was a profoundly wearied man.

★ ★ ★

17

WE TRIED, WE TRIED

R onald Reagan's craziest idea turned out to be his most brilliant. In September 1982, two days after the president rebuked Nitze for his walk in the woods, a friend visited and offered inspiration. "Dr. Teller came in," wrote Reagan in his diary, referring to the physicist who had convinced Nitze that a hydrogen bomb could work. "He's pushing an exciting idea that nuclear weapons can be used in connection with Lasers to be non-destructive except as used to intercept and destroy enemy missiles far above the earth."

Six months later, that exciting idea turned into a blockbuster speech. The United States was to devote billions of dollars to the Strategic Defense Initiative, essentially a giant shield that would swat down enemy nukes. Reagan believed SDI could work, would work, and must work.

Nitze had no idea the speech was coming, and neither did most of Reagan's top aides, many of whom would have tried to scuttle it. They knew the Soviets would see such a shield as an offensive weapon. After all, it would be almost impossible to build a shield that would actually stop a deliberate first strike—thwarting thousands of Soviet missiles heading toward America's major cities. If it worked at all, it would be much more useful as a backup to an initial American strike. The United States would fire its thousands of weapons at the Soviet Union, blowing up most of its silos. Some Soviet weapons would survive for a retaliatory launch, but the shield could block those. The shield thus might nullify the principle of mutually assured destruction, which had kept peace for a generation. "Reagan did not tell anyone because no one [would have] agreed with him," recalled the presidential adviser Martin Anderson.

Nitze was a skeptic from the start. Soon after Reagan gave his speech, Nitze followed with one of his own, at the World Affairs Council in Philadelphia, laying out the criteria such a system would have to meet to prove useful. Most important, it would have to be effective. Somehow, we would have to build and launch defensive missiles that would be able to hit incoming missiles—a task roughly equivalent to shooting bullets at bullets. Next, the system would have to be hard to knock down: SDI would do little good if based in, say, a space station that could easily be destroyed. Last, the system would have to be relatively inexpensive. If it were cheaper for the Soviets to fire off a missile than for the United States to shoot it down, then the shield would just spur the arms race. Nitze laid out these points in his speech, and the press soon dubbed them the Nitze criteria.

These were criteria for a rational discussion in a rational world. But Ronald Reagan believed in a dream: the missile shield, promptly nicknamed Star Wars, would magically work and magically keep everyone safe. He also genuinely hoped to rid the world of nuclear weapons—an eventuality Nitze considered extremely unlikely—in which case Star Wars would have the second purpose of thwarting the lone madman who launches a single missile when no one is looking.

With his president believing in a mirage, and the Soviets taking it seriously, Nitze decided the rational thing was to try to trade the mirage for something real. He would help lead a massive sting operation against the Soviets, who had been deluded by a naïve, if earnest, American president. Having seen the Soviet reaction to Reagan's speech, Nitze wrote a memo declaring that the country "should translate this initiative into Soviet movement on the issues of greatest interest to us—the stabilizing reduction of strategic . . . and intermediate range offensive nuclear forces." In other words, the United States would promise not to build SDI if the Soviets agreed to massive arms cuts.

It was a good plan, with one obvious flaw: a decade and a half before, the United States had signed, and Paul Nitze had negotiated, the ABM treaty outlawing future defenses. Star Wars, whether possible or impossible to build, appeared to be illegal.

Eventually, the State Department decided to investigate the issue; the department's legal counsel Abraham Sofaer was instructed to work with Nitze to figure out "the maximum amount of room the president could have under the treaty." Sofaer pored through the negotiating record and consulted closely with Nitze. The two men ultimately concluded that the treaty did indeed ban the "deployment" of a missile defense system. But read carefully, it did not ban the testing or development of missile defense systems based on "physical principles" that had not existed when the two parties made the initial commitment—including, perhaps, some systems based in outer space. This was soon called the "broad interpretation."

When announced, the reinterpretation caused an explosion in Washington. The Reagan administration was not just building more weapons, it was destroying the limitations established by the presidents who had come before. The press pummeled Sofaer, and Nitze too. Congress was furious. Senator Carl Levin of Michigan declared that the legal adviser had written things that were "not true," "wrong," or "a fabrication." To some of Nitze's friends, his endorsement of the broad interpretation was his second great sin, equal to his betrayal of Paul Warnke. He had negotiated the ABM treaty, the unambiguous point of which was to limit missile defense systems in order to prevent a destabilizing of the arms race. "I'll never understand why Paul did that," said John Rhinelander, a close friend and former protégé who had helped negotiate the treaty with Nitze in the early 1970s.

Moscow's response was even angrier. The Soviets saw Nitze's support for the broad interpretation as a sign of his fundamental mendacity. His country was reneging on the most significant arms deal the two sides had ever signed, and Nitze was reneging on an agreement that he had personally negotiated. "When Nitze joined the broad interpretation of the ABM treaty, I was immediately told by my superiors in the Foreign Ministry how wrong it was to conspire with him in the woods," Kvitsinsky said.

The criticism overwhelmed Sofaer. Nitze considered it old hat. He told the forty-seven-year-old lawyer, whose career had been a string of successes up to this point, to ignore all the incoming fire. "They attack you, but you have the chance to do great things."

Nitze also continued to justify his position to the end, and a section of his memoirs is devoted to it. When the journalist David Callahan wrote a long, critical book about him, *Dangerous Capabilities,* the antihero responded in a letter that took issue with only one substantial point: Callahan's dismissal of the legal case for the broad interpretation.

Kennan, meanwhile, wrote to Bundy that he considered the Nitze criteria "quite obscure" and the debate quite unfortunate. On the back of a copy of Nitze's speech, he scrawled a cranky note criticizing what he saw as an effort at dealing with "employment in California, [by] build[ing] superfluous missiles there at vast expense."

EARLY ON THE MORNING of March 11, 1985, mournful music began to play on Russian radio stations. Listeners expecting the usual state-run programming heard Chopin instead. The semi-comatose General Secretary Konstantin Chernenko had died in the night.

By late afternoon, the Central Committee had gathered. Everyone paid their grudging respects to the dead leader and then waited eagerly to hear who would take his place. Foreign Minister Andrei Gromyko stepped up to the podium. He represented the old guard: a plodding, difficult seventy-five-year-old hard-liner who first came to prominence under Stalin. But the man he was about to thrust into power was of an entirely different generation and style. He said the name—"Mikhail Sergeyevich Gorbachev"—and the room burst into sustained applause. The Soviet Union had a new leader and the Cold War suddenly had a new direction.

Neither Nitze nor Kennan understood immediately Gorbachev's significance. Whenever anyone expressed enthusiasm for the new man, Nitze would point out that he was still a communist. Kennan, writing in the *New York Times,* declared that Gorbachev "should produce a much higher order of vigor, flexibility, and thoughtfulness in the leading positions." But he added that the Politburo was a collective body, and "it is not to be expected that the advent of Gorbachev will in any way affect Soviet positions at the arms control talks."

Soviets grasped the magnitude of the change more quickly. Gorbachev was soon cleaning out the top leadership, implementing economic reforms, and beginning a fierce crusade against alcohol. His surprising choice for foreign minister was a reformer named Eduard Shevardnadze. "Yes, this is the opening of a truly different stage in Soviet history," wrote Anatoly Chernyaev in his diary. "Probably something big will come out of it. Gorbachev does not seem to be one of those who stop a quarter of the way through."

Meanwhile, Nitze had grown close to a secretary of state for the second time in his career. The first time, with Dean Acheson, Nitze was too young for the position himself. Now, with George Shultz, he was too old.

Appointed in 1984 as special adviser to the secretary, Nitze made it his first task to educate his boss about weaponry. "George Shultz wouldn't take a step on arms control without Nitze," said Max Kampelman, a fellow negotiator. Education then turned into collaboration on a plan to reduce nuclear weaponry by 50 percent, the magic figure that Kennan had suggested at the outset of the Reagan administration. Nitze worked up a detailed proposal in which the United States would agree to abide by the ABM treaty for a decade, over which time both parties would halve their arsenals. His staffers were instructed to tell no one about their work.

Once he had come up with the proposal, Nitze plotted with National Security Adviser Robert McFarlane about how to handle the politics. Their plan was for McFarlane to run the idea by Reagan, knowing the president might sign off on it even if he did not grasp anything like its full implications. Then they would try to open a back channel with Moscow through Ambassador Dobrynin; that done, they would set out to enlist the support of the Joint Chiefs of Staff. Ultimately, they could present the agreement as virtually a done deal without Perle or Secretary of Defense Caspar Weinberger knowing about it. It was a sting operation on the American side that would set up the larger sting operation with the Soviets.

The first part of the plan worked. Reagan initialed his support, and Shultz dropped a hint to Dobrynin about setting up a private channel through Nitze. But the Russian ambassador missed the hint. The plot was stalled.

Undeterred, Nitze pressed the idea again in early fall 1985, this time bringing the proposal to Kvitsinsky. But his old friend had no desire to get lost in the woods a second time. Kennan's, and then Nitze's, bold idea was dead.

The death of this sweeping plan was the death neither of arms control nor of Nitze's influence. That November, Reagan and Gorbachev were scheduled to meet for the first time, in Geneva. Nitze's job was to brief the president on the fine points of weaponry.

Nitze deeply admired Ronald Reagan, but the president had never been an eager student of detail. Right before the summit, one of Reagan's biographers attended a meeting between the president and Nitze. "I got the impression of a man too polite to say that he thought the distinctions Paul Nitze drew between mobile MIRVed ICBMs (worth banning because of the stabilizing effect of a reduced target-to-warhead ratio) and mobile unMIRVed ICBMs (worth preserving because they would permit a Midgetman RV system to counteract deployment of the SS-25) might just as well differentiate two cans of spinach." As Kenneth Adelman, head of the Arms Control and Disarmament Agency, once said, Reagan "had no knowledge, no feel, and no interest in whether it was missiles, warheads, SEPs, throw-weights, none of that."

If Reagan showed little enthusiasm for nuclear acronyms, he also did not worry. Right before his meeting, he wrote in his diary about his preparations for the summit, noting how well he had napped during his massage that day. "I hope I'm ready and not over trained."

The summit turned out to be a great success. The adversaries decided nothing of great substance. But the two leaders bonded as they sat by a fireplace and chatted. Two men, both with real power this time, now seemed ready to take their own walk in the woods.

There were hints, though, of tension to come. Gorbachev, it seemed, was as unbudging in his opposition to missile defense as Reagan was adamant in his support of it. At one point, Reagan asked his counterpart whether he believed in reincarnation. Gorbachev demurred, but Reagan said he did—and he thought that in a past life he had been the inventor of the shield.

IN EARLY 1986, the historian Gregg Herken publicly and prominently linked the lives of Kennan and Nitze in a way no one had done before. In a well-written and perceptive piece published in *American Heritage,* "The Great Foreign Policy Fight," Herken traced the parallel paths of the two men. Though it cast Nitze and Kennan as opposites, through whose lives one could understand the central conflicts of the Cold War, the article actually united them: both hated it.

Perceiving a liberal bias, Nitze sent a marked-up version back to the author—spotted with blunt "not so"s in the margins. The piece, he felt, was too sympathetic to Kennan. "Dear Gregg," he wrote, "I sense that it is difficult for you to accept that someone might honestly have come to the conclusion that the Western world faced a long term problem with totalitarianism, particularly with the Soviet variety thereof." Fundamentally, he and Kennan disagreed on how to combat that threat. Kennan had wanted us to take very little action against Moscow; Nitze had wanted substantial action, particularly rearmament. Who was right? He was!

"We did in fact do a great deal and were in fact able to put off the worst dangers to the West."

As usual, Nitze refrained from attacking Kennan personally. "I've never criticized the honesty or sincerity of George's position. I merely disagree with him." But his frustration came through in the annotations. When Herken wrote "Of the two, Kennan was the first to oppose the [Vietnam] war and the only one to do so publicly," Nitze crossed off "first" and inserted "second." In the margins he declared, "I was in government, Kennan was not." Early in the piece, Herken wrote, "The two men embodied the clash between morality and pragmatism, ends versus means." In the margins, Nitze scrawled, "No! Later you point out that George was never that much interested in ends; he has not wanted to face up to the means necessary to accomplish his own ends."

Kennan, for his part, ignored the big themes and focused on technical errors, sending Herken a long memo specifying twenty-six mistakes in the rough draft he had received. He copied Nitze and John Lewis Gaddis on the letter and added a cover note. "While most of these taken individually are trivial, the number of them leaves me to wonder whether the author had more than the most fleeting familiarity with my life."

The letter revealed more about Kennan's sensitivity—and acute memory for detail—than about Herken's (genuinely impressive) scholarship. Most of the errors were trivial, and some were more Nitze's fault than Herken's.

Nitze's memory sometimes substituted drama for precision, and over the years he repeated a number of slightly spurious stories about Kennan, a few of which made it into *American Heritage*. Perhaps the most irksome to its subject was Nitze's claim that Kennan had told him in the summer of 1949 that two mobile marine brigades could serve the country's entire defense needs. All attributions of this view to Kennan come from people to whom Nitze fed the tale. The story never appeared elsewhere. No documents back it up, Kennan vehemently denied it, and it doesn't square with the views he expressed elsewhere that summer. Kennan no doubt hoped that copying Nitze on the letter would get his former colleague to stop telling the story. But if Nitze read Kennan's list of errata, he did not remember them. That story and others Kennan debunked would pop up again and again in the interviews Nitze gave and the oral histories he recorded.

Herken's article circulated widely in Washington. Clark Clifford sent a copy to Paul Warnke with a note attached. "On p. 65 is a fascinating piece on Kennan and Nitze. They both end up frustrated. I thought you might find it interesting."

FEW LIVES HAVE A SINGLE DAY as intense as Paul Nitze's October 12, 1986. Phyllis, his beloved wife of fifty-four years, was dying of emphysema, and he was finding it harder and harder to concentrate. Set to turn eighty in three months, he had flown to Iceland with President Reagan for another round of negotiations with Gorbachev at the Hofdi House, a white art-nouveau building on the outskirts of Reykjavík. For more than forty years, since he had walked in the radioactive rubble of Hiroshima, Nitze had obsessed over the forces unleashed by the Manhattan Project. He had studied these powers as closely as anyone alive. If any nonscientist understood them, he did. And though it was his job to talk about them dispassionately, they still haunted him. Now, in Iceland, he suddenly had the best chance of his life to entomb the horrors deep underground.

Reagan and Gorbachev would not have been meeting in Reykjavík had they not hit it off in Geneva the previous autumn. Nor would this summit have occurred if not for the April meltdown of four nuclear reactors in Chernobyl, Ukraine. That disaster, which spread fallout across the Soviet Union and throughout Europe, gave the Soviet high command a new, visceral sense of nuclear calamity. The reactor contained a fraction of the power of one large weapon, yet months later workers in Kiev were still raking up chestnut leaves and sending them off as radioactive waste. That summer, when Gorbachev received the summit briefing papers from his staff, he threw them aside and exclaimed, "Simply crap!" It was the typical stuff—how to score small points and maneuver to get a faint edge—and he was sick of it. He wanted to make some kind of grand proposal.

In late September, Reagan agreed to the meeting, and two weeks later, the two leaders were flying to Iceland. As the Soviets left, Anatoly Chernyaev prepared a memo for his boss. "The main goal of Reykjavik, if I understood you correctly in the South, is to sweep Reagan off his feet by our bold, even 'risky' approach to the central problem of world politics."

Nitze suspected a trap. He had heard rumblings that Gorbachev might offer a serious deal. But the Soviet leader would not mean it, or he would rig it so the United States would have to reject it and appear set on war. He was thus pleasantly surprised when, at the first meeting, on the morning of October 11, Gorbachev offered real concessions, proposing to eliminate the Soviet SS-20s threatening Europe and reducing all weaponry by 50 percent. After that first conversation, the nine-man American team gathered in a tiny acrylic bubble inside the U.S. embassy. There were eight chairs, so Ken Adelman, the head of the Arms Control and Disarmament Agency, sat on the floor, up against the president's knee. "Boy, this place would look great if it was filled up with goldfish," said Reagan. When they got down to business, Nitze called the Soviet proposal "the best we have received in 25 years."

At eight that evening, Nitze sat down to work out the details with the lead Soviet negotiator, Marshal Sergei Akhromeyev, a veteran of World War II who had been wounded at the siege of Leningrad and who later led the invasion of Afghanistan. He was the toughest man Nitze ever negotiated with, and probably the smartest. At one dinner during the Geneva negotiations, he described how he had fought to protect the same road against the Nazis for eighteen months, never going inside a building, even when the temperature dropped to twenty degrees below zero. Secretary of State Shultz gushed and started to exclaim his wonder at the marshal's devotion to country. "Mr. Secretary, there was that," Akhromeyev said. "But I knew that if I had left that road, Stalin would have had me shot."

Now Akhromeyev's boss was gentler and the terrain was different. But he would handle this task with the same tenacity and resilience. He met with Nitze in a conference room with a long table in the elegant Hofdi House, flanked by beverages and a buffet.

"Good evening. I hope that today we will be able to make real progress," began Nitze, according to a transcript of the meeting. The first order of business was how exactly to reduce armaments by 50 percent. The Soviets wanted to cut each category of weapons by 50 percent. Nitze, however, did not like that idea, for the same reason that he had not liked so many proposed arms deals over the past sixteen years. The Soviets were starting with more heavy ICBMs, and if both sides simply halved their numbers, the Soviets would still have more heavy ICBMs. Wouldn't it be better for the two sides to reduce to equal levels?

Nitze and Akhromeyev argued the point back and forth. The conversation was intense but respectful, with each side yielding a bit when they hit an impasse. Here is a typical exchange.

Nitze: "We do not agree with that."

Akhromeyev: "Yes, we should record specifically that our opinions differ on this question."

Nitze: "Maybe we should try to liquidate this difference of opinion?"

They just kept on talking. They made progress, and then they would get stuck. They would make more progress, and then get stuck again. Eventually, they hit the issue of missile defense. Here Akhromeyev was adamant. If the Soviets were to reduce their offensive arsenals so massively, they could not have the United States building space weapons or a shield. Nitze offered to share any missile defense technology created by the United States, a proposal the Soviets considered ridiculous.

At two A.M., Akhromeyev declared, "Right now I suggest we take a break." They would resume the talks in one hour.

NITZE STEPPED OUTSIDE into the frigid night with one of his colleagues, jumped in a car, and drove to their hotel. They woke up Secretary of State Shultz, who was so cold he put a sweater on over his pajamas, and then a robe over that. They asked Shultz what to do, as well as how to settle a dispute between Nitze, who wanted to give some ground, and another member of the delegation, General Ed Rowny, who did not. Shultz told Nitze to do whatever he thought was right. "This is your working group, and you're the boss."

When they returned, it became clear that Akhromeyev had woken up his bosses too, and that they had told him to yield. He picked up the debate with the declaration that "we offer to prepare an agreement for the 50 percent reduction of US and Soviet strategic weapons to an equal number of carriers and warheads for both sides." It was a breakthrough.

Soon the two sides were negotiating limits upon particular types of missiles, as well as challenges in verification. They made progress and more progress. Issues that had sucked away hundreds of hours during past talks were resolved in minutes. And then, finally, they hit the inevitable and very familiar bump: missile defense. It was now 6:30 in the morning and Akhromeyev had had enough. "We brought closer our positions on strategic weapons quite well, but completely disagreed on the ABM. This makes strategic weapons impossible. . . . Thank you for your cooperation."

Nitze hustled back to report everything to Shultz. He had just worked intensely through the night—ten hours straight—and his adrenaline was pumping. He met the secretary at a few minutes past seven and explained what had happened, noting all the breakthroughs. "Damn good! It's what we came for!" exclaimed Shultz. "A terrific night's work, Paul."

"I haven't had so much fun in years," responded Nitze.

Now it was up to Gorbachev and Reagan.

BEFORE THE NEXT MEETING later that morning, the U.S. team huddled in the one private location they could find in Hofdi House, a small bathroom. Three men stood in the tub. When Reagan walked in, he said, "I'll take the throne," and sat on top of the toilet.

When the two leaders met that morning, they immediately returned to their haggling. Nothing mattered except missile defense. If they could resolve that, everything else would fall into place. Reagan could not understand why the Soviets objected to it, particularly since he offered to share the technology if it worked. Gorbachev knew that, if he could not kill SDI, his defense establishment would press ahead with its own, potentially quite dangerous, space weapons systems. And he also understood that SDI actually became more dangerous if built in tandem with substantial weapons reductions. If both sides had massive numbers of nuclear bombs, they could easily overwhelm a proto-defense. But SDI could offer a decisive advantage if each side had only a few weapons.

The rest of the morning session was more of the same. Gorbachev insisted that the United States agree to restrict its research on missile defense technology to laboratories for a decade. Reagan said he simply could not do that. As Richard Perle would later argue, restricting SDI research to a laboratory was like restricting submarine tests to land. The leaders broke for lunch and agreed they would meet again at three. There would be one more chance for the great settlement. Hundreds of journalists waited outside.

When they returned, both sides had come up with radical new proposals that involved eliminating all offensive weapons within the next ten years. Gorbachev, however, continued to insist that the United States restrict its work on SDI to a laboratory for a decade. Reagan said that although he would agree not to deploy SDI for a decade, he needed to be able to test components wherever he wanted.

Discussion grew heated, and the two sides decided to take another break. On one floor, Gorbachev paced, intensely aware of how close he was to a deal. Below him, Reagan asked his top advisers whether he should agree to Gorbachev's terms. Nitze and Shultz said yes. We had come so far; the Soviets had conceded so much. We should close the deal now. But Perle counseled no. Confining research to a laboratory would kill SDI.

The principals returned and tried one final time. Reagan began by reading his proposal to Gorbachev. "The U.S.S.R. and the U.S. pledge for a period of ten years not to exercise their right to withdraw from the unlimited ABM Treaty and, during that period, to comply strictly with all its provisions, while at the same time continuing research, development, and testing permitted by the ABM Treaty."

Gorbachev responded tartly. "Your formula omits any mention of laboratory testing. Was this done specifically?" Reagan bobbed and weaved. Gorbachev snapped, "What I'm asking is, did you omit the mention of the laboratories deliberately or not?"

"Yes it was deliberate. What's the matter?"

Reagan began making an old point that building missile defense was just a way to protect against nuclear maniacs. "Our aim is to safeguard ourselves from a revival of missiles that have been destroyed, in order to make a kind of gas mask against nuclear missiles."

"Yes, I've heard all about gas masks and maniacs, probably ten times already. But it still does not convince me," Gorbachev said in exasperation.

Each recited his now familiar arguments; each appealed to domestic politics, suggesting that colleagues would allow no further retreat. But none of it worked, and eventually there was simply no way forward. The issue of restricting missile defense research was insurmountable.

"It's too bad we have to part this way," said Reagan. "We were so close to an agreement. I think you didn't want to achieve an agreement anyway. I'm very sorry."

"I am also very sorry it's happened this way," said Gorbachev. "I wanted an agreement and did everything I could, if not more."

"I don't know when we'll ever have another chance like this and whether we will meet soon."

"I don't either."

It was over. They had failed—on what now look like the most absurd grounds. Missile defense research was not going to lead to a workable missile defense, whether confined to a laboratory or not. And none of the people in the debate even knew exactly what "laboratory" meant in this context. No one had bothered to define the word upon which the greatest arms deal ever had been shipwrecked.

Nitze and Shultz drove to a downtown hotel to talk with the press. Nitze was exhausted, run down, and crushed. "We tried, we tried. By God, we tried. And we almost did it."

WHEN NITZE RETURNED to Washington, he had lost his voice and he was angry. Looking back on the talks a few days later, he declared that their failure seemed like a setup. He speculated to his friend Charles Burton Marshall that the Soviets had actually wanted the talks to fail. They wanted to bring SDI into disrepute by blaming it for the collapse of the peace deal. He was angry at the euphoria he had felt at the Soviet proposals; he thought he and his colleagues had been "taken in."

Marshall speculated that the Soviets had taken such an adamant position against SDI because they had discovered their own form of defense and wanted to protect their monopoly; perhaps it was something involving high-energy X-rays. Nitze thought that possible too.

It turned out, though, that the Soviet Union had offered so many concessions because Gorbachev understood that his regime was on the verge of collapse. He knew by 1986 that the USSR could not afford its weapons— nor could it afford a race in space. The Soviet Union was like a snake that had broken its jaw trying to swallow an elephant. The system was dying, and Reykjavík was one of the USSR's last chances to survive. Right before the summit, Gorbachev had told the Politburo, "If we don't back down on some specific, maybe even important, issues, if we won't budge from the positions we've held for a long time, we will lose in the end. We will be drawn into an arms race that we cannot manage. We will lose, because right now we are already at the end of our tether."

Reykjavík, in some ways, was like the inverse of Stalin and Kurchatov's explosion of the atomic bomb in 1949. On that day, the United States had lost its monopoly over the atomic weapon. From then on, the springs of the arms race became ever more tightly wound and ever more dangerous.

After Reykjavík, the springs loosened: slowly at first, and then ever so quickly. Gorbachev hadn't offered his grand proposals in Iceland because he had a hidden program in high-energy X-rays. He had done it because the

Soviet Union's economy was imploding. Alexei Obukhov, who was deputy foreign minister under Gorbachev, remembers a sudden shift in his concerns. In Iceland, he worried about space weapons. Soon thereafter he worried that, besides a few boxes of salt, the delicatessen below his apartment had entirely empty shelves. It wasn't long before America's adversary of four decades was waving a giant white flag of surrender.

In December 1987, fourteen months after the apparent failure in Iceland, Nitze was negotiating the final touches on an INF treaty that eliminated all intermediate-range and short-range ground-based nuclear weapons from Europe. It was a far better deal for the United States than the one Nitze had negotiated in the woods with Kvitsinsky. Playing his usual role, Nitze trudged to Capitol Hill to defend it. A few of his old enemies, among them Jesse Helms, argued against it. But the agreement went through. The Soviet Union was commencing one of the greatest going-out-of-business sales in history. Soon, American inspectors would be heading to Soviet military bases—from which even Soviet civilians had long been banned—to observe missiles being dismantled.

With the signing of the INF Treaty, the two sides had accomplished half of the dream deal of Reykjavík. The second half—massive reductions in strategic nuclear weapons—was the last cause of Nitze's career. As he worked on what were called the START negotiations in 1988, he knew it was a chance for him to untie the Gordian knot that he himself had wrapped together so carefully over the years. Here was his chance to officially reverse the great arms buildup he had done so much to start with NSC-68, pushed with the Gaither Report, and driven to a peak with his aggressive bugle blowing in the 1970s.

Ultimately, Nitze, personally, would not succeed. The negotiations were too complicated to finish in Reagan's final year. And Nitze was beginning to slow down. Viktor Koltunov, one of the Soviet negotiators, remembers a late-night session in Moscow especially well. Around one A.M., Nitze quietly stepped out of the conference room where the talks were going on. A short while later, the delegations took a break. In the hallway outside the room, they found Nitze curled up, shoes off, asleep on the couch. They walked by quietly and respectfully, in awe of the eighty-one-year-old man who had done so much through the years and now simply needed a little rest.

When George H. W. Bush became president, Nitze yearned to continue his work. But the new administration had little interest in him.

"Nitze was old and crotchety," said one top aide to Secretary of State James Baker. Two weeks after the inauguration, Nitze wrote to his sister, "It is rather Kafka-like. Whenever they decide to talk to me, I will make up my mind what to do."

A few months later, they still were not talking to him. Baker had offered him a big office and the title of ambassador at large emeritus—but nothing to do. It was exactly the opposite of the sort of position in which he had thrived throughout his career. So he resigned. And, naturally, Nitze did not go silently. He left office on May 1 and, on May 3, his wry, smiling face was atop the front page of the *New York Times*: "Reagan Arms Adviser Says Bush Is Wrong on Short-Range Missiles." More interviews, and more darts, would follow.

The START talks did indeed end with an agreement—but it was anticlimactic, coming in July 1991, just weeks before a coup started the process by which the Soviet Union disappeared. People were not going to end the arms race. Events would.

ALMOST FORTY-FIVE YEARS before the Soviet Union collapsed, George Kennan accurately predicted the closing act. "If anything were ever to occur to disrupt the unity and efficacy of the Party as a political instrument," wrote X, "Soviet Russia might be changed overnight from one of the strongest to one of the weakest and most pitiable of national societies."

The whole thesis of that famous article had been that our adversary appeared strong, but the strength rested on savagery and illusion. Properly contained, the Soviet order would eventually rot from the inside out.

> Who can say with assurance that the strong light still cast by the Kremlin on the dissatisfied peoples of the western world is not the powerful afterglow of a constellation which is in actuality on the wane? This cannot be proved. And it cannot be disproved. But the possibility remains (and in the opinion of this writer it is a strong one) that Soviet power, like the capitalist world of its conception, bears within it the seeds of its own decay, and that the sprouting of these seeds is well advanced.

The seeds took much longer to sprout than Kennan thought or hoped. But when at last they did, they were like acorns that had slowly germinated and then suddenly burst through the stones above. Every seventy years or so, historians have noted, Western civilization turns upside down. It happened in 1776, 1848, 1917—and in 1989. First came the bloodless revolution in the Baltics, where the Soviet regimes in Latvia, Estonia, and Lithuania collapsed. In November, hordes of young Germans took their axes to the Berlin Wall. That same year the greengrocers of Eastern Europe took down the party signs from their windows, and the tyrants in Poland, Hungary, Czechoslovakia, Bulgaria, and Romania toppled from their pedestals. The iron curtain was rolled up as swiftly as it had descended. "We have literally no time even to be astonished," said Václav Havel, the Czech playwright-turned-dissident-turned-president.

The next year, the USSR's ethnic republics began to defy Moscow's authority. Gorbachev survived the August 1991 coup of orthodox Soviets against him, but after that he was a ghost. By the end of the month, Nitze's negotiating partner at Reykjavík, Marshal Akhromeyev, had become so depressed by the course of events in his country that he committed suicide. At the end of 1991, Boris Yeltsin deposed Gorbachev and suddenly the USSR ceased to exist. Its demise was accompanied by less violence than the average revolution in Guatemala.

Kennan had not gotten it all right. But he had foreseen how fast change would come once it began, and he had even perceived the potential role of ethnicity. In *The Cloud of Danger,* in 1977, he wrote:

> This nationalistic restlessness in the constituent republics is not a serious short-term problem for the regime, but it is a hard one to cope with; for both tolerance and repression tend to enhance rather than to dispel it. If, therefore, the regime does not have to fear it excessively in the short term, it has to recognize that it has still not found the answer to it. And this, too, is disturbing for anyone within the regime who has any historical sense; because the very similar nationalistic restlessness that prevailed among certain of these minority people in the Tsarist time proved, when that regime came under severe pressure, to be one of the major factors that conduced to its downfall.

Unlike many other students of Russia and Sovietism, he had seen how perilously loose was Gorbachev's grip on power. In February 1991, he wrote in the *Washington Post* of his doubt that "what we know as the Soviet Union can any longer be governed from a single center at all." And on the *MacNeil/Lehrer NewsHour* right after the August coup, he declared that neither Gorbachev nor the country would recover. "Kennan was the one person in the United States who really got it," said James Billington, a historian of Russia and later the librarian of Congress, who was in Moscow at the time. And the endgame in Moscow was not all that Kennan foresaw. Just before Warren Zimmermann headed off to serve as U.S. ambassador to Yugoslavia in 1989, Kennan explained to him that the country would soon shatter and that the United States would get pulled into the disaster.

As the Cold War ended, Kennan changed, in the minds of many, from pesky dissident to sage. Forgotten were his cries about the nuclear danger. What people remembered now was that this man had designed the strategy that ended up winning the Cold War. In 1989, he won the Presidential Medal of Freedom. President Bush's deputy chief of staff, James Cicconi, had the task of notifying the recipients that year. One of them, the baseball star Ted Williams, refused to come because he did not want to appear in public on crutches. Kennan, reached in Norway, responded with utter dignity and his customary grace: "I would be honored to be anywhere that the president of the United States wants me to be."

"George is a happy man now," wrote Arthur Schlesinger Jr. in his diary. "He basks in an atmosphere of belated but heartfelt recognition and approval." After he testified before the Senate Foreign Relations Committee on April 4, 1989, everyone in the room, including the committee members, broke into spontaneous applause. Asked by Senator Claiborne Pell when that had last happened, the committee clerk said 1966—when Kennan had testified about Vietnam.

Kennan had created the concept of containment, which, whether he liked it or not, had guided America's foreign policy for half a century. Although the idea had provided the justification for so many initiatives that Kennan disapproved of, the essential strategy had nonetheless won out. Even hard-liners gave him grudging credit. According to Richard Perle, Kennan had been "right for an instant—if wrong forever after." When Bill Clinton came to power in 1993, aides began trying to come up with a new name for his amorphous post–Cold War foreign policy. They called the quest "the Kennan sweepstakes."

AS THE SOVIET UNION CRUMBLED, Nitze stayed focused on the tasks at hand. "He didn't live in the past; he lived in the present," said George

Shultz, reflecting on meetings he had with his partner in the early 1990s to discuss reconstructing what was now Russia.

But eventually Nitze did begin to bask somewhat in the attention awarded to the men who had designed America's Cold War strategy. "Paul Nitze's mind and his memory of his experiences are a national treasure," declared a Senate resolution. Newspapers and magazines ran adoring profiles. The *Time* reporter Strobe Talbott published *The Master of the Game,* a meticulous history of Nitze's career as an arms negotiator. The School of Advanced International Studies renamed itself after its cofounder.

In retrospect, his was a remarkable career. The United States had, for the most part, followed his militant version of containment: arming itself, but never actually trying to roll back the Soviet Union. On nuclear arms policy, he had long pursued two objectives: making the United States a less tempting target for the Soviets and negotiating deals that would make an attack less likely. And whether he could take credit for it—or whether success came in spite of him—Moscow never did launch. "I've come to the conclusion we did it pretty goddam well," he said in a 1995 interview. "The Cold War achieved the eventual triumph of freedom over tyranny, and that was a very important triumph. Thank God for the Cold War, and thank God that it turned out the right way."

Until the end of his life, Kennan kept in his home office a newspaper front page from the day the Berlin Wall came down. But he was far less enthusiastic about the final result than Nitze was. Yes, the nuclear danger had now diminished. But victory, if it was that, had come at a great cost: to civil society, to our economy, and even to an orderly Russia.

In his view, the conflict had gone on too long and been too militarized. American belligerence had merely encouraged Soviet belligerence, which had encouraged the arms race. In 1992, he published an op-ed in the *New York Times,* "The G.O.P. Won the Cold War? Ridiculous." His argument was one he had made many times before: "The suggestion that any Administration had the power to influence decisively the course of a tremendous domestic upheaval in another great country on another side of the globe is simply childish." He could have retold his story about the fly on the nose of the ox who returns to the village to proclaim, "We've been plowing."

For his part, Nitze was in no position to seek credit for spending the Soviets into oblivion, as many Republicans liked to do after the conflict ended. After all, he had advocated passionately in the Reagan years for cost-saving arms deals. But he could feel vindicated in the principle he had articulated in the 1950s: respond to every problem, day to day, and assume that your efforts will help things work at the end. If you looked at the arms race at any given moment, the future seemed hopeless. Surely, at some point, either the Soviet Union or the United States would launch a strike that would destroy the world. But was it possible to imagine that the United States could survive the next decade? Yes. And could doing so reduce the odds of catastrophe in the decade after that? Yes. That pragmatic approach—despite a few terrifying episodes and a lot of wasted money— had helped to keep the world from Armageddon.

A few years after the Cold War ended, Nitze published a book called *Tension Between Opposites: Reflections on the Practice and Theory of Politics*. The premise came from Heraclitus: one way to seek truth was to think about the way tension works in a bow or a guitar, which depend on strings being pulled simultaneously in opposite directions. In the first chapter, Nitze quoted from his 1953 commencement speech at his son's boarding school:

> The great problems with which all of us have been wrestling . . . include the individual versus society, change versus continuing order, force versus consent, the East versus the West, power versus responsibility. In each case the answer is to be found not in the elimination of one of the opposites or in any basic compromise between them but in striving for a harmony in the tension between opposites.

One could make the same point about the harmony between Nitze's and Kennan's viewpoints during the Cold War. They pulled in different directions but, as suggested by the toasts they gave at Kennan's eightieth birthday party, the two men complemented each other. Kennan's ideas and methods were not practical and could do little to help solve day-to-day problems. He could not, for example, have been an effective arms negotiator. Nonetheless, he played a crucial role, both in framing the conflict and then serving as his nation's conscience as those horrifying weapons hypnotized the superpowers more and more. Kennan, the outsider, accurately foresaw how the Cold War would play out. Nitze, the insider, helped bring about the Cold War's end by behaving as if Kennan's prophecy would never come true.

EPILOGUE

Old age, and the fall of the Soviet Union, released Nitze's inner liberal. In January 1991, ten days before America began bombing Iraq, he said that the United States could contain that country with a blockade and sanctions; war was not necessary. He also joined the board of the Environmental Defense Fund, focusing on acid rain because he thought it a narrow enough issue that he could master it in the time he had remaining. He worked for an international treaty to ban land mines, and another to ban chemical weapons.

His new political endeavors solidified the position in the Washington establishment that his many years of public service had already earned him. At his ninetieth birthday party, a grand fete in Washington's Metropolitan Club, Supreme Court justice Sandra Day O'Connor read some verses she had written that summed up the way many people there felt.

Paul Nitze—a name we all know
A man whose life leaves us aglow
Aglow with amazement that he,
In only 90 years, could be
A scholar, investor, author
Diplomat and aristocrat,
Navy Secretary, pundit.
All matters he met with true grit.

There is more to tell than space permits.
The traits we most admire—it fits
Husband, father, skier, dancer
Horseman, donor, and romancer,
At tennis and bridge he stars too.
He surpasses us all—so what's new?
Paul, we salute you, entreat you,
To see that just ninety's too few.

In October 1999, Nitze invited his friend Jurek Martin of the *Financial Times* over for coffee and declared that after years of quiet contemplation he had decided that we should eliminate our entire nuclear arsenal. Martin went home, typed up Nitze's argument as he remembered it, read it back for approval over the telephone, and then sent it to the *New York Times* op-ed page.

In Nitze's prime, the piece would never have met his standards for rigorous thinking. The argument was composed of blunt assertion, and it passed over the complicated attendant questions, such as how to deal with future blackmailers. "Why would someone who spent so many years negotiating with the Soviet Union about the size of our nuclear arsenal now say we no longer need it?" Nitze asked in the piece.

I know that the simplest and most direct answer to the problem of nuclear weapons has always been their complete elimination. My "walk in the woods" in 1982 with the Soviet arms negotiator Yuli Kvitsinsky at least addressed this possibility on a bilateral basis. Destruction of the arms did not prove feasible then, but there is no good reason why it should not be carried out now.

But if the piece was simple, it came from an honest and sound heart. Five years before, Nitze had written that the country needed to place much less reliance on such armaments. In a study group the year after that, he had joined in concluding that the country should start to move toward nuclear renunciation.

Nitze was touched by the warm letter that Kennan wrote in response to his op-ed, with the author noting how pleasant it was to find them finally in agreement after their half century of contrasting views. But Nitze's conversion was based on the facts at the time; he certainly did not think his past judgment had been in error. Not long afterward, talking with the journalist James Srodes, he said: "[Kennan] always thought that I hijacked our Cold War policy of containment away from him." He paused and then chuckled: "And I did, of course."

THE END OF THE COLD WAR gave George Kennan a chance to reflect in a way he had never done before. He published a book of political philosophy—one that showed him to be a true conservative, in that he did not want significant changes in either the environment or the culture. He followed that with a work about the hard-laboring agrarian past of the Kennan line, *An American Family*. It was published when he was ninety-six years old; he labored to find the strength to depress the keys on his typewriter while working on it. And then came the last intellectual project of his life: a deep analysis of his religious faith.

Kennan had rarely discussed the subject publicly, but he had long pondered it. Raised a Presbyterian, Kennan maintained a certain distance from formal religion for most of his adult life. But age and a sense of his own mortality had pulled him closer to Christianity. In October 2002, he sent a twenty-page letter to his children.

The beginning was personal. He avowed his deep feelings of connection to Helmuth von Moltke and observed that the barrenness of secular Soviet ceremonies made him yearn for Christian ones. But most of the letter was didactic. He wrote, for example, how he had taken a skeptical historian's eye to the Gospels. Not only were they based on hearsay, but by focusing so intently on miracles, they emphasized merely the authors' own shallowness, and not the greatness of their subject. St. Paul, he wrote, was a courageous man and a great leader. But Kennan disliked him for distorting the historical record. And Paul, he argued, had clearly overstated his personal intimacy with Jesus.

But the letter's most compelling passages involved his vision of the human spirit and his answer to the fundamental question surrounding Christianity: if God is all-powerful, why is there evil in the world?

To Kennan, the answer was one provided by a small but passionate group of spiritual thinkers through history: God is not all-powerful. "I can see this whole range of human predicament as something beyond divine motive or control—rather as a limitation, if you will, on the almightiness of the divine power. But this, to my mind, is no reason for the abandonment of what we call faith."

It was classic Kennan. He did not explain away evil or pain; after all, he had spent his life brooding on them. And he even seemed to be bringing his realism to religion. One nation cannot control others; and one all-powerful God does not control us. As with so much else that he wrote, Kennan's words were profound and moving:

> At no time in my life have I ever been devoid of the awareness that I was accompanied, surrounded, and penetrated by some sort of tremendous spirit—the Holy Spirit, if one wishes to call it that, and one that stood in some intimate essentially benevolent if critical relationship to all that I was doing or experiencing. Without that awareness, life would have lost all hope and meaning.

IN LATE SEPTEMBER 2001, I visited my grandfather in his home in Georgetown. As he often did, he sat in his study, leaning back deeply in an oversized easy chair. A cane rested by his side. Books were stacked on the side table next to a small silver bowl of nuts and a glass of red wine. He moved slowly and had grown a light, scratchy beard. He talked infrequently and with great effort, and I would often come just to sit near him and keep him company. Sometimes I would read to him.

This day, he started by saying how shaken he had been by the terrorist attacks on the Pentagon and the World Trade Center. I nodded, and told him I agreed. After waiting for a bit, I decided to ask a question. Looking over his bookshelf, I noticed the complete works of Conrad, each conspicuously worn. I was a little taken aback. "How, Gramps," I asked, "did you have time to read all of these books when you were negotiating all the arms treaties?"

"Missiles are boring," he replied deliberately. "Conrad is interesting." He then began to reflect a bit over his life. Again he paused for a second. "Sometimes I think I have had so much more luck than I deserve." That evening, I wrote down another nugget of wisdom he passed on that day: "I keep going because I still find it interesting."

Three years later, in the summer of 2004, we had our last conversation. I came by to tell him of my engagement and plans for a wedding that

I knew he was far too frail to attend. "Is she kind?" he asked. Yes, I replied. He came back with the last sentence he ever said to me. "Tell me about her."

On October 19, 2004, he let go his grip on life.

KENNAN GAVE ONE final public interview, in 2002, when he was ninety-eight, warning that the United States should not rush into Iraq. "War has a momentum of its own, and it carries you away from all thoughtful intentions when you get into it. Today, if we went into Iraq, like the president would like us to do, you know where you begin. You never know where you are going to end."

His body was frail, though, and he knew it was time to tie up his most important loose end. One day he put on his coat and tie and told his nurse, Betsy Barrett, that he wanted to pray for his mother, who, he said, had died knowing that she would never know her son. He went to his church and spent fifteen minutes on his knees. He never mentioned her again.

Kennan was determined to be alert for his hundredth birthday. As the day neared, he tried to stay sharp by folding little pieces of paper and trying to keep track of them. But he knew he was losing control of his mind, just as his wife of more than seventy years had. Annelise was of sound body, but she could no longer remember what she had done during the day.

One of the last things Barrett remembers is Kennan tenderly looking at Annelise, who he knew could no longer understand him. He wished, he said, that "we could go down the steps and out through the door together."

He died, at age 101, on March 17, 2005, just 149 days after the death of his lifelong rival and friend.

NOTES

The following abbreviations appear in the endnotes and bibliography.

AFOH: Air Force Oral History
AHN: Anina Hilken Nitze (Paul's mother)
BRB: boiler room boxes (Boxes found in the boiler room of SAIS; these files are now in the possession of the Library of Congress.)
CBW: C. Ben Wright
CEB: Charles Eustis Bohlen
CFR: Council on Foreign Relations
DGA: Dean Gooderham Acheson
FHTG: *From Hiroshima to Glasnost*
FRUS: Foreign Relations of the United States
GFK: George F. Kennan
GFKFBI: George Kennan file held by the Federal Bureau of Investigation
GFKP: George F. Kennan papers
GFKP OF: George F. Kennan papers, Office Files (These files were examined before the Princeton Library made them public; thus, the box numbering system is likely different from the one in current use.)
HSTL: Harry S. Truman Library
JEK: Joan Elisabeth Kennan (Kennan's daughter)
JEKP: Joan Elisabeth Kennan Private Papers
JH: Jeanette Hotchkiss (Kennan's sister)
JLG: John Lewis Gaddis
JRO: J. Robert Oppenheimer
LOC: Library of Congress
LP: Lana Peters (Svetlana Alliluyeva/Svetlana Stalin)
memcon: memorandum of conversation

MOTG: *Master of the Game*
MSOW: *Measures Short of War*
MV1: *Memoirs: Volume 1*
MV2: *Memoirs: Volume 2*
NARA: National Archives and Records Administration
NSA: National Security Archive
NYT: *The New York Times*
OH: oral history
OOY: *Only One Year*
PFC: Personal Filing Cabinet
PHN: Paul Henry Nitze
PHNP: Paul Henry Nitze Papers
PHNFBI: Paul Henry Nitze file held by the Federal Bureau of Investigation
PHNPP: Paul Henry Nitze personal papers
RG: Record Group
SAIS: School of Advanced International Studies
SOS: Secretary of State
TBO: *Tension Between Opposites*
TEY: *The Early Years*
USSBS: United States Strategic Bombing Survey
WAN: William Albert Nitze (Paul's father)

PAGE   PROLOGUE

1   *Nitze arrived just*: Walter Pozen, author interview, Dec. 10, 2008.
1   *"Among those born"*: PHN remarks at Kennan birthday, PHNP LOC, box 29,
     folder 5.
2   *"it may be best"*: Gregg Herken, "The Great Foreign Policy Fight," *American
     Heritage*, April/May 1986, 66–79.
2   *Nitze smiled and*: PHN, *TBO,* 131.
3   *Nitze still wanted to win*: Ronald Steel, author interview, March 27, 2005.
3   *sent a letter*: PHN to Louis Halle, Nov. 10, 1983, PHNP LOC, box 29, folder 5.
3   *"Nitze was a God"*: Aleksandr Savelyev, author interview, Feb. 12, 2009.
3   *"Presidents came and went"*: George Shultz, author interview, Jan. 26, 2009.
6   *"They both were"*: Alexander Bessmertnykh, e-mail to author, Jan. 16, 2009.

1. NOW IS THE TIME TO LIVE

7   *He stood on*: JEK, author interview, March 8, 2008.
7   *marking each victory*: Ilya Ehrenburg, *The War,* 173; and Gabriel Temkin,
     My Just War, 205.
7   *Soviet citizens had swarmed*: Robert Tucker, OH, NSA, Nov. 30, 1995.
7   *on a cloudless day*: Ralph Parker, *Conspiracy Against Peace*, 5.
7   *thousands*: GFK to SOS, May 9, 1945, FRUS: 1945, vol. 5, 849.
7   *it had supplied wartime*: Robert Tucker, OH, NSA, Nov. 30, 1995.
8   *"Now is the"*: ibid.

8 *"if I'd played"*: *Chicago Daily Tribune*, "Won't Destroy Germany or Its People: Stalin," May 10, 1945, 1.

8 *Amid the frenzy*: GFK, *MVI*, 240–42.

8 *"The aftermaths of"*: GFK to JH, 1943, GFKP, box 7R.

8 *Terrified that the*: GFK to SOS, May 9, 1945, FRUS: 1945, vol. 5, 849.

9 *Everything in his life*: JEK, author interview, Jan. 6, 2009.

9 *He enjoyed making*: JEK, author interview, March 8, 2008.

10 *"As always Russia"*: GFK to JH, Oct. 8, 1944, GFKP, box 7R.

11 *The crowd quieted*: JEK, author interview, March 8, 2008.

11 *"Congratulations on the"*: GFK, *MVI*, 241.

11 *he would stay up*: Heidi Nitze, author interview, Dec. 24, 2008.

11 *He delighted in*: PHN, AFOH, 5.

11 *After work, he*: Paula Zurcher, author interview, April 3, 2008.

12 *"PHN collects people"*: Letter from PPN to friend, n.d., PHNPP.

12 *As he liked*: PHN, *FHTG*, 23–25.

12 *The Nitzes had*: PHN, *TEY*.

12 *His father pinned*: ibid.

12 *In spring 1937*: ibid.

13 *About an hour*: George Ball and John Kenneth Galbraith, "The Interrogation of Albert Speer," *Life*, Dec. 17, 1945, 57.

13 *Speer probably knew*: PHN to AHN, June 16, 1945, PHNP LOC, box 165, folder 5.

13 *His statues would*: Geoffrey Barraclough, "Hitler's Master Builder," *New York Review of Books*, Jan. 7, 1971.

13 *As German production*: John Kenneth Galbraith, "Albert Speer Was the Man to See," *NYT*, Jan. 10, 1971.

13 *Hitler had spent*: Hugh Trevor-Roper, *The Last Days of Hitler*, 201.

14 *When answering, he*: Galbraith, "Albert Speer Was the Man to See."

14 *Commanding an awe-inspiring*: Minutes of Meeting with Albert Speer, May 17, 1945, NARA, RG 243, box 6.

14 *"I wanted to"*: Minutes of Meeting with Reichminister, May 19, 1945, NARA, RG 243, box 6.

14 *"The second visible"*: ibid.

15 *Ball later recalled*: George Ball, *The Past Has Another Pattern*, 63.

15 *"We were always"*: Galbraith, "Albert Speer Was the Man to See."

15 *"Paul, if you've got"*: Paul Nitze, OH, HSTL, June 11, 1975, 81.

15 *"So now the"*: Joachim Fest, *Speer*, 280.

16 *George Kennan knew Germany*: Anders Stephanson, *Kennan and the Art of Foreign Policy*, 119.

16 *Bad Nauheim*: Charles Burdick, *An American Island in Hitler's Reich*, 34–35.

16 *Kennan's friends there*: ibid., 75–85.

16 *But Kennan had*: GFK to Robert Murphy, May 10, 1945, GFKP, box 28, folder 6.

16 *Now he sought not*: GFK, "Noble Man," *New York Review of Books*, March 22, 1973.

17   *Kennan, however, believed*: GFK, *MV1*, 258.

17   *A dismembered Germany*: GFK to CEB, Jan. 26, 1945, GFKP, box 28.

17   *"We should accept"*: ibid.

17   *His final letters*: Helmuth von Moltke, *Letters to Freya*, 405–407.

18   *The Soviet government, wrote Kennan*: GFK, *MV1*, 541.

19   *In a letter home*: PHN to AHN, undated, PHNPP.

19   *one of the Survey's assistants*: Richard C. S. Trahair, *Encyclopedia of Cold War Espionage*, 156.

20   *Colleagues remember him*: Murray Bovarnick, author interview, Nov. 11, 2007.

20   *A devout communist*: Philip Knightley, "The Spy Files," *Independent*, Nov. 17, 2006, 16.

20   *One was the result*: Benjamin B. Fischer, "Farewell to Sonia, the Spy Who Haunted Britain," *International Journal of Intelligence and Counterintelligence*, Jan. 2002, 61.

21   *Japan would, as he later*: PHN, *Vital Speeches of the Day*, Sept. 15, 1995, 723.

21   *"Certainly the testimony"*: PHNP LOC, box 166, folder 4.

21   *Two days before*: Gregg Herken, *Counsels of War*, 4.

21   *As the mushroom cloud*: Lansing Lamont, *Day of Trinity*, 242.

2. CHARMING, WITTY, AND URBANE

23   *"One moves through"*: GFK, *MV1*, 4.

24   *As the story was told*: Grace Warnecke, author interview, April 9, 2008.

24   *an indifferent stepmother*: GFK, JEK interview, n.d., JEKP.

24   *The only keepsake*: JH, JEK interview, n.d., JEKP.

24   *"in some way or"*: GFK, JEK interview, n.d., JEKP.

24   *"George, stop thinking"*: CBW, *George F. Kennan: Scholar-Diplomat*, 2.

24   *built the wrong*: JEK, author interview, March 15, 2008.

25   *The discipline did*: JEK, author interview, March 8, 2008.

25   *At Camp Highlands*: Timothy Bachmann, e-mail to author, April 25, 2008.

25   *The two were*: GFK, JEK interview, n.d., JEKP.

25   *"The net is drawn"*: GFK to JH, 1919, GFKP, box 7R.

26   *In a riotous 1922*: GFK to JH, Nov. 1, 1922, GFKP, box 7R.

26   *"Now do you"*: GFK to JH, Nov. 10, 1922, GFKP, box 7R.

26   *But that fleeting*: GFK, *MV1*, 12. Ultimately, Kennan graduated in 1925 with a degree in history and a GPA of 2.72, putting him 83rd in a class of 219.

27   *She befriended*: PHN, *TEY*.

27   *"by far the"*: PHN, *AFOH*, 27.

27   *"absolutely immense vitality"*: ibid.

27   *He worked in*: Paula Zurcher, author interview, April 3, 2008.

27   *"They're arguing"*: Peter Nitze, author interview, March 6, 2008.

27   *They failed*: Glenn Millikan to PHN, March 27, 1922, BRB, box 1.

28   *"You must have"*: Elizabeth Paepcke to PHN, July 10, 1985, Elizabeth Paepcke Papers, University of Chicago Library, box 244, folder 3.

28   *"All of them"*: PHN to AHN, July 29, 1922, BRB, box 1.

28   *When Nitze was sanctioned*: PHN, *TEY*.

28   *he responded by sending*: PHN, AFOH, 15.

28   *"If one looks"*: PHN, BRB 46.

29   *When Winthrop was asked to join*: PHN, *Jottings*.

29   *At one dinner*: Robert Merry, *Taking on the World*, 37.

29   *Nitze drank*: PHN, memo for file, BRB 45.

29   *"We were the darndest"*: PHN to AHN, Oct. 22, 1925, PHNPP.

29   *his thesis*: PHN, "The Supreme Court, Rate Regulation, and the Value Con-
     cept," April 16, 1928, PHNPP. The topic was Supreme Court decisions gov-
     erning state regulation of prices.

30   *This time*: PHN, *TEY*.

30   *He spent the next*: PHN, *Jottings*.

30   *"I am also"*: letter to AHN, n.d., PHNPP.

30   *"Now in the"*: GFK, *Sketches from a Life*, 9.

30   *Nitze and Calder*: interview about life of Alexander Calder, PHNP LOC, box
     20, folder 2, 4–10.

30   *quite scandalous*: PHN, *Jottings*.

31   *"I wouldn't have"*: PHN to AHN, 1929, PHNPP.

31   *Another friend*: Ann Nitze, author interview, March 2, 2008.

31   *In the late 1920s*: Walter Isaacson and Evan Thomas, *The Wise Men*, 145.

31   *"I perceived in"*: GFK to JH, Sept. 3, 1928, GFKP, box 7R.

31   *"Go back to"*: Isaacson and Thomas, *Wise Men*, 146.

32   *"I will probably"*: GFK to JH, Sept. 3, 1928, GFKP, box 7R.

32   *"She is simply"*: GFK to JH, April 12, 1932, GFKP, box 7R.

32   *1917 Pierce-Arrow*: PHN, *Jottings*.

32   *Nitze crossed*: Elizabeth Bouvier, e-mail to author, Oct. 2, 2008.

33   *The man's leg*: PHN to WAN, n.d., PHNPP.

33   *"I am convinced"*: Alexander Whiteside to PHN, June 11, 1928, BRB, box 1.

33   *"I can't bear"*: Mary Ames to PHN, n.d., BRB, box 1.

33   *"You say I"*: ibid.

33   *Afterward, Pratt asked*: PHN, *Jottings*.

34   *"Phyllis Pratt seems"*: PHN to AHN, 1932, BRB.

34   *"I had arrogantly"*: PHN, fiftieth-wedding anniversary toast, 1982, PHNPP.

34   *"Most of us look"*: GFK, *MV1*, 60.

34   *His daughter would*: JEK, author interview, Jan. 6, 2009.

35   *On his third*: GFK, *MV1*, 90–91.

35   *Not long after*: ibid., 92.

35   *The morning the*: ibid., 98.

35   *"There is only one"*: GFK, diary entry, April 19, 1942, GFKP OF, box 1R.

35   *"What do I actually want"*: GFK, diary entry, April 20, 1942, GFKP OF,
     box 1R.

36   *Within "about five seconds"*: PHN to AHN, Feb. 26, 1929, PHNPP.

36   *Dillon pointed to*: ibid.

37   *For three years*: PHN, AFOH, 89. Fittingly, asked late in life what fault he was
     most inclined to forgive, Nitze responded: "Recklessness."

37   *He thought a*: Zurcher, author interview, April 3, 2008.
37   *the old man called*: WAN speech at PHN and PPN wedding, 1932, PHNPP.
37   *Years later, he*: W. Scott Thompson, e-mail to author, Dec. 24, 2007.
37   *William Nitze and*: PHN, AFOH, 25.
38   *"It was kind"*: ibid., 99.
38   *At around one A.M.*: "Barge Cargoes Blow Up," *NYT*, July 30, 1916.
38   *Five nights later*: Chad Millman, *The Detonators*, 98.
39   *On Christmas Eve of 1930*: ibid., 196.
39   *The decoder would turn*: ibid., 200.
40   *"Forrestal indicated"*: "Paul Henry Nitze," FBI Report, April 9, 1948,
      PHNFBI.
40   *"filling stations, advertising"*: GFK, "The Prerequisites," GFKP, box 19R.
40   *"The only solution"*: ibid.
41   *In late October 1943*: GFK, *MV1*, 156.
42   *The two talked*: PHN, *TBO*, 120.

3. A STRANGE INTENSITY, A STRANGE BEAUTY

43   *"The hour was"*: Warner Wells, ed., *Hiroshima Diary: The Journal of a Japa-
      nese Physician, August 6–September 30, 1945*, 1.
44   *wanted to limit*: Wilson Miscamble, *From Roosevelt to Truman*, 227.
44   *In 1942*: JLG, *We Now Know*, 93.
44   *George Koval*: William J. Broad, "A Spy's Path," *NYT*, Nov. 12, 2007.
44   *Harriman declared that*: W. Averell Harriman, Conversation Notes, Aug. 8,
      1945, Harriman Papers, LOC, box 181.
45   *With that, Harriman*: Tsuyoshi Hasegawa, *Racing the Enemy*, 193.
45   *he had ordered a*: David Holloway, *Stalin and the Bomb*, 129.
45   *A friend who worked*: PHN, OH, HSTL, June 11, 1975.
45   *the day after*: Gian Gentile, "Shaping the Past Battlefield," *Journal of Military
      History*, Oct. 2000, 1085.
45   *One week later*: PHN, *FHTG*, 38.
45   *"This was the"*: ibid.
45   *The aide returned*: PHN, AFOH, 171.
46   *Rumors flew among*: John Hersey, *Hiroshima*, 72.
46   *Even President Truman*: "Awful Responsibility," *Time*, Aug. 20, 1945.
46   *"With weapons of "*: PHN, OH, HSTL, Aug. 4, 1975.
46   *His report for*: USSBS, *The Effects of Atomic Bombs on Hiroshima and Naga-
      saki*, 30.
46   *He was struck*: ibid., 9.
46   *Years later*: PHN, OH, HSTL, Aug. 4, 1975.
47   *"Flash burns were"*: USSBS, 23.
47   *"The eyebrows of"*: Hersey, *Hiroshima*, 29.
47   *He would almost*: Peter Nitze, author interview, March 6, 2008.
47   *"If we see"*: Turner Catledge, "Our Policy Stated," *NYT*, June 24, 1941, 1.
47   *"I like Stalin"*: Robert Ferrell, *Dear Bess*, 522.

48　*"He didn't just"*: Simon Sebag Montefiore, *Young Stalin,* 179.

48　*One early poem*: ibid., 17.

48　*His alcoholic father*: ibid., 29.

48　*"She took what"*: Lana Peters, author interview, Sept. 30, 2007.

49　*discolored teeth*: Vladislav Zubok and Constantine Pleshakov, *Inside the Kremlin's Cold War,* 10.

49　*"an old battle-scarred tiger"*: GFK, *MV1,* 279.

49　*"hundreds of portraits"*: Brooks Atkinson, "Eisenhower and Stalin Review Parade of 40,000 in Red Square," *NYT,* Aug. 13, 1945.

49　*"His words were few"*: GFK, *MV1,* 279.

49　*"I do hope"*: GFK to Doc Matthews, Aug. 21, 1945, GFPP, box 28, folder 6.

50　*According to Japanese*: Russell Brines, "Prince Konoye—Japan's Inscrutable Leader," *Washington Post,* Sept. 15, 1940.

50　*"The impression"*: PHN interview with Prince Konoye, PHNP LOC, box 166, folder 5.

50　*"How much longer"*: ibid.

50　*"If there are"*: PHN to AHN, Dec. 45, PHNP LOC, box 165, folder 5.

51　*After they left*: Mark Gayn, *Japan Diary,* 30.

51　*Among these was one*: "The Prince and Death," *Time,* Dec. 24, 1945.

51　*He noted the city's rhythms*: GFK, *Sketches from a Life,* 113.

51　*"a great, sad city"*: ibid.

52　*As they raced*: GFK, *MV1,* 277.

52　*Afterward, Pepper described*: Claude Pepper, "Stalin Voices Aim for Amity and Aid of U.S. in the Peace," *NYT,* Oct. 1, 1945.

53　*Nitze tried to convince*: Gregg Herken, *Counsels of War,* 46.

53　*"There is nothing"*: GFK to SOS, Sept. 30, 1945, FRUS: 1945, vol. 5, 885.

54　*He lashed out*: GFK, diary entry, Dec. 2, 1945, GFKP, box 1R.

54　*he squirmed through*: GFK, diary entry, Dec. 8, 1945, GFKP, box 1R.

54　*A group of Americans*: Norma Odom, author interview, Feb. 4, 2008.

54　*He had even inserted*: Vladislav Zubok, *A Failed Empire,* 52.

55　*Tonight they were just*: Lynn Boyd Hinds and Theodore Otto Windt, *The Cold War as Rhetoric,* 75.

55　*As his foreign minister*: Zubok and Pleshakov, *Inside the Kremlin's Cold War,* 53.

55　*The speech was broadcast*: Zubok, *A Failed Empire,* 52.

56　*"We should welcome receiving"*: State Department to GFK, Feb. 22, 1946, FRUS: 1946, vol. 6, 696.

56　*"both make and destroy"*: Martha Mautner, author interview, April 10, 2008.

4. DECEIT, CORRUPTION, PENETRATION, SUBVERSION

58　*A cold, sinus*: GFK, *MV1,* 292.

58　*She gave it a quick*: Martha Mautner, author interview, April 10, 2008.

59　*The telegram went out*: GFK to SOS, Feb. 22, 1946, FRUS: 1946, vol. 6, 696.

59   *declaring it a brilliant*: John Gimbel, *The Origins of the Marshall Plan*, 131.

59   *The president read it*: George Elsey, author interview, Nov. 6, 2006.

59   *"floundering"*: Louis Halle, *The Cold War as History*, 105.

60   *"Kennan tied everything"*: Elsey, author interview, Nov. 6, 2006.

60   *did have logical shortcomings*: Anders Stephanson, *Kennan and the Art of Foreign Policy*, 50.

60   *to penetrate everything*: Kennan used some form of the word "penetrate" eight times in the essay; later scholars were intrigued by what they saw as evidence of repressed sexuality in early Cold War tracts.

61   *"If none of my"*: GFK, *MV1*, 294.

61   *"My reputation was made"*: GFK, *MV1*, 295.

61   *Using a back channel*: Allen Weinstein and Alexander Vassiliev, *The Haunted Wood*, 283–85.

62   *"Some of us"*: GFK to SOS, March 20, 1946, FRUS: 1946, vol. 6, 723.

62   *Two weeks after*: GFK to Elbridge Durbrow, March 7, 15, 1946; GFK Personnel File, 1945–1949, RG 59, NA.

62   *A new job*: Giles O. Harlow and George C. Maerz, eds., *MSOW*, xiv.

63   *"Perhaps the whole idea"*: ibid., 213–14.

63   *"The problem of meeting"*: ibid., 128.

63   *He quoted Gibbon*: ibid., 254.

63   *"Does not significance"*: GFK, reading notebook, 1946, GFKP, box 1R, 32.

64   *"I believe that there"*: Harlow and Maerz, *MSOW*, 215.

64   *Alexander Hamilton was right*: ibid.

64   *"there is a little bit"*: ibid., 168.

64   *Kennan obliged*: Walter Isaacson and Evan Thomas, *The Wise Men*, 384.

64   *But, wary of making*: ibid.

65   *He tried desperately*: PHNP LOC, box 165, folder 6. *Reader's Digest* then often ran summaries of sophisticated essays.

65   *"I am deeply"*: Barton Leach to PHN, Aug. 28, 1946, PHNP LOC, box 165, folder 6.

65   *Rear Admiral Ralph Ofstie*: R. A. Ofstie to PHN, March 10, 1946, PHNP LOC, box 166, folder 3.

66   *If anything, the preponderance*: Robert Newman, *Truman and the Hiroshima Cult*, 40.

67   *The location would cause*: Margot Lindsay, author interview, June 2, 2006.

67   *Kennan liked dealing*: GFK, diary entry, Feb. 1958, GFKP, box 3R.

67   *To the slight irritation*: Tish Alsop, author interview, Nov. 25, 2006.

67   *In early 1946, Kennan*: GFK, reading notebook, 1946, GFKP, box 1R, 60.

5. AVOID TRIVIA

69   *Paul Nitze hustled down*: PHN, *TBO*, 166.

69   *When he was a*: Forrest C. Pogue, *George C. Marshall: Education of a General*, 138.

70   *Nitze would later describe*: PHN, interview for memoirs, April 20, 1982, PHNP LOC, box 118, folder 11, 24.

70   *Chip Bohlen, who became*: CEB, *Witness to History*, 268.

70   *"George you don't want"*: PHN, OH, HSTL, Aug. 4, 1975.

70   *In the last days*: Greg Behrman, *The Most Noble Adventure*, 24.

70   *As the new year*: Tony Judt, *Postwar*, 86.

71   *It snowed in Saint-Tropez*: Behrman, *Most Noble Adventure*, 25.

71   *Reports of cannibalism*: Judt, *Postwar*, 86.

71   *"We are threatened"*: ibid., 88–89.

71   *A high-level group*: Joseph M. Jones, *The Fifteen Weeks*, 133.

71   *led to one of Stalin's*: Vladislav Zubok, *A Failed Empire*, 75. Citing documents from Russian archives.

71   *The United States should*: Harlow and Maerz, *MSOW*, 198–99.

71   *"It must be"*: Jones, *Fifteen Weeks*, 22.

72   *"was embarking"*: PHN, *FHTG*, 50.

72   *"with courage and guts"*: PHN, OH, NSA, June 12, 1995.

73   *That winter, Nitze told*: PHN, *FHTG*, 48.

73   *a secret memo that Forrestal*: "Memorandum to Mr. Clifford," March 6, 1947, PHNP LOC, box 98, folder 3.

73   *dressed in a*: Walter Isaacson and Evan Thomas, *The Wise Men*, 413.

74   *To begin with*: GFK memo, Dec. 15, 1947, GFKP, box 23, folder 50.

74   *"It would be"*: GFK to SOS, May 23, 1947, FRUS: 1947, vol. 3, 226.

74   *"To talk about"*: Behrman, *Most Noble Adventure*, 56, citing Charles L. Mee, *The Marshall Plan*, 90.

74   *The day after*: CEB, *Witness to History*, 264.

74   *At first, the plan confused*: Zubok, *A Failed Empire*, 72.

75   *"Marshall 'plan.' We"*: PPS Memo, July 21, 1947, FRUS: 1947, vol. 3, 335.

75   *then the* New York Times: GFK, *MV1*, 356.

75   *A month after it ran*: Wilson Miscamble, *George F. Kennan and the Making of American Foreign Policy*, 64.

76   *when George Marshall summoned*: GFK, *MV1*, 356.

77   *Reader's Digest, for example*: Lynn Boyd Hinds and Theodore Otto Windt, *The Cold War as Rhetoric*, 194.

77   *"like one who has inadvertently"*: GFK, *MV1*, 356.

77   *"containment" was rendered*: Ernest May, ed., *American Cold War Strategy*, 124.

77   *He devoted fourteen consecutive*: Ronald Steel, *Walter Lippmann and the American Century*, 444.

78   *Friends referred to them*: ibid., 343.

78   *Armstrong had learned about the affair*: ibid., 363.

78   *Kennan would ascribe*: Wilson Miscamble, author interview, June 9, 2005.

78   *"bewilderment and frustration"*: GFK, *MV1*, 360.

78   *Lippmann declared*: Walter Lippmann, *The Cold War: A Study in U.S. Foreign Policy*, 9.

78   *Lippmann lumped*: ibid., 44.

79   *he drafted a letter*: GFK to Walter Lippmann, April 6, 1948, GFKP, box 17, folder 7.

79   *after being briefed*: Martha Mautner, author interview, Nov. 23, 2007.

79   *According to a report*: 80th Cong., 2nd sess., Report no 2173, Foreign Aid
      Appropriations Bill, 1949, June 3, 1948, PHNP LOC, box 98, folder 2.
79   *"I pointed out"*: GFK, diary entry, Jan. 23, 1948, GFKP, box 1R.
80   *collapsed from exhaustion*: PHN to AHN, 1947, BRB 7.
80   *"It really has become"*: ibid.
80   *huge stacks of paper*: PHNP LOC, box 96, folder 3.
80   *"He is young, able"*: Will Clayton to Paul Hoffman, April 6, 1948, PHNP
      LOC, box 97, folder 3.
80   *"I know of no"*: PHN to AHN and WAN, Dec. 27, 1947, PHNP LOC, box 97,
      folder 3.
80   *"I don't mind"*: PHN to AHN and WAN, Jan. 30, 1948, PHNP LOC, box 97,
      folder 3.
80   *"backed by more"*: James Reston, "Vandenberg Lauds Work Put into Fram-
      ing ERP Bill," *NYT,* Jan. 10, 1948.
81   *"any derogatory information"*: G. A. Nease memorandum for the director,
      April 8, 1948, PHNFBI.
81   *"Pulses are things"*: Hearings before the Subcommittee of the Committee on
      Appropriations, House of Representatives, 80th Cong., 2nd sess., Foreign
      Aid Appropriation Bill for 1949, part 1, April 20, 1948, 103.
81   *"I believe not"*: ibid., 105.
81   *After half an hour*: PHN, *FHTG,* 65.

6. ARCHITECT OF THE COLD WAR

83   *Late one moonless night*: Nicholas Bethell, *The Great Betrayal,* 1–3.
83   *"My real mission"*: GFK, *MSOW,* 131.
83   *"He knew that"*: Walter Pozen, author interview, Feb. 28, 2008.
83   *"Political warfare is"*: PPS Memorandum, May 4, 1948, FRUS: 1945–1950,
      Emergence of the Intelligence Establishment, doc. 269.
84   *If the Kremlin*: ibid.
84   *"Time is running out"*: GFK to Robert Lovett and George C. Marshall, May
      19, 1948, FRUS: 1945–1950, *Emergence of the Intelligence Establishment,*
      doc. 276.
84   *His top choice*: GFK to Robert Lovett, June 30, 1948, FRUS: 1945–1950,
      Emergence of the Intelligence Establishment, doc. 294.
84   *to import an ex-Nazi*: Christopher Simpson, *Blowback,* 115.
84   *Kennan had known Hilger*: GFK, review of Gustav Hilger's *The Incompatible
      Allies, New York Herald Tribune Book Review,* Nov. 1, 1953.
85   *Although he played*: Robert Wolfe, "Gustav Hilger: From Hitler's Foreign Of-
      fice to CIA Consultant," paper presented analyzing newly released CIA
      records under the Nazi War Criminal Records, Interagency Working Group,
      NARA, June 2006, http://www.fas.org/sgp/eprint/wolfe.pdf, accessed on
      Jan. 24, 2009.
85   *he certainly took pleasure*: Klaus Mehnert to GFK, Dec. 15, 1948, GFKP, box
      28, folder 10.
85   *Kennan thanked Wisner*: Robert Wolfe, "Gustav Hilger: From Hitler's For-

eign Office to CIA Consultant," paper presented analyzing newly released CIA records under the Nazi War Criminal Records, Interagency Working Group, NARA, June 2006, http://www.fas.org/sgp/eprint/wolfe.pdf, accessed on Jan. 24, 2009.

85   *Kennan was directly involved*: Margot and Franklin Lindsay, e-mail to author, Feb. 18, 2009.

85   *Not long after the infiltrators*: Bethell, *Great Betrayal*, 74–82.

85   *"everyone was arrested"*: Franklin Lindsay, author interview, June 2, 2006.

86   *Others survived only*: Gregory Mitrovich, *Undermining the Kremlin*, 44.

86   *The KGB's understandable suspicion*: Ron Rosenbaum, "Kim Philby and the Age of Paranoia," *NYT Magazine*, July 10, 1994.

86   *At its Addiction Research Center*: Evan Thomas, *The Very Best Men*, 212.

86   *he gave his blessing*: GFK to Robert Lovett, May 25, 1948, FRUS: 1945–1950, *Emergence of the Intelligence Establishment*, doc. 279.

86   *Nitze recalled that when Forrestal*: PHN, essay on James Forrestal, Aug. 1985, PHNPP.

87   *Nitze would sometimes deliver*: PHN, *TBO*, 89.

87   *"Forrestal was annoyed"*: ibid., 90.

87   *"He could have been"*: PHN, essay on Forrestal, Aug. 1985, PHNPP.

87   *"He felt that"*: GFK to John Osborne, July 31, 1962, GFKP, box 31, folder 8.

87   *"There is no method"*: Jeffery M. Dorwart, *Eberstadt and Forrestal*, 149.

88   *Watching people, he said*: PHN, *TBO*, 97.

88   *the doctors began*: Admiral M. D. Willcutts, "Report on the Death of James Forrestal," part 1, 35.

88   *They considered, but rejected*: ibid., 41.

88   *"I was shocked to"*: GFK to Forrestal, April 7, 1949, Forrestal Papers, box 83.

88   *Nitze wrote*: PHN, *TBO*, 108.

88   *"had, I thought"*: GFK to Osborne, July 31, 1962, GFKP, Box 31, folders; also, Townsend Hoopes and Douglas Brinkley, *Driven Patriot*, 274.

88   *When he returned*: Admiral M. D. Willcutts, "Report in the Death of James Forrestal," part 2, 176.

89   *His bathrobe sash*: ibid., part 1, 62.

89   *upstairs, a razor blade*: ibid., 81.

89   *"There is great joy"*: PHNP LOC, box 24, folder 5.

89   *"He was an architect"*: Ronald Steel, "A Self-Made Man," *New York Review of Books*, Aug. 13, 1992.

89   *In May, communists*: A. C. Sedgwick, "Athens Bomb Kills Minister; Red Plot on Cabinet Alleged," *NYT*, May 2, 1948.

89   *carefully leaked word*: Martin Walker, *The Cold War*, 57.

90   *The rescue*: Andrei Cherny, *The Candy Bombers*.

90   *And it terrified Kennan*: Robert Merry, *Taking on the World*, 174.

90   *Nitze later recalled*: Wilson Miscamble, *George F. Kennan and the Making of American Foreign Policy*, 154.

90   *"the early abandonment"*: GFK to SOS and undersecretary of state, Aug. 12, 1948, FRUS: 1948, vol. 2, 1289.

90   *In a letter*: GFK to Anders Stephanson, Nov. 15, 1985, GFKP OF, box 71.

91 *On the cover*: GFK to SOS and undersecretary of state, Aug. 12, 1948, FRUS: 1948, vol. 2, 1288.

91 *"Here, for the first time"*: GFK, *MV1*, 437.

92 *Once again, Kennan sought*: Hannah Gurman, *The Dissent Papers*, 81–83.

92 *already extracting uranium*: Vladislav Zubok, *A Failed Empire*, 63.

92 *was already leaning*: Wilson Miscamble, *From Roosevelt to Truman*, 314.

92 *Nitze, characteristically*: PHN, undated memorandum to self, PHNP LOC, box 140, folder 8.

93 *Only one man*: Robert Beisner, *Dean Acheson*, 27.

93 *"Twenty guys"*: ibid., 83.

93 *"Though it once"*: Philip Hamburger, "Mr. Secretary," *New Yorker*, Nov. 12, 1949, 39.

93 *and told him the horse's name*: Ronald L. McGlothlen, *Controlling the Waves*, 111.

93 *"an old horse pulling"*: Bob Woodward, *The Secret Man*, 20.

94 *"I couldn't find"*: PHN, Draft of *TBO*, PHN BRB.

94 *"I really have no"*: GFK to DGA, Jan. 3, 1949, GFKP OF, box 57.

94 *The secretary liked to*: John Lamberton Harper, *American Visions of Europe*, 248.

94 *"opened my hand"*: PHN, *TBO*, 153.

95 *Sometimes, the rest*: Walter Isaacson and Evan Thomas, *The Wise Men*, 405.

95 *unloading his emotional burdens*: GFK interviewed by JLG, Dec. 13, 1987, GFKP OF, box 62.

95 *His country pursued*: Miscamble, *George F. Kennan*, 349–50.

95 *Kennan believed*: JLG, *Strategies of Containment*, 29.

95 *policy toward Japan*: Miscamble, *George F. Kennan*, 247–48.

96 *According to Joseph Alsop*: Robert Merry, *Taking on the World*, 173.

96 *"By this act"*: PPS paper, June 30, 1948, FRUS: 1948, vol. 4, 1080.

96 *partly because of*: Zubok, *Failed Empire*, 74.

96 *It was one*: Miscamble, *George F. Kennan*, 189–97.

97 *When the junior man*: "Meeting 121," PPS Minutes of Meetings 1949, NARA, RG 59, box 32, Planning Staff Files.

97 *"No one can both"*: GFK, diary entry, Sept. 2, 1949, GFKP, box 1R.

97 *"Washington is hot"*: PHN to AHN, Aug. 12, 1949, BRB 1.

7. WHAT WE ARE ABOUT

98 *Igor Kurchatov had stopped*: Gregg Herken, *Brotherhood of the Bomb*, 89.

98 *a small city*: Arkadi Kruglov, *The History of the Soviet Atomic Industry*, 121.

98 *"The fireball"*: David Holloway, *Stalin and the Bomb*, 217.

98 *"It worked"*: Richard Rhodes, *Dark Sun*, 366.

99 *done by prisoners*: Holloway, *Stalin and the Bomb*, 172.

99 *the abbreviation*: Kruglov, *History of the Soviet Atomic Industry*, 123.

99 *The reward for success*: Holloway, *Stalin and the Bomb*, 213–18.

99 *Six days later*: Charles Ziegler, "Waiting for Joe-1," 213.

99 *Soon, scientists testing*: David McCullough, *Truman*, 747.

99 *"that our vaunted"*: Gordon Arneson, "The H-Bomb Decision," *Foreign Service Journal*, May 1969, 28.

99 *"When will the Russians"*: Raymond Ojserkis, *Beginnings of the Cold War Arms Race*, 57.

99 *Truman snapped*: McCullough, *Truman*, 748.

100 *On September 13*: GFK, diary entry, Sept. 21, 1949, GFKP, box 1R.

100 *"would be stripped"*: GFK to undersecretary of state, July 18, 1946, FRUS: 1946, vol. 1, 862.

100 *"confidently risk"*: ibid., 863.

100 *"we quietly"*: ibid., 864.

100 *"Our effort must"*: GFK, 1946 notebook entry, GFKP, box 1R.

100 *"We must be"*: ibid.

101 *"drifting toward a"*: GFK diary entry, Sept. 26, 1949, GFKP, box 1R.

102 *"I face the work"*: GFK diary entry, Sept. 30, 1949, GFKP, box 1R.

102 *Later, Kennan sent*: GFK to SOS, Nov. 18, 1949, FRUS: 1949, vol. 1, 585.

102 *Nitze scrawled "no"*: PHN, notes on GFK memo, NA RG 59, PPS box 50.

102 *He was nearly thrown out*: Kai Bird and Martin Sherwin, *American Prometheus*, 46.

103 *He believed it*: ibid., 100.

103 *He did not speak*: Richard Rhodes, *The Making of the Atomic Bomb*, 107.

103 *He described himself*: Herken, *Brotherhood of the Bomb*, 25.

103 *On the train ride back*: Fred Kaplan, *Wizards of Armageddon*, 83.

103 *Like Nitze, his skills*: Rhodes, *Dark Sun*, 303.

103 *"I feel I have"*: Truman to DGA, May 7, 1946, Box 201, cited in Bird and Sherwin, *American Prometheus*, 332.

104 *"I have no hope"*: Teller to Leo Szilard, July 2, 1945, JRO Papers, LOC, box 71.

104 *"I neither can"*: Bird and Sherwin, *American Prometheus*, 325.

104 *He offered a wager*: Herken, *Brotherhood of the Bomb*, 212.

104 *They talked physics*: PHN, AFOH, 234.

104 *"be there first"*: ibid., 235.

104 *Oppenheimer tried to save*: JRO to GFK, Nov. 17, 1949, JRO papers, LOC, box 43.

105 *He joined the*: memo by undersecretary of state, FRUS: 1949, vol. 1, 599.

105 *To opponents of*: Steven Rearden, *Paul Nitze on Foreign Policy*, 18.

105 *"Real question is"*: PHN, notes, NARA, RG 59, PPS box 50.

105 *"was tempted, day before yesterday"*: GFK to DGA, Dec. 21, 1949, DGA papers, Yale University.

106 *the State Department's historical*: GFK memo, Jan. 20, 1950, FRUS: 1950, vol. 1, 22.

106 *"I fear that"*: ibid., 38.

106 *"the effort to achieve"*: GFK, notes on international control of atomic energy, NARA, RG 59, PPS box 50.

107 *"All of us"*: Wilson Miscamble, *George F. Kennan and the Making of American Foreign Policy*, 304.

107 *Nitze's final argument*: PHN memo, Dec. 19, 1949, FRUS: 1949, vol. 1, 611.

107 *"My own inclination"*: GFK to CEB, Nov. 17, 1949, GFKP, box 28.

107   *"is 42, studious"*: "People of the Week," *U.S. News & World Report,* Dec. 30, 1949, 37.

107   *"Nitze operates more"*: Wallace Deuel, "America's New Policy Planner," *Washington Star,* Jan. 15, 1950, PHNP LOC, box 146.

108   *"One who has worked"*: PHN to James McDonald, Jan. 16, 1950, PHNP LOC, box 8, folder 6.

108   *"Dearest Paul"*: AHN to PHN, Jan. 11, 1950, PHNPP.

108   *His secretary came in*: Gordon Arneson, "The H-Bomb Decision," *Foreign Service Journal,* May 1949, 27.

108   *"We have known"*: GFK draft speech, Nov. 18, 1949, JRO Papers, LOC, box 43, folder "George F. Kennan, correspondence 1949–1966."

109   *The press statement*: Arneson, "The H-Bomb Decision," 27.

109   *"Any American steps"*: Zubok, *Failed Empire,* 150.

109   *Outside his hotel room*: GFK, *MV1,* 478–79.

109   *"I began to feel"*: GFK diary entry, GFKP, box 2R, Diaries 1950–1955, folder 1-F-1950, 23.

109   *"the night is restless"*: GFK, *Sketches from a Life,* 134.

110   *"incidentally, all of"*: GFK, diary entry 1950, GFKP, box 2R, Diaries 1950–1955, folder 1-F-1950, 17–19.

110   *"relaxed equanimity"*: GFK to SOS, FRUS: 1950, vol. 2, 598–624.

110   *A decade later*: "George Frost Kennan: Special Inquiry," FBI, Field Office File 161–153, Feb. 14, 1961.

110   *"Their attitude toward"*: GFK, diary entry 1950, GFKP, box 2R.

111   *At a meeting in December*: PPS meeting minutes, Dec. 16, 1949, FRUS: 1949, vol. 1, 414.

111   *A month and a half*: PPS meeting minutes, Feb. 2, 1950, FRUS: 1950, vol. 1, 142.

111   *"recent Soviet moves"*: PHN, "Recent Soviet Moves," FRUS: 1950, vol. 4, 1099.

111   *"treated on Capitol Hill"*: Ronald Steel, *Walter Lippmann and the American Century,* 468.

111   *But Nitze persuaded*: David Callahan, *Dangerous Capabilities,* 104.

111   *More deviously*: Ernest May, *American Cold War Strategy,* 11.

111   *His estimates thus*: Robert Beisner, *Dean Acheson,* 239.

112   *"For the past six weeks"*: PHN to AHN and WAN, April 11, 1950, PHNPP.

112   *"he liked it with"*: George Elsey, author interview, Nov. 6, 2006.

112   *eventually release it*: PHN to Evan Thomas, Feb. 21, 1985, PHNP BRB 21.

112   *the paper consistently*: Anders Stephanson, "Liberty or Death: The Cold War as U.S. Ideology," in Odd Arne Westad, ed., *Reviewing the Cold War,* 81.

113   *"still seeking to achieve"*: Report to president by National Security Council, Nov. 23, 1948, FRUS: 1948, vol. 1, part 2, 662.

113   *"With the preparation"*: GFK to Norman Graebner, May 16, 1959, GFKP, box 31, folder 5.

113   *"the only person"*: PHN, interview for memoir, June 3, 1986, PHNP, box 120, folder 3.

113 *At the appointed hour*: Memcon, State Department, March 22, 1950, FRUS: 1950, vol. 1, 204.

114 *"Johnson listened"*: DGA, *Present at the Creation*, 373.

114 *Nitze crossed out*: James Hamilton Isbell, "The Unexpected Paul Nitze," MA Thesis, University of Alabama in Huntsville, 1996, PHNPP, 4.

115 *"It was one of"*: PHN, AFOH, 248.

115 *"It is good"*: GFK, speech, June 11, 1950, JRO Papers, LOC, box 43, folder 14.

115 *"We've got to get back"*: Peter Nitze, author interview, March 6, 2008.

8. CONFINED TO KOREA

116 *frantic retreat*: Bong Lee, *Unfinished War*, 65.

117 *Most likely because of*: memcon by the ambassador at large, June 25, 1950, FRUS: 1950, vol. 7, 157.

117 *"I would probably"*: GFKP, 1955 interview inserted into 1950 diary entry, GFKP, box 2R, folder 1-F-1950.

117 *34,000 monuments*: Paul French, *North Korea*, 67.

117 *In the South*: David Halberstam, *The Coldest Winter*, 70–80.

117 *Finally, after a top spy*: Christopher Andrew and Vasili Mitrokhin, *The World Was Going Our Way*, 263.

118 *At the Sunday evening*: memcon by the ambassador at large, June 25, 1950, FRUS: 1950, vol. 7, 159.

118 *"to keep out"*: GFK, diary entry, June 29, 1950, GFKP, box 2R.

118 *drafting a paper*: memorandum of National Security Council consultants' meeting, June 29, 1950, FRUS: 1950, vol. 1, 330.

118 *"My whole framework"*: GFK, diary entry, July 3, 1950, GFKP, box 2R.

118 *The first confrontation*: Paul Nitze, OH, HSTL, Aug. 5–6, 1975.

118 *"Guys, sweat soaked"*: Halberstam, *Coldest Winter*, 147.

119 *"I just sensed"*: Donald Knox, *The Korean War: Pusan to Chosin*, 71, quoted in David McCullough, *Truman*, 787.

119 *As they and the rest*: Draft PPS memo, July 25, 1950, FRUS: 1950, vol. 7, 469.

119 *The Kremlin, they argued*: ibid., 471.

119 *"emphatic dissent"*: Allison to PHN, July 24, 1950, FRUS: 1950, vol. 7, 460.

119 *"If we have the opportunity"*: Dulles to PHN, July 14, 1950, FRUS: 1950, vol. 7, 386.

119 *"the course upon"*: GFK to SOS, Aug. 21, 1950, FRUS: 1950, vol. 7, 624.

119 *"By permitting General MacArthur"*: ibid.

120 *"was the most civilized"*: Robert Merry, *Taking on the World*, 37.

120 *large dog*: ibid., 99.

120 *When in Paris*: ibid., 238.

120 *After one dinner party*: Walter Pozen, author interview, Feb. 28, 2008.

120 *"as resembling the priestess"*: Joseph Alsop, *I've Seen the Best of It*, 274.

121 *He flew to Tokyo*: Joseph Alsop, "The Battle: First Phase," *Washington Post*, Aug. 14, 1950.

121 *It was only at*: Joseph Alsop, "The Battle: Second Phase," *Washington Post*, Aug. 16, 1950.

121   *Thucydides in his pocket*: Alsop, *I've Seen the Best of It,* 340.

121   *"Beautiful, just beautiful"*: Joseph Alsop, "The Battalion," *Washington Post,* Aug. 28, 1950.

121   *"I like going"*: Joseph Alsop, "Baker Company," *Washington Post,* Aug. 30, 1950.

122   *"Like Tolstoy"*: GFK to Alsop, Oct. 20, 1950, GFKP OF, box 57.

122   *He carried only*: John S. D. Eisenhower and Joanne Thompson Eisenhower, *Yanks,* 86.

122   *Descending regally*: "Over the Mountains: Mountains," *Time,* July 10, 1950.

122   *"The greatest man"*: ibid.

122   *"opening up communications"*: GFK, *MV1,* 382.

123   *"Mr. Prima Donna"*: McCullough, *Truman,* 949.

123   *A bugle would sound*: Roy E. Appleman, *Disaster in Korea,* 158.

123   *One American soldier vividly*: ibid., 182.

124   *"a failure to act"*: PHN, speech, Nov. 30, 1950, PHNP LOC, box 193, folder 1.

124   *The president stood erect*: Anthony Leviero, "Truman Gives Aim," *NYT,* Dec. 1, 1950.

124   *All went well*: McCullough, *Truman,* 820–21.

124   *"Always has been"*: John T. Woolley and Gerhard Peters, The American Presidency Project Online, http://www.presidency.ucsb.edu/ws/?pid=13673, accessed on Jan. 23, 2009.

124   *Horrified, Nitze suggested*: PHN, interview with Christopher Jones, cited in Christopher Jones, *Paul H. Nitze,* 107.

125   *In July, the PPS*: "The Question of U.S. Use of Atomic Bombs in Korea," July 15, 1950, NARA, RG 59, PPS papers, 1947–1953, box 20, "Korea 1947–50."

125   *Worse, it would align*: PHN, PPS memo, Nov. 4, 1950, FRUS: 1950, vol. 7, 1042.

125   *"The real question"*: memorandum of discussion at a Department of State–Joint Chiefs of Staff meeting, March 27, 1953, FRUS: 1952–1954, vol. 15, part 1, 817.

125   *"Why aren't you"*: GFK memo of conversation with CEB, Dec. 1, 1950, GFKP OF, box 58.

126   *The secretary, looking worn*: Walter Isaacson and Evan Thomas, *The Wise Men,* 542.

126   *"The Secretary told this"*: GFK diary entry, Dec. 1, 1950, GFKP, box 2R.

126   *"In international, as in private"*: Robert Beisner, *Dean Acheson,* 413.

127   *After the Inchon landing*: Kim Il Sung and Pak Hon-Yong to Joseph Stalin, Sept. 29, 1950, Cold War International History Project, http://www.wilsoncenter.org and http://tinyurl.com/2xgnas, accessed on Jan. 23, 2009.

127   *With the North Koreans retreating*: Stalin to Kim Il Sung, Aug. 28, 1950, Cold War International History Project, http://www.wilsoncenter.org and http://tinyurl.com/2o23sk, accessed on Jan. 23, 2009.

127   *to send planes*: Aleksandr Vasilevsky to Stalin, Sept. 23, 1950, Cold War International History Project, http://www.wilsoncenter.org and http://tinyurl.com/33xcvu, accessed on Jan. 23, 2009.

127   *crews went without*: Jon Halliday, "Air Operations in Korea," in William J. Williams, ed., *A Revolutionary War,* 152.

127 *"Our pilots' work"*: Vasilevsky to Stalin, Sept. 23, 1950, Cold War International History Project, http://www.wilsoncenter.org and http://tinyurl.com/33xcvu, accessed on Jan. 23, 2009.

127 *"point the finger"*: PHNP LOC, box 130, folder 3.

128 *decided to bury it*: Halliday, "Air Operations in Korea," in Williams, *A Revolutionary War*, 169.

128 *"Outright treachery"*: Joseph Goulden, *Korea*, 477.

128 *"This looks like"*: Halberstam, *Coldest Winter*, 602.

128 *Nitze helped write*: PHN, *FHTG*, 111.

128 *Outrage swept*: Beisner, *Dean Acheson*, 432.

128 *"1:50 Burning"*: ibid.

128 *"The papers today"*: GFK, diary entry, April 9, 1951, GFKP, box 2R.

129 *"the number one"*: memcon by Frank Corrigan and Thomas Cory, May 3, 1951, FRUS: 1951, vol. 7, 401–10.

129 *After the car ride*: PHN, *TBO*, 127. Nitze refers to Cory here, mistakenly, as Andrew Corry.

129 *quiet negotiation between*: GFK to deputy undersecretary of state, June 5, 1951, FRUS: 1951, vol. 7, part 1, 511.

129 *"I am writing to ask"*: GFK to Tsarapkin, May 26, 1951, GFKP, box 2R.

130 *joined Bohlen*: PHN, *FHTG*, 115.

9. THE FULL MERIDIAN OF MY GLORY

131 *"I should find it hard"*: GFK diary entry, April 2, 1951, GFKP 2R.

131 *"Here—there will be"*: ibid., April 3, 1951, GFKP 2R.

131 *"I have never been very good"*: ibid., April 6, 1951, GFKP 2R.

132 *"If dislike for one's self"*: ibid., Sept. 5, 1951, GKFP, 2R.

132 *"his mind functioned better"*: Wilson Miscamble, *George F. Kennan and the Making of American Foreign Policy*, 25, citing Dorothy Hessman, interviewed by CBW, Oct. 1, 1970, CBW papers, box 8, folder 15.

132 *"legalistic-moralistic"*: GFK, *American Diplomacy*, 95.

132 *A conflict between*: ibid., 65.

133 *"I sometimes wonder"*: ibid., 66.

133 *"an attitude of detachment"*: ibid., 103.

133 *"the happiest and"*: Robert Beisner, *Dean Acheson*, 119.

134 *The economist Thomas Schelling*: Thomas Schelling, author interview, April 28, 2008.

134 *"But here I"*: Vladislav Zubok and Constantine Pleshakov, *Inside the Kremlin's Cold War*, 17, citing Russian-language sources.

134 *Mossadegh had a reputation*: Michael Clarke, "Premier of Iran Airs Threat of Death, Faints After Talk," *NYT*, May 14, 1951.

134 *His shoulders slumped*: Stephen Kinzer, *All the Shah's Men*, 57.

135 *He found the leader*: PHN, *FHTG*, 131.

135 *"You know, I'm"*: PHN, OH, HSTL, Aug. 5–6, 1975.

135 *"He was canny"*: PHN, *FHTG*, 131.

135 *"famous, if mysterious"*: PHN to AHN, Dec. 1952, PHNPP.

136   *At the end of*: Kinzer, *All the Shah's Men*, 166–90.

136   *"the greatest mistake"*: Anne Karalekas, *History of the Central Intelligence Agency*, 31.

136   *"These were the"*: VOA Broadcast, June 1, 1952, "Daily Broadcast Content Reports and Script Translations 1950–5," NARA, RG 306.4.1.

137   *Recalling the incident*: GFK, *MV2*, 156.

137   *"There are many"*: VOA Broadcast, July 16, 1952, "Daily Broadcast Content Reports and Script Translations 1950–5," NARA, RG 306.4.1.

137   *Perhaps he could*: GFK, diary entry, Sept. 29, 1952, GFKP, box 2R.

137   *he told reporters*: Walter Hixson, *George F. Kennan*, 120.

137   *"Get those scorpions"*: Malcolm Toon, author interview, April 3, 2008.

138   *One official*: GFK, *MV2*, 158–59.

138   *John Lewis Gaddis*: GFK interviewed by JLG, Dec. 13, 1987, GFKP OF, box 62.

138   *"a childish"*: GFK to deputy undersecretary of state, June 18, 1952, FRUS: *The Intelligence Community, 1950–1955*, 284.

138   *"Placards portraying hideous"*: GFK, *MV2*, 123.

138   *he requested and received cyanide*: Peer de Silva, *Sub Rosa*, 71–74.

138   *"I would be asked"*: GFK, interview with JLG, Dec. 13, 1987, GFKP OF, box 62.

138   *"carried the pills to"*: Nancy Jenkins, memo for PHN files, May 27, 1980, PHNP LOC, box 29. All the men mentioned in the message are deceased and Jenkins does not remember the incident. Circumstantial evidence supporting the claim in the memo comes from a friend of Dean Acheson's who remembers him becoming upset, while secretary of state, because Kennan had had an affair abroad that could get him in political trouble.

138   *where he planned*: Anders Stephanson, *Kennan and the Art of Foreign Policy*, 259.

139   *"Don't be a boy"*: GFK diary entry, GFKP, box 2R.

139   *"Well, I was interned"*: GFK, *MV2*, 159.

139   *in fact, "obvious"*: Martha Mautner, author interview, April 10, 2008.

139   *they had rented*: JEK, author interview, Jan. 6, 2009.

139   *He went straight*: GFK, *MV2*, 164.

139   *The director of the institution*: JEK, author interview, March 8, 2008.

139   *"Kennan kicked out"*: Grace Warnecke, author interview, May 17, 2006.

139   *"Nay then, farewell!"*: GFK diary entry, GFKP, box 2R.

140   *One year later*: PPS memo, Jan. 29, 1951, FRUS: 1951, vol. 1, 38.

140   *Six months after*: Report by the NSC, FRUS: 1951, vol. 1, 147.

140   *"free world to"*: Christopher Jones, *Paul H. Nitze*, 126. Citing: Notes about why we should worry about possible peace, May 6, 1952, NARA, RG 59, Planning Staff files, box 7.

141   *In the summer of 1950*: GFK, diary entry, July 11, 1950, GFKP, box 2R.

141   *"My chief objection"*: PPS memo, Jan. 29, 1951, FRUS: 1951, vol. 1, 107.

141   *"Soviet actions in Korea"*: CEB memo, Sept. 21, 1951, FRUS: 1951, vol. 1, 171.

141   *"it seems to me"*: PPS memo about CEB, Sept. 22, 1951, FRUS: 1951, vol. 1, 174.

141 *"The way to peace"*: Dean Acheson, *Present at the Creation,* 753. Acheson was collapsing his time line for a literary effect. Bohlen had actually served as minister in Paris before the writing of NSC-68, and Kennan had traveled to Latin America in the winter of 1950. But Acheson's essential point was that he was choosing Nitze's position and letting him remain in the center of power.

142 *The explosion vaporized*: Richard Rhodes, *Dark Sun,* 509.

142 *If exploded in*: ibid., 510.

142 *A few months earlier*: PHN to SOS, June 9, 1952, FRUS: 1952–1954, vol. 2, part 2, 958–62.

142 *it's likely that*: PHN, *TBO,* 129.

142 *The ex-ambassador*: GFK, *MV2,* 168.

142 *"this did not endear"*: Robert Bowie, author interview, Aug. 2, 2005.

142 *FBI officials*: memo to A. H. Belmont, Jan. 21, 1953, GFKFBI.

142 *"Then I took"*: GFK, diary entry, July 29, 1953, GFKP, box 2R.

143 *"It was the first"*: LP, author interview, Sept. 30, 2007.

143 *He had decreed*: Vladislav Zubok, *A Failed Empire,* 85.

143 *To his twenty-six-year-old*: LP, author interview, March 30, 2008.

144 *Svetlana remembered a chaos*: LP, *Twenty Letters to a Friend,* 7.

144 *push the broken glass*: LP, author interview, March 30, 2008.

144 *His death would lift*: LP, *Twenty Letters to a Friend,* 9.

144 *"His face altered"*: ibid., 10.

144 *They wanted to move*: Emmet Hughes to president, March 10, 1953, FRUS: 1952–1954, vol. 8, 1114–15.

144 *Perhaps the new Soviet*: PHN to SOS, March 10, 1953, FRUS: 1952–1954, vol. 8, 1107.

145 *He helped craft*: Robert Bowie and Richard Immerman, *Waging Peace,* 116.

145 *there, indeed, was Eisenhower*: PHN, *FHTG,* 144–45.

145 *"Once you've seen"*: Strobe Talbott, *MOTG,* 60.

145 *"Put out your feelers"*: Melvyn Leffler, *For the Soul of Mankind,* 109–110, citing GFK to Allen [Dulles?], April 25, 1953, NA, RG 59, Records of Intelligence and Research Subject Files, 1945–1960, Lot 58, D 776, box 14.

146 *"the latest Truman-Acheson"*: Talbott, *MOTG,* 62.

146 *"asked that he"*: D. M. Ladd to Director, June 8, 1953, PHNFBI.

10. A FULLY CONVENTIONAL LIFE

147 *"Paul looks better"*: Phyllis Nitze to AHN, summer 1953, BRB.

148 *"the one meal"*: GFK, diary entry, June 21, 1958, GFKP, box 3R, folder 1-F-1958.

148 *"It turned out"*: GFK, *MV2,* 77.

148 *Kennan filed formal*: Walter Hixson, *George F. Kennan,* 142.

148 *Kennan decided that the job*: Doc Matthews, OH, HSTL, June 7, 1973, 31.

148 *When Dean Acheson*: Thomas Hughes, author interview, April 7, 2007.

148 *John Kennedy learned*: Priscilla McMillan, author interview, Dec. 27, 2008.

148 *Nitze too decided*: PHN, *Jottings.*

148   *Jealous and surprised*: ibid.

149   *The aging Albert Einstein*: Kai Bird and Martin Sherwin, *American Prometheus*, 376.

149   *Beth Straus*: Beth Straus, author interview, Oct. 6, 2006.

149   *von Neumann, for one, voted*: Bird and Sherwin, *American Prometheus*, 431.

149   *"Behind me"*: GFK, diary entry, GFKP, box 2R, folder 1-F-1953.

150   *nor was he keen*: JLG, *Strategies of Containment*, 125.

150   *Team A would argue*: FRUS: 1952–1954, vol. 2, part 1, 324–26.

150   *An Eisenhower biographer, Richard Immerman*: Richard Immerman, "Confessions of an Eisenhower Revisionist," *Diplomatic History*, Summer 1990, 319–42.

151   *He started with*: Robert Bowie and Richard Immerman, *Waging Peace*, 128.

151   *Kennan's most dramatic*: Task Force A, July 22, 1953, FRUS: 1952–1954, vol. 2, part 1, 399–412.

151   *"At my feet"*: GFK, *MV2*, 182.

152   *Oppenheimer sat*: Bird and Sherwin, *American Prometheus*, 498–99.

153   *"It is simply that"*: U.S. Atomic Energy Commission, *In the Matter of J. Robert Oppenheimer*, 353–68.

154   *"Since we have"*: Robert Merry, *Taking on the World*, 260.

154   *Beria was a vile*: Vladislav Zubok and Constantine Pleshakov, *Inside the Kremlin's Cold War*, 142.

154   *At the end*: Simon Sebag Montefiore, *Court of the Red Tsar*, 505.

154   *While Stalin was alive*: LP to author, April 27, 2008.

154   *"Beria was very clever"*: ibid.

154   *"Nobody was hated"*: ibid.

154   *With Stalin dead*: Melvyn Leffler, *For the Soul of Mankind*, 120.

155   *begging for his life*: William Taubman, *Khrushchev*, 256.

155   *"for that act alone"*: LP, author interview, March 30, 2008.

155   *"drab and somber"*: PHN, *FHTG*, 162.

155   *meant something closer to*: ibid., 163.

156   *This joyless country*: PHN to AHN, n.d., BRB.

156   *"I want us to"*: PHN to Joseph Alsop, June 1, 1954, PHNP LOC, box 17, folder 9.

156   *"in a position to issue"*: PHN, "Atoms, Strategy and Policy," *Foreign Affairs*, Jan. 1956, 190–91.

157   *"tactical atomic devices"*: CFR Study Group Reports, Nuclear Weapons and Foreign Policy, Nov. 8, 1954, CFR Papers, Records of groups, vol. 9, 1954–1955, 1954–1956, 10.

157   *"Once a war becomes nuclear"*: CFR Study group reports, Nuclear Weapons and Foreign Policy, May 4, 1955, 2.

157   *Nitze had inquired*: PHN to CEB, Sept. 1956, PHNP LOC, box 18, folder 14.

157   *"With proper tactics"*: Henry Kissinger, *Nuclear Weapons and Foreign Policy*, 152.

157   *Despite its dense prose*: Walter Isaacson, *Kissinger*, 88.

157   *"There are several hundred"*: PHN, "Limited Wars or Massive Retaliation?" *Reporter*, Sept. 5, 1957, 40–42.

157 *He scoffed at*: David Callahan, *Dangerous Capabilities*, 166.

158 *Asked fifty years later*: Henry Kissinger, author interview, July 11, 2008.

158 *"the common refuge"*: GFK, *MV2*, 261.

158 *impress fellow historians*: GFK to Herbert Butterfield, Dec. 17, 1956. GFKP, box 31, folder 2.

158 *a thorough debunking*: GFK, *Russia Leaves the War*, 210–14.

158 *He and Nitze had met*: PHN, LOC, box 34, folder 14.

158 *"I consider him"*: GFK, diary entry, Jan. 27, 1956, GFKP, box 3R.

159 *"How I wish"*: Adlai Stevenson to GFK, March 31, 1956, GFKP OF, box 71.

159 *Eventually, word started to circulate*: Hixson, *George F. Kennan*, 148.

160 *"It is clear that"*: GFK, diary entry, Aug. 23, 1956, GFKP, box 3R.

160 *"I found myself disgusted"*: GFK to PHN, Sept. 5, 1956, PHNP LOC, box 29, folder 4.

160 *"We thought you"*: LP, author interview, Sept. 30, 2008.

160 *He spoke passionately*: Taubman, *Khrushchev*, 270–75.

160 *Eventually the text ended up*: ibid., 283–84.

161 *Eastern Europe would soon*: Tony Judt, *Postwar*, 309–315.

161 *protesters tore down*: Evan Thomas, *The Very Best Men*, 142.

161 *"I think that the"*: Christopher Jespersen, *Interviews with George F. Kennan*, 3–16.

162 *"RUSSIAN GANGSTERS"*: "Out of the Darkness," *Time*, Nov. 12, 1956.

162 *Kennan, consulting with John Maury*: GFK, diary entry, Nov. 1, 1956, GFKP, box 3R.

163 *"The events of these recent"*: GFK, diary entry, Nov. 7, 1956, GFKP, box 3R.

163 *In a reprise of*: Jack Raymond, "US Revised Plan on Arms Is Ready," *NYT*, Jan. 13, 1957.

163 *CBS radio made*: PHN to AHN, Jan. 13, 1957, PHNPP.

163 *a British cartoon*: Derek Leebaert, *The Fifty-Year Wound*, 241.

163 *"But the position"*: PHN, "Atoms, Strategy, and Policy," *Foreign Affairs*, Jan. 1956, 187.

164 *"yet another agonizing"*: PHN to DGA, PHNP LOC, box 17, folder 4.

164 *"Is this right?"*: PHN, notes on "my favorite curve," PHNP LOC, box 102, folder 8.

165 *a gigantic underground office complex*: Leebaert, *Fifty-Year Wound*, 241.

165 *"Oh little Sputnik"*: Matthew Brzezinski, *Red Moon Rising*, 231.

165 *"Finally, assuming"*: PHN to John Foster Dulles, Nov. 16, 1957, John Foster Dulles Papers, box 3, folder 5.

165 *"The still top-secret"*: Chalmers Roberts, "Enormous Arms Outlay Is Held Vital to Survival," *Washington Post and Times Herald*, Dec. 20, 1957.

166 *"I'd rather not comment"*: PHN, interview for memoir, PHNP LOC, box 119, folder 1.

166 *"George Kennan is going"*: McMillan, author interview, Dec. 27, 2008.

166 *Russia Leaves the War also*: GFK, *MV2*, 12. In the memoirs, he seems to confuse the Benjamin Franklin Award, which he won for a magazine article in *Harper's*, with the Francis Parkman Prize.

166   *"Many a man"*: GFK, speech notes, GFKP, box 19, March 12, 1957.

167   *Recognizing his flight of fancy*: GFK, diary entry, July 28, 1957, GFKP, box 3R.

167   *The West should neither*: GFK, *Russia, the Atom, and the West*, 1–32.

167   *"No greater contribution"*: ibid., 36.

167   *"until we stop"*: ibid., 42.

167   *Nitze, commenting on the speech*: PHN speech before Third Annual Institute of the World Affairs Council of Milwaukee, Feb. 21, 1959, NSA, http://www .gwu.edu/~nsarchiv/NSAEBB/NSAEBB139/nitze03.pdf, accessed on Jan. 24, 2009.

167   *"They evidently believe"*: GFK, *Russia, the Atom, and the West*, 51.

168   *Afterward, 72 percent*: Kenneth W. Thompson, "The Kennan-Acheson Debate," *Commonweal*, April 6, 1958, 6.

168   *"futile—and lethal"*: DGA, "The Illusion of Disengagement," *Foreign Affairs*, April 1958, 374, quoted in Douglas Brinkley, *Dean Acheson*, 89.

168   *"I refused"*: PHN, personal memo, July 1982, PHNP LOC, box 29, folder 5.

169   *"I am now"*: GFK, diary entry, Jan. 12, 1958, GFKP, 3R.

169   *The rest of the group*: CFR Study Session on Military Strategy, Oct. 27, 1958, CFR papers, vol. 80.

169   *"I have no problems"*: PHN, speech to National Institute of Social Sciences, Oct. 20, 1981, PHN, BRB 46.

11. DEADLY SERIOUS EITHER WAY

170   *"How much time"*: PHN, *FHTG*, 181.

171   *"Reduction of arms"*: PHN notes, March 1961, PHNPP.

171   *only happened upon*: GFK diary entry, July 14, 1960, GFKP, 3R.

171   *"It is now nearly"*: GFK diary entry, Jan. 2, 1961, GFKP, 3R, black binder.

171   *"Had I taken"*: GFK to Walter Lippmann, Dec. 28, 1960, Lippmann papers, Yale University.

172   *One of the first*: Arthur Schlesinger Jr., *A Thousand Days*, 251.

172   *"Whatever you feel"*: GFK, OH, JFK Library, 42.

172   *He told Kennedy*: GFK to SOS, June 3, 1961, FRUS: 1961–1963, vol. 5, 81.

173   *Kennedy was weak*: Vladislav Zubok and Constantine Pleshakov, *Inside the Kremlin's Cold War*, 243.

173   *Why wait*: ibid., 247.

173   *Afterward, Kennedy*: David Halberstam, *The Best and the Brightest*, 76.

173   *"met a man who"*: Alistair Horne, *Harold Macmillan*, vol. 2, 1957–1968, 304.

173   *"tongue-tied"*: GFK, OH, JFK Library; also, "Role of Kennedy in 1961 assessed," *NYT*, Sept. 1, 1970.

173   *"This would not"*: PHN, notes on summary of conversation between Kennedy and Khrushchev, BRB 7.

174   *so poor*: William Taubman, *Khrushchev*, 21.

174   *"signed his own name"*: Dmitrii Shepilov, *The Kremlin's Scholar*, 65.

174   *"ugly, little man"*: PHN speech before Third Annual Institute of the World

Affairs Council of Milwaukee, Feb. 21, 1959, NSA, http://www.gwu.edu/~nsarchiv/NSAEBB/NSAEBB139/nitze03.pdf, accessed on Jan. 24, 2009.

174 *was not "sadistic"*: GFK to Theo Sommer, Aug. 9, 1979, GFKP OF, box 60, file Donhoff.

174 *"He's either all the way"*: Taubman, *Khrushchev*, xx.

174 *"never did stand up"*: Veljko Micunovic, *Moscow Diary*, 330.

175 *One of Khrushchev's speechwriters*: Zubok and Pleshakov, *Inside the Kremlin's Cold War*, 249.

175 *the communists christened*: "Texts of Reds' Communiqué and the East Germans' Decree About Berlin," *NYT*, Aug. 14, 1961.

175 *John Foster Dulles responded*: Derek Leebaert, *The Fifty-Year Wound*, 235.

176 *"If nothing's going on"*: David Callahan, *Dangerous Capabilities*, 222.

176 *"I have children"*: Arthur Schlesinger Jr., *Journals*, 111.

176 *At the time of*: memo from General Taylor, Oct. 4, 1961, NSA, http://www.gwu.edu/~nsarchiv/NSAEBB/NSAEBB56/BerlinC1.pdf, accessed on Jan. 24, 2009; also, Fred Kaplan, "JFK's First Strike Plan," *Atlantic Monthly*, Oct. 2001, 81–86.

176 *Nitze recommended four steps*: NSAM 109, Oct. 23, 1961, JFK Library, http://www.jfklibrary.org and http://tinyurl.com/azqvgj, accessed on Jan. 24, 2009.

177 *"have a tremendous"*: "Excerpts from Nitze Speech on Berlin," *NYT*, Sept. 7, 1961.

177 *Nitze mentioned the possibility*: Henry Brandon, diary entry, Sept. 15, 1961, Henry Brandon papers, LOC, box 5.

177 *"I supervised the engineers"*: PHN, personal notes, PHNP LOC, box 81, folder 4.

177 *"pulling down house"*: PHN, personal notes, Oct. 3, 1961, PHNPP.

178 *"would not protect"*: PHN, memcon, Oct. 9, 1961, PHNP LOC, box 83, folder 2.

178 *"The first side"*: Minutes of Meeting, Oct. 10, 1961, FRUS: 1961–1963, vol. 14, document 173.

178 *"Our war plans assumed"*: Vitalii Tsygichko, author interview, Feb. 12, 2009.

178 *The two men would meet*: GFK, OH, JFK Library, 120.

179 *"Unfortunately, however"*: Khrushchev to JFK, Sept. 29, 1961, FRUS: 1961–1963, vol. 6, document 7, http://www.state.gov/www/about_state/history/volume_vi/exchanges.html, accessed on Jan. 24, 2009.

179 *He reported*: Editorial note, FRUS: 1961–1963, vol. 14, document 137, http://www.state.gov/r/pa/ho/frus/kennedyjf/xiv/15863.htm, accessed on Jan. 24, 2009.

179 *"Unless the West"*: GFK to undersecretary of state, Sept. 22, 1961, FRUS: 1961–1963, vol. xiv, document 158, http://www.state.gov/r/pa/ho/frus/kennedyjf/xiv/15864.htm, accessed on Jan. 24, 2009.

180 *"Our prestige is already involved"*: PHN, meeting notes, Nov. 10, 1961, PHNPP.

181 *He mused*: GFK, MV2, 269.

181   *Young Foreign Service officers*: Lawrence Eagleburger, author interview, May 5, 2008.

181   *The local town council*: Walter Hixson, *George F. Kennan*, 202.

181   *pondered the past* : GFK, *MV2*, 270.

181   *He would ask his staff*: Gerald Livingston, author interview, Jan. 20, 2007.

181   *Everyone treated*: GFK, *MV2*, 273.

181   *After one memorable luncheon*: Livingston, author interview, Jan. 20, 2007.

182   *He declared that Khrushchev*: GFK, memo to Department of State, Sept. 3, 1961, FRUS: 1961–1963, vol. 16, document 96, http://www.state.gov/r/pa/ho/frus/kennedyjf/xvi/63673.htm, accessed on Jan. 24, 2009.

182   *"entirely a friendly"*: GFK, memo to Department of State, Sept. 15, 1961, FRUS: 1961–1963, vol. 16, Belgrade, Sept. 15, 1961, document 97, http://www.state.gov/r/pa/ho/frus/kennedyjf/xvi/63673.htm, accessed on Jan. 24, 2009.

182   *"he didn't realize"*: Eagleburger, author interview, May 5, 2008.

183   *"appalling ignorance"*: Max Frankel, "U.S. Envoys Warn on Cuts in Red Aid," *NYT*, June 15, 1962.

183   *"most careful thought"*: Charles A. Owens Jr., "Aiding Russians by Testing," letter, *NYT*, July 2, 1962.

183   *Even if he did not*: Livingston, author interview, Jan. 20, 2007.

183   *"He was a better writer"*: Robert Cleveland, author interview, April 30, 2008.

184   *He had grim news*: PHN, *FHTG*, 215–16.

185   *"deadly serious either way"*: PHN, meeting notes, Oct. 17, 1962, BRB.

185   *"We have been waiting"*: Dean Rusk, as told to Richard Rusk, *As I Saw It*, 245; also, JLG, *We Now Know*, 181.

185   *"all plans vague, grandiose"*: PHN, meeting notes, Nov. 4, 1961, BRB 7.

185   *"the top priority"*: Michael Beschloss, *The Crisis Years*, 6, quoted in Ronald Steel, *In Love with Night*, 78.

185   *"We should increase"*: Alexsandr Fursenko and Timothy Naftali, *Khrushchev's Cold War*, 5.

185   *By the spring*: Taubman, *Khrushchev*, 541.

185   *Each ship carried*: ibid., 549–50.

186   *no "Pearl Harbor"*: PHN, *FHTG*, 223.

186   *"It would be better"*: Ernest May and Philip Zelikow, *The Kennedy Tapes*, 190.

186   *"maybe better to go"*: PHN, meeting notes, White House PM, Oct. 18, 1962, BRB.

186   *"If you encounter mush"*: PHN, meeting notes, Ball's Office, Oct. 18, 1962, BRB.

186   *"a sophomoric seminar"*: PHN, interview with Blight, Welch, Rearden, Smith, May 6, 1987, BRB.

187   *he wrote his name*: PHN, meeting notes, Oct 20, 1962, BRB.

187   *"I just don't"*: May and Zelikow, *Kennedy Tapes*, 177–78.

188   *"Can we take care"*: ibid., 222–23; also, Sheldon Stern, *Averting the Final Failure*, 145–46.

188 *"We will not prematurely"*: Robert Kennedy, *Thirteen Days*, 152.

189 *"If we have this"*: May and Zelikow, *Kennedy Tapes*, 357.

189 *As Nitze spoke*: Michael Dobbs, *One Minute to Midnight*, 50.

189 *"Escalate blockade"*: PHN, meeting notes, lunch with McNamara, Oct. 25, 1962, BRB.

190 *He ended the talk*: GFK, briefing notes, Oct. 27, 1962, GFKP, box 24, folder 33.

190 *"liquidating such a danger forever"*: Dobbs, *One Minute to Midnight*, 204.

190 *"Unless we can return"*: PHN, meeting notes, Ball's office, Oct. 27, 1962, BRB.

191 *He had spent*: Dobbs, *One Minute to Midnight*, 43.

191 *He had become*: Tsygichko, author interview, Feb. 12, 2009.

191 *He might run for president*: Anatoly Dobrynin, *In Confidence*, 90.

191 *"The Soviet government"*: Dobbs, *One Minute to Midnight*, 331.

191 *"Nothing that has gone on"*: GFK, appearance on *Meet the Press*, Aug. 18, 1963, GFKP, box 261, folder 15.

191 *Soviet missiles were aimed*: Andrian Danilevich, in John G. Hines, Ellis M. Mishulovich, and John F. Shull, *Soviet Intentions, 1965–1985*, vol. 2: *Soviet Post–Cold War Testimonial Evidence*, 31.

192 *"sent a chill"*: Robert S. McNamara, "Forty Years After 13 Days," *Arms Control Today*, Nov. 2002, 4.

192 *In a 1965 interview*: Callahan, *Dangerous Capabilities*, 271.

192 *"I knew them all"*: PHN, interview for memoirs, PHNP LOC, box 119, folder 3.

192 *"a dove from the start"*: Arthur Schlesinger Jr., *Robert Kennedy and His Times*, 507.

193 *But in return*: PHN, "Basis for Substantive Negotiations with U.S.S.R.," Feb. 1963, NARA, RG 59, Records of Ambassador-at-Large Llewellyn E. Thompson 1961–1970, File 67D2, no. 5.

193 *"Kennedy expected to name"*: Jack Raymond, "Kennedy Expected to Name Nitze to Gilpatric's Post in Pentagon," *NYT*, March 16, 1963.

193 *But Kennedy twisted*: PHN, AFOH, 319.

193 *"The man doesn't know"*: Carl Kaysen, author interview, March 12, 2006.

193 *paid a visit to Nitze*: PHN, 1963 meeting notes, PHNP LOC, box 81, folder 1.

194 *Kennan mailed the letter*: GFK to JFK, Oct. 22, 1963, GFKP, box 31.

194 *profound sadness*: Constance Goodman, interview with author, March 15, 2008.

12. ABOUT 60/40

195 *The conference goers*: Harold Brown, author interview, Jan. 19, 2009.

196 *Donald Rumsfeld unearthed it*: Strobe Talbott, *MOTG*, 86–87.

196 *wrestled a colleague down*: "How Silly Can You Get," *Time*, July 17, 1964.

196 *"Mr. Chairman"*: Nominations of Paul H. Nitze and William P. Bundy, "Hearings Before the Committee on Armed Services," United States Senate, Eighty-eighth Congress, First Session, Nov. 7 and 14, 1963, 67.

196   *Nitze take an oath*: "Senators Question Nitze Sharply on Past Views," *NYT*, Nov. 8 1963.

197   *"Nitze opposed in"*: "Nitze Opposed in Navy Job for Alleged Pacifist Views," *NYT*, Nov. 1, 1963.

197   *"The Navy is"*: "Anchors Away," *Time*, Oct. 25, 1963.

198   *When he read*: William Thompson, author interview, May 24, 2007.

198   *He set up a special*: PHN, "Instructions for the Coordination and Control of the Navy's Clandestine Intelligence Collection Program," Dec. 7, 1965, NSA, http://www.gwu.edu/~nsarchiv/NSAEBB/NSAEBB46/, accessed on Jan. 24, 2009.

198   *He spent hours*: David Ignatius, "The Old Pro," *Wall Street Journal*, Aug. 1, 1985.

198   *"You made any mistake"*: Thompson, author interview, May 24, 2007.

198   *"The service secretaries"*: James Mann, *Rise of the Vulcans*, 16.

198   *"I've never said this"*: PHN, personal memo, May 9, 1983, BRB 45.

200   *We should fight*: Elmo Zumwalt, *On Watch*, 39.

200   *In one June 1964 memo*: Edward J. Marolda and Oscar Fitzgerald, *The United States Navy and the Vietnam Conflict*, vol. 2, *From Military Assistance to Combat, 1959*, 369.

200   *If we did send*: Stewart Alsop, *The Center*, 162.

200   *In February 1965*: Kai Bird, *The Color of Truth*, 306.

200   *"Even if it fails"*: ibid., 308.

200   *a dandified aviator*: Larry Berman, *Lyndon Johnson's War*, 18.

200   *"a saxophone player"*: Walter Isaacson and Evan Thomas, *The Wise Men*, 647.

201   *He then headed to Saigon*: PHN, *FHTG*, 258.

201   *"You offer no alternative"*: ibid., 259.

201   *Nitze kept private notes*: PHN, meeting notes, July 22, 1965, BRB 55.

202   *"Paul, what is your view"*: meeting notes, July 22, 1965, FRUS: 1964–1968, vol. 3, document 76, http://www.state.gov/www/about_state/history/vol_iii/070.html, accessed on Jan. 24, 2009.

202   *"was to pin"*: Brown, author interview, Jan. 19, 2009.

202   *"40 percent"*: PHN, *FHTG*, 260.

203   *He confided*: GFK, diary entry, Jan. 20, 1965, GFKP, box 5R.

203   *"The provocation"*: GFK, diary entry, Feb. 7, 1965, GFKP, box 5R.

203   *He began by asserting*: GFF, "Testifying before Senate Foreign Relations committee," Feb. 10, 1966, GFKP, box 263, folder 6.

205   *The next day*: PHN, meeting notes, BRB 1.

205   *"hauling sacks like Santa Claus"*: Constance Goodman, author interview, March 15, 2008.

206   *"Something has come up"*: ibid.

206   *"We have a tremendous defection"*: GFK, interview with JLG, Dec. 13, 1987, GFKP OF, box 62.

206   *she was Svetlana Alliluyeva*: LP, *OOY*, 199.

206   *Svetlana fell in love*: ibid., 17–20.

206   *"What have you cooked up"*: ibid., 37.

207 *"Every week"*: LP, author interview, Sept. 30, 2008.

207 *"Why, yes, it's next door"*: LP, *OOY*, 192.

207 *did not even know*: Robert Rayle, author interview, June 12, 2008.

208 *The nuns told*: Marvin Kalb, author interview, Sept. 9, 2008.

208 *"I had a feeling"*: LP to author, May 9, 2008.

208 *"Hello there, everybody"*: "News Summary," *NYT*, April 22, 1967.

208 *"a visiting queen"*: Olga Carlisle, "Dictator's Daughter," *NYT*, Sept. 24, 1967.

209 *"complete self-possession"*: CEB to GFK, Dec. 21, 1967, GFKP OF, box 58.

209 *When the CIA gave her*: Rayle, author interview, Sept. 28, 2007.

209 *"She's so nice"*: Sylvan Fox, "Life, The Times to Serialize Stalin Daughter's Memoirs," *NYT*, April 23, 1967.

13. THE OTHER SIDE OF THE BARRICADES

210 *Radicals tried to provoke*: Robert McNamara, *In Retrospect*, 304.

211 *would self-immolate*: PHN, meeting notes, Oct. 21, 1967, PHNP LOC, box 85, folder 3.

211 *None of their rifles*: McNamara, *In Retrospect*, 303.

211 *burst in and rape*: Leslie Gelb, author interview, March 18, 2006.

211 *"Warren Christopher and I share"*: PHN, *Jottings*.

211 *Christopher remembers*: Warren Christopher, *Chances of a Lifetime*, 52–54.

211 *The two were unquestionably*: description of meeting on Jan. 10, 1968, "Supplementary Detailed Staff Reports on Intelligence Activities and the Rights of Americans," Book III: "Final Report of the Select Committee to Study Governmental Operations with Respect to Intelligence Activities," April 23, 1976, http://www.aarcl.library.org/publib/church/reports/book2/pdf/churchb2-2D-dissent.pdf, accessed March 26, 2009.

211 *"303 Committee"*: Mort Halperin, author interview, May 30, 2008.

211 *But Christopher says*: Warren Christopher, author interview, May 13, 2008.

212 *"take young men"*: GFK to James Russell, Oct. 11, 1950, GFKP, box 29.

212 *He foresaw nothing*: GFK, "Rebels Without a Program," *NYT Magazine*, Jan. 21, 1968, 69. For more discussion of the topic of freedom within constraints, see Danielle Goldman, *I Want to Be Ready*.

213 *"I wonder whether"*: Wendy Kennan, author interview, March 26, 2008.

213 *"the end of the world"*: JEK, author interview, Jan. 6, 2009.

214 *"an old-fashioned voice"*: Norman Podhoretz, "George Kennan and the Students," *Harper's*, Oct. 1968, 104.

214 *dressed in a gray suit*: Walter Hixson, *George F. Kennan*, 249.

214 *"God knows"*: Israel Shenker, "Kennan Analysis Coolly Received," *NYT*, Dec. 4, 1968.

214 *an FBI informant*: Notes from the meeting appear in GFKFBI.

214 *"is to deny"*: GFK, *Democracy and the Student Left*, 94.

214 *in front of a Zayre*: Pete Earley, *Family of Spies*, 66–72.

215 *the first American ship*: Mitchell Lerner, "A Dangerous Miscalculation," *Journal of Cold War Studies*, vol. 6, no. 1 (Winter 2004), 3.

215 *"sweated peach pits"*: PHN, interview with Frank Vandiver, Sept. 20, 1990, PHNPP.

215 *The options were limited*: Halperin, author interview, May 30, 2008; also, Bradley K. Martin, *Under the Loving Care of the Fatherly Leader,* 129.

215 *"to be throwing dirt"*: PHN, interview with Frank Vandiver, Sept. 20, 1990, PHNPP.

215 *His notes from*: PHN, notes, Jan. 31, 1969, PHNP LOC, box 85, folder 4.

216 *"more than one million"*: Earley, *Family of Spies,* 73. Recent documents suggest that the timing of Walker's turning and the capture of the *Pueblo* was a coincidence—but a very serendipitous one for Moscow.

216 *"I can't find words"*: "McNamara Deeply Moved as President Pays Him Tribute," *Washington Post and Times Herald,* Feb. 29, 1968.

216 *one of the leading*: "Heirs Apparent," *Time,* Dec. 8, 1967.

216 *"I am sorry that LBJ"*: DGA to PHN, Jan. 22, 1969, LOC PHN, box 17.

216 *he made Nitze sit*: PHN, *FHTG,* 261–62.

216 *"Clifford was acutely aware"*: George Elsey, author interview, Nov. 6, 2006.

217 *"What are you"*: *Armed Forces Management,* Oct. 1968, 771, quoted in David Callahan, *Dangerous Capabilities,* 307.

217 *Clifford would begin the meeting*: Elsey, author interview, Nov. 6, 2006.

217 *"fire-breathing hawk"*: PHN, *FHTG,* 274.

217 *He had played semi-pro*: Bart Barnes and Patricia Sullivan, "Gentle Senator, Presidential Hopeful, Empowered U.S. Antiwar Movement," *Washington Post,* Dec. 11, 2005.

218 *The* New York Review: GFK, "Introducing Eugene McCarthy," *New York Review of Books,* April 11, 1968.

218 *"I do not feel"*: PHN to LBJ, March 16, 1968, FRUS: 1964–1968, vol. 6, document 133, http://www.state.gov/r/pa/ho/frus/johnsonlb/vi/13702.htm, accessed on Jan. 24, 2009.

218 *"I had no idea"*: PHN, *FHTG,* 278.

218 *"You take Nitze"*: conversation between LBJ and Richard Russell, March 22, 1968, FRUS: 1964–1968, vol. 6, document 150, http://www.state.gov/r/pa/ho/frus/johnsonlb/vi/13703.htm, accessed on Jan. 24, 2009.

219 *the percentage of Americans*: Doris Kearns Goodwin, *Lyndon Johnson and the American Dream,* 336.

219 *"Defects of old speech"*: PHN, notes, PHNP LOC, box 85, folder 5.

220 *"an absolute incontinent"*: Jerry Sanders, *Peddlers of Crisis,* 141.

221 *"Nitze explodes again"*: notes of meeting, Sept. 16, 1968, FRUS: 1964–1968, vol. 7, document 15, http://www.state.gov/r/pa/ho/frus/johnsonlb/vii/21590.htm, accessed on Jan. 24, 2009.

221 *a list of Americans residing*: CBW, *George F. Kennan: Scholar-Diplomat,* 31; also, SOS to General Counsel at Berlin, April 12, 1932, FRUS: 1932, vol. 2, 523.

221 *"on whom there"*: report, April 14, 1970, GFKFBI.

221 *"he had a weekly"*: memo, Dec. 27, 1951, GFKFBI.

221 *"You will recall that George"*: memo from D. M. Ladd, March 28, 1951, GFKFBI.

221 *with advanced degrees*: Ken Clawson, "Top FBI Official Forced Out in Policy Feud with Hoover," *Washington Post,* Oct. 2, 1971.

221 *the only liberal Democrat*: "William C. Sullivan, Ex-F.B.I Aide, 65, Is Killed in a Hunting Accident," *NYT,* Nov. 10, 1977.

222 *He was in charge*: David Garrow, *Bearing the Cross,* 310.

222 *accumulated a large*: GFKP OF, box 71.

222 *"I must say"*: GFK to William Sullivan, Dec. 11, 1970, GFKP OF, box 71.

222 *"probably would read"*: Robert Novak, *The Prince of Darkness,* 210.

223 *"hell of a good guy"*: Henry Kissinger and Melvin Laird, Non-Classified, Memorandum of Telephone Conversation Kissinger Telephone Conversations, Digital NSA, Dec. 19, 1969.

223 *The Arizona senator believed*: Melvin Laird, author interview, Feb. 21, 2006.

223 *"any objections to Paul Nitze"*: Carl Marcy to William Fulbright, May 15, 1969, William Fulbright papers; Vera Ekechukwu, e-mail to author, Jan. 29, 2007.

224 *None of the four interns*: Edward Luttwak, author interview, May 22, 2008.

225 *Appraising the odds*: PHNP LOC, box 74, folder 11.

225 *"Psychologically I think"*: PHN, interviews for memoir, PHNP LOC, box 119, folder 11.

225 *"payoff for his ABM testimony"*: Henry Kissinger and Melvin Laird, Non-Classified, Memorandum of Telephone Conversation, Kissinger Telephone Conversations, Digital National Security Archive, May 2, 1969.

226 *"The extreme unhappiness"*: GFK, diary entry, Aug. 19, 1968, GFKP, box 6R.

226 *"in part a certainty"*: ibid.

227 *"I thought that"*: GFK, diary entry, Oct. 10, 1968, GFKP, box 6R.

227 *he told Kissinger*: Henry Kissinger, author interview, July 11, 2008. Kissinger recalled that the key sign for Kennan was that the U.S. government had decided to allow people to use foreign currency to buy Chinese goods in Hong Kong.

227 *"Now I had to get"*: LP, *OOY,* 436.

228 *The KGB gave Svetlana*: Christopher Andrew and Vasili Mitrokhin, *The Sword and the Shield,* 616.

228 *"cuckoo bird"*: George Kennan, *Siberia and the Exile System,* vol. 2, 153. This is a book by George Frost Kennan's relative with the same name.

228 *and sent an agent*: Christopher Andrew and Oleg Gordievsky, *KGB,* 479.

228 *"How can one"*: James Hudson, *Svetlana Alliluyeva: Flight to Freedom,* 160.

228 *"Two KGB officers"*: Donald Jameson to GFK, Oct. 12, 1967, GFKP OF, box 64.

228 *"You are all present"*: LP, *OOY,* 340.

228 *she bought the first house*: LP, *The Faraway Music,* 37.

229 *Svetlana fell immediately in love*: ibid., 51–63.

229 *"I see [similarities] every day"*: LP to GFK, June 15, 1970, GFKP OF, box 68.

229 *His widow believed*: LP, *Faraway Music,* 76.

229 *to confront Svetlana directly*: LP to ASK, May 23, 1970, GFKP OF, box 68.

229 *Eventually, Kennan was able to*: LP, *Faraway Music,* 76–77.

14. THIS DELEGATION IS A DISASTER

231 *In October 1969*: Jeremi Suri, "The Nukes of October," *Wired,* March 2008, 162.

232 *Instead of just counting missiles*: Strobe Talbott, *MOTG,* 121.

232 *Alexei Obukhov, a young member*: Alexei Obukhov, author interview, Feb. 12, 2009.

233 *Nitze declined the offer*: PHN, *FHTG,* 299.

233 *bureaucratic rival*: The most interesting moment in the Laird-Kissinger tussle came when Kissinger prepared for his covert 1971 trip to China. Learning about the trip from National Security Agency intercepts, Laird decided to yank his rival's tail by announcing that he would visit Taiwan to tour its defense installations at exactly the same time.

233 *information from the confidential*: Dale Van Atta, *With Honor,* 199.

233 *"I have seen more Talmudic"*: Henry Kissinger and Gerard Smith, Non-Classified, Memorandum of Telephone Conversation, Kissinger Telephone Conversations, Digital NSA, April 29, 1970.

233 *"this delegation is a disaster"*: Henry Kissinger and Melvin Laird, Non-Classified, Memorandum of Telephone Conversation, Kissinger Telephone Conversations, Digital NSA, March 18, 1971.

234 *Nitze was a suspect*: memorandum on distribution of OSD Task Force Study, Jan. 14, 1969, PHNP LOC, box 168, folder 2.

234 *"What about Nitze"*: Stanley Kutler, *Abuse of Power,* 31.

234 *confused him with*: Daniel Ellsberg, *Secrets,* 243.

234 *It is not clear*: It must have reached him by the fall because, in November, Nixon and Kissinger discussed naming Nitze as U.S. representative to NATO. Richard Nixon and Henry Kissinger, Non-Classified, Memorandum of Telephone Conversation, Kissinger Telephone Conversation, Digital NSA, Nov. 16, 1971.

234 *"You've got to know"*: Ralph Earle, author interview, Sept. 6, 2005.

234 *"Then what is wrong"*: Vladislav Zubok, *A Failed Empire,* 242, citing Russian-language sources.

235 *Given the political benefits*: Henry Kissinger, *White House Years,* 1217.

235 *during the final days and hours*: Raymond Garthoff, author interview, June 19, 2008.

235 *And just before*: PHN, *FHTG,* 326.

235 *Frustrated and angry*: ibid., 328.

235 *At 1:30 in the morning*: ibid., 327.

236 *"took the heart out"*: GFK, *MV2,* 306.

236 *"the story of a sensitive"*: Ronald Steel, "Man Without a Country," *New York Review of Books,* Jan. 4, 1968.

237 *"Half of us"*: GFK, *MV1,* 139.

237 *"talk[ing] in tense low tones"*: ibid., 43.

237 *"He paced wretchedly"*: ibid., 98.

237 *"It will be easily understood"*: ibid., 112.

238 *"I can think of no"*: GFK to JH, summer 1943, GFKP, box 7R.

238   *"Again, with my proclivity"*: GFK to Marion Donhoff, March 15, 1965, GFKP, box 31, folder 11.

239   *Throughout his life*: Walter Pozen, author interview, Feb. 28, 2008.

239   *And he always expressed*: JEK, author interview, March 15, 2008.

239   *Right before the SALT*: Zubok, *Failed Empire*, 242, citing Russian-language sources.

240   *During the crisis*: ibid.

240   *One night the Nitzes*: PHN, undated recollections of GFK, BRB 5.

240   *Looking for a way*: David Callahan, *Dangerous Capabilities*, 354.

240   *"You know the president doesn't like"*: Henry Kissinger and William Clements; Non-Classified, Memorandum of Telephone Conversation; Kissinger Telephone Conversations, Digital NSA, March 9, 1973.

241   *Worse, Kissinger had given Newhouse*: Callahan, *Dangerous Capabilities*, 357.

241   *"Needless to say"*: PHN to Robert Murphy, April 15, 1974, Robert D. Murphy papers, Hoover Library, box 120, folder 24.

241   *"until the Office"*: Strobe Talbott, *MOTG*, 139–40.

241   *He disclosed the existence"*: Callahan, *Dangerous Capabilities*, 367.

242   *"It was a terrible scene"*: Richard Perle, author interview, April 6, 2007.

242   *If Kissinger did not know*: Henry Kissinger, *Years of Upheaval*, 1152. Kissinger begins the section on Nitze with effusive praise, calling him "one of our nation's most distinguished public servants and ablest theorists on national defense."

242   *"It is with deep gratitude"*: Draft memo from Helmut Sonnenfeldt to PHN, NARA, RG 59.31, General Records of the Department of State, Office of the Counselor, subject files of Helmut Sonnenfeldt, 1955–1977, box 12, file 3, "SALT June–Sept. 1974."

242   *A few days later*: Bernard Gwertzman, "Kissinger Puts Off His Visit to Soviet for Talks on Arms," *NYT*, Dec. 10, 1975.

242   *Four months later*: Elmo Zumwalt, memo to PHN, April 2, 1976, PHNP LOC, box 43, folder 14.

243   *describing Kissinger as a "traitor"*: Callahan, *Dangerous Capabilities*, 359.

243   *Nitze found out*: Elmo Zumwalt, *On Watch*, 28.

243   *According to Melvin Laird*: Laird, author interview, Feb. 21, 2006.

243   *At one of their first meetings*: Zumwalt, *On Watch*, 309.

243   *"K. feels that U.S."*: ibid., 319.

243   *Angered, Kissinger called Laird*: ibid., 239.

243   *Zumwalt became convinced*: ibid., 432–34.

244   *Kissinger denounced*: Gordon Chaplin, "Zumwalt's Next War," *Washington Post*, Feb. 15, 1976.

244   *Lawn learned*: Jack Lawn, author interview, July 16, 2008.

244   *Eventually, the Zumwalts*: Mouza Zumwalt, author interview, June 11, 2008.

244   *Told about this account*: Jessica P. LePorin, e-mail to author, April 2, 2009.

244   *The point of détente*: JLG, *Strategies of Containment*, 272–81.

245   *In a September 1973*: Henry Kissinger and GFK; Non-Classified, Memorandum of Telephone Conversation; Kissinger Telephone Conversations, Digital NSA, Sept. 14, 1973.

245 *"What in the name"*: Murrey Marder, "Summit Clouded by Watergate," *Washington Post*, July 4, 1974.

246 *"Henry understands my views"*: JLG, *Strategies of Containment*, 281.

246 *"I thought [Kennan] understood"*: Kissinger, author interview, July 11, 2008.

246 a 1976 interview: George Urban, "From Containment to Self-Containment," *Encounter*, Sept. 1976, 10–43.

247 *"He's on their side"*: PHN, notes on "A Conversation with George Kennan," PHNP LOC, box 29, folder 5.

247 *"Dear Mr. Kennan"*: George Krimsky to GFK, Aug. 5, 1975, GFKP OF, box 68, folder LP.

248 *The letter came with*: GFK, memorandum to self, Aug. 20, 1975, GFKP OF, box 68, folder LP.

248 *The affair had begun*: George Krimsky, author interview, June 22, 2008.

249 *"just a pretext"*: Don Oberdorfer, "U.S. Retaliates, Expels Soviet Reporter," *Washington Post*, Feb. 6, 1977.

249 *"The real reason"*: "When A.P. Correspondent," *Time*, Feb. 21, 1977, http://www.time.com/time/magazine/article/0,9171,918656,00.html, accessed on Jan. 24, 2009.

249 *He wrote her back*: GFK to LP, May 14, 1977, GFKP OF, box 68, folder LP. Svetlana was now going by "Lana Peters."

15. YOU CONSTANTLY BETRAY YOURSELF

251 *Nitze put the point*: PHN, "Deterring Our Deterrent," *Foreign Policy*, Winter 1976–1977, 206.

252 *Brezhnev fought desperately*: Vladislav Zubok, *A Failed Empire*, 245–46, citing Russian-language sources. Chernyaev's diaries have been donated to the National Security Archive. But, as of 2009, many years' worth, including 1975, have not yet been translated into English. Also, Nikolai Detinov, author interview, Feb. 11, 2009.

252 *On the final day*: Melvyn Leffler, *For the Soul of Mankind*, 248.

252 *He had carefully worked*: W. Scott Thompson, e-mail to author, July 27, 2008.

253 *The morning of his trip*: ibid.

253 *"He was a lion"*: Walter Slocombe, author interview, June 29, 2005.

253 *"was giving a presentation"*: Barry Blechman, author interview, May 21, 2008.

253 *young people*: James Woolsey, author interview, Nov. 27, 2006.

253 *"Nitze was typically"*: Strobe Talbott, *MOTG*, 149.

253 *When Nitze returned home*: W. Scott Thompson, e-mail to author, July 22, 2008.

254 *Now he had written*: CBW, "Mr. 'X' and Containment," *Slavic Review*, March 1976, 1.

254 *Wright was an admirer*: CBW, author interview, Aug. 19, 2008.

255 *top Soviet officials translated*: Alexei Obukhov, author interview, Feb. 12, 2009.

255 *"These discussions are confidential"*: James Millar to CBW, Nov. 7, 1975, CBW personal papers.

256 *In the clearest test case*: Wilson Miscamble, *George F. Kennan and the Making of American Foreign Policy*, 93.

256 *"Mr. Kennan said that"*: GFK, speech, "Soviet Way of Thought and Effect on For. Policy," Jan. 7, 1947, GFKP, box 18R.

256 *"I stand, as I see"*: GFK, "George F. Kennan Replies," *Slavic Review*, March 1976, 32.

256 *"reject plans to make"*: GFK, "National Power and Foreign Policy: Council on Foreign Relations Study Group," Oct. 30, 1946, GFKP, box 18R.

257 *On more than one occasion*: Priscilla McMillan, author interview, Sept. 14, 2008.

257 *"I do not miss Princeton"*: LP to ASK, April 26, 1976, GFKP OF, box 68.

258 *"George, you deserve"*: LP to GFK, April 28, 1976, GFKP OF, box 68.

259 *"Cherry's mouth froze"*: Richard Pipes, author interview, March 11, 2006.

259 *"It was like Walt Whitman"*: Anne Hessing Cahn, *Killing Détente*, 158.

260 *because they felt pressure*: Author interview with Team A member who insisted on anonymity, July 28, 2008.

260 *"are not doing"*: Bernard Gwertzman, "Kissinger Says Idea of Supremacy Makes No Sense in a Nuclear Age," *NYT*, Jan. 11, 1977.

260 *according to his son*: Ed Paisley, author interview, Aug. 28, 2008.

260 *And his empty*: William Corson, Susan Trento, and Joseph Trento, *Widows*, 121.

260 *It also carried*: "CIA Related Documents Retained by Mr. Paisley on His Boat or at His Apartment," CIA, FOIA request, personal files of author.

261 *extraordinary collection of interviews*: John G. Hines, Ellis M. Mishulovich, and John F. Shull, *Soviet Intentions, 1965–1985*, vol. 1: *An Analytical Comparison of U.S.-Soviet Assessments During the Cold War*, and vol. 2: *Soviet Post–Cold War Testimonial Evidence*.

261 *weapons manufacturers drove decisions*: Pavel Podvig, author interview, Jan. 13, 2009.

261 *"everything was militarized"*: Vitalii Tsygichko, author interview, Feb. 12, 2009.

262 *"We considered that"*: Andrian Danilevich, in Hines, Mishulovich, and Shull, *Soviet Intentions*, vol. 2: *Soviet Post–Cold War Testimonial Evidence*, 29.

262 *"We never had"*: ibid., 61.

262 *"The doctrine was"*: Tsygichko, author interview, Feb. 12, 2009.

262 *The scenario "terrified" Brezhnev*: Danilevich, in Hines, Mishulovich, and Shull, *Soviet Intentions*, vol. 2: *Soviet Post–Cold War Testimonial Evidence*, 27.

263 *"I have nothing to market"*: W. Scott Thompson, author interview, Oct. 19, 2008.

264 *"never the same after that"*: Leslie Gelb, author interview, May 18, 2006.

264 *In Warnke's view*: Paul C. Warnke, "Apes on a Treadmill," *Foreign Policy*, Spring 1975, 12.

264 *There would be hearings*: PHN, *FHTG,* 354.

264 *On February 9, 1977*: PHN, Senate testimony, Feb. 9, 1977, Warnke papers, box 23, folder 6.5, 78.

264 *A passerby*: Ron Rosenbaum, conversation with author, Nov. 9, 2007.

264 *On this day, Nitze's tone*: PHN, Senate testimony, Feb. 28, 1977, Warnke papers, box 23, folder 9.5, 174.

265 *"I [don't] think"*: ibid., 175.

265 *"I think he has"*: ibid., 178.

265 *"Mr. Nitze, in your"*: David Callahan, *Dangerous Capabilities,* 394.

265 *"tended to look for fights"*: Harold Brown, author interview, Jan. 19, 2009.

265 *Nitze's description*: PHN, *FHTG,* 355.

266 *Immediately after the hearings*: Stephen Warnke, author interview, Feb. 22, 2006.

266 *"Dear George," he wrote*: PHN to GFK, March 7, 1977, GFKP OF, box 68.

266 *"a real and crucial parting"*: GFK, *Cloud of Danger,* ix.

267 *"in one breath"*: ibid.

267 *they were the inevitable*: ibid., 5.

267 *"Our political philosophy"*: PPS, "Review of Current Trends in U.S. Foreign Policy," Feb. 24, 1948, FRUS: 1948, vol. 1, part 2, 510.

268 *"Even if the Soviet leaders"*: GFK, *Cloud of Danger,* 186.

268 *After all, they simultaneously*: ibid., 88.

268 *"I see no reason"*: ibid., 190.

269 *Ronald Steel dubbed it*: Ronald Steel, "Russia, the West, and the Rest," *New York Review of Books,* July 14, 1977.

269 Pravda *declared*: Leopold Labedz and Melvin Lasky, *The Use and Abuse of Sovietology,* 223.

269 *"George didn't leave much"*: W. Scott Thompson, author interview, Oct. 19, 2008. Thompson was sitting next to Bruce and Marshall.

269 *"a debate between two parties"*: Martin Herz, ed., *Decline of the West,* 69.

270 *"policy is old-fashioned"*: ibid., 116.

270 *Nitze's typed copy*: PHN, comments on speech by GFK, PHNP LOC, box 29, folder 5.

271 *"My means and energies"*: GFK to James Reston, Nov. 28, 1978, GFKP OF, box 69.

271 *"For more than thirty years"*: Strobe Talbott, *MOTG,* 153.

272 *"[Nitze] has the"*: GFK, interview with JLG, Aug. 8, 1982, GFKP OF, box 62.

272 *"Whatever Professor Gaddis says"*: JLG, e-mail to author, Feb. 21, 2009.

273 *Nitze began to shake*: Strobe Talbott, *MOTG,* 155.

273 *"Paul Nitze is worth"*: C. Robert Zelnick, "Paul Nitze: The Nemesis of SALT II," *Washington Post,* June 24, 1979.

273 *"because the administration"*: Kenneth Bacon, "Fighting a Treaty: Nitze, Long a Backer of Arms Curbs, Now Is a Key Critic of SALT," *Wall Street Journal,* June 20, 1979.

273 *"Henry Kissinger we will"*: C. Robert Zelnick, "Paul Nitze: The Nemesis of SALT II," *Washington Post,* June 24, 1979.

273 *Kennan, on the other hand*: GFK to Frank Church, Feb. 26, 1979, GFKP OF, box 59.

274 *After the 1962*: Gloria Duffy, "Crisis Mangling and the Cuban Brigade," *International Security*, Summer 1983, 67–87.

274 *In fact, the charge*: Vladislav Zubok, *A Failed Empire*, 264.

274 *"It was so distorted"*: Ralph Earle, author interview, June 23, 2008.

275 *"we would not have"*: Detinov, author interview, Feb. 11, 2009.

275 *He talked extensively*: PHNP LOC, box 144, folder 1.

16. I AM WORRIED ABOUT EVERYTHING

276 *He had hung his coat*: William Casey to Caspar Weinberger, Dec. 8, 1981, available online from NARA, CIA Records Search Tool, http://www.foia.cia .gov/search-archive.asp, accessed on March 26, 2009.

276 *"His manner sparkled"*: George Shultz, *Turmoil and Triumph*, 501.

277 *"I had a particular philosophy"*: PHN, interview with Academy of Achievement, Oct. 20, 1990, http://www.achievement.org/autodoc/printmember/ nit0int-1, accessed Jan. 24, 2009.

277 *"He was convinced"*: Harold Brown, author interview, Jan. 19, 2009.

277 *"I feel like George Kennan"*: Nancy Jenkins, e-mail to author, Oct. 10, 2008.

278 *Kennan had a firm routine*: Christopher Kennan, author interview, March 9, 2006.

278 *Kennan believed that a declaration*: Walter Hixson, *George F. Kennan*, 271– 72; also, Don Oberdorfer, "George Kennan Urges Tougher Stance on Iran," *Washington Post*, Feb. 28, 1980.

278 *A few weeks before*: GFK to Walt Rostow, Dec. 26, 1980, GFKP OF, box 69.

278 *"The only morality"*: Edmund Morris, *Dutch*, 436.

279 *"We have gone on piling"*: GFK, *The Nuclear Delusion*, 175–76.

279 *The* Washington Post *ran*: Don Oberdorfer, "Kennan Urges Halving of Nuclear Arsenals," *Washington Post*, May 20, 1981.

279 *Two days after that*: Don Oberdorfer, "George Kennan's 30-Year Nightmare of Our 'Final Folly,' " *Washington Post*, May 24, 1981.

279 *the entire text*: GFK, "We Got Ourselves into This Mess," *Washington Post*, May 24, 1981.

279 *"probably our most distinguished"*: James Reston, "A Day to Remember," *NYT*, May 24, 1981.

279 *"Kennan later equated"*: GFK interview with JLG, Sept. 4, 1984, GFKP OF, box 62, p. 10.

279 *a senator asked Nitze*: PHN, AFOH, 351.

280 *"If there are enough"*: Robert Scheer, *With Enough Shovels*, front cover.

280 *"Depending upon certain assumptions"*: "Hearings on Nomination of Eugene V. Rostow to Be Director, Arms Control and Disarmament Agency," Senate Committee on Foreign Relations, Ninety-Seventh Congress, First Session; June 22–23, 1981, 48–49.

280 *"mad welter"*: GFK, *Nuclear Delusion*, 206.

281 *In June 1982*: Arthur Schlesinger Jr., *Journals*, 464.

281 *"In 1941"*: Vojtech Mastny and Malcolm Byrne, *A Cardboard Castle?*, 467–68.

281 *During the early 1980s*: Valery Yarynich, author interview, March 20, 2009; also, Vitalii Kataev, in John G. Hines, Ellis M. Mishulovich, and John F. Shull, *Soviet Intentions, 1965–1985*, vol. 2: *Soviet Post–Cold War Testimonial Evidence*, 100; and Varfolomei Korobushin, in ibid., 107.

281 *Who would issue*: Bruce Blair, *Global Zero Alert for Nuclear Forces*, 45; also, Blair, author interview, March 20, 2009.

282 *nearly foolproof way*: Vitalii Tsygichko, author interview, Feb. 12, 2009.

282 *The [Soviet leadership] had"*: Andrian Danilevich, in Hines, Mishulovich, and Shull, *Soviet Intentions*, vol. 2: *Soviet Post–Cold War Testimonial Evidence*, 28.

283 *"We could say simply"*: GFK to McGeorge Bundy, Jan. 18, 1982, GFKP OF, box 59.

283 *"be the most important article"*: ibid.

283 *"On this issue"*: David Shribman, "How the Call for Shift in Nuclear Strategy Evolved," *NYT*, April 9, 1982.

283 *His final draft*: PHN, "A-Arms and NATO," *NYT*, April 13, 1982.

283 *"Mac was a great success"*: Peter Nitze, author interview, March 6, 2008.

283 *"would really have"*: Viktor Koltunov, author interview, Feb. 13, 2009.

284 *"Let us acknowledge it"*: Barbara Tuchman, "The Alternative to Arms Control," ACIS Working Paper No. 36, presented to the Subcommittee on Strategic and Theater Nuclear Forces, Senate Committee on Armed Services, Ninety-seventh Congress, Second Session, April 26, 1982, 75.

284 *"a stroke of genius"*: Strobe Talbott, *MOTG*, 168.

284 *"an inveterate problem solver"*: "Arms and the Man," *Time*, Dec. 21, 1987.

284 *The SS-20s were essential*: Gelii Batenin, in Hines, Mishulovich, and Shull, *Soviet Intentions*, vol. 2: *Soviet Post–Cold War Testimonial Evidence*, 7.

284 *"the SS-20 was a breakthrough"*: Danilevich, in Hines, Mishulovich, and Shull, *Soviet Intentions*, vol. 2: *Soviet Post–Cold War Testimonial Evidence*, 33.

285 *"It came so quickly"*: Richard Perle, *Hard Line*, 89–91.

285 *it was demonstrably*: ibid., 94.

285 *The Intermediate-Range*: Ray Moseley, "Gray Silence Shrouds Geneva Scene," *Chicago Tribune*, Dec. 1, 1981.

285 *Kvitsinsky was*: Strobe Talbott, *Deadly Gambits*, 94.

285 *"In each session"*: PHN to Elizabeth Paepcke, Feb. 21, 1982, Elizabeth Paepcke Papers, University of Chicago Library, box 244, folder 3.

286 *"This horse has already"*: Pavel Palazchenko, *My Years with Gorbachev and Shevardnadze*, 15.

286 *Kvitsinsky's deputy, Nikolai Detinov*: Nikolai Detinov, author interview, Feb. 11, 2009.

286 *A few days later*: Michael McGwire, *Perestroika and National Security*, 103.

286 *"Was Kraft correct"*: PHN, handwritten memo, PHNP LOC, box 102, folder 1.

287 *Kvitsinsky's chauffeur let them off*: PHN, *FHTG,* 376

287 *Kvitsinsky was initially quite excited*: Detinov, author interview, Feb. 11, 2009.

288 *"the most flagrant disobedience"*: Richard Burt, author interview, July 14, 2008.

288 *Shultz nodded*: ibid.

288 *Richard Perle was off*: Jay Winik, *On the Brink,* 197.

288 *Soon the two*: Richard Perle, author interview, April 6, 2007.

288 *"an act of intellectual"*: Talbott, *MOTG,* 176.

289 *Because, Nitze said*: ibid., 177.

289 *Reagan allowed Nitze*: Richard Perle, author interview, Jan. 22, 2009.

289 *Kvitsinsky was instructed*: Yuli Kvitsinsky, *Memoirs,* translated from the Russian by Tatyana Gassel-Vozlinskaya.

289 *"depicted Nitze as a shrewd"*: Yuli Kvitsinsky, e-mail to author, Oct. 10, 2008.

289 *convinced that there*: Detinov, author interview, Feb. 11, 2009.

290 *someone on his staff leaked*: Bernard Gwertzman, author interview, Feb. 9, 2009. Gwertzman did not remember exactly who had given him the story, but he did not think it was Rostow, who has been described in other works as having done so.

290 *U.S. Aide*: Bernard Gwertzman, "U.S. Aide Reached Arms Agreement Later Ruled Out," *NYT,* Jan. 16, 1983.

290 *"Your brother is"*: Elizabeth Paepcke to PHN, Oct. 17, 1983, Elizabeth Paepcke Papers, University of Chicago Library, box 244, folder 3.

290 *Before even determining*: W. Scott Thompson, author interview, Oct. 19, 2008. Thompson was, at the time, working as assistant director of the United States Information Agency.

291 *The writer Günter Grass*: Derek Leebaert, *The Fifty-Year Wound,* 504.

291 *"Mieux un Pershing"*: Morris, *Dutch,* 504.

291 *"almost ran that baby"*: Burt, author interview, July 14, 2008.

291 *"The most important method"*: PHN interview with *Der Spiegel,* n.d., personal copy, BRB.

291 *"Breaking the Spell"*: GFK, "Breaking the Spell," *New Yorker,* Oct. 3, 1983.

292 *"Finally, all this"*: PHN to Louis Halle, Nov. 10, 1983, PHNP LOC, box 29, folder 5.

293 *"Being a man of integrity"*: Yuli Kvitsinsky, e-mail to author, Oct. 10, 2008.

293 *"Dear Svetlana"*: GFK to LP, Jan. 29, 1983, GFKP OF, box 68.

293 *"There is a PATTERN"*: LP to GFK, Feb. 9, 1983, GFKP OF, box 68.

294 *"OH, HOW I WOULD LOVE"*: LP to GFK, July 27, 1983, GFKP OF, box 68.

294 *"I do not know"*: LP to GFK, Nov. 23, 1983, GFKP OF, box 68.

294 *"It is true"*: GFK to LP, Dec. 8, 1983, GFKP OF, box 68.

17. WE TRIED, WE TRIED

295 *"Dr. Teller came in"*: Ronald Reagan, *The Reagan Diaries,* 100.

295 *Nitze had no idea*: Strobe Talbott, *MOTG,* 208.

295 *Some Soviet weapons*: Aleksandr G. Savel'yev, and Nikolai N. Detinov, *The Big Five*, 86.

296 *"Reagan did not tell"*: Martin Anderson, author interview, Sept. 22, 2008.

296 *"should translate"*: PHN, *FHTG*, 402.

297 *"the maximum amount of room"*: Abraham Sofaer, author interview, Jan. 13, 2009.

297 *"not true"*: Robert Bowie, "Don't overlook the ABM 'Scandal,'" *Christian Science Monitor*, Dec. 26, 1986.

297 *"I'll never understand"*: John Rhinelander, author interview, July 3, 2008.

297 *The criticism overwhelmed*: Sofaer, author interview, Jan. 13, 2009.

297 *When the journalist*: PHN to David Callahan, Oct. 9, 1990, Elizabeth Paepcke Papers, University of Chicago Library, box 175, folder 11.

298 *"quite obscure"*: GFK to McGeorge Bundy, March 4, 1985, GFKP OF, box 59.

298 *By late afternoon*: Anatoly Chernyaev, *My Six Years with Gorbachev*, 21–22.

298 *"it is not to be expected"*: "Succession in Moscow: What the Specialists Are Saying; Experts on Soviet Differ on How Much of an Impact Gorbachev Will Have," *NYT*, March 12, 1985.

298 *"Yes, this is"*: Anatoly Chernyaev, "The Diary of Anatoly Chernyaev: 1985," NSA, 93, http://www.gwu.edu/~nsarchiv/NSAEBB/NSAEBB192/index.htm, accessed on Jan. 24, 2009.

299 *"George Shultz wouldn't"*: Max Kampelman, author interview, Oct. 29, 2008.

299 *The first part*: Steven Pifer, e-mail to author, Jan. 28, 2009.

299 *But his old friend*: Talbott, *MOTG*, 260–68.

299 *"I got the impression"*: Edmund Morris, *Dutch*, 552–54. Morris fictionalized some minor parts of his book, particularly when describing Reagan's youth. But this reference is legitimate: Edmund Morris, author interview, March 26, 2009.

300 *"had no knowledge"*: Kenneth Adelman, OH, Miller Center for Public Affairs, Sept. 30, 2003, http://millercenter.org/scripps/archive/oralhistories/detail/3204, accessed on Jan. 25, 2009.

300 *At one point*: Memorandum of Conversation, Nov. 20, 1985, Cold War: Geneva (Reagan-Gorbachev) Summit 5 Session, Margaret Thatcher Foundation, http://www.margaretthatcher.org/archive/displaydocument.asp?docid=109215, accessed on Jan. 24, 2009.

300 *Gregg Herken publicly*: Gregg Herken, "The Great Foreign Policy Fight," *American Heritage*, April/May 1986, 65–80.

301 *"While most of"*: GFK to Herken, JLG, and PHN, Nov. 3, 1985, PHNP BRB 21.

302 *"On p. 65"*: Clark Clifford to Paul Warnke, Warnke papers, box 12, folder 2.

302 *months later workers in Kiev*: Richard Rhodes, *Arsenals of Folly*, 238.

302 *"Simply crap"*: Chernyaev, *My Six Years with Gorbachev*, 78.

302 *"The main goal"*: ibid., 81.

302 *Nitze suspected a trap"*: PHN, *FHTG*, 429.

303 *"Boy, this place"*: Adelman, OH, Miller Center for Public Affairs, Sept. 30, 2003, http://millercenter.org/scripps/archive/oralhistories/detail/3204, accessed on Jan. 24, 2009.

303 *When they got*: Rhodes, *Arsenals of Folly,* 248.

303 *At one dinner*: Adelman, OH, Miller Center for Public Affairs, Sept. 30, 2003, 37.

303 *"Good evening"*: Soviet-American Summit, Oct. 11–12, 1986, NSA, http://www.gwu.edu/~nsarchiv/NSAEBB/NSAEBB203/Document17.pdf, accessed on Jan. 24, 2009.

304 *Shultz told Nitze*: PHN, *FHTG,* 430.

304 *"This is your"*: George Shultz, *Turmoil and Triumph,* 764.

304 *"We brought closer"*: Soviet-American Summit, Oct. 11–12, 1986, NSA, http://www.gwu.edu/~nsarchiv/NSAEBB/NSAEBB203/Document17.pdf, accessed on Jan. 24, 2009.

305 *"I haven't had"*: Shultz, *Turmoil and Triumph,* 764–65.

305 *"I'll take the throne"*: Ed Rowny, OH, Miller Center for Public Affairs, May 17, 2006, 15, http://millercenter.org/scripps/archive/oralhistories/detail/3521, accessed on Jan. 24, 2009.

305 *Gorbachev knew*: Pavel Podvig, author interview, Jan. 13, 2009.

306 *Confining research*: Richard Perle, author interview, Oct. 4, 2008.

307 *"We tried"*: Talbott, *MOTG,* 325.

307 *Marshall speculated*: Steven L. Rearden, memo of conversation with PHN and Charles Burton Marshall, Oct. 15, 1986, PHNP LOC, box 161, F8.

307 *"If we don't back down"*: Chernyaev, *My Six Years with Gorbachev,* 84.

307 *Alexei Obukhov*: Alexei Obukhov, author interview, Feb. 12, 2009.

308 *Soon, American inspectors*: Viktor Koltunov, author interview, Feb. 13, 2009.

308 *to untie the Gordian knot*: Ronald Steel, "Always in the Game," *Washington Post,* Aug. 28, 1988.

308 *They walked by quietly*: Koltunov, author interview, Feb. 13, 2009.

309 *"It is rather Kafka-like"*: PHN to Elizabeth Paepcke, Jan. 31, 1989, Elizabeth Paepcke Papers, University of Chicago Library, box 244, folder 4.

309 *"Reagan Arms"*: Michael Gordon, "Reagan Arms Adviser Says Bush Wrong on Short-Range Missiles," *NYT,* May 3, 1989.

310 *"We have literally"*: Joint Meeting of the House and Senate to hear an address by his excellency Václav Havel, president of the Czechoslovak Socialist Republic, One Hundred-first Congress, Second Session, Feb. 21, 1990; also Aviezer Tucker, *The Philosophy and Politics of Czech Dissidence from Patocka to Havel,* 167.

310 *"This nationalistic"*: GFK, *Cloud of Danger,* 185. GFK would point to this passage in a Sept. 13, 1991, letter to JLG.

310 *"what we know"*: GFK, "If the Kremlin Can't Rule," *Washington Post,* Feb. 3, 1991.

310 *"Kennan was the one"*: James Billington, author interview, July 14, 2006.

311 *Just before Warren Zimmermann*: Warren Zimmermann, "Prophet with Honor," *New York Review of Books,* Aug. 13, 1996.

311 *"I would be honored"*: James Cicconi, author interview, Nov. 12, 2008.

311 *After he testified*: Don Oberdorfer, "Revolutionary Epoch Ending in Russia, Kennan Declares," *Washington Post,* April 5, 1989.

311 *"George is a happy"*: Arthur Schlesinger Jr., *Journals,* 583–84.

311 *"right for an instant"*: Richard Perle, author interview, April 6, 2007.

311 *"He didn't live"*: George Shultz, author interview, Jan. 26, 2009.

312 *"I've come to"*: PHN OH, NSA, June 12, 1995, http://www.gwu.edu/~nsarchiv/coldwar/interviews/episode-24/nitze1.html, accessed on March 3, 2009.

312 *In his view, the conflict*: GFK, "The Failure of Our Success," *NYT,* March 14, 1994.

312 *"The suggestion that"*: GFK, "The G.O.P. Won the Cold War? Ridiculous," *NYT,* Oct. 28, 1992.

EPILOGUE

314 *"Paul Nitze—a name"*: Sandra Day O'Connor, Toast for PHN, Jan. 16, 1997, PHNPP.

315 *In October 1999*: Jurek Martin, author interview, April 24, 2008.

316 *"[Kennan] always thought"*: James Srodes, "Paul H. Nitze: 1907–2004," *American Spectator,* Dec. 2004–Jan. 2005, 62.

316 *Raised a Presbyterian*: Grace Warnecke, author interview, Dec. 11, 2006.

316 *twenty-page letter*: GFK, "Notes on Religion," October 2002, personal memo given to author.

318 *"War has a momentum"*: Albert Eisle, "George Kennan Speaks Out About Iraq," History News Network, Sept. 26, 2002, http://hnn.us/articles/997.html, accessed on March 26, 2009.

318 *"we could go down"*: Betsy Barrett, author interview, April 17, 2008.

BIBLIOGRAPHY

BOOKS

Abella, Alex. *Soldiers of Reason: The RAND Corporation and the Rise of the American Empire*. New York: Harcourt, 2008.

Acheson, Dean. *Present at the Creation: My Years in the State Department*. New York: Norton, 1987.

Alliluyeva, Anna, and Sergei Alliluyev. *The Alliluyev Memoirs: Recollections of Svetlana's Aunt and Grandfather*. New York: G. P. Putnam's Sons, 1968.

Alliluyeva, Svetlana. *The Faraway Music*. New Delhi: Lancer International, 1984.

———. *Only One Year*. New York: Harper & Row, 1969.

———. *Twenty Letters to a Friend*. New York: Harper & Row, 1967.

Allin, Dana H. *Cold War Illusions: America, Europe and Soviet Power 1969–1989*. New York: St. Martin's Press, 1994.

Alsop, Joseph, with Adam Platt. *I've Seen the Best of It*. New York: Norton, 1992.

Alsop, Joseph, and Stewart Alsop. *We Accuse: The Story of the Miscarriage of American Justice in the Case of J. Robert Oppenheimer*. New York: Simon & Schuster, 1954.

Alter, Jonathan. *The Defining Moment: FDR's Hundred Days and the Triumph of Hope*. New York: Simon & Schuster, 2007.

Amis, Martin. *Koba the Dread: Laughter and the Twenty Million*. New York: Hyperion, 2002.

Andrew, Christopher, and Oleg Gordievsky. *KGB: The Inside Story*. New York: Vintage International, 1990.

Andrew, Christopher, and Vasili Mitrokhin. *The World Was Going Our Way: The KGB and the Battle for the Third World*. New York: Perseus, 2005.

Appleman, Roy E. *Disaster in Korea: The Chinese Confront MacArthur*. College Station: Texas A&M University Press, 1989.

Atkinson, Rick. *An Army at Dawn: The War in North Africa, 1942–1943*. New York: Henry Holt, 2002.

Ausland, John C. *Kennedy, Khrushchev, and the Berlin Crisis*. Oslo: Scandinavian University Press, 1996.

Austin, Anthony. *The President's War: The Story of the Tonkin Gulf Resolution and How the Nation Was Trapped in Vietnam*. Philadelphia: J. B. Lippincott, 1971.

Ball, George. *The Past Has Another Pattern*. New York: Norton, 1982.

Behrman, Greg. *The Most Noble Adventure: The Marshall Plan and How America Helped Rebuild Europe*. New York: Free Press, 2007.

Beisner, Robert. *Dean Acheson*. Oxford, Eng.: Oxford University Press, 2006.

Berman, Larry. *Lyndon Johnson's War: The Road to Stalemate in Vietnam*. New York: Norton, 1991.

Bethell, Nicholas. *Betrayed*. London: Hodder & Stoughton, 1984.

Biagi, Enzo. *Svetlana: An Intimate Portrait*. New York: Funk & Wagnalls, 1967.

Bird, Kai. *The Color of Truth*. New York: Simon & Schuster, 1998.

Bird, Kai, and Martin J. Sherwin. *American Prometheus: The Triumph and Tragedy of J. Robert Oppenheimer*. New York: Vintage, 2006.

Blight, James G., and David A. Welch. *On the Brink*. New York: The Noonday Press, 1989.

Bohlen, Charles E. *Witness to History: 1929–1969*. New York: Norton, 1973.

Bowie, Robert R., and Richard H. Immerman. *Waging Peace: How Eisenhower Shaped an Enduring Cold War Strategy*. New York: Oxford University Press, 1998.

Brandon, Henry. *Special Relationships*. New York: Atheneum, 1998.

Brandt, Ed. *The Last Voyage of USS Pueblo*. New York: Norton, 1969.

Brinkley, Douglas. *Dean Acheson*. New Haven: Yale University Press, 1994.

Brodie, Bernard, ed. *The Absolute Weapon*. New York: Harcourt, 1946.

Brzezinski, Matthew. *Red Moon Rising*. London: Bloomsbury, 2007.

Brzezinski, Zbigniew. *Power and Principle*. New York: Farrar, Straus & Giroux, 1983.

Bucar, Annabelle. *The Truth About American Diplomats*. Moscow: Literaturnaya Gazeta Publishers, 1949.

Bundy, McGeorge. *Danger and Survival*. New York: Vintage Books, 1988.

Burdick, Charles. *An American Island in Hitler's Reich*. Menlo Park, Calif.: Markgraf, 1987.

Burke, Michael. *Outrageous Good Fortune*. Boston: Little, Brown, 1984.

Burr, William, ed. *The Kissinger Transcripts*. New York: New Press, 1998.

Cahn, Anne Hessing. *Killing Détente: The Right Attacks the CIA*. University Park: Pennsylvania State University Press, 1998.

Callahan, David. *Dangerous Capabilities: Paul Nitze and the Cold War*. New York: HarperCollins, 1990.

Carroll, James. *House of War*. Boston: Houghton Mifflin, 2006.

Cherny, Andrei. *The Candy Bombers: The Untold Story of the Berlin Airlift and America's Finest Hour*. New York: Penguin, 2008.

Chernyaev, Anatoly. *My Six Years with Gorbachev*. University Park: Pennsylvania State University Press, 2000.

Chomsky, Noam. *On Power and Ideology*. Boston: South End Press, 1987.

Christopher, Warren. *Chances of a Lifetime*. New York: Scribner, 2001.

Clifford, Clark, and Richard Holbrooke. *Counsel to the President: A Memoir*. New York: Random House, 1991.

Coffey, John W. *Political Realism in American Thought*. Lewisburg, Pa.: Bucknell University Press, 1977.

Congdon, Lee. *George F. Kennan: A Writing Life*. Wilmington: ISI Books, 2008.

Corson, William R., Joseph Trento, and Susan Trento. *Widows: Four American Spies, the Wives They Left Behind, and the KGB's Crippling of American Intelligence*. New York: Crown, 1989.

Craig, Campbell. *Destroying the Village: Eisenhower and Thermonuclear War*. New York: Columbia University Press, 1998.

Dallas, Gregory. *The War That Never Ended*. New Haven: Yale University Press, 2005.

Davies, John Paton, Jr. *Dragon by the Tail: American, British, Japanese and Russian Encounters with China and One Another*. New York: Norton, 1972.

Day, Clarence. *This Simian World*. New York: Knopf, 1968.

Department of Defense. *Soviet Military Power*. 6th ed. Washington, D.C.: U.S. Government Printing Office, 1987.

———. *Soviet Military Power: An Assessment of the Threat*. 7th ed. Washington, D.C.: U.S. Government Printing Office, 1988.

DeSantis, Hugh. *The Diplomacy of Silence: The American Foreign Service, the Soviet Union, and the Cold War, 1933–1945*. Chicago: University of Chicago Press, 1979.

De Silva, Peer. *Sub Rosa*. New York: Times Books, 1978.

Dippel, John V. H. *Two Against Hitler: Stealing the Nazis' Best-Kept Secrets*. New York: Praeger, 1992.

Dobbs, Michael. *One Minute to Midnight*. New York: Knopf, 2008.

Dobrynin, Anatoly. *In Confidence*. Seattle: University of Washington Press, 1995.

Donhoff, Marion. *Before the Storm*. New York: Knopf, 1990.

Dorwart, Jeffery M. *Eberstadt and Forrestal: A National Security Partnership, 1909–1949*. College Station: Texas A&M University Press, 1991.

Drell, Sidney, and George Shultz, ed. *Implications of the Reykjavik Summit on its Twentieth Anniversary*. Stanford: Hoover Institution Press, 2007.

Earley, Pete. *Comrade J*. New York: Penguin, 2007.

———. *Family of Spies*. Toronto: Bantam, 1988.

Ebon, Martin. *Svetlana: The Incredible Story of Stalin's Daughter*. New York: Signet, 1967.

Ehrenburg, Ilya. *The War: 1941–1945*. New York: World, 1964.

Eisenhower, Dwight D. *The White House Years: Mandate for Change, 1953–1956*. Garden City, N.Y.: Doubleday, 1963.

———. *The White House Years: Waging Peace, 1957–1961*. Garden City, N.Y.: Doubleday, 1965.

Eisenhower, John S. D., with Joanne Thompson Eisenhower. *Yanks: The Epic Story of the American Army in World War I*. New York: Simon & Schuster, 2001.

Ellsberg, Daniel. *Secrets: A Memoir of Vietnam and the Pentagon Papers*. New York: Penguin, 2002.

Etzold, Thomas H., and John Lewis Gaddis. *Containment: Documents on American Policy and Strategy, 1945–1950*. New York: Columbia University Press, 1978.

Feifer, Gregory. *The Great Gamble: The Soviet War in Afghanistan*. New York: Harper, 2009.

Ferrell, Robert, ed. *Dear Bess: The Letters from Harry to Bess Truman, 1910–1959*. Columbia: University of Missouri Press, 1998.

Fest, Joachim. *Speer*. Orlando, Fla.: Harcourt, 1999.

Fordham, Benjamin. *Building the Cold War Consensus*. Ann Arbor: University of Michigan Press, 1998.

French, Paul. *North Korea: The Paranoid Peninsula*. London: Zed Books, 2005.

Friedland, Roger, and Harold Zellman. *The Fellowship*. New York: Harper Perennial, 2006.

Friedrich, Otto. *Blood and Iron: From Bismarck to Hitler, the Von Moltke Family's Impact on German History*. New York: HarperCollins, 1995.

Fursenko, Aleksandr, and Timothy Naftali. *Khrushchev's Cold War*. New York: Norton, 2006.

Gaddis, John Lewis. *The Long Peace*. Oxford, Eng.: Oxford University Press, 1987.

———. *Russia, the Soviet Union, and the United States: An Interpretive History*. New York: Wiley, 1978.

———. *Strategies of Containment*. New York: Oxford University Press, 2005.

———. *The United States and the Origins of the Cold War, 1941–1947*. New York: Columbia University Press, 1972.

———. *We Now Know*. Oxford, Eng.: Oxford University Press, 1997.

Galbraith, John Kenneth. *A Life in Our Times*. Boston: Houghton Mifflin, 1981.

Gardner, Lloyd. *Architects of Illusion*. Chicago: Quadrangle, 1970.

Garrow, David. *Bearing the Cross: Martin Luther King, Jr., and the Southern Christian Leadership Conference*. New York: Harper, 2004.

———. *The FBI and Martin Luther King, Jr.* New York: Penguin, 1981.

Garthoff, Raymond L. *Detente and Confrontation*. Washington, D.C.: Brookings Institution, 1985.

———. *Deterrence and the Revolution in Soviet Military Doctrine*. Washington, D.C.: Brookings Institution, 1990.

———. *The Great Transition*. Washington, D.C.: Brookings Institution, 1994.

———. *A Journey Through the Cold War*. Washington, D.C.: Brookings Institution, 2001.

Gayn, Mark. *Japan Diary*. New York: William Sloan Associates, 1948.

Gellman, Barton. *Contending with Kennan*. New York: Praeger, 1984.

Gimbel, John. *The Origins of the Marshall Plan*. Stanford, Calif.: Stanford University Press, 1976.

Goldman, Danielle. *I Want to Be Ready: Improvised Dance as a Practice of Freedom*. Ann Arbor: University of Michigan Press, 2010.

Goodwin, Doris Kearns. *Lyndon Johnson and the American Dream*. New York: St. Martin's Griffin, 1976.

Goulden, Joseph C. *Korea*. New York: Times Books, 1982.

———. *Truth Is the First Casualty*. Chicago: Rand McNally, 1969.

Goure, Leon. *War Survival in Soviet Strategy*. Miami, Fla.: University of Miami, Center for Advanced International Studies, 1976.

Graham, Thomas, Jr. *Disarmament Sketches*. Seattle: University of Washington Press, 2002.

Gromyko, Andrei. *Memoirs*. New York: Doubleday, 1989.

Grose, Peter. *Operation Rollback*. Boston: Houghton Mifflin, 2000.

Haines, Gerald K., and Robert E. Leggett. *CIA's Analysis of the Soviet Union, 1947–1991*. Washington, D.C.: Center for the Study of Intelligence, 2001.

Halberstam, David. *The Best and the Brightest*. New York: Ballantine, 1969.

———. *The Coldest Winter*. New York: Hyperion, 2007.

Halle, Louis. *The Cold War as History*. New York: Harper & Row, 1967.

Hanhimaki, Jussi, and Odd Arne Westad. *The Cold War: A History in Documents and Eyewitness Accounts*. Oxford, Eng.: Oxford University Press, 2003.

Harlow, Giles, and George Maerz, eds. *Measures Short of War: The George F. Kennan Lectures at the National War College, 1946–1947*. Washington, D.C.: National Defense University Press, 1991.

Harper, John Lamberton. *American Visions of Europe*. Cambridge, Eng.: Cambridge University Press, 1994.

Harriman, W. Averell, and Ellie Abel. *Special Envoy*. New York: Random House, 1975.

Hasegawa, Tsuyoshi. *Racing the Enemy*. Cambridge, Mass.: Belknap Press, 2005.

Haynes, John Earl, and Harvey Klehr. *Venona*. New Haven: Yale University Press, 2000.

Healy, Denis. *The Time of My Life*. New York: Norton, 1989.

Herken, Gregg. *Brotherhood of the Bomb*. New York: Holt, 2002.

———. *Counsels of War*. New York: Knopf, 1985.

———. *The Winning Weapon*. Princeton: Princeton University Press, 1981.

Hersey, John. *Hiroshima*. New York: Knopf, 1946.

Hersh, Seymour. *The Price of Power*. New York: Summit, 1983.

Herz, Martin F., ed. *George Kennan and His Critics*. Washington, D.C.: Ethics and Public Policy Center of Georgetown University, 1978.

Hinds, Lynn Boyd, and Theodore Otto Windt. *The Cold War as Rhetoric: The Beginnings, 1945–1950*. New York: Praeger, 1991.

Hines, John G., Ellis M. Mishulovich, and John F. Shull. *Soviet Intentions, 1965–1985*. Vol. 1: *An Analytical Comparison of U.S.-Soviet Assessments During the Cold War*. Vol. 2: *Soviet Post–Cold War Testimonial Evidence*. Germantown, Md.: BDM Federal, 1995.

Hitchcock, William. *The Struggle for Europe*. New York: Doubleday, 2002.

Hixson, Walter L. *George F. Kennan: Cold War Iconoclast*. New York: Columbia University Press, 1989.

Holloway, David. *Stalin and the Bomb*. New Haven: Yale University Press, 1994.

Hoopes, Townsend, and Douglas Brinkley. *Driven Patriot: The Life and Times of James Forrestal*. Annapolis: Naval Institute Press, 1992.

Horne, Alistair. *Harold Macmillan*. Vol. 1: *1894–1956*. Vol. 2: *1957–1986*. London: Macmillan, 1988 and 1989.

Hudson, James. *Svetlana Alliluyeva: Flight to Freedom*. New York: Tower, 1967.

Hughes, Emmet John. *The Ordeal of Power*. New York: Atheneum, 1963.

Immerman, Richard H. *John Foster Dulles*. Wilmington: Scholarly Resources, 1999.

Institute for Strategic Studies. *The Military Balance 1970–1971*. London: Institute for Strategic Studies, 1970.

International Institute for Strategic Studies. *The Military Balance 1995–1996*. London: Oxford University Press, 1995.

Isaacson, Walter. *Kissinger*. New York: Touchstone, 1992.

Isaacson, Walter, and Evan Thomas. *The Wise Men*. New York: Touchstone, 1986.

Jespersen, T. Christopher, ed. *Interviews with George F. Kennan*. Jackson: University Press of Mississippi, 2002.

Jones, Joseph M. *The Fifteen Weeks (February 21–June 5, 1947)*. New York: Viking Press, 1955.

Judt, Tony. *Postwar: A History of Europe Since 1945*. New York: Penguin, 2005.

Kahn, Herman. *On Escalation*. New York: Praeger, 1965.

———. *On Thermonuclear War*. Princeton: Princeton University Press, 1960.

Kaplan, Fred. *The Wizards of Armageddon*. New York: Simon & Schuster, 1983.

Keefer, Edward C., David C. Geyer, and Douglas E. Selvage. *Soviet-American Relations: The Détente Years, 1969–1972*. Washington, D.C.: U.S. Government Printing Office, 2007.

Kennan, George. *Siberia and the Exile System*, vol. 2. New York: Century, 1891.

Kennan, George F. *American Diplomacy, 1900–1950*. Chicago: University of Chicago Press, 1951.

———. *An American Family: The Kennans*. New York: Norton, 2000.

———. *Around the Cragged Hill: A Personal and Political Philosophy*. New York: Norton, 1993.

———. *At a Century's Ending: Reflections 1982–1995*. New York: Norton, 1996.

———. *The Cloud of Danger*. Boston: Little, Brown, 1977.

———. *The Decline of Bismarck's European Order: Franco-Russian Relations, 1875–1890*. Princeton: Princeton University Press, 1979.

———. *Democracy and the Student Left*. New York: Little, Brown, 1968.

———. *The Fateful Alliance: France, Russia, and the Coming of the First World War*. New York: Pantheon, 1984.

———. *From Prague After Munich: Diplomatic Papers, 1938–1940*. Princeton: Princeton University Press, 1968.

———. *The Marquis de Custine and His Russia in 1839*. Princeton: Princeton University Press, 1971.

————. *Memoirs*. Vol. 1: *1925–1950*. New York: Pantheon, 1967.

————. *Memoirs*. Vol. 2: *1950–1963*. New York: Pantheon, 1972.

————. *The Nuclear Delusion: Soviet-American Relations in the Atomic Age*. New York: Pantheon, 1983.

————. *Realities of American Foreign Policy*. Princeton: Princeton University Press, 1954.

————. *Russia and the West Under Lenin and Stalin*. New York: Mentor, 1960.

————. *Russia, the Atom, and the West*. New York: Harper & Brothers, 1957.

————. *Sketches from a Life*. New York: Norton, 1989.

————. *Soviet-American Relations 1917–1920*. Vol. 1: *Russia Leaves the War*. Princeton: Princeton University Press, 1956.

————. *Soviet-American Relations, 1917–1920*. Vol. 2: *The Decision to Intervene*. Princeton: Princeton University Press, 1958.

————. *Soviet Foreign Policy, 1917–1941*. Malabar, Fla.: Robert E. Krieger, 1960.

Kennan, George F., et al. *Encounters with Kennan*. London: Cass, 1979.

Kennan, George F., and John Lukacs. *George F. Kennan and the Origins of Containment, 1944–1946: The Kennan-Lukacs Correspondence*. Columbia: University of Missouri Press, 1997.

Kennedy, Robert F. *Thirteen Days*. New York: Norton, 1969.

Kerr, Andy. *A Journey Amongst the Good and the Great*. Annapolis: United States Naval Institute, 1987.

Kimbrough, Emily. *The Innocents from Indiana*. New York: Harper & Brothers, 1950.

Kinzer, Stephen. *All the Shah's Men: An American Coup and the Roots of Middle East Terror*. Hoboken, N.J.: Wiley, 2003.

Kissinger, Henry A. *Diplomacy*. New York: Simon & Schuster, 1994.

————. *Nuclear Weapons and Foreign Policy*, abridged edition. New York: Norton, 1969.

————. *White House Years*. Boston: Little, Brown, 1979.

————. *Years of Upheaval*. Boston: Little, Brown, 1982.

Koch, Stephen. *Double Lives: Spies and Writers in the Secret Soviet War of Ideas Against the West*. New York: Free Press, 1994.

Kruglov, Arkadi. *The History of the Soviet Atomic Industry*. London: Taylor & Francis, 2002.

Kuklick, Bruce. *Blind Oracles*. Princeton: Princeton University Press, 2006.

Kutler, Stanley. *Abuse of Power: The Nixon Tapes*. New York: Simon & Schuster, 2000.

Labedz, Leopold, and Melvin Lasky. *The Use and Abuse of Sovietology*. New Brunswick, N.J.: Transaction, 1989.

LaFeber, Walter. *America, Russia, and the Cold War, 1945–2006*. 10th ed. New York: McGraw-Hill, 2008.

Lamont, Lansing. *Day of Trinity*. New York: Atheneum, 1965.

Leary, William M., ed. *The Central Intelligence Agency*. Tuscaloosa: University of Alabama Press, 1984.

Lee, Bong. *The Unfinished War*. New York: Algora, 2003.

Leebaert, Derek. *The Fifty-Year Wound*. Boston: Little, Brown, 2002.

Leffler, Melvyn. *For the Soul of Mankind: The United States, the Soviet Union, and the Cold War.* New York: Hill & Wang, 2007.

Leites, Nathan. *The Operational Code of the Politburo.* New York: McGraw-Hill, 1951.

Lettow, Paul. *Ronald Reagan and His Quest to Abolish Nuclear Weapons.* New York: Random House, 2005.

Lilienthal, David E. *The Journals of David E. Lilienthal,* vol. 2. New York: Harper & Row, 1964.

Lind, Michael. *Vietnam: The Necessary War.* New York: Touchstone, 1999.

Lippmann, Walter. *The Cold War: A Study in U.S. Foreign Policy.* New York: Harper, 1947.

Loftus, John. *The Belarus Secret.* New York: Knopf, 1982.

Lukacs, John. *George Kennan: A Study of Character.* New Haven: Yale University Press, 2007.

Mailer, Norman. *The Armies of the Night.* New York: Signet, 1968.

Manchester, William. *American Caesar.* Boston: Little, Brown, 1978.

Mann, James. *Rise of the Vulcans.* New York: Penguin, 2004.

Marolda, Edward J., and Oscar Fitzgerald. *The United States Navy and the Vietnam Conflict.* Vol. 2: *From Military Assistance to Combat, 1959–1965.* Washington, D.C.: Naval Historical Center, 1986.

Marshall, Charles Burton. *The Cold War: A Concise History.* New York: Franklin Watts, 1965.

Martin, Bradley K. *Under the Loving Care of the Fatherly Leader.* New York: Macmillan, 2006.

Mastny, Vojtech, and Malcolm Byrne. *A Cardboard Castle?* Budapest: CEU Press, 2005.

Matlock, Jack. *Reagan and Gorbachev: How the Cold War Ended.* New York: Random House, 2004.

May, Ernest, ed. *American Cold War Strategy: Interpreting NSC 68.* Boston: Bedford/St. Martin's, 1993.

May, Ernest, and Philip D. Zelikow. *The Kennedy Tapes.* Cambridge, Mass.: Belknap Press, 1997.

Mayers, David. *George Kennan and the Dilemmas of U.S. Foreign Policy.* Oxford, Eng.: Oxford University Press, 1988.

McCullough, David. *John Adams.* New York: Simon & Schuster, 2001.

———. *Truman.* New York: Simon & Schuster, 1992.

McGlothlen, Ronald L. *Controlling the Waves: Dean Acheson and U.S. Foreign Policy in Asia.* New York: Norton, 1993.

McGwire, Michael. *Perestroika and National Security.* Washington, D.C.: Brookings Institution Press, 1991.

McMillan, Priscilla. *The Ruin of J. Robert Oppenheimer.* New York: Penguin, 2005.

McNamara, Robert. *Blundering into Disaster.* New York: Pantheon, 1986.

———. *In Retrospect.* New York: Vintage, 1996.

Meacham, Jon. *Franklin and Winston.* New York: Random House, 2003.

Mee, Charles, Jr. *The Marshall Plan: The Launching of the Pax Americana*. New York: Simon & Schuster, 1984.

Merry, Robert W. *Taking on the World: Joseph and Stewart Alsop—Guardians of the American Century*. New York: Penguin, 1996.

Micunovic, Veljko. *Moscow Diary*. New York: Doubleday, 1980.

Millis, Walter, ed. *The Forrestal Diaries*. New York: Viking Press, 1951.

Millman, Chad. *The Detonators: The Secret Plot to Destroy America and an Epic Hunt for Justice*. New York: Little, Brown, 2006.

Mills, Nicolaus. *Winning the Peace*. Hoboken, N.J.: Wiley, 2008.

Miscamble, Wilson D. *From Roosevelt to Truman*. Cambridge, Eng.: Cambridge University Press, 2007.

———. *George F. Kennan and the Making of American Foreign Policy 1947-1950*. Princeton: Princeton University Press, 1992.

Mitrovich, Gregory. *Undermining the Kremlin: America's Strategy to Subvert the Soviet Bloc, 1947-1956*. Ithaca: Cornell University Press, 2000.

Moïse, Edwin. *Tonkin Gulf and the Escalation of the Vietnam War*. Chapel Hill: University of North Carolina Press, 1996.

Montefiore, Simon Sebag. *Stalin: The Court of the Red Tsar*. New York: Vintage, 2005.

———. *Young Stalin*. London: Weidenfeld & Nicolson, 2007.

Morris, Edmund. *Dutch*. New York: Modern Library, 1999.

Newhouse, John. *Cold Dawn: The Story of SALT*. New York: Holt, Rinehart & Winston, 1973.

———. *War and Peace in the Nuclear Age*. New York: Knopf, 1989.

Newman, Robert P. *Truman and the Hiroshima Cult*. East Lansing: Michigan State University Press, 1995.

Niebuhr, Reinhold. *Moral Man and Immoral Society*. New York: Charles Scribner's Sons, 1932.

Nitze, Paul H. *From Hiroshima to Glasnost*. New York: Grove Weidenfeld, 1989.

———. *Tension Between Opposites: Reflections on the Practice and Theory of Politics*. New York: Charles Scribner's Sons, 1993.

Nitze, Paul H., James E. Dougherty, and Francis X. Kane. *The Fateful Ends and Shades of SALT*. New York: Crane, Russak, 1979.

Nitze, Paul H., Leonard Sullivan, Jr., and the Atlantic Council Working Group on Securing the Seas. *Securing the Seas*. Boulder, Colo.: Westview Press, 1979.

Nitze, William A. *Arthurian Romance and Modern Poetry and Music*. Chicago: University of Chicago Press, 1940.

Novak, Robert. *The Prince of Darkness*. New York: Crown, 2007.

Ojserkis, Raymond P. *Beginnings of the Cold War Arms Race: The Truman Administration and the U.S. Arms Build-up*. Westport, Conn.: Praeger, 2003.

Palazchenko, Pavel. *My Years with Gorbachev and Shevardnadze*. University Park: Pennsylvania State University Press, 1997.

Parker, Ralph. *Conspiracy Against Peace*. Moscow: Literaturnaya Gazeta Publishers, 1949.

Perle, Richard. *Hard Line*. New York: Random House, 1992.

Perret, Geoffrey. *Old Soldiers Never Die*. Holbrook, Mass.: Adams Media Corporation, 1996.

Perry, Roland. *Last of the Cold War Spies*. Cambridge, Mass.: Da Capo Press, 2005.

Pipes, Richard. *Vixi: Memoirs of a Non-Belonger*. New Haven: Yale University Press, 2003.

Pogue, Forrest C. *George C. Marshall: Education of a General*. London: MacGibbon and Kee, 1964.

Radzinsky, Edvard. *Stalin*. New York: Doubleday, 1996.

Reagan, Ronald. *An American Life*. New York: Simon & Schuster, 1990.

———. *The Reagan Diaries*. New York: HarperCollins, 2007.

Rearden, Steven L. *The Evolution of American Strategic Doctrine: Paul H. Nitze and the Soviet Challenge*. Boulder, Colo.: Westview Press, 1984.

Rhodes, Richard. *Arsenals of Folly*. New York: Knopf, 2007.

———. *Dark Sun: The Making of the Hydrogen Bomb*. New York: Simon & Schuster, 1995.

———. *The Making of the Atomic Bomb*. New York: Simon & Schuster, 1986.

Rounds, Frank. *A Window on Red Square*. Boston: Riverside Press, 1953.

Ruddy, T. Michael. *The Cautious Diplomat: Charles E. Bohlen and the Soviet Union, 1929–1969*. Kent, Oh.: Kent State University Press, 1986.

Rusk, Dean, as told to Richard Rusk. *As I Saw It*. New York: Norton, 1990.

Sakharov, Andrei. *Memoirs*. New York: Knopf, 1990.

Sanders, Jerry W. *Peddlers of Crisis*. Boston: South End Press, 1983.

Savel'yev, Aleksandr G., and Nikolai N. Detinov. *The Big Five: Arms Control Decision-Making in the Soviet Union*. Trans. Dmitri Trenin. Westport, Conn.: Praeger, 1995.

Scheer, Robert. *With Enough Shovels*. New York: Random House, 1982.

Schlafly, Phyllis, and Chester Ward. *The Gravediggers*. Alton, Ill.: Pere Marquette Press, 1964.

Schlesinger, Arthur M., Jr. *Journals 1952–2000*. New York: Penguin, 2007.

———. *Robert Kennedy and His Times*. Boston: Houghton Mifflin Harcourt, 2002.

———. *A Thousand Days: John F. Kennedy in the White House*. Boston: Houghton Mifflin, 1965.

Scoblic, J. Peter. *U.S. vs. Them*. New York: Viking, 2008.

Seaborg, Glenn. *Kennedy, Khrushchev and the Test Ban*. Berkeley: University of California Press, 1981.

Sereny, Gitta. *Albert Speer: His Battle with Truth*. New York: Knopf, 1995.

Service, Robert. *Stalin*. Cambridge, Mass.: Belknap Press, 2004.

Sevareid, Eric. *Not So Wild a Dream*. New York: Atheneum, 1979.

Shapiro, Ian. *Containment: Rebuilding a Strategy Against Global Terror*. Princeton: Princeton University Press, 2007.

Shepilov, Dmitrii. *The Kremlin's Scholar*. New Haven: Yale University Press, 2007.

Sherwin, Martin J. *A World Destroyed*, 3rd ed. Stanford, Calif.: Stanford University Press, 2003.

Shesol, Jeff. *Mutual Contempt*. New York: Norton, 1997.

Shimko, Keith L. *Images and Arms Control*. Ann Arbor: University of Michigan Press, 1991.

Simpson, Christopher. *Blowback*. New York: Weidenfeld & Nicolson, 1988.

Smith, Gerard. *Doubletalk: The Story of SALT I*. New York: Doubleday, 1980.

Smith, Perry McCoy. *The Air Force Plans for Peace 1943–1945*. Baltimore: Johns Hopkins Press, 1970.

Smyser, W. R. *From Yalta to Berlin*. New York: St. Martin's, 1999.

Solzhenitsyn, Aleksandr. *The Gulag Archipelago*. New York: HarperCollins, 2002.

Speer, Albert. *Inside the Third Reich*. New York: Macmillan, 1970.

Spengler, Oswald. *Decline of the West*. New York: Oxford University Press, 1991.

Steel, Ronald. *In Love with Night: The American Romance with Robert Kennedy*. New York: Touchstone, 2000.

———. *Pax Americana*. New York: Viking, 1967.

———. *Walter Lippmann and the American Century*. Boston: Little, Brown, 1980.

Stephanson, Anders. *Kennan and the Art of Foreign Policy*. Cambridge, Mass.: Harvard University Press, 1989.

Stern, Sheldon. *Averting the Final Failure*. Stanford, Calif.: Stanford University Press, 2003.

Steury, Donald P. *Intentions and Capabilities: Estimates of Soviet Strategic Forces, 1950–1983*. Washington, D.C.: Center for the Study of Intelligence, 1996.

Sullivan, William C. *The Bureau: My Thirty Years in Hoover's FBI*. New York: Norton, 1979.

Suri, Jeremi. *Henry Kissinger and the American Century*. Cambridge, Mass.: Belknap Press, 2007.

———. *Power and Protest*. Cambridge, Mass.: Belknap Press, 2003.

Talbott, Strobe. *Deadly Gambits*. New York: Knopf, 1984.

———. *Endgame: The Story of SALT Two*. New York: Harper & Row, 1979.

———. *The Master of the Game*. New York: Knopf, 1988.

Taubman, William. *Khrushchev*. New York: Norton, 1993.

Temkin, Gabriel. *My Just War: The Memoir of a Jewish Red Army Soldier in World War II*. Novato, Calif.: Presidio Press, 1998.

Thayer, Charles. *Bears in the Caviar*. Philadelphia: Lippincott, 1950.

Thomas, Evan. *The Very Best Men*. New York: Touchstone, 1995.

Thompson, Kenneth W., and Steven L. Rearden, eds. *Paul H. Nitze on Foreign Policy*. Lanham, Md.: University Press of America, 1989.

———. *Paul H. Nitze on the Future*. Lanham, Md.: University Press of America, 1991.

Trahair, Richard C. S. *Encyclopedia of Cold War Espionage, Spies, and Secret Operations*. Westport, Conn.: Greenwood Press, 2004.

Trevor-Roper, Hugh. *The Last Days of Hitler*. New York: Macmillan, 1947.

Tucker, Aviezer. *The Philosophy and Politics of Czech Dissidence from Patocka to Havel*. Pittsburgh, Pa.: University of Pittsburgh Press, 2000.

Tyroler, Charles III. *Alerting America: The Papers of the Committee on the Present Danger*. Washington, D.C.: Pergamon Brassey, 1984.

U.S. Atomic Energy Commission. *In the Matter of J. Robert Oppenheimer: Transcript of Hearing before Personnel Security Board, Washington, D.C., April 12, 1954, Through May 6, 1954*. Washington, D.C.: U.S. Government Printing Office, 1954.

U.S. Strategic Bombing Survey. *The Effects of Atomic Bombs on Hiroshima and Nagasaki*. Washington, D.C.: U.S. Government Printing Office, 1946.

Van Atta, Dale. *With Honor: Melvin Laird in War, Peace, and Politics*. Madison: University of Wisconsin Press, 2008.

Von Moltke, Helmuth James. *Letters to Freya*. New York: Vintage Books, 1995.

Walker, Martin. *The Cold War*. New York: Holt, 1993.

Warner, Wells, ed. *Hiroshima Diary: The Journal of a Japanese Physician, August 6–September 30, 1945*. Chapel Hill: University of North Carolina Press, 1995.

Weinberger, Caspar. *In the Arena*. Washington, D.C.: Regnery, 2001.

Weinstein, Allen, and Alexander Vassiliev. *The Haunted Wood: Soviet Espionage in America—The Stalin Era*. New York: Random House, 1999.

Wells, Tom. *Wild Man: The Life and Times of Daniel Ellsberg*. New York: Macmillan, 2001.

Westad, Odd Arne, ed. *Reviewing the Cold War*. London: Frank Cass, 2000.

Williams, William J., ed. *A Revolutionary War: Korea and the Transformation of the Postwar World*. Chicago: Imprint, 1993.

Winik, Jay. *On the Brink*. New York: Simon & Schuster, 1996.

Woodward, Bob. *The Secret Man: The Story of Watergate's Deep Throat*. New York: Simon & Schuster, 2006.

Yergin, Daniel. *Shattered Peace*. Boston: Houghton Mifflin, 1977.

Yoder, Edwin. *Joe Alsop's Cold War: A Study of Journalistic Influence and Intrigue*. Chapel Hill: University of North Carolina Press, 1995.

Zaloga, Steven. *The Kremlin's Nuclear Sword*. Washington, D.C.: Smithsonian Institution Press, 2002.

Zubok, Vladislav. *A Failed Empire: The Soviet Union in the Cold War from Stalin to Gorbachev*. Chapel Hill: University of North Carolina Press, 2007.

Zubok, Vladislav, and Constantine Pleshakov. *Inside the Kremlin's Cold War*. Cambridge, Mass.: Harvard University Press, 1996.

Zumwalt, Elmo R., Jr. *On Watch*. New York: Quadrangle, 1976.

Zumwalt, Elmo R., Jr., and Elmo Zumwalt III. *My Father, My Son*. New York: Dell, 1986.

PERIODICALS

"Anchors Aweigh." *Time* 82, no. 17 (25 Oct. 1963): 25.

Arneson, Gordon. "The H-Bomb Decision." *Foreign Service Journal* 15, no. 6. (May 1969): 27–29.

"Awful Responsibility." *Time* 46, no. 8 (20 Aug. 1945): 29.

Ball, George, and John Kenneth Galbraith. "The Interrogation of Albert Speer." *Life* 19, no. 25 (17 Dec. 1945): 57–66.

Barraclough, Geoffrey. "Hitler's Master Builder." *New York Review of Books* 15, no. 12 (7 Jan. 1971): 6–15.

Citron, Zachary. "The Conversion of Paul." *New Republic* 200, no. 5 (30 Jan. 1989): 33.

"Creating Axis." *Time* 75, no. 8 (22 Feb. 1960): 24.

Duffy, Gloria. "Crisis Mangling and the Cuban Brigade." *International Security* 8, no. 1 (Summer 1983): 67–87.

Eisle, Albert. "George Kennan Speaks Out About Iraq." *History News Network* (26 Sept. 2002), http://hnn.us/articles/997.html. Accessed on March 26, 2009.

Fischer, Benjamin. "Farewell to Sonia, the Spy Who Haunted Britain." *International Journal of Intelligence and Counterintelligence* 15, no. 1 (Jan. 2002): 61–76.

Gentile, Gian P. "Shaping the Past Battlefield." *Journal of Military History* 64, no. 4 (Oct. 2000): 1085–112.

Hamburger, Philip. "Mr. Secretary." *New Yorker* 25 (12 Nov. 1949): 39.

"Heirs Apparent." *Time* 90, no. 23 (8 Dec. 1967): 26.

Herken, Gregg. "The Great Foreign Policy Fight." *American Heritage* 37, no. 3 (April/May 1986): 65–80.

"How Silly Can You Get." *Time* 84, no. 3 (17 July 1964): 26–27.

Immerman, Richard. "Confessions of an Eisenhower Revisionist: An Agonizing Reappraisal." *Diplomatic History* 14, no. 3 (Summer 1990): 319–42.

Kaplan, Fred. "JFK's First Strike Plan." *Atlantic Monthly* 288, no. 3 (Oct. 2001): 81–86.

Kennan, George F. "Breaking the Spell." *New Yorker* 59, no. 33 (3 Oct. 1983): 44–53.

———. "George F. Kennan Replies." *Slavic Review* 35, no. 1 (March 1976): 32–36.

———. "Introducing Eugene McCarthy." *New York Review of Books* 10, no. 7 (11 April 1968): 14–16.

———. "Noble Man." *New York Review of Books* 20, no. 4 (22 March 1973): 3–6.

———. "Review of Gustav Hilger's *The Incompatible Allies.*" *Herald Tribune Book Review* (1 Nov. 1953).

Lerner, Mitchell. "A Dangerous Miscalculation: New Evidence from Communist-Bloc Archives about North Korea and the Crises of 1968." *Journal of Cold War Studies* 6, no. 1 (Winter 2004): 3.

McNamara, Robert. "Forty Years After 13 Days." *Arms Control Today* 32, no. 9 (Nov. 2002): 4–8.

Nitze, Paul H. "Atoms, Strategy and Policy." *Foreign Affairs* 34, no. 2 (Jan. 1956): 190–91.

———. "Deterring Our Deterrent." *Foreign Policy,* no. 25 (Winter 1976–77): 195–210.

———. "Limited Wars or Massive Retaliation?" *Reporter* (5 Sept. 1957): 40–42.

———. "Was Truman Right to Drop the Bomb? A Weapon Beyond War." *Vital Speeches of the Day* 61, no. 23 (15 Sept. 1995): 723.

"Out of the Darkness." *Time* 68, no. 20 (12 Nov. 1956): 48–50.

"Over the Mountains: Mountains." *Time* 55, no. 2 (10 July 1950): 12–15.

"People of the Week." *US News & World Report* (30 Dec. 1949): 37.

Podhoretz, Norman. "George Kennan and the Students." *Harper's* (Oct. 1968): 104–7.

Rosenbaum, Ron. "Kim Philby and the Age of Paranoia." *New York Times Magazine* (10 July 1994): 29.

Srodes, James. "Paul H. Nitze: 1907–2004." *American Spectator* 37, no. 10 (Dec. 2004/Jan. 2005): 62.

Steel, Ronald. "A Self-Made Man." *New York Review of Books* 39, no. 14. (13 Aug. 1992): 33–36.

———. "Man Without a Country." *New York Review of Books* 9, no. 12. (4 Jan. 1968): 8–15.

———. "Russia, the West, and the Rest." *New York Review of Books* 24. no. 12 (14 July 1977): 19–22.

Suri, Jeremi. "The Nukes of October." *Wired* 16, no. 3 (March 2008).

Thompson, Kenneth W. "John F. Kennedy and Revisionism." *Virginia Quarterly Review* (Summer 1994): 430–43.

———. "The Kennan-Acheson Controversy." *Commonweal* (6 April 1958): 6.

"The Prince and Death." *Time* 45, no. 24 (24 Dec. 1945): 36.

Urban, George. "A Conversation with George F. Kennan." *Encounter* 47 (Sept. 1976): 10–43.

Warnke, Paul. "Apes on a Treadmill." *Foreign Policy*, no. 18 (Spring 1975): 12–29.

"When A.P. correspondent . . ." (untitled article). *Time* 109, no. 8 (21 Feb. 1977): 2.

"Winds of Freedom." *Time* 58, no. 9 (27 Aug. 1951): 27.

Wohlstetter, Albert J. "The Delicate Balance of Terror." *Foreign Affairs* 37, no. 1 (Jan. 1959): 211–34.

Wright, Ben C. "Mr. X and Containment." *Slavic Review* 35, no. 1 (March 1976): 1–31.

Ziegler, Charles. "Waiting for Joe-1: Decisions Leading to the Detection of Russia's First Atomic Bomb Test." *Social Studies of Science* 18, no. 2 (May 1988): 213.

Zimmermann, Warren. "Prophet with Honor." *New York Review of Books* 43, no. 13 (8 Aug. 1996).

NEWSPAPERS

"Acheson Renews Defense of Hiss." *New York Times*, 26 Jan. 1950.

Alsop, Joseph. "Baker Company." *Washington Post*, 30 Aug. 1950.

———. "The Battalion." *Washington Post*, 28 Aug. 1950.

———. "The Battle: First Phase." *Washington Post*, 14 Aug. 1950.

———. "The Battle: Second Phase." *Washington Post*, 16 Aug. 1950.

———. "The Odds." *Washington Post*, 23 Aug. 1950.

Bacon, Kenneth. "Fighting a Treaty: Nitze, Long a Backer of Arms Curbs, Now Is a Key Critic of SALT." *Wall Street Journal*, 20 June 1979.

"Barge Cargoes Blow Up." *New York Times*, 30 July 1916.

Barnes, Bart, and Patricia Sullivan. "Gentle Senator, Presidential Hopeful, Empowered U.S. Antiwar Movement." *Washington Post*, 11 Dec. 2005.

Berger, Marilyn. "An Appeal for Thought." *New York Times*, 7 May 1978.

Bowie, Robert. "Don't Overlook the ABM 'Scandal.'" *Christian Science Monitor*, 26 Dec. 1986.

Brines, Russell. "Prince Konoye—Japan's Inscrutable Leader." *Washington Post*, 15 Sept. 1940.

Broad, William J. "A Spy's Path." *New York Times*, 12 Nov. 2007.

Carlisle, Olga. "Dictator's Daughter." *New York Times*, 24 Sept. 1967.

Catledge, Turner. "Our Policy Stated." *New York Times*, 24 June 1941.

Chaplin, Gordon. "Zumwalt's Next War." *Washington Post*, 15 Feb. 1976.

Clawson, Ken. "Top FBI Official Forced Out in Policy Feud with Hoover." *Washington Post*, 2 Oct. 1971.

Clarke, Michael. "Premier of Iran Airs Threat of Death, Faints After Talk." *New York Times*, 14 May 1951.

Deuel, Wallace. "America's New Policy Planner." *Washington Star*, 15 Jan. 1950.

"Excerpts from Nitze Speech on Berlin." *New York Times*, 8 Sept. 1961.

Finney, John W. "The Long Trial of John Paton Davies." *New York Times*, 31 Aug. 1969.

Fox, Sylvan. "Life, The Times to Serialize Stalin Daughter's Memoirs." *New York Times*, 23 April 1967.

Galbraith, John Kenneth. "Albert Speer Was the Man to See." *New York Times*, 10 Jan. 1971.

Goldhaber, Samuel. "NAC Protesters Disrupt CFIA Visiting Committee." *Harvard Crimson*, 10 April 1970.

Gordon, Michael. "Reagan Adviser Says Bush Wrong on Short-Range Missiles." *New York Times*, 3 May 1989.

Gwertzman, Bernard. "Kissinger Puts Off His Visit to Soviet for Talks on Arms." *New York Times*, 10 Dec. 1975.

———. "Kissinger Says Idea of Supremacy Makes No Sense in a Nuclear Age." *New York Times*, 11 Jan. 1977.

Hill, Ira L. "Mary C. Ames to Wed H. G. Cushing." *New York Times*, 19 Jan. 1930.

Ignatius, David. "The Old Pro." *Wall Street Journal*, 1 Aug. 1985.

"Kennan Suggests 1,000,000-GI Europe Buildup." *Stars and Stripes*, 22 Sept. 1968.

Klemesrud, Judy. "For Stalin's Daughter, a Quiet Question." *New York Times*, 6 March 1973.

Knightley, Philip. "The Spy Files." *London Independent*, 17 Nov. 2006.

Luther, Claudia. "Paul Nitze, 97; Key Player in U.S. Foreign Policy During Cold War." *Los Angeles Times*, 21 Oct. 2004.

"Lyle H. Munson, 55, Publisher of Right-Wing Books, Is Dead; Involved in Davies Case." *New York Times*, 2 Nov. 1973.

Marder, Murrey. "Carter to Inherit Intense Dispute on Soviet Intentions." *Washington Post*, 2 Jan. 1977.

———. "Summit Clouded by Watergate." *Washington Post*, 4 July 1974.

"McNamara Deeply Moved as President Pays Him Tribute." *Washington Post and Times Herald*, Feb. 29, 1968.

"Moscow May Day Comes to Havana." *Christian Science Monitor*, 1 May 1961.

"News Summary." *New York Times*, 22 April 1967.

"Nitze Opposed in Navy Job for Alleged Pacifist Views." *New York Times*, 1 Nov. 1963.

"Nixon Announcement on SALT Progress." *Washington Post*, 21 May 1971.

Oberdorfer, Don. "George Kennan's 30-Year Nightmare Of Our 'Final Folly.'" *Washington Post*, 24 May 1981.

———. "George Kennan Urges Tougher Stance on Iran." *Washington Post*, 28 Feb. 1980.

———. "Kennan Urges Halving of Nuclear Arsenals." *Washington Post*, 20 May 1981.

———. "U.S. Retaliates, Expels Soviet Reporter." *Washington Post*, 6 Feb. 1977.

Pepper, Claude. "Stalin Voices Aim for Amity and Aid of U.S. in the Peace." *New York Times*, 1 Oct. 1945.

Raymond, Jack. "Kennedy Expected to Name Nitze to Gilpatric's Post in Pentagon." *New York Times*, 16 March 1963.

———. "U.S. Revised Plan on Arms Is Ready." *New York Times*, 13 Jan. 1957.

Reston, James. "Vandenberg Lauds Work Put Into Framing ERP Bill." *New York Times*, 10 Jan. 1948.

Roberts, Chalmers. "Enormous Arms Outlay Is Held Vital to Survival." *Washington Post and Times Herald*, 20 Dec. 1957.

Sedgwick, A. C. "Athens Bomb Kills Minister; Red Plot on Cabinet Alleged." *New York Times*, 2 May 1948.

Shenker, Israel. "Kennan Analysis Coolly Received." *New York Times*, 4 Dec. 1968.

"Stalin Sets a Huge Output Near Ours in 5-Year Plan." *New York Times*, 10 Feb. 1946.

"Texts of Red's Communiqué and the East Germans' Decree About Berlin." *New York Times*, 14 Aug. 1961.

Trohan, Walter. "Reds Get Our Bomb Plans." *Chicago Tribune*, 4 Feb. 1950.

"Truman Gives Aim." *New York Times*, 1 Dec. 1950.

"William C. Sullivan, Ex-F.B.I Aide, 65, Is Killed in a Hunting Accident." *New York Times*, 10 Nov. 1977.

Zelnick, C. Robert. "Paul Nitze: The Nemesis of SALT II." *Washington Post*, 24 June 1979.

MANUSCRIPTS

Gurman, Hannah. "The Dissent Papers: The Voice of Diplomats in the Cold War and Beyond." Unpublished PhD dissertation, Columbia University, 2009.

Hamilton, James Isbell. "The Unexpected Paul Nitze." MA thesis, University of Alabama in Huntsville, 1996.

Jones, Christopher. "Paul H. Nitze, The State Department Policy Planning Staff, and the Origins of American Atomic Strategy, 1949–1953." MA thesis, University of Virginia, 1996.

Nitze, Paul. "The Early Years." Personal manuscript given to family.

———. "Jottings." Personal manuscript given to family.

U.S. Central Intelligence Agency (1976). "Intelligence Community Experiment in Competitive Analysis: Soviet Strategic Objectives, an Alternate View: Report of Team 'B.'" Washington, D.C.: U.S. Government Printing Office. Declassified September 16, 1992.

Willcutts, Admiral M. D. "Report on the Death of James Forrestal," part 1.

———. "Report on the Death of James Forrestal," part 2.

Wright, C. Ben. "George F. Kennan: Scholar-Diplomat." Unpublished PhD dissertation, University of Wisconsin, 1972.

PAPERS, LETTERS, COLLECTIONS

George C. Marshall Library: George C. Marshall, C. Ben Wright
Georgetown University: Paul Warnke
Hoover Library: Robert Murphy
Library of Congress: Joseph Alsop, Charles Bohlen, Daniel Boorstin, Henry Brandon, W. Averell Harriman, Philip Jessup, Hans Morgenthau, Paul H. Nitze, J. Robert Oppenheimer, John Osborne
Seeley G. Mudd Manuscript Library, Princeton, N.J.: George Ball, William Bundy, Allen Dulles, John Foster Dulles, James Forrestal, George F. Kennan, Arthur Krock, David Lilienthal
University of Chicago: Elizabeth Paepcke, Walter Paepcke
Yale University: Dean Acheson, Walter Lippmann

INTERVIEWS

Kenneth Adelman, Tish Alsop, Jonathan Alter, Annelise Anderson, Martin Anderson, Nancy Arneson, Timothy Bachmann, Betsy Barrett, Francis Bator, Lucius Battle, Alexander Bessmertnykh, James Billington, Bruce Blair, Barry Blechman, Frederic Bohen, Murray Bovarnick, Robert Bowie, Harold Brown, Mary Bundy, William Burr, Richard Burt, David Callahan, James Cicconi, Robert Cleveland, Norm Clyne, Elliot Cohen, Philip Coyle, Fred Cushing, Kenneth Dam, Carla Davis, Nikolai Detinov, Larry Diamond, Michael Dobbs, Sidney Drell, Vladimir Dvorkin, Lawrence Eagleburger, Ralph Earle, Daniel Ellsberg, George Elsey, John Lewis Gaddis, Mark Garrison, Raymond Garthoff, Jeanne Gaylor, Leslie Gelb, Dean Godson, Constance Goodman, Thomas Graham, David Greenberg, Fred Greenstein, Ann Gruner, Hannah Gurman, Bernard Gwertzman, Mort Halperin, Hermann Hatzfeldt, John Haynes, Gregg Herken, Richard Hornik, Thomas Hughes, Paul Ignatius, Fred Iklé, Richard Immerman, Walter Isaacson, Zup James, Nancy Jenkins, Marvin Kalb, Max Kampelman, Nicholas Katzenbach, Carl Kaysen, Christopher Kennan, Joan Kennan, Wendy Kennan, Donald Kennedy, Howard Kerr, Henry Kissinger, Henry Knoche, Viktor Koltunov, George Krimsky, Yuli Kvitsinsky, Melvin Laird, Donald Lamm, Jack Lawn, Derek Leebaert, Robert Legvold, Nicholas Lemann, Franklin Lindsay, Margot Lindsay, Gerald Livingston, Jim Lowenstein, Edward Luttwak, Andrew Marshall, Jurek Martin, Jack Matlock, Martha Mautner, Martin Mayer, Priscilla McMillan, Wilson Miscamble, Edwin Moise, Robert Newman, Ann Nitze, Heidi Nitze, Peter Nitze, William Nitze, Robert Norris, Alexei Obukhov, Norma Odom, Robert Ordonez, Ed Paisley, Pavel Palazchenko, Lana Peters, Richard Perle, Steve Pifer, Richard Pipes, Pavel Podvig, Walter Pozen, George Rathjens, Robert Rayle, Steve Rearden, John Rhinelander, Walter Roberts, Chuck Robinson, Peter Robinson, Ron Rosenbaum, Henry Rowen, Frank Ruocco, Aleksandr Savel'yev, Thomas Schelling, Alan Schwartz, Jeff Shesol, George Shultz, Robert Silvers, Christopher Simpson, Walter Slocombe, Ann Smith, Fred Smith, Helmut Sonnenfeldt, Abraham Sofaer, Theodore Sorensen, Ronald Steel, Anders Stephanson, Beth Straus, Don Straus, Strobe Talbott, Evan Thomas, Kenneth Thompson, John Thompson, Scott Thompson,

William Thompson, Malcolm Toon, Robert Tucker, Vitalii Tsygichko, William Van Cleave, Freya von Moltke, Charles Wardell, Grace Warnecke, Stephen Warnke, Kenneth Weisbrode, Craig Whitney, Robert Wiley, Peter Wilson, Paul Wolfowitz, James Woolsey, C. Ben Wright, Valery Yarynich, Felicity Yost, Marilyn Young, Wendy Young, Vladislav Zubok, Mouzzetta Zumwalt, Paula Zurcher

INTERVIEW AND ORAL HISTORY TRANSCRIPTS

The Academy of Achievement, Washington, D.C.: Paul Nitze
John F. Kennedy Library, Boston, Ma.: George F. Kennan
Miller Center for Public Affairs, Charlottesville, Va.: Kenneth Adelman, Ed Rowny
The National Security Archive, Washington, D.C.: Paul Nitze; Robert Tucker
Harry S. Truman Library, Independence, Mo.: Doc Matthews, Paul Nitze
U.S. Air Force Historical Research Center, Maxwell Air Force Base, Ala.: Paul Nitze

MISCELLANEOUS

CFR Study Group Reports. "Nuclear Weapons and Foreign Policy." Nov. 8, 1954, CFR Papers, Records of groups, volume IX. 1954–1955, 1954–1956.
Hotchkiss, Jeanette. Undated interview with Joan Kennan.
Kennan, George Frost. "Notes on Religion." Oct. 2002 letter given to author.
Kennan, George Frost. Personal file held by the Federal Bureau of Investigation.
Kennan, George Frost. Undated interview with Joan Kennan.
Nitze, Paul Henry. Papers from his personal filing cabinets. In author's possession.
Nitze, Paul Henry. Personal file held by the Federal Bureau of Investigation.

AUTHOR'S NOTE

That one of my two subjects was a relative has, of course, affected my research. In the simplest respect, it has given me access to an archive of documents that no one has ever seen before. My favorite moment while reporting this book came one day in the spring of 2008, when I went to the Nitze School of Advanced International Studies where he used to keep his office. One Saturday morning when no one else was around, I asked a janitor if I could see his papers.

"Of course," he said and took me toward the elevator. I expected to head to a familiar filing cabinet on the sixth floor. But he pressed "4," took me down an unfamiliar hallway, opened a solid door at the far end, and then pointed at a gigantic boiler, humming loudly, with pipes sprawling everywhere. And behind it were fifty long-abandoned cardboard boxes containing the documents from much of Nitze's life. Apparently, that janitor was the only person in the building who knew about them. In those boxes, I found many of the details and documents that inform this book.

My connection to Nitze has given me access to more than documents: I have also conducted many interviews with important figures from the Cold War who sat with me only because of my grandfather. For better or worse, my personal connection has also surely affected the way some of these people talked to me. While I was spending a week doing research at a conservative think tank, one of the fellows jubilantly introduced me to someone at a cocktail party: "This fellow's writing a book about Paul Nitze, who was his grandfather, and George Kennan, whose grave we piss on."

My relation to Nitze also undoubtedly affected the preconceptions with which I started the book. I grew up in a house with the ten-inch models of the Russian ICBMs that Nitze used to carry around in the 1970s, and I learned at an early age that George Shultz was a hero and that Jimmy Carter was a villain. Had I never known Nitze, I might have begun with the preconception that he was the hard-line demon so often portrayed in modern Cold War histories. That Paul Nitze—far less complex than the real one—would not have seemed worthy of a book.

It's also true, of course, that writing about someone you knew and admired means that there's always a faint sense that he is looking over your shoulder. Fortunately, I'm certain that my grandfather would chiefly have wished that the book be as rigorous and accurate as possible. As it happened, while I worked up one of my final drafts, in my mother's old house in New Hampshire, I found the copy of my grandfather's memoirs that he had given me when I was fourteen. A few years before, I had written a paper for a sixth-grade class about his arms control negotiations, which he claimed to like. "For Nicky / This may give you some ideas for further essays. Congratulations for all your good work. / Gramps."

Despite so personal a connection, I have made every effort to hold nothing back. I have concealed no interesting secrets. If I have cut Paul Nitze slack, I have done so unconsciously.

George Kennan wrote far more books, letters, and essays than Nitze did. His memoirs are intensely revealing, unlike Nitze's. Eight writers have produced full studies of Kennan's life; two have done so for Nitze. More important, thanks to the generosity of Kennan's family and his estate, I have been able to read decades' worth of the private diaries and personal letters that he kept in his office and house, most of which have not been written about before. I feel, thus, that I have had about equal access to the two men's lives.

The question I have been asked most often while working on the project is, "Who was right?" And my answer, even as I come to an end, is "Both of them." Each was profoundly right at some moments, and profoundly wrong at others.

But I have learned two things for certain. First, no matter whether you think his ideas right or wrong, Paul Nitze set an example of how to live and work. He was knocked down endlessly, and each time he got up. He had a passion for everything he did in his life, right until the very end. "Each year I get is a gift, perhaps an undeserved one, but one I'm going to use," he told me a couple of years before he died, as we walked to Stanley's Fish Market in Northeast Harbor.

Second, no matter what you think of Kennan's choices or views, no one felt deeper, thought harder, or wrote more beautifully about diplomacy. He spent an absolutely extraordinary amount of time in his 101 years with his mind focused, trying to understand himself and the world around him: from the remarkable teenage poet to the centenarian folding up bits of paper. He left behind a treasure chest of essays, books, letters, and ideas—deeply felt works that tell us much about a farsighted man, his country, and his epoch.

One cannot play the Cold War backward to learn how it would have turned out if neither Kennan nor Nitze had been born. Perhaps there would have been a final clash between the two superpowers. Perhaps the United States and the Soviet Union would never have entered into— or would have found a way to end—their ruinous arms race. But there's one thing I feel confident saying after several years immersed in the worlds of these two men: America is a richer place because of the examples set by Paul Nitze and George Kennan.

ACKNOWLEDGMENTS

Many brilliant and generous people helped with this book. I'll start with my editor at Henry Holt, John Sterling. I had been told going into this process that book editors don't edit. But it's just not true. John did a superb job at every stage: from the initial conversations about conception to his careful line-by-line edit. Any clunky sentences found in this manuscript are entirely my responsibility.

Timothy Dickinson, a dear friend, and a man more knowledgeable about these matters (and all matters) than anyone else I know, also deserves immense thanks. He is a gentleman of great patience: after completing each chapter, I would call him and read it aloud. He would listen and interject whenever he found a mistake or an awkward phrase. I'm serious when I say that I'll miss the days when I could pick up my phone to hear "You have six new messages"—all from Timothy.

Rafe Sagalyn, my agent, likewise, deserves substantial gratitude for this project. He saw the potential for this book, and guided me along the way. He also gets credit for coming up with a title I really like, after much discussion of genuinely bad ones.

My father, Scott Thompson, told me this would be a good idea for a book as we sat one afternoon discussing Kennan's obituary, and he was the first person to read every chapter. He also gets credit for teaching his five-year-old son about the perilous balance of power.

Lincoln Caplan, my boss at *Legal Affairs*, saw immediately that this book had promise. Then, at a crucial stage, Linc did a close—and extremely smart—read that identified several important problems with the first draft.

Several other people also played crucial roles in helping this project, and, without them, I do not know if I could have completed it. Eliot Cohen opened up his collection of Nitze papers at SAIS; John Lewis Gaddis read the entire manuscript carefully and generously shared some documents that he has collected during his marvelous research into Kennan's life; John Haynes helped me to win access to a huge swath of my grandfather's papers at the Library of Congress that I initially thought was closed; Christopher Kennan allowed me access to his father's diaries and private papers; Joan Kennan not only read the manuscript very carefully, she was willing to share a collection of personal documents and to sit for endless interviews; Lana Peters was also extremely kind in engaging in a half dozen interviews and sending me scores of letters about Kennan; Grace Warnecke also took her keen eyes to the manuscript and shared some wonderful photographs with me.

I also have a collection of extremely talented friends and colleagues who helped in reading and editing the manuscript. I'd like to start by thanking everyone who read the manuscript from beginning to end and offered comments throughout: Gregg Herken, Wilson Miscamble, Marshall Moriarty, Roger Pasquier, Steve Rearden, Heidi Thompson Saunders, John Swansburg, Phyllis Thompson, Maynard Toll, and Ed Wilson. Their comments saved me from errors, led to new insights, and often gave me the confidence to keep going. I would also like to deeply thank Wendy Kennan, William Nitze, and Walter Pozen. They, too, read the manuscript start to finish and offered extremely important insights into men they knew far better than I could.

Another group of people read parts of the manuscript and offered extremely helpful comments: Larry Berman, Barry Blechman, Harold Brown, Taylor Bynum, Andrei Cherny, Mario del Pero, Michael Dobbs, Raymond Garthoff, Ann Gruner, Hannah Gurman, David Hans, Walter Isaacson, Nancy Jenkins, Gerry Livingston, Edward Luttwak, Priscilla McMillan, Chad Millman, Edwin Moîse, Heidi Nitze, Peter Nitze, Richard Perle, Steve Pifer, Daniel Roth, Martin Sherwin, Anders Stephanson, Strobe Talbott, Bill Thompson, Steven Warnke, Ken Weisbrode, C. Ben Wright, and Mouzetta Zumwalt.

Other people to whom I owe heartfelt thanks include Chris Anderson, Bob Cohn, Thomas Goetz, Mark Horowitz, and Jacob Young at *Wired*, who encouraged this project and helped me create the time for it, even when it conflicted with my day job. I am very grateful as well to Steve Clemons, Steve Coll, Andres Martinez, and Rachel White for bringing me, and this project, back into the New America Foundation.

Betsy Barrett showed me Kennan's house. Paul Barron shared papers from the George C. Marshall Foundation with me. David Bernstein offered me shelter during a very interesting reporting trip to Moscow. David

Callahan helped a great deal when I was getting started. Sarah Fallon saved the lead. Jonathan Safran Foer convinced me that the title was the right one when I started to waver. Connie Goodman was always willing to answer my random questions about her former boss. Yuli Kvitsinsky guided me in my Moscow reporting. Daniel Linke helped me sort through Kennan's archive before he was able to officially organize it. Mandy MacCalla and David Brady gave me an invaluable grant at the Hoover Institution. Thayer McKell opened up SAIS to me and was a constant and friendly presence as I pored over papers in the office next to her. Vanessa Mobley provided terrific guidance early in the process. Richard Perle spent hours talking with me and was helpful in connecting me to other sources. Richard Pipes was very helpful in vetting several documents. Pavel Podvig spent more time than could have reasonably been expected in helping me understand complicated military matters. Josh Rosenblum's computer skills saved me from despair at a crucial moment. Noah Shachtman has allowed me to use his wonderful DangerRoom blog to vet ideas. Chris Suellentrop and Jeremi Suri both edited stories that contribute to the final product.

Other people who were very helpful in different ways include Margaret Barr, Alexander Bessmertnykh, William Burr, Peter Canellos, Carl DeTorres, Julia Gardner, Martin Goldman, Lilita Gusts, Jeff Howe, Maili Holiman, Michael Hogan, Emi Ikkanda, Jon Kelly, Steven Levy, Mark Lord, Tarek Masoud, Parvin Moyne, Frank Rose, Marisol Salazar, Jenny Schuessler, and Zack Sturges. I would like to thank, too, the staff who handle FOIA requests at the CIA, Defense Department, Department of Justice, and State Department.

I also had a marvelous group of research assistants, starting with Faith Smith and Carolina Astigarraga. In not long, I'll be helping them research their books. I also received excellent assistance from Erica DeBruin, Katie Drummond, Shelley DuBois, Tanya Gassel, Marina Kameneva, Benjamin Katcher, Sameer Popat, and Katherine Tiedemann. Erik Malinowski and Rachel Swaby both deserve great credit for taking their keen *Wired* fact-checking skills to this manuscript.

I would like to thank my mother, Nina Moriarty, who has always provided constant, and absolute, loving support—and who has taught me an immense amount about both my family and family in general. And my wife, Danielle Goldman: my most insightful reader, emotional and intellectual companion, best friend, and source of my favorite footnote.

Lastly, I need to give thanks to my son, Ellis Martin Thompson. His impending arrival inspired me to hit my deadlines, and his actual arrival has brightened every moment since then. I end with something he wrote this morning, partially with his forehead, after deciding that Daddy had typed enough: "z6u5k65kkkkkkkkk65kkkkkp.z√`ej4zj pppppppppe kk`".

INDEX

ABOUT THE AUTHOR

NICHOLAS THOMPSON is an editor at *Wired Magazine*, a fellow at the New America Foundation, and a regular contributor to CNN. He has written articles for *The New York Times*, *The Washington Post*, and numerous other publications. A grandson of Paul Nitze's, he lives in New York City with his wife and son.